D1282837

Hitler's Economy

Hitler's Economy

Nazi Work Creation Programs, 1933–1936

DAN P. SILVERMAN

HARVARD UNIVERSITY PRESS

Cambridge, Massachusetts
London, England
1998

Library of Congress Cataloging-in-Publication Data

Silverman, Dan P., 1935–
    Hitler's economy : Nazi work creation programs, 1933–1936 / Dan P.
Silverman.
        p.   cm.
    Includes bibliographical references and index.
    ISBN 0-674-74071-8 (cloth : alk. paper)
    1. Labor policy—Germany—History—20th century.
    2. Germany—Economic policy—1933–1945.
    3. Germany—Economic conditions—1918–1945.
    4. Germany—Politics and government—1933–1945.
    5. National socialism.
    I. Title.
    HD8450.S55   1998
    331.12′042′094309043—dc21   97-44972

Contents

Contents

Preface

Hitler's rapid conquest of unemployment, a feat more brilliant than any of his later *Blitzkrieg* victories on the battlefield, constituted National Socialism's strongest claim to legitimacy. When Hitler came to power on January 30, 1933, official labor market statistics counted over six million German workers—about 34 percent of the labor force—as jobless. Hitler reduced unemployment by over one-third during his first year in power. Within eighteen months, unemployment had been cut by 60 percent. One is inclined to agree with economist Gerhard Kroll's observation that "a reduction of unemployment by a third in one year borders on the miraculous."[1] Economics is not religion; "miracles" have to be explained. How did the National Socialists, who had little respect for traditional economic expertise, bring off this *Wirtschaftswunder* and put Germany back to work? How did a system now generally recognized as brutal, barbaric, and chaotic apparently conquer unemployment so effectively and efficiently, before the rearmament program took hold of the German economy?

The Nazi Third Reich continues to attract attention in large measure because, in the minds of many, it represents the incarnation of evil. Viewed from this perspective, German National Socialism had nothing positive to offer—it was nothing but mindless brutality of the worst order. But there is another side to this story. Coming to power less than fourteen years after Germany had been humiliated by the Treaty of Versailles and at a time when over a third of Germany's active labor force was unemployed, Hitler and the Nazis supposedly restored to the German people their work, their bread, and their national dignity.

Nazi leaders always claimed that outsiders misrepresented and distorted the essence of German National Socialism by their preoccupation with the terror and violence that seemed to accompany every Nazi policy or program. In 1934, for example, Joseph Goebbels, the Nazi propaganda wizard, criticized the picture of Nazi Germany presented to the world by "Marxist emigrants." Among these "unteachables," cautioned Goebbels, German National Socialism "is still regarded as a form of intellectual barbarism, its constructive ideas as products of an over-heated fantasy, its methods of reconstruction as sheer brutality, its intellectual background as a menace to culture, and its striving for order and discipline as a threat to individual libery."[2]

Today, most of us would agree that the "Marxist emigrants" and countless others who left their German homeland during the 1930s understood only too well the nature of the regime that had taken power on January 30, 1933. But a question remains unanswered. Could a pack of barbarians have engineered the most effective economic recovery among the industrialized nations during the 1930s? Would such uncivilized leaders not have destroyed any "spontaneous" recovery that might have been in progress when Hitler took power? If the Nazis did contribute significantly to Germany's rapid recovery, was success achieved simply through a combination of rearmament and the barbaric application of coercive measures? Or did a new and potentially fruitful, culturally nourishing political and socioeconomic movement rejuvenate Germany's economy before somehow going off the track?

Historians have attributed Germany's miraculous 1933–1936 economic recovery to a combination of an economic upturn that had begun before Hitler came to power, public expenditures on rearmament and work creation, a highly effective propaganda campaign that created the impression of a successful Nazi "battle for work," and Nazi manipulation of labor market statistics. The role of direct work creation programs in the recovery has never been rigorously assessed. Work creation is often written off as nothing more than hidden rearmament. Among the thousands of published works on National Socialist Germany, there exist few archive-based studies of Nazi economic policy and programs between 1933 and 1936. Perhaps historians assumed that since Hitler was interested only in preparing Germany for war, there was little need for a close examination of Nazi economic programs prior to the Four Year Plan of 1936. In contrast, this study presumes that, even if rearmament was Hitler's only "economic" goal, the years prior to 1936 were years of relatively modest rearmament expenditure and need to be studied from the point of view of work creation policy rather than rearmament policy.

General works on German economic policy during the National Socialist era generally focus on the "rearmament economy" or the "war economy."[3] The handful of works on Reich economic recovery policies and work creation programs (e.g., the Papen program, the Gereke *Sofortprogramm*, the Reinhardt program) tend to deal in a static fashion only with the theory or administrative structure of those programs, without illuminating the dynamics of Nazi economic policy by examining the implementation of policies and programs.[4] Only a few local case studies provide some insight into the manner in which the Hitler government, governments of the Länder and Prussian provinces, and municipal officials actually implemented economic recovery programs.[5]

Nazi direct work creation programs are my focal point. Based on extensive research in national, regional, and local archives, this book examines the conception and implementation of Reich, regional, and local work creation programs. I evaluate the validity of Nazi labor market statistics, emphasize the importance of regional and local initiative, and compare the Nazi economic achievement—the so-called economic miracle—with recoveries in Britain and the United States during the 1930s.

The aim of this work is to enhance the historical record on Nazi economic policy and to provide at least partial answers to some important questions for which answers are long overdue. How and why did Germany's recovery during the first three years of the Nazi regime outstrip the economic rebound in other industrial nations such as Great Britain and the United States? At what financial and human cost was Germany's rapid economic recovery achieved between 1933 and 1936, and who paid that price? Was economic recovery itself tainted with the same brutality that characterized other aspects of the National Socialist regime? To answer these questions, I examine and evaluate various explanations of Germany's economic recovery. I reassess the importance of rearmament and "motorization" in Germany's recovery, hotly debated issues over the years, in the context of the historical record. My aim in the process is to contribute to our understanding of the internal dynamics of the Nazi regime in the early years of the Third Reich.

I wish to thank the directors and staffs of the following archives for their cooperation and most cordial assistance in making available their collections:

Federal Republic of Germany, Bundesarchiv (both Koblenz and Potsdam); Berlin Document Center; Geheimes Staatsarchiv Preußischer Kulturbesitz, Berlin (Dahlem); Nordrhein-Westfälisches Staatsarchiv Detmold; Stadtarchiv Duisburg; Nordrhein-Westfälisches Hauptstaatsarchiv, Düsseldorf (and Zweigarchiv Kalkum); Stadtarchiv Düsseldorf; Bayerisches Hauptstaatsarchiv, Munich; Nordrhein-Westfälisches Staatsarchiv Münster; Staatsarchiv Nürnberg; Stadtarchiv Nürnberg; Hauptstaatsarchiv Stuttgart; Landeshauptstadt Stuttgart, Stadtarchiv; Hessisches Hauptstaatsarchiv Wiesbaden; and the Staatsarchiv Würzburg. This book was completed with the assistance of a research grant from the Deutscher Akademischer Austauschdienst, a Travel to Collections grant from the National Endowment for the Humanities, a research fellowship from the German Marshall Fund of the United States, and a research grant from the College of the Liberal Arts Research and Graduate Office of the Pennsylvania State University. The Pennsylvania State University provided a sabbatical leave during the 1989–90 academic year.

Thanks also to the publishers of the following articles of mine, from which I have borrowed in writing this book: "Fantasy and Reality in Nazi Work-Creation Programs, 1933–1936," *Journal of Modern History*, 65: 113–151, © 1993 by The University of Chicago, all rights reserved; and "National Socialist Economics: The *Wirtschaftswunder* Reconsidered," in *Interwar Unemployment in International Perspective*, ed. Barry Eichengreen and T. J. Hatton (Dordrecht, The Netherlands: Kluwer Academic Publishers, 1988), pp. 204–215.

Hitler's Economy

Introduction

Over forty years after the demise of the Third Reich, the historian Charles S. Maier conceded that the impulses leading to Germany's economic recovery remained difficult to explain.[1] Why have historians found it so difficult to explain Germany's economic recovery during the early years of Hitler's regime? Is the recovery under Hitler more difficult to explain than Germany's failure to recover under Hitler's predecessors? A review of the present state of theory about the recovery of the German economy and labor market may provide some answers to these questions.

Historians reluctant to credit the Nazis with the recovery have argued that Hitler "benefited from the fact that the depression was coming to an end" and simply rode the crest of an autonomous "natural" upswing in the German economy.[2] Hitler and the Nazis also allegedly reaped the benefits of work creation initiatives of their predecessors Franz von Papen and General Kurt von Schleicher. Most widely held is the skeptical view that Nazi "work creation" programs in 1933 and 1934 were nothing more than disguised rearmament. It is true that Hitler told members of his cabinet on February 8, 1933, that "the next five years in Germany must be devoted to the rearmament of the German people. Every publicly sponsored work creation measure must be considered from the point of view of whether it is necessary in terms of the rearmament of the German people . . . for the next four to five years the guiding principle must be: everything for the Wehrmacht." But Reich labor minister Franz Seldte's response, "that beside the purely military requirements there were also other projects of value to

1

the national economy which ought not be neglected," is generally ignored and deserves more consideration than it has received.[3]

After years of debate over the timing and amount spent by the Nazis on rearmament, it now seems unlikely that the labor market recovery of 1933–1935 was induced by a "rearmament boom." The debate highlighted the difficulty in defining "rearmament." Military expenditure, however defined, was relatively low during the key recovery years, 1933 through 1935. Once the upswing was well under way, rearmament contributed substantially to sustaining it.[4] Richard J. Overy, moreover, has cautioned that "military expenditure is not the same thing as expenditure on armaments," and that "rearmament expenditure" does not necessarily go entirely into industry and productive employment. Overy estimates that of a total "military expenditure" of RM (Reichmarks) 4.8 billion from 1933 to 1935, only about RM 600 million was spent on "military investment" in 1933 and 1934, and another RM 1.9 billion in 1935. Military expenditure represented only 1.9 percent of Germany's GNP (gross national product) in 1933 and 4 percent in 1934, "reaching economically significant levels only in 1935–6."[5] There exists no systematic study of the employment effect of Nazi rearmament expenditures. Prior to the middle of 1935 the employment effect seems to have been modest in comparison to the total number of unemployed, the total amount by which unemployment decreased, and the total amount by which employment increased between January 1933 and June 1935.[6]

If a "rearmament boom" did not drive the vigorous labor market recovery of 1933–1935, then some combination of "autonomous recovery" and government intervention in the form of direct and indirect work creation programs must have played a significant role. Overy rightly regards the portion of the recovery attributable to the autonomous working of the business cycle as conjectural, but he estimates that direct work creation accounted for 20 percent of the 2.8 million increase in employment during 1933–34, largely concentrated in the winter and spring.[7] Overy's estimate may also be conjectural, but in any case it does not differentiate between the impact of Hitler's direct work creation programs and those of his predecessors.

The extent to which the Hitler government merely capitalized on its predecessors' direct work creation programs needs to be clarified.[8] Hitler inherited from Heinrich Brüning, Franz von Papen, and Kurt von Schleicher a deflationary fiscal policy and modest direct work creation programs of approximately RM 1,098 million, including RM 269 million in projects undertaken by the German railways and post office. Of this total, the Gereke

Sofortprogramm, which is supposed to have financed some rearmament during 1933, came to RM 500 million, of which RM 400 million was earmarked for projects sponsored by the Länder and local governments.[9] Many Länder (state) and local governments, however, refused to initiate work creation projects under the program. They considered the terms of borrowing onerous and expected to get a more favorable deal from the Hitler government. At the end of December 1933, only 58 percent of the RM 600 million available under the Gereke program had been paid out.[10]

Local authorities who expected easier borrowing terms under Nazi work creation programs received virtually no assistance from the Hitler government for at least six months. The first major Nazi work creation measure was the June 1, 1933, "Reinhardt program" (after Fritz Reinhardt, a Nazi state secretary in the Reich finance ministry), which earmarked credits of RM 1 billion for large-scale public works projects. Because these projects became effective only after many months of planning and preparation, the original Reinhardt program was supplemented on September 21 by a "second Reinhardt program" consisting of RM 500 million in direct Reich budget expenditures for housing repair and renovation that supposedly could be executed immediately.

Placed in the context of antidepression measures taken by Hitler's predecessors, the Hitler government's 1933 work creation programs raise important political and economic questions. Policies enacted under Heinrich Brüning's chancellorship between 1930 and 1932 were brutally deflationary, and chancellor Franz von Papen's 1932 program relied largely on indirect methods such as tax certificates and employment premiums to induce businesses to hire additional workers. Of Hitler's immediate predecessors in the chancellor's office, only General Kurt von Schleicher ventured to propose a deficit-financed work creation program, the so-called *Sofortprogramm.* Devised by Reich Commissioner for Work Creation Günter Gereke, the program was launched only a few weeks prior to Hitler's appointment to the chancellorship.

During the summer and fall of 1932, the Nazis had demanded work creation programs costing between RM 3 billion and RM 10 billion. Reichsbank president Hans Luther was willing to finance only RM 500 million for Gereke's program. Yet, even RM 500 million was too much for Germany's traditional conservatives, who eventually decided that Hitler was better than Schleicher. How, then, could Hitler's government launch a RM 1 billion deficit-financed work creation program when its predecessors had been either unwilling or unable to launch comparable, or even smaller, efforts to put Germany's unemployed back to work? And why did the Nazis, once in power, delay and scale back their work creation programs to a fraction of what they had demanded of non-Nazi governments in 1932?

The question of whether Hitler's predecessors, particularly Brüning, were unwilling or unable to launch substantial deficit-financed employment programs for the jobless has formed the core of a virtually endless discussion among economic historians. Until the German economist Knut Borchardt began to explore the question well over a decade ago, it was widely believed that as the economic crisis engulfed Germany during 1929–1930, chancellor Heinrich Brüning deliberately chose a ruinous deflationary fiscal policy that only added to the human misery of unemployment and hunger. Brüning allegedly rejected feasible "Keynesian" reflationary fiscal alternatives for various nefarious reasons. Most frequently cited were his alleged desire to free Germany from the shackles of Versailles by proving that Germany could no longer meet its reparations obligations, and his supposed determination to destroy the social welfare system developed during the Weimar years.[11]

Borchardt has argued forcefully that, given Germany's objective economic situation in the final Weimar years, Brüning did what he had to do. Regardless of who held the chancellorship, there were no alternatives, no "room to maneuver" in German economic policy. German real wages were excessive, and had to be reduced in order to restore corporate profitability and competitiveness. Excessive wages meant higher unemployment. The budget had to be balanced. Massive deficit spending would only discredit the regime, destroy the German currency, and possibly ignite another round of hyperinflation. In any case, the German government could not have borrowed to finance massive deficit spending. Germany's capital markets had collapsed, and foreign lending to Germany had dried up. Germany's bank laws, still subject to international control, and the international moratorium agreement on debt repayment severely restrained the financing of job creation programs. Germany's deepening political crisis and growing opposition to the entire "Weimar system" ruled out agreement on any job creation program that might have shored up the existing regime or granted political advantage to one side or another. Brüning, argued Borchardt, had no realistic alternative to the deflationary policy that he pursued.[12]

Borchardt's argument unleashed a debate that ultimately became a full-blown "Borchardt controversy."[13] Borchardt's principal critic, Carl-Ludwig Holtfrerich, has argued that Brüning's problem was his "lack of determination" rather than a "lack of options or of political force to pursue expansionary economic policies after July 1931."[14] Brüning deliberately ignored calls for such a program from key members of his own cabinet and senior civil servants in the finance and economics ministries. Their proposals would have counterbalanced the inflationary side effects of deficit spending financed by the Reichsbank with price and cost reductions, defense of the mark exchange rate, and a relatively high discount rate. By the end of 1931, argued Holtfrerich, the imminent prospect of long-term unemployment frightened German voters much more than the theoretical chance of inflation induced by deficit spending. Voters increasingly turned to the Nazis, who "promised employment and economic growth as well as a radical abolition of the Versailles Treaty."[15]

Holtfrerich argues rather convincingly that a number of influential personalities in government, finance, and the labor movement proposed deficit-financed work creation programs that Brüning rejected. He is less convincing in demonstrating that these programs, if implemented, would have worked. Did proponents of these plans believe they would actually put six million Germans back to work, or were they simply trying to save the Weimar republic by showing disillusioned voters that the government cared about their plight? Borchardt argued that work creation proposals made in late 1931 came too late to forestall the labor market catastrophe of 1931–32, and that the amount of deficit spending proposed (no more than RM 2 billion, or 2.3 percent of the 1929 gross national product) was insufficient to change the direction of the economy. Holtfrerich has admitted that the work creation programs recommended by officials in Brüning's government would have come too late to head off the catastrophic collapse of the labor market during the winter of 1931–32. But, he argued, the trough of the cycle would have been reached earlier, and a government more democratically oriented than Hitler's might have benefited from the earlier upturn.[16]

Because Germany's capital market was exhausted and foreign loans were unavailable, the key player in any work creation program financed by government deficit spending would have been the Reichsbank, the lender of last resort. Brüning or any other chancellor contemplating a massive work creation program would first have had to convince the Reichsbank to finance it. Under Hans Luther's leadership, the Reichsbank refused to provide any Weimar government with a blank check.[17] Luther agreed to provide only RM 500 million for the Schleicher/Gereke *Sofortprogramm* in December 1932. Why was the Reichsbank prepared to finance a RM 1 billion program for Hitler in June 1933? Why was Hitler's "room to maneuver" so much greater than that of his predecessors? And why did RM 1 billion for work creation in 1933 seem to work miracles, when experts such as Borchardt argue that an expenditure of RM 2 billion between mid-1931 and mid-1932 would have been too small to turn the German economy around?[18]

Answers to these questions must consider changes in both the economic and the political climate between 1932 and 1933. Hitler's appointment as Reich chancellor on January 30, 1933, seemed to open the way for new men with new ideas for an aggressive war against unemployment. The Nazi Führer, however, either had less "room to maneuver" than one might imagine, or had no desire to entrust untried people with Germany's economic future. For the presidency of the Reichsbank, he brought Hjalmar Schacht back for a return engagement. Schacht's record as head of the Reichsbank during the post-1923 stabilization reassured the German and international financial community that there would be no wild experiments with money creation under a Hitler government. Hitler's finance minister, Lutz Graf Schwerin von Krosigk, a holdover from the last Weimar governments who served Hitler until 1945, was a fiscal conservative determined to balance the Reich budget. Hitler's first economics minister, Alfred Hugenberg, boasted impeccable credentials as a fiscal conservative. As the only cabinet minister to oppose outright the June 1, 1933, Reinhardt work creation program, he lived up to his reputation. These appointments in no way signaled a huge Nazi work creation program financed by radical monetary expansion. Personnel changes initiated by Hitler do not explain the fact that it became possible to finance larger work creation programs after January 30, 1933. Germany's financial leadership had not changed. It was the objective economic situation that had begun to change.

Before Hitler took power, sometime after the middle of 1932, the depression bottomed out in Germany, and the economy began a natural conjunctural upswing. The perception that the depression had bottomed out was a decisive factor in convincing the fiscally conservative Reichsbank and Reich finance ministry to finance a work creation program of major proportions. The change in attitude was becoming evident several months before Hitler came to power, just as Papen's work creation program was taking shape. Papen's August 28, 1932, Münster speech announced a new program to combat unemployment. Papen's speech calmed big business, which had feared that the government would introduce a massive public works program financed by special property taxes or compulsory loans to the state.[19]

Papen's Münster program relied for the most part on indirect work creation measures. Firms hiring additional workers obtained tax relief and permission to reduce contract wages of their employees. But Papen's program did include a direct work creation component calling for the expenditure of RM 167 million on earthmoving projects (mainly canals and roads), suburban settlements, agricultural land improvement, and agricultural settlements.[20]

It fell to Papen's finance minister, Krosigk, to explain how and why the government and Reichsbank could now drop its opposition to credit creation (*Vorfinanzierung*, prefinancing) for direct work creation, and gamble that deficit-creating tax relief to business in 1932–33 would be repaid in future years after the economy had recovered. The finance minister acknowledged that the Reich government still had little confidence that work creation programs in and of themselves could combat unemployment successfully. The economy had to revive itself so as to give the free forces that still remained "a certain amount of elbow-room." "The moment this happens, and only in so far as it does happen," explained Krosigk, "could a work creation program be appropriate and bring relief." Apparently that time had come. Krosigk admitted the risk of issuing tax certificates and work creation bills that the government would have to redeem a few years later, but he believed it was now a risk worth taking, "since in their [government's] view, a good bit of progress has already been made on the way to warding off the crisis, and solid ground will soon have been reached; beginning next spring, a general improvement in the economy can be expected."[21] Once the economy had bottomed out and the beginnings of an upswing were visible, the benefits of credit expansion and deficit spending outweighed the risks.

The economic conditions believed to be necessary for successful economic stimulation through public work creation programs were beginning to appear prior to Hitler's appointment to the chancellorship, but the political consensus required for such action was disintegrating. Perhaps the lack of consensus among the political parties of the Weimar constitutional system could have been overcome or simply ignored by substituting authoritarian leadership for the constitution. Hitler's predecessors, Brüning, Papen, and Schleicher, were already moving in the direction of authoritarian government. But those intriguing against the Weimar system could not agree on who or what should be substituted, and none but Hitler possessed the broad popular support that could make possible a return to an authoritarian system without either a civil war or military putsch. Only Hitler, controlling the largest party in the Reichstag, could lead a "legal" revolution.

With his observation that "the Third Reich obviously was not Weimar in politics, and that is why it was not Weimar in economics either," Gerald Feldman sought the key to understanding Hitler's success in putting Germany back to work.[22] Feldman was elaborating on Hjalmar Schacht's claim in 1949 that "work creation at the beginning of the 1930s could only be implemented by authoritarian regimes."[23] German industrial leaders, claimed Feldman, "did not oppose work creation and reflation if it were done under the right conditions," the "right conditions" being government action to contain or reduce wages, and the termination of legalized collective bargaining. By August 1933, businesspeople who had resisted work creation two years earlier were now doing their part to support the Hitler government's battle for jobs. The new attitude reflected not only an improved economic outlook but also the fact that under the developing Nazi dictatorship, "the price of insurance against unpleasant forms of government intervention had risen considerably."[24] By destroying the German trade unions, Hitler had finished the job begun by Brüning. In return, the government expected industry to cooperate in providing jobs for the unemployed. If that cooperation had not been forthcoming, implied Feldman, German industrialists might have faced unpleasant consequences from a brutal Nazi regime.

German big business hoped to restore profitability by destroying organized labor. Hitler sought to eliminate a perceived threat to his political power by destroying organized labor. Hitler and big business thus shared a common interest. But there would be a price to pay if the scheme were to work. Deprived of their right to organize and bargain collectively, workers would have to be provided with jobs. Over six million unemployed workers posed an intolerable threat to the stability of the Hitler government. With its limited financial resources, the government could only do so much with public works programs. Like it or not, German employers, be they industrialists or farmers, would have to furnish work and bread. By providing strong leadership and a new sense of direction, Hitler convinced many employers that cooperation was worth the gamble. Economic recovery may have continued with or without Hitler, but neither Hitler nor the industrialists wanted economic recovery to occur under the detested Weimar system.

Was deficit-financed public work creation, then, one of those undertakings in which "the Nazi government used repression to escape from its unfulfillable promises to the German population"?[25] It may be stretching logic to argue both that the promise of bread and work was "unfulfillable" in the months following January 1933, and that "Hitler also benefitted from the chance fact that the depression was coming to an end."[26] It is not this inconsistency that concerns us here, but rather the question of how Hitler and the Nazis put Germany back to work before the rearmament program took hold of the economy. Did the Nazis misrepresent their success through the manipulation of labor market statistics? Did the Nazi government use repression against both labor and employers to make good on its promise of bread and jobs? Was National Socialist work creation the one decent, constructive program of the regime, or was it, too, characterized by the brutality that pervaded every other aspect of the Nazi dictatorship?

1

National Socialist Labor Market Statistics: Fact or Fiction?

Can we accept at face value the labor market statistics provided by a regime that perfected the "Big Lie" propaganda technique? The Nazis used labor market statistics to glorify Hitler's accomplishments and to predict even greater triumphs in the future. According to official labor market statistics, Hitler achieved an "economic miracle" during his first three years as leader of the German nation. This alleged miracle occurred before rearmament under the 1936 Four Year Plan took hold of the German economy. Was this astonishing feat simply the result of cooked labor market statistics? Does the propaganda function of Nazi statistics invalidate the statistics themselves?

Twenty years ago Timothy W. Mason suggested that the miraculous recovery of the labor market under Hitler was more appearance than reality. He argued that the 1933 reclassification of hundreds of thousands of emergency relief workers as "employed" represented an illegitimate "statistical manipulation," a triumph of propaganda designed to credit the Nazis with an illusory improvement in the labor market.[1] Michael Kater asserted in 1983 that recent scholarship in eastern and western Europe had shown that labor market figures published by the Nazis were "often deceptive because of inconsistent arithmetic or outright falsification."[2] These warnings aroused suspicion but produced no formal, systematic challenges to the validity of Nazi labor market statistics. Harold James endorsed Nazi labor market statistics when he argued recently that Germany's economic recovery resulted from "a dramatic revival in economic activity" unaided by "statistical manipulation," a "statistical conjuring trick," or "jiggery-pokery with numbers."[3]

The Nazis did manipulate labor market statistics. Manipulation took the form of changes in the criteria for classifying the labor force as either employed or unemployed, and alterations in the procedures for registering the unemployed and processing labor market statistics. The impact of manipulation on published labor market statistics has never been established clearly, and there may have been valid theoretical arguments for the classification changes made by the Nazis. This study will examine the management of labor market statistics by the Nazis and will judge the extent to which this management may have affected the validity and reliability of those statistics.[4]

Dictatorial regimes are noted for their attempts to restrict the circulation of accurate information to a select few within the system. Those who lie outside the inner circle are treated to a barrage of propaganda designed to enhance the prestige of the regime. Statistical information provided by modern dictatorships must be used with extreme caution, but it need not be summarily rejected. While Mussolini's penchant for exaggeration is now well documented, experts doubt that Italy's Fascist government falsified labor market statistics for political reasons.[5] Similar arguments have been advanced in the German case. C. W. Guillebaud assumed that if the Nazis had wished to hide the truth about unemployment rates, they would have ceased publication of the statistics—just as they eventually discontinued publication of the Reich budget in order to maintain the secrecy of military expenditures. Gerhard Kroll, for whom the steep decline in unemployment during 1933 "borders on the miraculous," nevertheless felt that "it would be a mistake" to assume deliberate Nazi alteration of unemployment statistics. The mass of statistics, he argued, was too large to be falsified in a credible manner, and such altered statistics would have been useless for official internal use.[6]

These purely logical arguments against the possibility of doctored statistics are by no means conclusive. Proof of deliberate alteration of labor market statistics requires evidence that "incorrect" figures resulted from willful activity by the responsible authorities. I have been unable to uncover archival evidence of deliberate alteration of labor market statistics. Nevertheless, the accuracy and reliability of labor market statistics may have suffered from the disorganization and reduced competence attendant upon the nazification of two institutions responsible for collecting and recording relevant statistics, the Statistisches Reichsamt (Reich Statistical Office) and the Reichsanstalt für Arbeitsvermittlung und Arbeitslosenversicherung (Reich Institution for Placement and Unemployment Insurance, RfAA).[7] Moreover, changes made after January 30, 1933, in the method of classifying the "employed" and "unemployed" may have served to reduce the unemployment rate by artificial means. Finally, Nazi revisions of regulations governing unemployment insurance coverage and eligibility altered the number of persons who were likely to be counted in official labor market statistics.

The Reich Statistical Office traced its roots to 1872, when, shortly after the creation of the Second German Empire, the Imperial Statistical Office (Kaiserliche Statistisches Amt) was established directly under the supervision of the imperial chancellor, Otto von Bismarck. Seven years later, supervision of the office was transferred to the head of the Reich interior department. Operation of the statistical office was vested in a director, who, from 1902, held the title of president. Under the Weimar Republic, the imperial statistical office was renamed the Reich Statistical Office. In 1923, Ernst Wagemann was named president of the office.

Born to a German family living in Chile in 1884, Wagemann took his university studies in Berlin and entered the imperial civil service. Prior to his 1923 appointment to the presidency of the Reich Statistical Office, he had directed the statistical department of the war food office from 1916 to 1918 and had held positions in the Reich economics ministry after the war. In 1925, Wagemann founded the prestigious Institut für Konjunkturforschung (IfK) and, until 1933, served as both president of the Reich statistical office and director of the Institut.[8]

Hitler's formation of his first cabinet on January 30, 1933, placed Wagemann in a perilous position. The fact that Wagemann had joined the Nazi party did not protect him from the purging of civil servants deemed undesirable under the new regime. In this case, however, it was a rabid German nationalist, Alfred Hugenberg, rather than the Nazis, who forced Wagemann to give up his post at the statistical office. Until he was forced to resign on June 26, 1933, Hugenberg held the portfolios for both economics and agriculture in Hitler's first cabinet, and he sought to become an "economic dictator" who "would now have the opportunity to implement his grand design for the reorganization of the German economy."[9] Hugenberg seemed intent on settling old scores and weeding out those who might try to thwart his plans for economic reform and recovery.

In Hugenberg's view, personal and policy considerations earmarked Wage-

mann for dismissal. Wagemann's brother-in-law, who was the former IG Farben executive and onetime Reich economics minister Hermann Warmbold,
had opposed agrarian demands for protection when the matter came before
the Papen cabinet in 1932. As agriculture minister, Hugenberg sought concessions aimed at relieving Germany's farmers. Hugenberg opposed the June
1933 Reinhardt work creation program because he believed it threatened to
unleash inflation. In 1932, Wagemann had advanced a plan for monetary
expansion that was universally denounced as inflationary.[10]

In mid-March 1933, Hugenberg suspended Wagemann from his duties
at the Reich statistical office and ordered him to step down as president
of the IfK. Hugenberg's judgment of Wagemann was not shared by the
leading personalities of the Nationalsozialistische Deutsche Arbeiterpartei
(NSDAP), including Hitler, nor was it shared by most of Germany's economic leadership, who appreciated Wagemann's efforts to provide them
with reliable statistical material. By the middle of June, Hugenberg himself
had worn out his welcome in Hitler's cabinet. Representatives of the new
Nazi labor organization, the German Labor Front (Deutsche Arbeitsfront,
DAF), now sat on the IfK board of trustees. Apparently unable to salvage
Wagemann's position at the statistical office, the DAF trustees were determined to keep him as director of the IfK. At a meeting on June 16, 1933,
they changed the IfK charter, separating the directorship of the IfK from
the presidency of the Reich statistical office. After revising the charter to
read "The director of the IfK is elected by the board of directors," they
elected Wagemann director.[11]

In establishing the IfK in 1925, Wagemann sought to provide a source
of statistical information and analysis associated with, but independent of,
official Reich and Länder authorities. With the rise of the Nazis to power
and the "coordination" of all autonomous organizations, Wagemann's hope
for an independent statistical operation was diminished. Yet he continued
to press his case, making the necessary compromises with National Socialism. "The IfK," wrote Wagemann, "will, as before, be driven by the
endeavor to reflect as accurately as possible processes of movement in the
national economy and the world economy." He did recognize that the advent
of National Socialism required some adjustment in the IfK's attitudes. Liberal individualism had to be abandoned in favor of "close contact between
the individual branches of the economy, between the private economy and
the national economy, in other words: the adjusting of the individual interest
to the welfare of the whole promotes the spirit of the new state leadership.

The IfK regards it as its foremost task to facilitate for the individual a view of the total economy over and above the narrow circle of his own interests."[12]

How, or if, this new attitude affected the validity of IfK statistics is unclear. Wagemann's statement of purpose reflected the attitude expressed by the German Labor Front after Robert Ley's Nazi organization replaced the trade unions and workers' associations in 1933. According to the DAF, unions had used the statistics they compiled to promote their own interests. "The union statistics," claimed the DAF, "were thus an exact mirror-image of the liberalism that shaped the *Systemzeit*," and were useless for compiling the total picture required for an economic policy benefiting the entire nation.[13] Neither Wagemann nor the DAF explained how statistics reflecting the "National Socialist spirit" differed from "liberal" statistics.

As a step toward unitary handling of economic statistics, the Prussian Land statistical office was dissolved in 1934, and its personnel largely absorbed by the Reich statistical office. Reich efforts to monopolize and centralize statistical collection and reporting, however, were not entirely successful, because other Land statistical offices continued to function. In an effort to pursue "a more thorough investigation of the economic situation in particular regions," Wagemann set out to establish branches of the IfK in various German cities.[14] By 1937, there was an IfK branch in Essen, another was soon to be opened in Breslau, and negotiations were under way for a branch in Munich.

The estimated RM 50,000 annual cost of the Munich IfK office was to be shared by the IfK, the Bavarian Land government, and Bavarian chambers of commerce and industry. Although Wagemann had apparently discussed such a possibility ten years earlier, he lost interest when it became clear that an IfK branch would have to be attached to the Bavarian statistical office. The 1937 discussions broke down when Wagemann indicated that a Munich office of the IfK would operate independently of the chamber of industry and trade and the Bavarian statistical office. Ultimately, regional leaders of government, industry, and the NSDAP decided that the opening of an IfK branch in Munich was unnecessary. The economy's development, they argued, had been "subordinated to political influences." Business cycle research was superfluous, since business cycles had been all but eliminated by National Socialist "steering" of the economy. Furthermore, they claimed, the requirements of a steered economy had stimulated improvements in the collection and analysis of official Reich statistics. Because the IfK now (1937) relied on official Reich statistics for its analysis of employment, unemployment, imports, exports, production, consumption, and population trends, Wagemann's organization no longer functioned as an independent statistical collection agency.[15]

Official German labor market statistics originated from two sources. The Reich Institution for Placement and Unemployment Insurance (RfAA), through its regional and local employment offices, collected and published statistics on the registered unemployed. The Reich workers' insurance system (Krankenkasse) collected statistics on employed workers covered by the system. Since the RfAA did not count the unemployed who failed to register with the employment offices, either because they were "discouraged" or ineligible for benefits, and because not all workers were covered under the insurance system (after August 1933, agricultural, forestry, and domestic labor in particular), neither the official unemployment statistics nor the official employment statistics present a completely accurate picture of Germany's labor market (see Appendix, Table 1).[16]

The RfAA was particularly susceptible to the nazification efforts of the Hitler regime. Because of the agency's functional connection to the German labor market, the RfAA's personnel included many admitted and alleged communists, socialists, and Jews. The RfAA was established in 1927 as an autonomous, self-governing public body under the supervision of the Reich Labor Ministry. In addition to administering unemployment insurance (made compulsory under the 1927 act), the RfAA compiled and published labor market statistics, served as a placement office for the unemployed, provided vocational guidance and rehabilitation, and furnished funds for crisis relief *(Krisenunterstützung)* and productive unemployment assistance *(wertschaffende Arbeitslosenfürsorge)* in the form of emergency public works *(Notstandsarbeiten)* undertaken to reduce unemployment.

After January 30, 1933, the nazification of the RfAA began with a sweeping purge of the agency's personnel under terms of the "Law for the Restoration of the Professional Civil Service" (Gesetz zur Wiederherstellung des Berufsbeamtentums, BBG) of April 7, 1933. The number of RfAA civil servants, salaried employees, and wage workers who were dismissed, demoted, transferred, or involuntarily retired during 1933–34 under the terms of the BBG totaled 3,455, of whom 3,037 were dismissed. At least an equal number of salaried employees were fired under terms of their labor contract in cases in which there was no legal basis for dismissal under the BBG. Thus, in 1933–34, at least 6,000 (22 percent) of the RfAA's staff of 26,606 were dismissed. It has been estimated that during the same year, as many as 11,000 new employees were hired, but it is not clear how many of these were replacements for those dismissed. In hiring, firing, and promotion, political reliability and racial desirability were the main criteria for selection.[17]

After routine inspections during 1932 had uncovered irregularities in the collection of statistics by some local RfAA employment offices, RfAA president Friedrich Syrup ordered unannounced monthly examinations of statistical computations in the local employment offices.[18] The drastic purge of the RfAA after the Nazi takeover further compromised the efficiency and competence of the RfAA, particularly since seasoned experts were replaced with inexperienced personnel whose competence was less important than their political reliability and racial acceptability. Training and cram courses for new salaried employees produced meager results because instruction in Nazi ideology and race theory consumed a disproportionate amount of the curriculum.[19]

Quality-control procedures within the RfAA broke down completely with Hitler's assumption of the chancellorship. Quality control examination of the employment offices was suspended for at least six or seven months. When resumed in September 1933, the examination of offices was no more than a perfunctory procedure. During the fiscal year April 1, 1933, to March 31, 1934, only 42 of the 360 local and 13 district offices were evaluated even on this limited scale. Four years later, Syrup eviscerated examinations designed to assure the accuracy of AA labor market statistics.[20]

Personnel purges, the breakdown of discipline, reduced competency levels, and relaxation of examination procedures in the RfAA cast doubt upon the reliability of German labor market statistics after January 30, 1933. Into an already chaotic situation, the National Socialist government introduced changes in the statistical classification of Germany's labor force, which were both questionable theoretically and extremely confusing to untrained and often unqualified personnel. Errors in the classification of some members of the labor force occurred prior to the Nazi takeover, but uncertainty about the classification regulations intensified as a result of changes in classification criteria during 1933 and 1934. Reich cabinet approval of the June 1, 1933, Law for the Reduction of Unemployment (Gesetz zur Verminderung der Arbeitslosigkeit) occasioned new classification regulations and a revision of forms used to record and report labor market statistics. The "simplified" statistical reporting methods introduced by the RfAA on October 1, 1933, were in fact quite complex.[21]

Confusing regulations produced errors in statistical record-keeping at local employment offices. "Welfare unemployed" (*Wohlfahrtserwerbslose*, WE) who enlisted in the Voluntary Labor Service were counted in RfAA statistics as "looking for work," but were not counted as either "unemployed" or "employed."[22] Beginning July 31, 1933, emergency relief workers, Labor Service volunteers, and agrarian Land Helpers were no longer counted as "unemployed." This seemingly straightforward classification change, however, produced a nightmare for employment office workers trying to classify emergency relief workers who were employed on large earthmoving projects *(Tiefbauarbeiten-Erdarbeiten)* under section one, paragraph one, number seven, of the June 1, 1933, work creation law. Such workers received no wage but continued to receive either unemployment insurance benefits, crisis support, or local welfare support, as well as one warm meal a day and coupons for the purchase of some basic necessities. Regulations implementing the June 1 law stipulated that these particular emergency relief workers were to be counted in different ways for three specific purposes: (1) in the productive unemployment statistics, as "employed" through the reporting employment office; (2) in the labor market statistics, as "looking for work" through the person's hometown employment office; and (3) in the unemployment insurance or emergency relief statistics, as a primary relief recipient through the hometown employment office. These emergency relief workers could thus be considered simultaneously as "employed," "looking for work," and "on relief." Beginning July 31, 1933, emergency relief workers appeared in published official statistics as "employed."[23] The classification of applications for unemployment insurance benefits as "first applications," "new applications," and "applications for resumption" also confused employment office employees. Discrepancies between monthly totals and daily figures could not be ironed out, because statistics were not always entered on the proper forms on a daily basis.[24]

Errors made in recording and computation cast doubt on the reliability of Nazi labor market statistics. Moreover, post–January 1933 revisions of the regulations governing unemployment insurance coverage and eligibility altered the scope and inclusiveness of German labor market statistics. At the end of April 1933, an estimated 2,673,724 persons worked in segments of the labor market that were "exempt" from unemployment insurance coverage. Neither the exempt workers nor their employers contributed to the compulsory unemployment insurance fund, and such workers could not collect unemployment compensation if they found themselves out of work.

By May 1934, Nazi regulations exempting previously covered agricultural, fishery, forestry, and domestic labor had increased the number of exempt workers by 1,384,458, up to an estimated 4,058,182. The government regarded these new exemptions as "job creation" measures. Relieved of costly contributions to the unemployment fund, employers of such workers would hire additional personnel.[25]

The employment effect of the new exemptions is not clear, but the Nazis either inadvertently or intentionally contributed to the statistical improvement in the labor market outlook simply by changing the rules of the game. "Official" labor market statistics counted as "unemployed" only those jobless persons who reported to RfAA employment offices. Persons who are not covered by unemployment insurance or who are ineligible for unemployment benefits are less likely to register than those who are covered and eligible. As the ranks of the "official" unemployed declined, the number of "invisible" unemployed grew in 1933. Estimates of the number of discouraged workers ran as high as two million.[26] Oscar Weigert, author of the 1927 unemployment insurance law, suggested in 1934 that labor market statistics were "no longer complete" because unemployed persons not entitled to benefits failed to report to employment offices. In London, the Royal Institute for International Affairs noted that changes in registration procedures and statistical methods rendered German labor unemployment statistics suspect. The Institute suggested that "employment figures afford a better basis for measuring the degree of recovery."[27]

Employment statistics provide no better measure of German economic recovery than do unemployment statistics. Official employment statistics were compiled by the Reich compulsory health insurance offices (Krankenkassen). Persons currently gainfully employed and covered by compulsory workers' health insurance were counted as "employed." Theoretically, each participant in the German labor market encompassed by official labor market statistics could be counted as either "employed" or "unemployed."

The Nazis made important changes in the classification scheme. Beginning with the July 31, 1933, statistics, those who were enrolled in various types of government job creation programs, such as Land Helpers *(Landhilfer)*, Labor Service volunteers *(Arbeitsdienstwillige)*, emergency relief workers *(Notstandsarbeiter)*, and public relief workers *(Fürsorgearbeiter)* were removed from the "unemployed" category and, with the exception of Labor Service volunteers discussed later, were counted as "employed."

By the simple stroke of the pen, the Nazis seemingly reduced the ranks of the "unemployed" by 619,000. The historian Timothy W. Mason considered this reclassification scheme as illegitimate "statistical manipulation," a triumph of propaganda designed to give the Nazis credit for an illusory improvement in the labor market.[28] At the time, the government vigorously denied that the dramatic decline in unemployment during Hitler's first months as chancellor simply reflected changes in the classification system and methods of computing the unemployment rate. RfAA president Syrup, the trustee of German labor market statistics, assured key Reich cabinet ministers that "The amazing decline of the unemployment figures during this year [1933] is in no way to be attributed to changes in the statistical methods; rather, it completely corresponds to an actual improvement in the labor market." Syrup also claimed that verification and inspection procedures guaranteed the accuracy of official labor market statistics.[29]

The defining characteristics of "official" German unemployment statistics can now be stated clearly. Unemployment figures provided by the RfAA merely reflected the number of unemployed who reported to local employment offices seeking either employment or unemployment benefits. Monthly changes in these totals to some extent represented real improvement or deterioration of the German labor market, but to an undetermined extent such changes also reflected the impact of revised regulations governing coverage and eligibility for unemployment compensation benefits.

Official labor market statistics provided neither an entirely accurate count of the true number of unemployed and employed nor an entirely accurate indicator of the extent of labor market improvement or deterioration in any given month. Given the apparent shortcomings of "official" monthly labor market statistics, an alternate source of statistics might serve as a check against the accuracy of the official numbers. The "coordination" *(Gleichs-chaltung)* of competing power centers and independent institutions by the Nazis during 1933 left little in the way of independently prepared "unofficial" labor market statistics. There were, however, sources of statistics other than the RfAA and the Krankenkassen. The Reich Statistical Office conducted occupational censuses in 1907, 1925, and the middle of June 1933. Beginning in October 1933, Ernst Wagemann's Institut für Konjunkturforschung (IfK) published its own monthly estimate of German employment. Finally, a check on official unemployment statistics for a portion of the unemployed can be obtained by comparing monthly district welfare authority (Bezirksfürsorgeverbände) estimates of the number of locally supported "welfare unemployed" (*Wohlfahrtserwerbslose*, WE) with official statistics provided by local RfAA offices.

The 1933 Statistical Office census listed 5,900,000 persons as unemployed, and 14,239,000 as actually working. The occupational census, then, indicated about 800,000 more unemployed than the official RfAA statistics for May to June, and between 900,000 and one million more employed than official Krankenkassen statistics.[30] Although useful, this snapshot of the German labor market in June 1933 needs to be supplemented by a continuing labor market series that can be compared with official figures on a monthly basis. Much more interesting are the monthly attempts to count the number of welfare unemployed, which produced significant discrepancies between figures provided by local welfare authorities and estimates of local RfAA labor exchanges. Undercounting of WE could work against local welfare authorities, who received Reich assistance *(Reichswohlfahrtshilfe)* on the basis of the number of "recognized welfare unemployed." Local and regional administrative officials sought explanations for the discrepancies that, they believed, caused their districts to lose Reich welfare assistance to which they were entitled.[31]

From the end of August 1930 to the end of July 1932, monthly statistics on the number of WE were compiled by both the district welfare authorities and the local employment offices (Arbeitsämter, AA) of the RfAA. The data of these two agencies "differed not insignificantly from one another for various reasons."[32] Monthly statistics on WE published by the Statistisches Reichsamt between August 1930 and July 1932 indicate that the district welfare authorities consistently counted more WE than did the AA. In some cases, relief recipients did not report to the AA on the day of the count for one reason or another (illness, having found work, having moved), and were thus not counted by the AA. They may, however, have been counted as supported by district welfare authorities who were not aware of the recipients' new status or failure to report to the AA. After regulations of August 2, 1932, established the AA statistics on the number of WE as the basis for distribution of Reich welfare assistance *(Reichswohlfahrtshilfe)* to local welfare authorities, the Reich statistical office ceased to publish monthly WE statistics provided by the welfare district authorities.[33]

Local welfare authorities, however, continued to count their WE and continued to note significant discrepancies between their figures and the official

AA numbers. In September 1933, the Deutscher Gemeindetag, representing German municipal governments, asked the larger cities to report each month the number of "recognized" WE, as computed by local welfare authorities, "in order to approximate our survey with the official [AA] survey." This apparent challenge to official WE statistics lasted only until January 1934, when the Deutscher Gemeindetag asked cities to report the "official" WE figures provided by the AA and discontinue reporting the estimates provided by local welfare authorities. The organization explained that the differences between the two estimates were "no longer very significant," and felt it desirable that the count of recognized WE be based on "the most uniform statistics possible."[34]

Contrary to the Gemeindetag's claim, significant differences between the two counts of WE continued well into 1934. The organization may have been under pressure to discontinue an operation that cast doubt upon the validity of official labor market statistics. Local authorities, however, were not easily silenced. They wanted an independent count of WE and continued to report estimates provided by local welfare boards. The Gemeindetag admitted in April 1934 that "in some cases the figures for recognized WE provided by local welfare boards do not agree with RfAA figures," but it instructed cities to report the local AA figure on their response cards.[35] The "coordinated" National Socialist system could not tolerate two sets of statistics.

Although there is no independent series against which official unemployment statistics can be checked, monthly estimates of employment published by the IfK beginning in October 1933 do provide a series against which the official Krankenkassen employment statistics can be compared. It may thus be possible to assess the reliability of German employment statistics and to examine the relationship between the decline in unemployment and the increase in employment during the early years of the Nazi regime.

The IfK's employment estimates are of particular interest because they distinguish between "regular" employment ("real" private sector jobs) and *zusätzliche* employment (supplementary or substitute employment of Land Helpers, emergency relief workers, public relief workers, and members of the Labor Service) (see Appendix, Table 2). IfK estimates of "regular" employment consistently differed significantly from official statistics on the number of employed (see Appendix, Table 3). Much of this apparent discrepancy probably had more to do with changes made in the labor market classification system during 1933 than with actual "undercounting" or "overcounting" by one agency or the other. The precise impact of changes in classification regulations is, however, difficult to establish.

Between the end of June and the end of July 1933, reclassification struck 619,000 persons (land helpers, emergency relief workers, welfare employed, and labor service volunteers) from the list of the "unemployed," and presumably added the same number to the list of "employed." This administrative change was in no obvious way reflected in official labor market statistics for the month June 30–July 31, 1933, which showed unemployment declining by 393,101 while total employment increased by 128,685 (see Appendix, Table 4).[36] In the unlikely event that the June–July period brought no downturn in "real" unemployment, the official "unemployment" figure should have dropped by 619,000, the number deleted from the rolls. One could interpret the June–July decline in unemployment as unusually large compared with the previous month, but the June–July increase in total employment was virtually unchanged from the May–June gain. If 619,000 persons "vanished" from the official unemployment statistics on July 31, 1933, where, statistically, did they go? The presumption that they were all added to the ranks of the officially "employed" cannot be sustained. To begin with, the 262,992 persons enrolled in the Labor Service on July 31 were no longer counted as "unemployed," but neither were they counted as "employed," even though, until April 30, 1935, they were counted as insured by the national workers' health insurance service.[37] Members of the labor service were, in effect, statistically deleted from the German labor force. Adding these 262,992 labor service workers to the June–July recorded increase in "employed" (+128,685) produces a total increase of 391,677, almost precisely the equivalent of the 393,101 decrease in official unemployment for that month. Although many will find this precise balance aesthetically pleasing, it is most likely completely fortuitous.

Those who would attempt to correct the Nazi labor market statistics might refer to similar operations performed on 1930s labor market statistics for the United States. Michael R. Darby believed (as did Germany's National Socialist government) that emergency relief workers should have been counted as "employed" rather than "unemployed."[38] He attempted to correct American employment and unemployment statistics by adding federal emergency relief workers to the standard Bureau of Labor Statistics (Lebergott) employment series for 1929–1943 and subtracting emergency relief workers from the standard BLS/Lebergott unemployment series.

Aside from questions about the theoretical appropriateness of counting emergency relief workers as employed, it is not at all clear that the "true" count can be established merely by subtracting such persons from one column and adding them to the other. Assuming that it is not legitimate to count employees of "federal contra-cyclical programs" as "employed," what happens when one applies Darby's technique to German labor market statistics? One would presumably reverse Darby's procedure and add 619,000 to the official July 31, 1933, unemployment figure and subtract 356,008 (262,992 Labor Service volunteers have already been "deducted" from the total 619,000) from the official employment total. This procedure yields the unlikely result that unemployment during July had increased back to the level of May 31 and that employment had decreased back to the level of early May.[39]

There seems to be no rigorous correlation between the number of persons affected either by reclassification schemes or by monthly changes in employment and unemployment figures. The first strikingly sharp break in labor market statistics occurred prior to the June–July 1933 reclassification schemes, in February and March, with a 6.70 percent decline in unemployment as compared with a decline of only 1.54 percent between February and March 1932 (see Appendix, Table 1). The February–March statistical development has received little attention and is not easily explained. Reich labor minister Seldte may have been correct in attributing most of the early 1933 improvement in the labor market to normal seasonal fluctuations, assisted by unusually favorable weather conditions.[40] In any event, attempts to "correct" the Nazi labor market statistics produce questionable results.

There are theoretical as well as practical objections to counting workers on federal emergency relief projects as "employed." Jonathan R. Kesselman and N. E. Savin have pointed out that Darby's "corrected" unemployment series rests on several dubious implied hypotheses. Darby claimed that the "corrected" data revealed the American economy's "true" speed of adjustment from high unemployment rates to the "natural rate." A similar claim would presumably be made for "corrected" German unemployment statistics; "otherwise," as Kesselman and Savin observed with reference to Darby's work, "the corrected figures merely reclassify relief workers from the unemployed to the employed category," and have no theoretical significance.[41]

Kesselman and Savin were not merely arguing that emergency relief workers really were "unemployed"; they were also contesting Darby's inferred hypothesis that the "corrected" data measure how many persons would have been unemployed in the absence of the work creation programs. (Mason appears to have made the same inference for corrected German labor market statistics.) The case for reclassification of emergency relief workers as "employed" (presumably in either Germany or the United States), they argue, requires support from three underlying hypotheses: (1) that the natural-rate hypothesis be appropriate for the high unemployment setting of the 1930s; (2) that the natural unemployment rate for the 1930s be close to that of other decades; and (3) that work relief jobs displaced private sector and regular public jobs one for one, or, putting it another way, that an equivalent number of private sector or regular public sector jobs would have arisen in the absence of work relief programs. Without this latter behavior, "the government could have reduced the unemployment rate . . . to any desired level by expanding work relief programs." In that case, the "corrected" data would not convey an accurate picture of the economy's natural convergence to full employment.[42] Kesselman and Savin found no theoretical or empirical support for either the natural-rate hypothesis or the 100 percent displacement hypothesis for the United States during the 1930s, and they concluded that theoretical justification for counting American emergency relief workers as "employed" was lacking. On this basis, it seems equally inappropriate to consider German emergency relief workers as employed during the 1930s.

With this review of some of the practical and theoretical problems associated with the use of Nazi labor market statistics, it is now possible to outline the development of the German labor market between 1933 and 1936. Table 1 in the Appendix, "Development of the German labor market, 1928–1938," indicates an initial sharp reduction in unemployment in March 1933, before Hitler's government had either formulated a work creation program or manipulated the statistics. As Seldte suggested, this early sharp improvement in the labor market may have reflected the normal seasonal improvement enhanced by unusually favorable late winter and early spring weather conditions. It is also conceivable, though rather improbable, that the Nazi "victory" in the March 5 Reichstag elections (notwithstanding the fact that the Nazis won only 44 percent of the vote in a not entirely free election), coupled with the passage of the March 23 Enabling Act that created a Nazi dictatorship, spurred employer confidence sufficiently to encourage a wave of new hiring during March. The next significant acceleration in the decline of unemployment, which came during July and August 1933, must be attributed partially to the changes in classification that became effective during these months. It is highly improbable that the RM 1 billion Reinhardt program had any impact on the July and August labor market statistics, since the allocation of Reinhardt funds was not set until the end of June. It is not clear what portion of July's 8.09 percent decline in unemployment and August's 7.61 percent decline can be attributed to the natural upswing of the economy. In July and August 1932, the labor market had already reversed the 1930 and 1931 trends by registering unemployment declines of 1.53 percent and 3.12 percent respectively.

Trends in employment during 1933 did not exactly mirror trends in unemployment on a monthly basis. For the most part, when unemployment declined, employment rose, but not by the same magnitude. Employment might have been expected to rise most dramatically during July and August, as the impact of Nazi reclassification schemes was presumably reflected in official labor market statistics. This was not the case, however. The most remarkable monthly increase in employment, 9.25 percent, occurred in June 1933, when unemployment declined by 3.61 percent. This extraordinary monthly percentage gain in employment was unmatched in any other month during the entire decade from 1928 to 1938. In contrast, the monthly increases in employment during July and August 1933, as the reclassification schemes took effect, were only 0.97 percent and 2.09 percent respectively. The unusually large employment gain in June 1933 seems to be an anomaly for which no obvious statistical or economic explanation exists. Special hiring actions designed to provide jobs for Nazi "Old Fighters" may account for some of the June 1933 employment gains.

Nazi determination to hold on to the 1933 employment gains over the winter of 1933–34 seems to have paid dividends. Although unemployment rose sharply during December 1933, the onset of the seasonal deterioration was delayed (unemployment actually declined slightly in November 1933, as against an increase of 4.82 percent in November 1932); and the reduction of unemployment resumed without hesitation in January 1934 (contrasted to a 4.17 percent increase in unemployment a year earlier). It was in February and especially March 1934 that the truly remarkable break in unemployment occurred, as unemployment dropped by 10.61 percent and 17.03 percent respectively in these two months. The two Reinhardt programs of June and September 1933, particularly the second Reinhardt program for repair and renovation of housing, were now beginning to have a significant impact on economic activity.

The influence of these programs, particularly the housing program, seems to have been short-lived, as the decline in unemployment quickly fell back to much lower rates during the summer and early autumn of 1934. Compared to the previous winter, the winter of 1934–35 was a disaster, as unemployment registered very substantial increases during November (3.75 percent), December (10.71 percent), and January (14.16 percent). Employment, up 9.25 percent in June 1933, fell by 0.20 percent in June 1934, and rose slightly during the next four months (0.02 percent, 0.17 percent, 0.40 percent, 0.10 percent) until it began a three-month decline in November 1934. As 1934 drew to a close, the recovery of Germany's labor market remained hesitant at best. The permanence and irreversibility of Hitler's "economic miracle" seemed by no means assured. The unemployment rate had certainly fallen dramatically from 34 percent in January 1933, but between May 1934 and the end of March 1935, it appeared to be stuck at an eleven-month average of 14 percent.

From March 1935, open rearmament and compulsory military service drove Germany's labor market and economy in an upward direction. The Saar plebiscite of January 1935 (favorable to Germany) and the remilitarization of the Rhineland in March 1936 returned control over the western borderlands to Germany, and made it once again safe and attractive to invest in these important industrial regions. There were, nonetheless, some significant setbacks, and the unemployment rate again approached 14 percent during the winter of 1935–36.

Ideally, it would be useful to compare the development of German labor market statistics after the Nazi seizure of power with the development of other economic indicators. The reliability and usefulness of labor market statistics might be enhanced if, for example, it could be shown through regression analysis that their movement between 1933 and the end of 1935 correlated closely with the development of German industrial production. Unfortunately, any meaningful correlation is impossible because the basis for calculation changed throughout the 1930s. Changes in the definition and classification of "employed" and "unemployed" during 1933 were matched by changes in the calculation of German production statistics during the 1930s. For its annual statistical yearbook, the Reich statistical office utilized the quarterly production index generated by the IfK. The IfK modified the basis for its calculation of German production statistics a number of times during the 1930s. Industries were both added and deleted from the production index in March 1933 and June 1935, and seasonal correction of monthly statistics was dropped in June 1935.[43]

There is no evidence that the Nazis deliberately falsified labor market statistics during the years 1933 through 1935. Although authorities did "manipulate" both labor market and production statistics, the impact of that manipulation on the validity of the statistics remains unclear. Unemployment declined and employment rose at a very uneven pace between 1933 and 1936. There were "great spurts" forward as well as temporary periods of stagnation and setbacks. But the most pronounced monthly changes in labor market statistics do not seem to have been related to any of the changes made in the classification of the labor force as "employed" or "unemployed," changes in coverage and eligibility for unemployment benefits, or any other form of statistical manipulation. Even though they may not be entirely accurate for any given month, German labor market statistics for 1933 to 1936 provided a basically legitimate overview of the recovery process. Charges of statistical manipulation should not obscure the fundamental reality of the recovery of the labor market prior to the massive rearmament drive beginning in 1936. Statistics indicate that this recovery was incomplete and that it probably could not have been sustained without the transition to a rearmament economy.

Statistics can tell us what happened to the German labor market in the crucial years between 1933 and 1936, but they cannot explain why or show us how the recovery of the labor market took place. The following chapters will examine the origins and implementation of Nazi direct work creation programs, as well as the role that such programs played in Germany's economic recovery.

2

Financing Germany's Economic Recovery

Gerhard Kroll characterized the method of financing Germany's job creation and rearmament as "the truly essential phenomenon in overcoming the preceding conjunctural collapse."[1] Choosing a strategy for financing economic recovery confronted Hitler's government with a paradox. Catastrophic economic conditions seemed to demand unprecedented, innovative measures, but Hitler's government could not afford to gamble on wild economic experiments. Württemburg's Nazi economics minister Oswald Lehnich illuminated Hitler's dilemma with the observation that the new regime's opponents "hoped for dangerous experiments" that would fail.[2] As the Nazi regime sought to reestablish confidence among Germany's financial and industrial leadership, the financing of an ambitious economic recovery program had to find an acceptable middle ground between "more of the same" and "dangerous experiments."

During his first year as chancellor, Hitler rejected reckless financing of government expenditures. In 1933 he surrounded himself with fiscal conservatives such as Reichsbank president Hjalmar Schacht, Reich economics minister Alfred Hugenberg, and Reich finance minister Graf Lutz Schwerin von Krosigk, none of whom was a Nazi and each of whom was determined to avoid the potentially inflationary impact of unbalanced budgets and the creation of money and credit. Only after 1935 did Hitler feel free to spend recklessly. The financing of Nazi economic recovery programs drew upon credit-creation techniques already developed prior to Hitler's appointment to the chancellorship. What changed gradually after 1933 was the amount

28

of credit that the government was willing to create, and the government's commitment to retiring the debt created by that credit.[3]

Hitler told German industrialists in May that economic recovery required action by both the state and the private sector. The government's role was limited to encouraging private sector investment, mainly through tax incentives. He expressed willingness to provide significant public funding only for highway projects. Investment was unlikely if consumers refused to spend their money, and Hitler believed potential consumers were deferring purchases because they feared the social consequences of appearing better off than their less fortunate neighbors. National Socialist education and propaganda programs could "psychologically stimulate the economy" and develop a "lust for life" among consumers.[4]

In his government's first high-level meeting devoted to the matter of work creation on May 31, 1933, Hitler stressed that whatever plan was chosen, the Reich budget had to be balanced. A balanced budget meant reducing expenditures on social programs, because Hitler intended to reduce business taxes to promote investment.[5] A large work creation program undertaken without resort to deficit spending had to be financed outside the Reich budget. Fortunately, a means to this end, "prefinancing" *(Vorfinanzierung)* by means of "work creation bills" *(Arbeitsbeschaffungswechseln)*, was available. The method had already been developed prior to Hitler's chancellorship as a means of financing Günther Gereke's *Sofortprogramm*.[6]

Under the scheme of prefinancing with work creation bills, the Reich finance ministry distributed work creation bills (three months, renewable up to five years) to participating credit institutions (Deutsche Gesellschaft für öffentliche Arbeiten [Öffa], Deutsche Bau- und Bodenbank, Deutsche Rentenbank-Kreditanstalt, Deutsche Siedlungsbank, Reichs-Kredit-Gesellschaft) and public agencies. Contractors and suppliers who required cash in order to participate in work creation projects drew bills against the agency ordering the work or the appropriate credit institution. The appropriate credit institution then accepted (assumed liability for payment of) the bills, which, now treated as commercial paper, could be discounted at any one of a number of banks that had been joined in a special consortium. Consortium banks could rediscount the bills at the Reichsbank. The entire process of drawing, accepting, and discounting work creation bills provided the cash necessary to pay the contractors and suppliers. The Reich treasury undertook to redeem these bills, one-fifth of the total each year, between 1934 and 1938, as the economy and tax receipts recovered. As security for the bills, the Reich treasury deposited with the credit institutions a corresponding amount of tax vouchers *(Steuergutscheine)* or other securities. As the treasury redeemed work creation bills, the tax vouchers were to be returned to the treasury.[7]

The "work creation bill" has been characterized as "a sort of financial practical joke played on the German credit system."[8] This view may at first seem justified, given the manner in which the Nazis later abused a similar financing technique for rearmament through the issue of billions of Reich marks in "Mefo-bills" drawn on the Metallurgisches Forschungsgesellschaft, a government holding company. The Reich government cared little about the amount of Mefo-bills that it issued, and it had no intention of redeeming them, but this was not the Reich government's attitude with respect to the work creation bills issued between 1933 and 1935. Those who reluctantly had recourse to work creation bills as a means of financing jobs programs under both Schleicher and Hitler were fiscal and monetary conservatives. Reich economics ministers Hermann Warmbold, Alfred Hugenberg, Kurt Schmitt, and Hjalmar Schacht, Reich finance minister Krosigk, and Reichsbank presidents Hans Luther and Schacht, could hardly be described as practical jokesters. Harold James accurately described the early years of the Nazi era (up to 1936) as "a regime of fiscal conservatism," in which government borrowing was "rather restrained" and deficits "were always rather conservatively funded."[9]

Raising taxes to pay for work creation was the only alternative to financing through creation of credit. In 1933, however, Brüning-style tax increases were rejected by Germany's leading "Keynesian," Wilhelm Lautenbach, as well as by the Nazi party's economic expert in the Reich finance ministry, Fritz Reinhardt. Reinhardt believed that credit creation for purposes of job creation posed no inflationary threat and that it would be a far more responsible policy than the more "conservative" approach of tax increases and balanced budgets. Redeeming work creation bills would burden the 1934–1939 Reich budgets, but the decline in Reich expenditures for welfare support and other subsidies, claimed Reinhardt, would more than offset the redemption payments. The "surplus" would be used to reduce public debt and reduce taxes. Though he did not share Reinhardt's Nazi political perspective, Lautenbach also recommended stimulating demand by increasing public spending. This additional public spending had to be financed by an expansion of credit. Otherwise, he argued, the result would be not an increase in demand but merely a redistribution of demand accompanied by further disturbances in the economy.[10]

Legal restrictions on the activities of the Reichsbank virtually dictated recourse to work creation bills as a means of putting six million Germans back to work. The 1924 Reichsbank Law placed statutory limits on the expansion of central bank credit. The 40 percent minimum reserve in gold and foreign exchange against circulating notes restricted the central bank's credit-generating powers. The Reichsbank could not use government securities to meet its reserve requirement, nor could it engage in open-market activities to manipulate either the supply of central bank money or the interest rates at which government securities sold. To prevent a repetition of the hyperinflationary spiral of 1923, the 1924 law imposed a ceiling on the Reichsbank's discounting of Reich treasury bills. Commercial banks, not the Reichsbank, were expected to absorb Reich treasury issues.[11] Because the Reichsbank's legitimate function was to finance the real requirements of trade, commerce, and industry, the 1924 law placed no limit on the Reichsbank's discounting of commercial paper. Under the 1924 law, the Reichsbank could participate in the financing of public work creation programs only by invoking the Reichsbank's unlimited authority to rediscount commercial paper. Reich "work creation bills" had to be dressed up as "commercial paper."[12]

Public work creation programs in 1932 and 1933 were financed by work creation bills simply because, given the restrictive Reichsbank law, there was no other way to insure the Reichsbank's participation. The Reichsbank's inclusion in the scheme was essential both because the reserves of the public treasuries were exhausted and because large-scale borrowing on domestic and foreign capital markets was out of the question.[13] The Reichsbank's main role in financing public work creation programs between 1932 and 1935 took the form of offering rediscount privileges for various types of work creation bills. The Reichsbank's offer, however, did not necessarily mean that every outstanding bill would be presented to the Reichsbank. It was hoped and expected that, as the economy recovered, banks would view these bills as first-class securities bearing a reasonable rate of interest—that is, as securities worth holding in their own portfolios.[14] The employment of the work creation bill, then, far from being a practical joke, was viewed at the time as the most conservative, responsible, temporary means of financing the creation of jobs for Germany's six million unemployed.

During discussions of financing arrangements for Gereke's *Sofortpro-gramm* between December 1932 and February 1933, many questioned whether this temporary financing would ever be transformed into long-term consolidated debt on Germany's capital market, and whether the banks could be persuaded to take up work creation bills even with the necessary guarantees and rediscount privileges. Gereke professed optimism that it would not be necessary to renew all of the work creation bills until the final redemption date in 1938. He anticipated that at least a portion of the bills could be consolidated prior to 1938, thereby easing the bank consortium's dependence on Reichsbank rediscount privileges. But the Reichs-Kredit-Gesellschaft, one of the primary credit-issuing institutions for the *Sofort-programm*, warned that it would be difficult to obtain on Germany's capital market the long-term loan needed to retire the temporary financing. "Owing to the intrusions of recent years in the legal relationship between debtors and creditors," the institution observed, "banks recommending German fixed-interest securities often still encounter a strong attitude of rejection among the investing public."[15] The bank consortium, however, did take up significant amounts of work creation bills (with the intent of rediscounting them, rather than holding them in bank portfolios), to the point where Öffa felt that the volume of its normal business (and normal profits) with the banks was endangered. Öffa demanded—and obtained from the Reich finance minister—an increase on the interest spread (its profit margin) on work creation bills from ¾ percent to 1⅛ percent.[16]

Only after the major work creation programs were in place did the Reichsbank Act of October 27, 1933, remove the restrictions of the 1924 Act and effectively empower the Reichsbank to create money and credit without limit. Prior to Hitler's assumption of the chancellorship, claimed Schacht, the Reichsbank's main role lay in "taking up a defensive position against the defective economic and financial policy" of pre-Hitler govern-ments. With Hitler in power, the Reichsbank "left its former defensive posi-tion and took the field in the front line of the battle for work" and supported the Reinhardt program by promising rediscount privileges for RM 1 billion in work creation bills for the June 1, 1933, Reinhardt program.[17] And while the "Second Reinhardt Program" of September 1933 provided RM 500 million directly from the Reich budget for home repairs and enlargements, the Reichsbank stood ready to rediscount and/or prolong any "repair bills" *(Reparaturwechsel)* drawn by construction firms and handicraftsmen in need of financing for purchase of materials. Additionally, by August 1935, the

Reichsbank had provided the Reichsautobahnen corporation a rediscount credit of "several hundred million Reich marks" for construction of the *Autobahnen.*[18]

Although the potential now existed for a repetition of the 1923 hyper-inflation, that catastrophe was not repeated. In principle, the use of work creation bills to finance public job creation programs did not constitute fraud, and that use would not constitute fraud so long as the issue of such paper remained within reasonable limits, the Reich treasury's intent to redeem the paper remained firm, and commercial banks and other credit institutions stood ready to hold such paper as reserves. As long as these conditions were met, the use of work creation bills to finance job creation programs was not necessarily inflationary. Both Krosigk and Schacht were committed to payment of interest and redemption of work creation bills. They may have differed on the timing and schedule of redemption, but at least into early 1935 the record indicates no attempt to disregard the Reich treasury's redemption obligation (see Appendix, Table 5).

As the RM 1 billion Reinhardt program was being discussed and im-plemented in May and June 1933, the Reichsbank president, the Reich finance minister, and the Reich labor minister agreed on the need to avoid any depreciation of the currency and a price spiral resulting from an "unhealthy" increase in the money supply. The Reichsbank reluctantly agreed to support the required credit expansion, but only on the condition that the private sector and the national railway contributed funds of their own. The Reichsbank demanded that, as the sole agency responsible for the health of the currency, it retain control over the extent and type of any credit expansion. The Reichsbank rejected any work creation financing plan that strained the central bank's capacity for financing credits, violated the banking law, or required the granting of credits that were unlikely to be repaid in the foreseeable future.[19]

Given these constraints, it is remarkable that Schacht consented to redis-count up to RM 1 billion under the Reinhardt program. In his autobiog-raphy published many years later, Schacht conceded that "the first milliard which I had sanctioned for the Reinhardt programme was insufficient, as we knew from the first that it would be. Further funds had to be provided, and at the same time a way had to be found to avoid an undue increase in the holding of bills of exchange by the Reichsbank, and a correspondingly undue increase in the issue of bank-notes."[20] Schacht was admitting ret-rospectively that neither he nor the government's top leadership believed a

RM 1 billion work creation program would conquer German unemployment. But, believing that the depression had bottomed out, Reichsbank officials reluctantly gambled on repayment of prefinanced work creation credits out of rising tax revenues during the next five years as Germany climbed out of the depression.[21] Schacht was determined that the Reich finance ministry would uphold its end of the bargain and redeem the work creation bills in a timely fashion.

On February 16, 1934, the Reich finance minister informed Hitler that, in addition to increasing military outlays, the 1934–35 Reich budget would have to accommodate the redemption of RM 300 million in tax vouchers and RM 390 million in work creation bills. Budgets from 1935 through 1938 would be burdened by similar redemption costs.[22] The Reich treasury was obligated to redeem RM 120 million from the Gereke program between April 1 and June 30, 1934, and another RM 200 million from the Reinhardt program between July 16 and October 15, 1934.

This redemption schedule rested on two assumptions: that economic recovery would provide increased revenue to accommodate these redemption payments, and that the work creation projects financed by the work creation bills would have been completed. Krosigk argued that because neither assumption had been realized by early 1934 (by March 1934, only two-thirds of the Gereke program and about one-seventh of the Reinhardt program had been implemented), the redemption schedule should be adjusted. He sought to restrict redemption to bills that had circulated for at least a half year as of November 15, 1933 (Gereke program), or March 1, 1934 (Reinhardt program). Under the Reich finance ministry (RFM) plan, the 1934–35 budget year redemptions would total RM 53 million for the Gereke program and RM 28 million for the Reinhardt program, a saving of RM 225 million for the year. Any adjustment required negotiation between the Reich treasury on the one hand, and on the other, the Reichsbank, the five major participating credit institutions, and a consortium of 250 banks involved in the financing of work creation projects. The four credit institutions and the bank consortium accepted the Reich finance ministry's proposal, stipulating that the redemptions be completed in 1938 and that bills falling due could no longer be used as the basis for credits. The Reichsbank, however, initially balked, because it wished to be relieved of the largest share of its rediscount liability as quickly as possible. The Reichsbank eventually accepted the finance ministry proposal on March 2, 1934, with the stipulation that the base redemptions for 1935–1938 equal a full one-fifth of the total, and that the 1934 savings be added in equal installments to the 1935– 1938 payments, bringing the annual redemption for those years to RM 362 million.[23]

The fate of the work creation bills can be traced in statistical records of the Reich finance ministry and the Reichsbank. In May 1934, the finance ministry projected its schedule of work creation costs through 1938. The RFM met its redemption obligation during fiscal year 1934. As of January 1, 1935, the Reich treasury had redeemed work creation bills amounting to RM 269 million (Papen program, RM 187.9 million; Gereke program, RM 52.9 million; Reinhardt program, RM 28.2 million).[24] Redemption of work creation bills seems to have proceeded on schedule during 1935 and 1936 as well. By the end of March 1935, the five major participating credit institutions had paid out approximately RM 1,625 million for 1932–33 programs financed by work creation bills. Deducting the RM 269 million redeemed by the Reich treasury, approximately RM 1,356 million in work creation bills presumably remained outstanding. This figure virtually corresponds with the actual circulation of work creation bills on March 30, 1935, RM 1,307 million, 41 percent of which was held by the Reichsbank. By the end of June 1936, approximately RM 1,936 million had been paid out for work creation programs. The Reich treasury's redemption responsibility totaled RM 1,084 by the end of fiscal year 1936, leaving a balance of approximately RM 852 million in unredeemed work creation bills. At the end of August 1936, work creation bills in circulation came to RM 825 million, only 13 percent of which were held by the Reichsbank (see Appendix, Tables 6 and 7).[25]

The Reichsbank's holding of work creation bills represented only a small portion of its overall financing of work creation in the wider sense. By the end of 1934, the Reichsbank had taken up bills from work creation programs of the Reichsbahn and the Reichsautobahnen corporation in an amount nearly equal to that of the work creation bills issued under the Papen, Gereke, and Reinhardt programs. By October 1936, the Reichsbank admitted that its holding of Mefo-bills (used to finance rearmament) "exceeds that of all other work creation credits."[26]

During 1934, over half of the work creation bills in circulation, described by the Reichsbank as "first-class securities bearing a good interest rate, and exceptionally liquid," rested in the Reichsbank's portfolio. Why did private banks and credit institutions shy away from such securities? According to the Reichsbank, many industrial and commercial firms with which it maintained direct credit relationships discounted work creation bills at the

Reichsbank in order to avoid the costs of going through the bank consortium established for that purpose. Moreover, banks that had piled up massive "emergency credits" with the Reichsbank at the height of the crisis used funds coming in during 1933 and 1934 to reduce their balance at the Reichsbank, rather than increasing their holdings of work creation bills. According to the Reichsbank, most of the money pumped into the economy through the prefinancing of work creation was used both for the repayment of bank credits and for increasing cash reserves, bank balances, and savings account balances.[27]

The Reichsbank attributed the sharp 1935–36 decline in the percentage of work creation bills held by the Reichsbank partly to increasing redemptions by the Reich treasury. But the decline was also a sign of the increasing liquidity of the money market.[28] During 1935, funds that were seeking an investment outlet piled up at financial institutions, with a resulting demand for first-class securities. To avoid an exorbitant expansion of the issue of short-term Reich securities, as well as to provide relief for the shortage of discountable paper, the Reichsbank invoked a scheme previously used in 1927. It had the German Gold Discount Bank issue approximately RM 700 million in *"Solawechsel,"* three-month paper, which were sold to banks and other financial institutions. The Gold Discount Bank used funds thus sucked out of the money market to purchase and hold work creation bills. In this manner, money market liquidity was harnessed for financing work creation programs, and the Reichsbank was relieved of a portion of its rediscounting burden under the work creation programs.[29]

By the end of 1935, the Reichsbank's role in financing work creation was drawing to a close, and the central bank was preparing for its next task, the financing of rearmament. The flow of Mefo-credits into the economy during 1936 had some bearing on the amount of authentic work creation bills held at the Reichsbank. The resulting glut on the money market forced money-market rates down to the point where credit institutions regarded work creation bills bearing higher interest rates as a good investment. By the spring of 1936, banks had virtually no need to rediscount work creation bills at the Reichsbank, as the Mefo-bill had replaced the work creation bill as a source of market liquidity.[30]

The administration and distribution of the work creation credits was handled by five major credit institutions, the flagship of which was the Deutsche Gesellschaft für öffentliche Arbeiten AG (Öffa). Öffa was established on August 1, 1930, only after conventional financing methods through conventional Reich and Land institutions had proved inadequate during the economic crisis.[31] Until 1930, the regular Reich budget provided funds for work creation, in the form of productive unemployment relief *(produktiven Erwerbslosenfürsorge)* or value-creating unemployment relief, *(wertschaffende Arbeitslosenfürsorge)*. Productive unemployment relief, which stressed social goals and labor market policy, was not intended to stimulate a national economic recovery. The scheme was aimed at the long-term unemployed, and it was supposed to maintain their skills, test their willingness to work, and make them useful to society while preserving their self-esteem.[32]

Prior to July 1927, the Länder administered the Reich government's basic subsidy *(Grundförderung)* as well as the augmented subsidies *(verstärkten Förderung)* provided by both Reich and Land governments. After passage of the July 16, 1927, law on labor exchange and unemployment insurance (Gesetz über Arbeitsvermittlung und Arbeitslosenversicherung, A.V.A.V.G.), the newly created Reich Institution for Labor Exchange and Unemployment Insurance (Reichsanstalt für Arbeitsvermittlung und Arbeitslosenversicherung, RfAA) administered Reich subsidies, while the Länder retained administrative control over their funds. The creation of Öffa in 1930 produced three levels of funding administration: the RfAA for the Reich basic subsidy, Land authorities for augmented subsidies from the Länder, and Öffa for augmented subsidies from the Reich.[33]

The economic crisis forced the Länder as well as the Reich to find new ways to finance work creation. By 1927, Prussia could no longer fund work creation from the regular state budget and began funding such programs from loans under a special borrowing and lending authorization law that was approved annually by the Prussian Landtag. Repayment of the funds lent out was supposed to service the interest and principal payments on funds borrowed by Prussia. The Reich government funded productive unemployment relief projects from the regular budget until 1930, when occasional stoppage of payments and nonfulfillment of commitments forced the Reich to find a new method of funding. Long-term unemployment on an unprecedented scale was devastating the Reich budget. The creation of Öffa appeared to offer an alternative to massive budget deficits.[34]

Öffa did not immediately live up to its promise as an effective way of funding work creation projects. Before June 1933, Öffa lacked the financial resources required for the implementation of an effective, large-scale work creation program. Öffa's original capital consisted of a portfolio of RM 387 million in Reich loans to cities, towns, Länder, and mixed public and private enterprises. In return for handing over these loans to Öffa, the Reich government received 150,000 shares of Öffa stock. As trustee, Öffa administered another RM 372 million in Reich loans to various borrowers. Additional loan claims were to be transferred from the Reich to Öffa during 1931. The interest and principal payments on all of these loans were to be reloaned by Öffa to finance work creation projects throughout Germany.[35]

During its first eight months in operation (August 1930–March 1931), Öffa's income from interest and principal payments came to RM 35 million. During the same period, the credit institute loaned over RM 50.2 million for work creation projects. Given the rising rates of unemployment and municipal bankruptcy, income from Öffa's loan portfolio could not accommodate the ever-growing demand for large-scale work creation programs. However, this problem had been anticipated when Öffa was established. To supplement its loan portfolio, Öffa was supposed to obtain large foreign loans from which to fund work creation projects. Given the condition of international money markets by August 1930, it is not surprising that these foreign loans never materialized.[36]

Only after the failure of attempts to fund work creation out of "real" savings and borrowing did the Reich treasury and the Reichsbank resort to prefinancing by means of work creation bills. What viable alternative was available as unemployment neared the six million mark? Beginning with the September 1932 Papen program, Öffa's role in financing work creation grew rapidly. By the end of the 1933–34 business year(March 31, 1934), Öffa had financed RM 1.2 billion in work creation bills, of which RM 522.7 million was actually paid out during 1933–34. Öffa's share of the RM 1 billion Reinhardt program came to RM 596 million. The Nazis pumped over a half billion Reich marks into Öffa only after "coordinating" it by purging and packing Öffa's supervisory board with Nazi members in May 1933.[37]

Öffa and the RfAA held decisive power in deciding where Reich work creation funds would be spent. Öffa generally provided augmented subsidy *(verstärkten Förderung)* only for projects already approved for the highest allowable RfAA basic subsidy. Öffa also generally expected the appropriate Land authority to match its loan on the same terms. Öffa loans and RfAA subsidies could cover up to 80 percent of the total cost of a project. Projects lacking RfAA approval generally died on the drawing board. In the four years from 1932–33 to 1935–36, the RfAA paid out RM 764.8 million in basic subsidies for work creation projects.[38]

For bankrupt local governments, obtaining financing for the portion of work creation projects not covered by the RfAA's basic subsidy often proved impossible. The problem was aggravated when the RfAA reduced the rate from RM 3.00 per man-day to RM 2.50 for each man-day beginning March 1, 1934. The total to be made available for RfAA basic subsidies during fiscal year 1934–35 was limited to RM 250 million. The government hoped that reduced subsidy expenditures would steer sponsors into projects requiring the smallest capital expenditure and would divert emergency relief workers to the agricultural sector, where labor was scarce.[39] By April 1, 1934, the LAA had committed RM 223 million of the RM 250 million 1934–35 basic subsidy allocation, prompting Syrup to order a freeze on approval of basic subsidies for new projects. Complaints from LAA that the freeze had "destroyed confidence in the organic progress [of the economy] held by project sponsors, political authorities, and the general public," and a warning from the Nazi party's deputy Führer that "the limitation or elimination of funds for [RfAA] basic subsidies must have the most serious consequences," forced Syrup and the Reich finance minister to cancel the freeze and increase 1934–35 funding for RfAA emergency public works projects from RM 250 million to RM 310 million. The additional funds were to be directed to urban high-unemployment areas such as Berlin (RM 30 million) and a number of cities in Saxony (RM 10 million). To compensate for the additional subsidies for distressed areas, Syrup cut off basic subsidies for all projects sponsored by the Reich government, the Länder, the Reichsbahn, and the Reichsautobahnen corporation, as well as for projects having no value to the national economy.[40]

Sponsors of work creation projects, usually local governments, were hard hit by the reduction of the subsidy level from RM 3 per man-day to RM 2.50. Reduced basic subsidies meant that communities had to provide additional residual funding in order to finance work creation projects.[41] The increased demand for residual financing, which the RfAA estimated at RM 200 million for the remainder of the budget year (late July 1934 to the end of March 1935), could not be met by the credit institutions financing work creation, which held only an estimated RM 60 or 70 million in available funds.[42] As the winter of 1934–35 approached, regional and local officials demanded that unspent RfAA basic subsidy funds be used for the residual financing of projects approved for basic subsidies. RfAA president Syrup granted exemptions to the limit of RM 2.50 per man-day for basic subsidies and set aside approximately RM 2 million for interest-free residual financing loans, but he refused to release unspent basic subsidy funds for residual financing purposes. By January 1935, continuing pressure from regional and local officials forced Reich finance minister Krosigk to approve the use of uncommitted RfAA "basic subsidy" funds for "residual financing" in certain predefined "emergency zones." This special arrangement lasted only until April.[43]

In the spring of 1935, the RfAA's role as provider of basic financing for emergency relief works was sharply curtailed. On the basis of decisions taken at an April 10 meeting of cabinet ministers, Reich interior minister Wilhelm Frick ordered an end to budget outlays or borrowing for work creation by communes and communal organizations whose 1935–36 budgets could not be balanced or whose budgets were not on a sound long-term footing. "Even attempts to contribute to the war on unemployment through the use of communal funds must retreat before the need to balance the budgets," remarked Frick. In line with Frick's decree, RfAA president Syrup ordered LAA to stop approving new applications for basic subsidies.[44] Frick's decree, which was not released to the public, created widespread consternation among local authorities. Syrup requested and received assurances that the Reich propaganda ministry and Nazi party officials would cooperate in an effort to "avoid a political disturbance."[45]

The RfAA continued to supply large sums for public works, but not necessarily for RfAA-controlled emergency relief projects *(Notstandsarbeiten)*. For budget year 1936–37, Reich officials set the RfAA's emergency relief budget at only RM 100 million, RM 20 million of which was earmarked for the Saarland. At the insistence of the Reich finance minister, the RfAA was required to hand over another RM 500 million from its surplus income to finance construction of *Autobahnen*, ordinary Reich roads, and waterways.[46]

By 1936, "work creation" programs in the original sense of the word were a thing of the past. New grants for emergency relief works were now restricted to a handful of recognized "distressed areas," whose financial condition and labor market were so desperate that the basic subsidy system was of little use. These areas could not come up with the necessary residual financing even if a basic subsidy were granted. Special measures were required to mop up the remaining pockets of hard-core unemployment.[47] A limited work creation program that was financed through a scheme of relatively conservative, responsible "prefinancing" now gave way to an unlimited rearmament program recklessly "financed" by Mefo-bills, war, conquest, and plunder.

To ensure jobs for Germany's six million unemployed, Hitler's government had to prevent serious inflation during the recovery. Neither the government nor the Reichsbank wished to see thousands of new jobs and orders for goods and construction material eaten up by wage and price increases. The government sought to ensure the greatest possible employment effect from its expenditure on work creation. Having agreed to finance the job creation program through the Reichsbank's rediscount facilities, Reichsbank president Schacht had a vested interest in suppressing any hint that excessive credit creation was producing inflation. Significant price increases would discredit the government's financing policy in general. Labor would demand wage increases to compensate for the higher cost of living. On the one hand, meeting these demands would cost Hitler much of his support among the business community; on the other hand, rejecting demands for wage adjustments might precipitate widespread social unrest before the Nazis had cemented their grip on state power.

Financing an expansion of income and employment through credit expansion financed by central banks may be commonplace today, but it was "unorthodox by the standards of the 1930s," and was criticized as being inflationary.[48] Hitler's government never developed a consistently applied price control policy during the years of recovery from 1933 to 1936. Direct attempts to control prices antedated Hitler's government and were implemented sporadically through the period of recovery. A Reich Commissioner for Price Supervision was appointed under a decree of December 8, 1931, but the office was abolished and the duties and powers redistributed to the Reich economics ministry at the end of 1932. Hitler's government made no direct effort to control prices during 1933 and most of 1934. Responsibility for prices was generally turned over to the cartels, which sought to enforce "administered prices." Government intervention to "save the farmers" actually raised agricultural prices.

Karl Goerdeler, the former mayor of Leipzig, was appointed Reich Commissioner for Price Supervision when the office was revived on November 5, 1934. Goerdeler was empowered to regulate prices of all goods and services. Although Otto Nathan has claimed that the government regarded Goerdeler's position and powers as a temporary arrangement, it is quite possible that resistance to Goerdeler's efforts to roll back prices played a significant role in the government's decision to abolish his post on July 1, 1935, and to redistribute its responsibilities and authority to various Reich departments. As the demands of all-out rearmament under the Four Year Plan exceeded the capacity of the German economy, the government appointed Gauleiter Josef Wagner as Reich Commissioner for Price Formation on October 29, 1936. One month later, Wagner issued a "price stop" decree.[49]

Why did Hitler's government shy away from vigorous price controls during an economic recovery financed by the large-scale creation of credit? During 1933, Hitler sought to reassure Germany's business leadership that Nazi rule was consistent with the preservation of the free market system. Hitler still felt he needed the support and cooperation of Germany's industrialists. He could buy that support by keeping wages down during the recovery, but any rigorous effort to curb prices and profits would alienate the business community and perhaps slow down economic recovery.

The Nazis hoped to restore profitability to German business through reduced unit costs achieved by increasing output and sales volume, rather than through a general increase in prices (the slogan invoked was *"Mengenkonjunktur, nicht Preiskonjunktur,"* output boom, not price boom). The government did its part to bring about profitability by holding down wages during the recovery. Institution of the "performance wage" (*Leistungslohn*—payment on a piece-rate basis) resulted in increased labor productivity, thereby driving costs of production down and bringing corporate profits up. Some upward movement of prices was permitted, but only insofar as it was necessary to adjust price relationships between agricultural and manufactured products, and between goods with elastic and inelastic demand. Nazi price policy also aimed at curbing destructive cut-throat competition characterized by the reduction of prices below cost.[50]

"Historians since the war," wrote R. J. Overy, "armed with Keynesian theory and common sense, have seen that the danger of serious inflation was remote in the years of recovery from 1932 to 1936 with the existence of large unused resources and strict government control over the financial markets."[51] But Keynesian theory and common sense ignore the actual behavior of both the Reich government, which in some cases (notably agriculture) sought to raise prices during 1933, and German businesspeople, many of whom attempted to reverse years of losses by raising prices as soon as the 1933–34 work creation programs began to stimulate demand.

Although Reichsbank president Schacht made a substantial effort to minimize the inflationary impact of German economic policy under Hitler, it is a gross exaggeration to claim that "so long as Schacht held the rudder of economic policy in his hands, the danger of inflation was banished."[52] Kurt Mandelbaum's analysis of Nazi price policy in conjunction with Nazi wage policy concluded that German workers and consumers experienced "a very marked fall in real wage rates." "Had German policy seriously aimed at keeping real wages reasonably stable," observed Mandelbaum, "more [price control] interventions would have been required in the early period, given the wage stop." Mandelbaum's argument has been reinforced by Rüdiger Hachtmann's recent analysis indicating that official statistics grossly understated increases in the cost of living. Despite nominal wage increases, average weekly real net income for German workers barely improved between 1932 and 1935, and remained far below 1929 levels in 1938.[53]

Hitler had promised to save the farmers, who were being crushed under a massive debt burden. Hugenberg, Hitler's first minister for food and agriculture (as well as economics minister), argued that a successful agricultural relief program had to include immediate price increases for the farmers.[54] Hugenberg had his way, and prices paid to farmers were increased. To prevent these price increases from touching off a general inflationary spiral, it was necessary to place a cap on prices paid to farmers; trim the profit margins of processors, distributors, and retailers; and provide some state subsidies in order to absorb the price increases before they reached the consumer. Farm income was pushed up at the expense of businesses farther downstream in the agricultural industry. The policy worked in the sense of protecting consumers from disastrous increases in food prices. Nazi agricultural price policy reportedly raised agricultural wholesale prices by around 30 percent between April 1933 and November 1934, while the retail price of foodstuffs rose by only about 9 percent during the same period. The overall official cost of living had risen by 4.1 percent since the beginning of 1933.[55]

Hitler's government sought price stability only in sectors that were considered critical to the national economy and the rearmament of Germany. Stable prices of raw materials and construction materials were particularly vital to the success of Hitler's efforts to put Germany back to work and prepare the nation for war. Maintaining price stability during the 1933–1936 recovery required that certain conditions be met. Price increases of imported goods had to be either avoided or compensated for elsewhere. Price increases on scarce commodities had to be prevented by rationing or be offset by compensating price reductions in other goods. Price increases resulting from the use of more expensive substitutes had to be suppressed or minimized by profit squeezing, wage restraints, or state subsidies.[56] Because Germany was far from self-sufficient in food and raw materials, it proved virtually impossible to meet these conditions. Notwithstanding the slack in Germany's economy during the period 1933 through 1935, the combination of work creation programs, rearmament orders, and the effort to produce and utilize raw materials of domestic origin rather than less costly imports contributed to inflationary pressures.

In September 1933, Schacht had "absolutely no fear of inflation" arising out of the credit expansion taking place under the new work creation programs. His main concern was that the first signs of economic recovery would embolden businesspeople to execute very substantial increases in prices. "That," he warned, "is something that we could not want."[57] Firms had to resist the temptation to recover years of losses within a few months by raising prices sharply as the effects of the work creation programs became noticeable. The process of recovery and the rebuilding of reserves, asserted Schacht, would take years.

Schacht's concern that the stimulus of work creation funds would encourage businesses to raise prices was well founded. Only a month after the announcement of the June 1, 1933, Reinhardt program, "already observable price increases" had led the Reich finance minister to consider withholding to a later date half of the total RM 1 billion in credits.[58] Business pricing practices threatened to sabotage key elements of the Reinhardt program. Firms that were bidding on public works projects bloated their cost estimates and collaborated on submitting inflated bids. In January 1934, Reich economics minister Kurt Schmitt warned German business groups that he was "not inclined to countenance price increases for goods and services that will threaten Reich projects or reduce their efficacy."[59] A few months later, general inspector for German roads Fritz Todt ordered road construction firms to stop their collusion on submitting inflated bids. He claimed that the bid-riggers usually came from the part of the industry that "has become unhealthy as a result of its own mistakes." Todt reminded them that "work creation measures are not here for the purpose of quickly cleansing the old sins of the improper conduct of business, failed investments, and the like, or to guarantee prices such that the consequences of these old sins can now be erased in the shortest time." He suggested that owners of construction firms follow the example of their laborers on the *Autobahnen* construction sites, who earned little more for a forty-hour week than they were eligible to receive from unemployment support.[60]

By the beginning of 1935, the Reich commissioner for price supervision was receiving reports of significant price increases in the construction industry. Goerdeler, who, according to Arthur Schweitzer, was appointed price commissioner in November 1934 at Schacht's insistence, viewed such increases as "most objectionable from the viewpoint of the national economy and labor market policy." Price increases in the construction industry increased the financial burden of public works projects and meant "a reduction of the impact of the Reich government's work creation measures." Goerdeler attributed the price increases to "selfish exploitation of a boom for which the economy can thank the work creation measures of the Reich government."[61]

Goerdeler, as well as other officials in the Nazi government, made a distinction between "justifiable" and "unjustifiable" increases in prices. Agriculture had already been identified early in 1933 as an economic sector needing special treatment in the form of higher prices. Now Goerdeler argued that the forestry industry was also a special case in which price increases were needed. An adjustment of forestry prices was justifiable and "to a certain extent unavoidable, in order to bring the German forestry industry out of the unprofitable economy *(Verlustwirtschaft)*."[62] In both instances, only the primary producers of the products were entitled to price relief. Processors, distributors, and retailers who raised prices in these industries were "price gougers."

Goerdeler sought to roll back "unjustified" construction price increases to the level of July 1, 1933, beginning with all publicly financed projects. Public agencies that awarded construction contracts were to review their contracts and determine the prices prevailing on July 1, 1933. No range of prices was to be permitted; the single price selected was to be "the lowest replaceable price." If any decline in prices had occurred, the lower price was to be adopted. These prices were not to be exceeded in future contracts, even if some construction projects might not be carried out because of a lack of interest on the part of construction firms.[63]

Goerdeler's directive represented only a temporary emergency measure designed to stop what he regarded as "in part wild overpricing." As soon as the rollback had reestablished 1933 price levels, he promised a gradual relaxation of the regulations. His objective was to "return construction prices to the level that they had before the injection of large amounts of public funds." The economy had to experience a "natural" upswing if the improvement were to bring an increase in output rather than an increase in prices; somehow, the "artificial" upswing had to be transformed into a "natural" upswing. Just how this transition could be achieved was a critical problem for the economic and political leadership of all nations during the 1930s. Goerdeler believed that the first step was a price rollback. He apparently reasoned that when businesspeople realized they could not add to profits by raising prices, they would be forced to increase output in order to take advantage of improved economic conditions.

Goerdeler's attack on price increases, which provoked much resentment, undoubtedly contributed to the Hitler government's abolition of the office of Reich Commissioner for Price Supervision on July 1, 1935, and the redistribution of Goerdeler's powers to other Reich officials. World market prices for most raw materials rose during 1935. In Germany, foreign-determined wholesale prices of raw materials rose by 5.3 percent, but domestic-determined raw material wholesale prices declined by 0.1 percent. Domestic-determined prices might have fallen still further had it not been for attempts to replace imported goods with more expensive domestic-produced materials in the drive to achieve autarky.[64]

By the end of 1935, Germany's economy was feeling the demands of Hitler's rearmament program, and Schacht was determined to provide the necessary credits so long as the demands remained within what to him seemed reasonable bounds. Reich finance minister Krosigk claimed that prices of cartelized construction materials had risen by some 10 to 30 percent since 1933. He feared that rising prices of building materials combined with unending demands for construction of military facilities would bankrupt the Reich treasury. Schacht denied Krosigk's allegations, contending that the low prices of 1933 and the higher prices of December 1935 were not statistically comparable, especially since the 1933 figures represented prices driven to unprofitably low levels by cutthroat competition. Any increase in the price of building materials, argued Schacht, had resulted from measures taken by the government to raise wages and prices in certain cases. He claimed that the price index for building materials had risen not by the 10 to 30 percent alleged by Krosigk, but by only 0.66 percent. Schacht saw no possibility for reducing the prices of building materials and claimed that it would make little difference in the end price of construction projects even if those prices were reduced. Since building materials accounted for about a third of total construction costs, he argued, a 10 percent reduction in the price of building materials would save "only about 3 percent" in total construction costs.[65] Although Schacht apparently felt that a saving of "only" 3 percent was not worth the effort, the total amount saved would have been significant, given the exploding demand for military construction. Perhaps Schacht was concerned with the *political* price of trying for a 3 percent saving on construction costs.

Hitler's government had no real price policy from 1933 to 1936. The government, which undertook only sporadic efforts to control prices in a few sectors, generally confined its price actions to pleas that businesspeople should not take advantage of a recovering economy to raise prices unduly. This muted approach seemed appropriate while the government hesitated to offend business interests that held considerable influence in the "power cartel" during the first years of the Hitler regime. Price increases from the beginning of 1933 to the end of 1935 do not seem to have reduced the effectiveness of work creation measures during those years. The shortage of foreign exchange and raw materials, on the other hand, primarily inhibited the recovery of those industries not deemed essential to long-range rearmament plans. It was the implementation of the 1936 Four Year Plan to prepare Germany's economy and military for war, as well as the concentration of economic authority in the hands of Hermann Göring, that finally put an end to the government's essentially free-market price policy.

3

National Socialist Work Creation from Theory to Practice

"With Hitler," wrote Henry A. Turner, Jr., "it is misleading to speak of economic thought in the usual sense."[1] Though Hitler may have been an economic illiterate in the sense that "he never attained even a basic grasp of the formal discipline of economics,"[2] he did nevertheless have a "vision of the economy."[3] Many of Hitler's economic ideas followed the conventional wisdom of the time, and for good reason. Hitler did not wish to frighten Germany's industrial and financial leadership with the prospect of "wild experiments" with the economy under a Hitler government. Thus, Hitler rejected socialism, defended the right to hold private property, and generally favored individual initiative and free enterprise. Hitler spurned inflation as a means of financing work creation, condemning it as a hidden means of expropriation. These were mainstream ideas, and they told German voters nothing about how Hitler proposed to deal with the economic crisis if he became German chancellor.

Whether the Nazis held any clear economic ideas, concepts, or theories remains a matter of debate. A widespread assumption that National Socialism's ideological framework detailed no "Nazi" economic theory has led many historians to question the existence of any specifically "Nazi" economic policy during the early period of the Nazi era. Avraham Barkai, however, has steadfastly argued that "the widely accepted assumption, that the Nazis had nothing to offer with regard to economic principles and theory, is inadmissable." He contended that "it is not true that the economy was neglected within their [Nazi] ideological system." Moreover, argued Barkai, "it is not true that the Nazis were totally unequipped in the sphere

of economic policy when they seized power." The importance of Nazi economic ideology in defining Nazi economic policy, admitted Barkai, diminished over time. He conceded that "ideological aims and objectives played
a comparatively greater role in the earlier stages of the Nazi regime; later
these goals had to yield to the more urgent and pragmatic task of war
preparations." But ideological goals were relinquished only temporarily,
until victory on the battlefield could create the political and military conditions required for their realization.[4]

Barkai's distinction between an ideological beginning and a temporarily
pragmatic ending to Nazi economic policy is not well supported by an examination of early Nazi economic policy after January 1933, which, at the
higher levels of policy formulation, indicates a largely pragmatic approach
from the beginning. Nazi economic policy remained unpredictable so long
as the Nazi leadership encouraged the notion that there was no such thing
as "Nazi economic theory." In 1939, Reich economics minister and Reichsbank president Walther Funk explained that "dogma is the enemy of the
economic system. . . In Germany we pursue the economic policy of common
sense. We do what is necessary. Thereupon one does what is right, and what
is right is also good."[5] The question, as Harold James has pointed out, is
"what was common sense?"[6]

As he came closer to the chancellorship, Hitler refused to commit himself
on economic policy. Taking a clear position might alienate Nazi sympathizers or potential sympathizers.[7] "Nazi" economic policy prior to Hitler's
chancellorship and some months into his chancellorship was defined by bills
and resolutions introduced by the Nazi Reichstag fraction, and speeches
and writings of various economic spokespersons for the NSDAP. These
diverse sources provided an inconsistent picture of Nazi economic ideas and
policies. The Reichsbank, which would have to finance any Nazi economic
program should Hitler win the chancellorship, closely followed Nazi pronouncements and activities after the NSDAP's shocking gains in the September 1930 Reichstag elections.

The Reichsbank considered Gottfried Feder, who "had gained a deserved
reputation as a radical fanatic on monetary and credit questions," as the
NSDAP's chief economic theorist.[8] Feder's radical economic ideas can be
traced back to a February 1919 article in the *Süddeutsche Monatshefte* appropriately titled "Das Radikalmittel." It was here that Feder recommended
"the breaking of the thralldom of interest payments," the total elimination
of all interest payments.[9] Nearly twelve years later, the Reichsbank regarded

Feder as the "true originator" of the Nazi economic program and lamented that "it is a particular misfortune for this [National Socialist] party movement, that it has preserved as its economic inspiration a man who never has grasped the fundamentals of political economy."[10]

The Reichsbank followed Feder's activities closely, sending employees to monitor his speeches. During 1932 Feder "repeatedly" mentioned and discussed the "breaking of interest-slavery," renewed his support for the creation of a new form of money (often derisively referred to by his opponents as "Feder-Geld"), and continued to demand the nationalization of all banks, including the Reichsbank.[11] Feder's ideas continued to interest the Reichsbank after Hitler's consolidation of power. Early in 1934, Reichsbank president Schacht asked the bank's economic and statistical department whether Feder's positions had shifted since 1919. The verdict was mixed. Feder had brought greater precision to the centerpiece of his program, the breaking of interest slavery, "but the idea always remained basically unchanged." On the other hand, Feder seemed to have changed his mind about nationalizing the banks, including the Reichsbank. Now he wanted to nationalize only the banks' money and credit policy, not the banks themselves. And, Feder claimed, no responsible Nazi official ever intended to introduce a new form of money after the Nazi takeover. The Reichsbank's analysis, overestimating Feder's importance and influence in charting Nazi economic policy, concluded that the NSDAP's "economic ideologist," now a state secretary in the Reich economics ministry, would try to put "the essential points of the program" into practice.[12]

The Nazis made startling gains in the September 1930 Reichstag elections. Now, reasoned the Reichsbank, the Nazi leadership had to go through the motions of appeasing an electorate whose expectations had been raised by Nazi propaganda. The Nazi response was a flood of motions and interpellations in the Reichstag, which, taken together, could be considered a "National Socialist economic program." Most of the Nazi Reichstag motions were sheer fantasy. The motions dealing with economic policy represented a compromise designed to appeal to a broad spectrum of the electorate. The party that "ogles capitalist economic leaders" such as Gustav Krupp von Bohlen und Halbach, Fritz Thyssen, Emil Kirdorff, and the Mannesmann corporation sought support among socialist workers by supporting the Berlin metal workers' strike.[13]

In the NSDAP Reichstag motion 64.1, the Reichsbank found a watered-down version of Feder's old demand for the breaking of interest slavery. The Nazi Reichstag delegation demanded only that interest rates be capped at 5 percent, of which at least 1 percent was to be counted toward the amortization of the debt. A fifty-year limit was to be placed on the amortization of any debt. Motion 64.4, aimed at curbing "speculation," would sharply curtail the exchanges and eliminate the stock exchange altogether. Motion 66 would transform all large banks, including the Reichsbank, into state banks. Germany's capital shortage would be compensated for by the creation of money. The holdings of the "bank and exchange princes" (meaning Jews), and the property of anyone who had profited from the war, the hyperinflation, or the deflation during the stabilization, were to be expropriated without compensation. Funds obtained through such expropriations would be used "for the benefit of the entire German people." On the one hand, concluded the Reichsbank, the National Socialists would get the economy moving through inflation; and, on the other hand, they would punish the so-called "inflation criminals" *(Inflationsverbrecher)*. Omitted from the Nazi Reichstag motions was any proposal to nationalize large firms, "a concession to the economic leaders so popular among the National Socialists." "Nothing," asserted the Reichsbank, "illuminates more strikingly the double-dealing of the National Socialists."[14]

During the summer of 1932, the NSDAP circulated a *Wirtschaftliches Sofortprogramm* hatched by Gregor Strasser in preparation for the July Reichstag election campaign. In keeping with its strong anticapitalist tone, the *Sofortprogramm* promised to put Germany's unemployed back to work with a massive RM 10 billion public works program, financed by deficit spending and higher taxes on the rich. Hitler and the leaders of the party's "right wing" soon repudiated Strasser's "socialist" program in order to placate the party's newfound friends among the business community. But once again the astonishing results of the July 1932 elections (230 seats in the Reichstag) forced Hitler to show the electorate that their confidence in his leadership had not been misplaced. The Economic Reconstruction Program *(Wirtschaftliches Aufbauprogramm)* announced in October 1932 softened the *Sofortprogramm*'s strident anticapitalist tone and called for a deficit-financed RM 3 billion work creation program.[15]

In the context of a disintegrating, stalemated republic dominated by a conservative economic leadership, the mere suggestion of a massive deficit-financed, work creation program was highly unrealistic. Such proposals could not possibly enhance the party's standing with the economic and political elite who influenced Reich President Paul von Hindenburg in making and deposing Reich chancellors.

Attempts to formulate a party line on economic policy tended to exacerbate latent divisions within the NSDAP, fueled power struggles within the party, and threatened to divert energy from Hitler's main objective, the assumption of political power. At the end of 1931, responsibility for defining Nazi economic policy was being shared by Otto Wagener's economic policy department of the Reichsleitung setup in December 1930, and by an economic council established in November 1931 under Gottfried Feder's leadership. Hitler never defined the respective competencies of these two party agencies, and Wagener and Feder held rather divergent views on "national socialist" economics. A third party, Walther Funk, a business correspondent for the *Berliner Börsenzeitung*, who had helped Hitler establish contact with industrialists and businesspeople, served on Feder's Reich economic council.[16]

As Hitler inched closer to power during 1932, effective party organization became more critical. Between June and September 1932, NSDAP Reich organization leader Gregor Strasser undertook a general reorganization of the party apparatus. The reorganization affected the agencies that dealt with economic policy. Jurisdictional disputes between Wagener and Feder were first eliminated by making Feder's Reich economic council directly responsible to Hitler and by designating it "the supreme organ of the Party headquarters for all fundamental questions of national socialist economic policy." Funk joined the council as Feder's deputy chairman. Despite the impressive description of its authority, Feder's economic council continued to be overshadowed by Wagener's economic policy department of the Reichsleitung until September 1932, when Wagener left under circumstances that remain unclear even today. He was closely connected with the radical July *Sofortprogramm*, which had frightened Germany's business leaders. Power struggles within the Nazi hierarchy also played a role in Wagener's sudden departure.[17]

Wagener's ouster from the economic policy section was accompanied by a complete reorganization of the agency. Under Hitler's order of September 22, 1932, the department was divided into two entities, a main department IVa (state-controlled sectors of the economy) under Feder, and a main department IVb (private sector of the economy) under Funk. Feder's Reich economic council was declared the party's "supreme organ for economic questions," and the only function of the two economic policy departments was to implement directives ordered by the Reich economic council.[18] The council was reorganized. Funk and Feder became cochairmen, and membership now included representatives of various departments of the Reichsleitung, as well as leading businesspeople. Despite the council's official role as the party's highest authority on economic matters, "it was hardly an effective control organ," since it met only twice during 1932.[19] Shortly after the reorganization, publication of the NSDAP's October 1932 Constructive Economic Program *(Wirtschaftliches Aufbauprogramm)* sought to reassure business and financial leaders who had been frightened by the radical July *Sofortprogramm.*

Wagener's departure from the economic policy department and the department's reorganization and subordination to the Reich economic council reflected the party leadership's discomfort with the role that economic policy was playing in Nazi electoral strategy. As the NSDAP came closer to gaining power, the electorate was taking its economic pronouncements more seriously. The risk of alienating potential supporters with the "wrong" economic program was increasing. Hitler's reorganization of the party's economic policy apparatus in September 1932 came at a time when some party leaders apparently wished to de-emphasize economic issues in official publications and speeches by party members. Wagener was under attack from some of his party comrades, because some of them did "find it distasteful that economic policy assumes such a prominent position." Discussion of programs to end Germany's economic crisis merely pulled the party into an endless debate that diverted the party from its single goal, the attainment of power.[20] Apparently following the advice of Hjalmar Schacht, Hitler ordered a ban on discussions of the future economic order during the autumn of 1932.[21]

In the weeks during which the fate of the economic policy department was being debated and Hitler's September 22 reorganization order was being implemented, it was less clear than ever who spoke for the NSDAP on economic policy matters. In October, Gregor Strasser, Reich organization leader in the NSDAP Reichsleitung, sought to clarify the lines of authority. Strasser ordered that, while the reorganization of the party's economic policy apparatus was in progress, party economic experts and advisers were prohibited either from issuing any publications of their own or calling any meetings dealing with economic matters. During the reorganization period, all offices and agencies of the economic department were to obtain material on economic questions directly from the NSDAP Reichsleitung. This material, and this material alone, was to serve as the basis for preparation of statements and propaganda on all economic issues.[22]

Despite the turmoil within the party's economic policy apparatus during August, September, and October 1932, economic planning for the eventuality of a Nazi takeover became less rhetorical and more concrete. During mid-September, orders went out to prepare for the implementation of work creation projects. An expert adviser on work creation was to be appointed in each district (Kreis). These experts were to be technically trained persons familiar with the economic situation of their districts. They were to identify and prepare possible rural land improvement projects. Those projects that were suitable for immediate implementation by the Reich Voluntary Labor Service (Arbeitsdienst) were to be turned over to the party's labor service department. Projects that could be implemented only after a Nazi takeover of state power were to be collected in a special file by the Nazi district economic experts and held for later use.[23]

The NSDAP's setback in the November 6, 1932, Reichstag elections (down by two million votes and thirty-four seats from the July 31 peak) shocked the party's leadership. Had the Nazis missed their "window of opportunity"? Would the party now be able to convince the power brokers surrounding Reich president von Hindenburg that Hitler's appointment to the chancellorship was the only way out of a stalemated situation? Compounding the shock of the November 6 election disaster was Gregor Strasser's resignation as Reich organization leader on December 8. Having failed to convince Hitler to enter a coalition government, Strasser apparently felt he had no future in the NSDAP.[24] In Hitler's mind, those who were not with him were against him. Hitler now had two aims: to destroy the concentration of power that had developed in Strasser's office of Reich organization leader, and to identify the source of his party's electoral decline and make the necessary adjustments before it was too late. Hitler reconsidered the organization, leadership, and tactics of his party from the ground up. The result of this evaluation was Hitler's December 1932 "Memorandum on the internal basis for decrees aimed at creating an enhanced effectiveness of the movement."[25]

Hitler was concerned that the NSDAP's bureaucratic apparatus was holding back the party's drive to power. When it came to organization, Hitler believed, less was better. "The ideal situation," he wrote, "would be for a single bearer of knowledge and will to seize hold of the nation, without any intermediate command at all. Unfortunately," he admitted, "this is impossible." So, one must organize, but only what one must organize. "The dissemination of a *Weltanschauung* (worldview) requires not bureaucrats but fanatic apostles," concluded Hitler. "Wisdom thus dictates," reasoned Hitler, "that organization be extended only so far as necessary, and for the rest, individual capacity should be permitted the widest possible room for maneuver."[26]

Without specifying precisely what form the economic policy department would take or where it would fit into the party organizational scheme, Hitler indicated that it "can obviously only serve to advise all levels of the party, while simultaneously supervising all fundamental economic policy announcements within the party."[27] But, in an allusion that might well have included the economic policy apparatus as well as certain other departments of the party organization, Hitler came down in favor of a sharp separation between "administrative organizations" *(Verwaltungsorganisationen)* and "political leadership organizations" *(politischen Führungsorganisationen)*. This separation, argued Hitler, was necessary to insure that cumbersome administrative apparatus did not cripple the force of political decisions. Under this principle of separation, Hitler advised that the party put aside projects that could be carried out only after a National Socialist takeover of the state. Activities that were bound to fail because the prerequisite technical basis and personnel were lacking should be shelved. "In particular," warned Hitler, "the party organization is not a field of action for scholarly experiments." Such experiments, argued Hitler, would draw the party away from its mission of propagating the Nazi worldview and thereby "substitute eternally fluctuating and uncertain scholarly theories for its [NSDAP's] eternally correct *weltanschaulichen* fundamental principles."[28] These general ideas of the Führer found immediate expression in orders to reorganize the party's economic policy apparatus and redefine its mission in a rather restrictive manner.

In an order (*Verfügung* 3) issued on December 15, 1932, Hitler disbanded both the Reichsleitung's economic policy department and the party's Reich economic council. In their place, Hitler established a Third Commission for Economic Questions in the Political Central Commission (III. Kommission für Wirtschaftsfragen in der Politischen Zentralkommission). The new commission, like the disbanded economic policy department, was divided into two subcommissions: Unterkommission III A (Wirtschaftspolitik), chaired by Walther Funk, and Unterkommission III B (Wirtschaftstechnik u. Arbeitsbeschaffung), headed by Gottfried Feder. Feder's section essentially represented a combination and continuation of the old "technical engineering" section and the former "work creation" section of the now defunct economic policy department.[29]

Efforts to judge whether the reorganization favored Funk more than Feder or vice versa are rather fruitless. Hitler intended to downplay discussion of any economic matters until the Nazis had actually won political power in Berlin. In describing the duties of the Third Commission, and the activity of party leaders in general, Funk made it clear that the Gau economic advisers and the rest of the party's new economic apparatus were neither to conduct scientific economic research nor to construct theoretical "national socialist" economic systems and programs. "The future configuration of the economy, alleged specifically national socialist monetary systems, schemes for a complete economic order that will do away with all problems and evils, methods of finance that will end the crisis, and the like, have nothing to do with the political tasks of the movement," warned Funk. "The economy," he continued, "is favorable or unfavorable, money is either usable or not usable, financing is solid or not solid. But these things have nothing directly to do with the national socialist *Weltanschauung.*" Economic advisors were necessary only because the party found it necessary to take positions on specific current economic developments, the specific measures of non-Nazi governments, the specific proposals of competing parties, the specific attitudes and actions of powerful capitalist groups. They could also assist state and local governments controlled by Nazis, and Land parliaments in which the Nazis had substantial influence.[30]

Hitler's reorganization of his party's economic policy agencies was motivated by a desire to push divisive economic questions into the background and to exercise greater control over any economic policy statements emanating from organs or officials representing the party. Six days before Hitler's appointment to the chancellorship, Nazi commitment to any type of work creation program remained unclear. Feder now asserted that "a work creation program can make sense and have a goal only if the projects undertaken by it truly guarantee a lasting elimination of unemployment." He gave no indication that the NSDAP had a plan that could provide such a guarantee, but he did give vague assurance that the party would not support irresponsible financing of work creation.[31]

Hitler's appointment to the chancellorship on January 30, 1933, produced no immediate clarification of either "national socialist economics" or a "national socialist" approach to the reduction of unemployment. The

March 5, 1933, Reichstag elections would determine whether Hitler and the Nazis would be able to consolidate their political power and free themselves from interference from the conservatives who had helped Hitler obtain the chancellorship. Politics had to take precedence over economics, regardless of the demands of various interest groups for immediate economic relief. Discussion of economic problems had to be banished, or at least relegated to a subordinate place, during the March 1933 election campaign. Party speakers had to be able to handle economic questions competently, but they also had to know when to change the subject. "We are leading a political struggle," warned Funk. "The movement," he wrote, "has not yet gotten within its grasp all portions of the population that belong to it by virtue of blood and [race] value. The movement is not yet the state."[32]

Funk realized that the party propaganda machine would be called upon to explain and defend Nazi economic theory and policy. Opponents, he claimed, consistently "distort, misrepresent, and falsify" Nazi economic positions, insinuating that Nazi economic policies would endanger legitimate economic interests and destroy Germany's currency. This derogatory portrayal of Nazi economic theories and projected policies resulted from the "lying propaganda of opponents," aided and abetted by the "widespread and deep-seated lack of knowledge of so many who have concerned themselves with the subject." Attempting to counter such lies was a losing proposition, for the opposition was determined to distort any clarification of economic program that the party apparatus might publicize. "For these reasons," noted Funk, "the publication of accounts dealing with [Nazi] monetary theories and related discussions and projects was already expressly prohibited during the autumn of last year [1932] and likewise remains forbidden." To avoid statements that might cost the party votes, advised Funk, Nazi "speakers who lack mastery over the subject [of economic policy] preferably will not go into it, but, rather, limit themselves to a few short definitive sentences."[33] Funk's advice that slogans were more effective than reasoned analysis was not lost on Hitler, who regaled his audiences with such informative phrases as "The economy cannot save a people; rather, a people must save its economy."[34]

The fact that Hitler had been forced to accept non-Nazis in critical positions in his January 30 cabinet hampered Nazi campaigners in the March 1933 election. Alfred Hugenberg, Reich minister for food and agriculture as well as for economics, considered himself to be Germany's "economic czar." He was a traditional nationalist political and fiscal conservative, not a Nazi. As Reich food and agriculture minister, he favored the continuation of measures to bail out Prussia's great agrarian landowners; but, as Reich economics minister, he opposed any spending on direct work creation programs. Nazi election campaigners could not support a man who was not a Nazi and whose economic program provided no direct relief for Germany's army of unemployed. Funk advised party speakers to avoid the subject of economic policy. If they had to address economic issues, they were instructed to say "that we fight not for the policy of the present occupant of the economics ministry [Hugenberg], but for the [Nazi] movement and for the transfer of power to Adolf Hitler."[35]

Nazi coercion failed to produce a definitive Nazi victory in the March 5, 1933, Reichstag election. With 43.9 percent of the votes (88 percent of the eligible voters cast ballots), the NSDAP controlled 288 of the 647 Reichstag seats. Only the passage of the March 23, 1933, Enabling Act (made possible by the outlawing of the Communist Party and by support from the Catholic Center Party) gave Hitler and the Nazis virtual dictatorial powers for the next four years. Nazi speakers and publicists could now discuss "National Socialist" economic theory and policy more freely and in more detail than they had dared during the years of the struggle for power.

The Nazi party's economic leadership did not take advantage of this opportunity to develop a "National Socialist" economic theory or program. Slogans and propaganda, rather than reasoned, intellectually stimulating statements, continued to dominate Nazi discussion of economics. In December 1933, ambassador Werner Daitz of the NSDAP's foreign affairs office, admitted that the Nazi movement had no real economic program aside from the twenty-five-point program of 1920. National Socialism rejected scientific attempts to predict the economic future with curves and indicators. The economic future of a people, argued Daitz, cannot be constructed artificially; it must develop [organically].[36]

In articles written for the *Völkischer Beobachter* and other Nazi press organs, Dr. Fritz Nonnenbruch asserted that under National Socialism, "the [German] blood develops itself creatively in the reconstruction of the economy, and thereby creates a type of economy corresponding to the spirit of the race." Economic theory plays no role in Nazi economic reconstruction programs. National Socialism simply "does that which is practical. But in doing so, it [National Socialism] demands that everything that will be done is compatible with the spirit of the race. . . From this follows the emphasis on the way of thinking and the Führer principle in [the formulation of] economic policy. The true National Socialist way of thinking is found where people feel, think, and act in a racially authentic manner." Racially genuine behavior has nothing to do with reason, intellect, or judgment, argued Nonnenbruch; it simply comes down to the "trustworthiness of instinct and the courage to follow one's own instinct." A person endowed with correct instincts and the courage to follow them "may not be restricted by paragraphs and norms that would make it impossible for him to follow his instinct. He must be a Führer," proclaimed Nonnenbruch.[37]

Nonnenbruch was simply stating the obvious, that the familiar Nazi racial and leadership principles applied to the economy as well as every other aspect of German life. The question was, what did Hitler's correct racial instincts tell him to do with an economy that was in shambles and with six million workers who were in need of jobs? Foreign critics of National Socialism argued that programs devoid of an adequate theoretical foundation could never rehabilitate Germany's economy. Nonnenbruch argued that the Nazis had deliberately by-passed theories and proceeded directly to practical goals. The first and most important goal of Nazi economic policy was to "finally annihilate unemployment," to do away with unemployment forever. The "confusion" over Nazi economic policy arose because the policy "is so simple and clear and is too uncomplicated for overly intellectual brains." National Socialism simply reversed the usual approach to economic policy. "Instead of erecting theories and experiments on which the elimination of unemployment would then become dependent," argued Nonnenbruch, "National Socialism directly addresses the problem of eliminating unemployment, and stimulates the economy with its [National Socialist] arrangements and programs."[38] In other words, the elimination of unemployment is simple: just put people back to work!

Bernhard Köhler, head of the economic policy commission of the NSDAP Reichsleitung, reinforced the idea that National Socialist economics represented nothing more or less than practical action to solve the problem of unemployment. Köhler's speech to the Reichsverband der Wirtschaftsleiter on October 27, 1933, could not have reassured Germany's economic elite. "We did not smash Marxism in order to uphold capitalism," announced Köhler; "it [Marxism] was destroyed in order to replace Marxism and capitalism with socialism." Köhler reassured his audience that socialism as he defined it did not mean expropriation or nationalization of private property. That, he said, would represent an attempt to correct one injustice by perpetrating another. Köhler argued that the real injustice of capitalism was not that it denied property to so many, but that it denied work to so many. The problem facing Germany was not a question of one economic system or another; it was, said Köhler, "a question of right." The injustice of work denied had to be replaced by "the right to work."[39]

Köhler argued that, whereas the old system had sought in vain to create work indirectly by reviving the economy, the Nazis were reviving the economy by creating work. "Not the free economy, but only the political leadership," argued Köhler, "is in a position to eliminate unemployment," through such measures as marriage loans, large state investments in highway construction and other public works projects, and the Labor Service.[40] The Nazis, asserted Köhler, had promoted economic recovery not by increasing the amount of available capital, but by increasing the size of the available labor force. National Socialism was vanquishing capitalism by "eliminating the dominance of capital," by reversing the relationship between capital and labor. Prior to the Nazi takeover, a lack of capital and credit condemned a large segment of Germany's labor force to joblessness. This situation, argued Köhler, characterized all capitalist systems where the availability of work depended on the availability of capital seeking investment. The Nazis recognized that "labor power is the most important thing, for capital needs labor, and not the other way around," argued Köhler. National Socialism asserted "the right to life of the German people against impersonal loan capital's claim to power" by reversing the usual capitalist line of reasoning, by substituting *"Arbeitsdenken"* for *"Kapitaldenken."* Starting from work *(Arbeit)*, National Socialist policy increased national income and, finally, built up the stock of capital *(Kapital)*.[41]

Köhler's explanation of Nazi economic policy extended the attacks on "interest slavery" and "loan capital" in the party's twenty-five-point program of 1920 and Feder's theoretical works from the 1919–1933 period. Fritz Nonnenbruch provided a more interesting account of Nazi economic policy during the first ten months of Hitler's chancellorship. Nonnenbruch argued that Weimar economic policy during 1932 had been undermined and paralyzed by the conflicting priorities of agricultural protection and an industrial policy providing jobs for the unemployed. Policies that might have guaranteed the farmers' interests would have driven up the number of unemployed. Since coming to power, the Nazis had saved the farmers and reduced the number of unemployed. They had provided effective protection for farmers without touching off a crisis in other parts of the economy.[42]

Nonnenbruch did not explain how the Nazis had managed to reconcile

Germany's various economic interests behind an effective program. By some magic, Nazi economic policy was strong enough to be effective, without damaging the economic interests of any group. "No German," claimed Nonnenbruch, "can on November 12 [1933 Reichstag elections] maintain that he would be harmed [by Nazi policy] because of belonging to a certain profession or occupation." Most remarkable, however, was Nonnenbruch's assertion that National Socialism "had opened new possibilities for the development of the economy without employing the slightest bit of force." "Every measure that National Socialism takes up," wrote Nonnenbruch, "realizes a living desire in the people. It [National Socialism] has not yet forced the slightest thing on the people. . . Because National Socialism attends to the needs of the people, it has no need for compulsion."[43]

As the "battle for work" was giving way to open rearmament in 1935 and 1936, Nazi economic spokespersons continued to identify the "right to work" as the essence of "German socialism." According to Nazi publicists and mythmakers, the Nazi Führer had seized control of an economy in chaos, followed his racially sound instincts, and restored the right to work to six million unemployed Germans without resorting to force or coercion. The Nazis brought to German government not only a different policy but also a different style of leadership. Sound policy arising from the correct instincts of the Leader could now be implemented because, in contrast to the Weimar system, there was now a unity of will and purpose—a government economic policy based on a clear sense of direction and guaranteed not to change overnight.

This particular Hitler myth, like most myths, contained just enough truth to make it plausible to those who did not care to look too closely at reality.[44] Hitler refused to present the electorate with a clear economic program prior to his assumption of the chancellorship. He did not wish to alienate potential supporters by endorsing a particular economic program, and he had no clear idea of how he would deal with the economic crisis if he took over the government. On economic questions, Hitler seems to have lacked trustworthy instincts and the courage to follow them. His government included traditional, conservative business and financial leaders in the finance and economics ministries, and at the Reichsbank. He consulted with Germany's industrial, commercial, and financial leaders before endorsing any work creation program. Hitler certainly did not seize control of an economy in chaos on January 30, 1933, and he certainly did not put six million Germans back to work simply by following his "racially sound instincts."

When Hitler came to power, he had no concrete plan for massive public investment in work-creation projects. Two days before his cabinet approved the first Reinhardt work creation program of June 1, 1933, Hitler told a group of industrialists that government programs in housing and highway construction would provide the impetus for overcoming Germany's economic crisis.[45] Yet, only 10 percent of the RM 1 billion June 1, 1933, Reinhardt work creation program was earmarked for housing repair, and nothing was provided for road building. In October, RM 3 million of the housing repair fund was reallocated for repair of ships used in inland trade. In November, Reich finance minister Krosigk sought to reallocate RM 30 million of the housing repair fund to Reichsbahn projects.[46] The housing repair and renovation expenditures of the September 1933 "second Reinhardt program" stimulated recovery in the construction sector during the spring and summer of 1934, but the gains diminished swiftly as the second Reinhardt program exhausted itself. The net gain in housing units declined in 1935 from its 1934 level.[47]

The Hitler government's early appropriations for highway construction and housing investment do not suggest any strong commitment to an economic recovery led by these sectors. Those who have argued for the primacy of investment in roads and motorcars (R. J. Overy) and in housing (Charles S. Maier, G. F. R. Spencerley, Timothy W. Mason) as the "key industries," "initial impulse," or the "economic key" in the rapid decline of unemployment under Hitler have failed to notice this fundamental discrepancy between Hitler's words and the program that his cabinet enacted two days later.[48] There are at least two ways of explaining this curiosity. First, there is the possibility that Hitler played little or no role in drawing up Nazi work creation programs and that he was not informed of schemes that his bureaucrats were in the process of developing when he spoke to the industrialists on May 29. Second, many officials concerned with the formulation of economic policy in 1933 did not share Hitler's expressed optimism that investment in roads or housing would lead to anything close to full employment. In October 1933 Leopold Peill, president of the chamber of commerce and industry for the Aachen region, quite succinctly summed up the NSDAP's approach to the problem of mass unemployment: "The economic policymakers of the Party have earlier taken the position, and this position is correct, that in the Third Reich it will be impossible to reintegrate all of the industrial workers in the production process, because exports have declined extraordinarily. Therefore, many workers will have to be resettled in the countryside. After the completion of land reclamation projects, which in turn put people to work, there will be sufficient space for rural settlements in the southern part of the Westmark."[49]

Officials at the Reich Institution for Labor Exchange and Unemployment Insurance (Reichsanstalt für Arbeitsvermittlung und Arbeitslosenversicherung, RfAA) shared Piell's view. They believed that urban work creation projects such as road and street construction posed an "artificial" block to the "natural" movement of "surplus" labor out of the cities and back to the land. The president of one Land employment office (Landesarbeitsamt, LAA) cautioned in May 1933 that the "healthy migration from the city back to the countryside must not be restricted artificially through the provision of large-scale [urban] employment opportunities."[50] The RfAA tended to fund emergency relief projects that reflected the outlook of its top officials.

During 1933, land reclamation projects connected with the resettlement of urban industrial workers to rural areas, not roads and housing, spearheaded the Nazi battle for jobs. Large-scale resettlement presupposed that previously unused or unusable land be made fit for cultivation through land reclamation projects. Such projects provided short-term relief for those put to work on the reclamation projects, assured a longer-term solution to the disposition of industrial workers who could never return to their former jobs, and promised to reduce Germany's dependence on imported foodstuffs and raw materials. Land reclamation projects assumed a central place in both the Gereke *Sofortprogramm* and the 1933 Nazi work creation programs supported by the RfAA.[51]

Hitler's government had no labor market policy until April 1933, and when a policy did finally appear, Nazi labor market policy did not even originate with a Nazi.[52] Hitler's work creation programs bear the name of the Nazi state secretary in the Reich finance ministry, Fritz Reinhardt. It was not Reinhardt, however, but Stahlhelm leader and Reich minister of labor Franz Seldte who finally accepted the challenge of formulating a labor market plan. Seldte recognized that although the depression had bottomed out several months earlier, there was very little in the way of a conjunctural upswing. The German economy was simply sitting on the bottom. Noting the upcoming May 1 "Celebration of National Labor," he prodded the government into action with a memorandum to the Reich Chancellery, stressing the urgency of declaring how the Hitler government intended to put Germany back to work. On April 27, he proposed a RM 1.6 billion work creation program.[53] Seldte's initiative, for which he has never received due credit, ultimately emerged as the "Reinhardt program" of June 1, 1933.

His proposal came unexpectedly, forced the issue to the forefront, and sent other cabinet ministers scrambling for position and control of a billion-mark program. The allocation of funds reflected power struggles in Hitler's first cabinet.

Seldte proposed a "Four-Year Plan of Work Creation" designed to employ 470,000 to 700,000 jobless persons for up to one year. Dictated by social as well as economic considerations, Seldte's priorities emphasized *settlement* in every form—agricultural settlement, suburban settlement *(vorstädtische Kleinsiedlung)*, and owner-occupied housing *(Eigenheim)*. Settlement policy, or more accurately, resettlement policy, transcended job creation and renewed the German people's ties to their land. Housing construction, which Seldte felt had been neglected in previous work creation programs, came second on his list. Housing projects would alleviate Germany's severe housing shortage while providing additional jobs. Repair of public buildings, railway construction and electrification, road building, canal construction, postal service projects, agricultural improvements, regulation of rivers, renewal of the merchant marine fleet, and gas, water, and electricity projects rounded out Seldte's plan.[54]

High-level meetings to discuss Seldte's proposal with Hitler scheduled for May 11 and 18 were postponed because of the absence from Berlin of both the chancellor and the president of the Reichsbank, Hjalmar Schacht. Hitler wished to discuss the economic situation with Germany's leading businesspeople before committing himself to a program of action. This he did in his May 29 "discussion with industrial leaders on work creation," in which he singled out housing and road construction programs as the two keys to economic recovery. These delays afforded members of Hitler's cabinet an opportunity to clarify their positions on work creation and time to develop alternative proposals.[55]

A meeting of representatives of Reich ministries and agencies held at the Reich labor ministry (RAM) on May 9 produced requests for a RM 1.6 billion work creation program. Among the largest allocations, road construction (RM 300 million) replaced settlement (RM 270 million) as the highest priority. *Reichsbahn* projects and housing would get RM 270 million and RM 130 million respectively. Agricultural improvement was one of three categories allocated RM 100 million each. The Reich aviation and defense ministries deferred their requests.[56]

While government officials were meeting at the Reich labor ministry, the Reich finance ministry (RFM) was deciding what it was prepared to pay out for work creation programs and how the bill would be paid. The RFM agreed upon an "appropriate and feasible" program considerably smaller than Seldte's original proposal, and ignored priorities set in both Seldte's proposal and the May 9 discussions held at the Reich labor ministry. The RFM proposed nothing for either agricultural settlement or road construction. The RFM, in fact, opposed any publicly financed work creation program. Of a RM 950 million program, only RM 550 million was to come from public funds; the remainder would be provided by homeowners putting up four-fifths of the cost of home repairs. The Reich government, however, would provide debt service on only RM 350 million; RM 200 million for the repair of public buildings was to be loaned to communities, which would repay the Reich in five equal annual installments. Finally, the finance ministry expected the proceeds of a new department store tax, estimated at RM 70 million annually, to pay debt service on the Reich government's RM 350 million share. The work creation program that was discussed at the RFM would have cost the Reich government nothing, and, because all inflationary impact had been eliminated, probably would have contributed little to an economic revival.[57]

Reich economics minister and agriculture minister Alfred Hugenberg shared the finance minister's dream of a noninflationary path to recovery and disdain for publicly financed work creation projects. But Hugenberg lacked the finance minister's political acumen. Instead of proposing a sham program, he circulated to the cabinet a memorandum denouncing public works programs as inflationary and ineffective in combatting unemployment or raising national output. In a May 31 meeting of top government officials, Hugenberg alone refused to endorse the "artificial work creation" in what had now become the "Reinhardt program."[58]

Hitler's cabinet endorsed the first "Reinhardt program" later in the day on May 31. It included the categories contained in the RFM May 9 plan, added agricultural settlement, river regulation (later defined to include reclamation and improvement of agricultural land), and gas, water, and electricity projects, and it raised the total outlay to RM 1 billion. The "Reinhardt program" was really the "Seldte program" without provision for road construction.[59]

Apportioning the RM 1 billion among the various types of projects fell to a committee composed of Reichsbank president Hjalmar Schacht, Reich finance minister Schwerin von Krosigk, and Reich labor minister Franz Seldte. After receiving proposals from Reich ministers involved in the program, these three approved an apportionment scheme on June 27.[60] Reflecting the May 9 Reich finance ministry plan, the June 27 allocation provided nothing for road construction, although transportation minister Peter Paul Freiherr von Eltz-Rübenach had requested RM 100 million for ordinary roads, and an additional RM 50 million for *Autobahnen* in the event that the Reichsbahn did not finance these special highways. Hugenberg received none of the RM 200 million that he (as minister for food and agriculture) had requested for agricultural improvements and land reclamation. For agricultural resettlement he received more than he had requested, apparently because Seldte was pushing this program. It is not clear how resettlement was to occur without land reclamation. This outcome can be regarded as a payback for Hugenberg's refusal to endorse any work creation expenditures and must have been a factor in his resignation from the cabinet shortly thereafter. The amount allocated to repair of public buildings (RM 200 million) and private housing (RM 100 million) coincided with proposals put forth by both the Reich finance ministry (May 9) and the Reich labor ministry (June 8).[61]

A program that initially lacked provision for road building and agricultural land reclamation and furnished only RM 100 million for repair of private housing (nothing directly for new housing; some would be built in conjunction with resettlement programs) could not put five million (end of May 1933) unemployed Germans back to work. The original Reinhardt program priorities reflected both political and economic considerations, and foreshadowed the outcome of power struggles within the Nazi hierarchy. Work creation spending priorities were modified once these political questions were resolved.

Two days after the June 27 allocation of Reinhardt program funds, Hugenberg, who, as both Reich economics minister and food and agriculture minister, fancied himself as Germany's "economic dictator," was pressured to resign his posts. After the trusted Nazi Richard Darré replaced Hugenberg as Reich food and agriculture minister, projects for the improvement and reclamation of agricultural land were incorporated in the Reinhardt program by expanding the category "river regulation" *(Flußregulierung)* to include any necessary or desirable ancillary land reclamation work.[62]

Large sums were also earmarked for roads following the resolution of "certain differences of opinion" between Hitler and the Reich transportation minister. Hitler favored new superhighways *(nur-Autostraßen)*, whereas Eltz-Rübenach supported the extension of the existing road network as the

only financially responsible option.[63] Conflicting interests also set supporters of new superhighways against advocates of extension and modernization
of Germany's railway system. The creation of the "Gesellschaft Reichsautobahnen" on June 27, 1933, and the appointment of Fritz Todt as general
inspector of German roads three days later resolved the competition
between rails and superhighways, and initiated the transfer of most of the
Reich transportation minister's jurisdiction over roads to Todt.[64] After
refusing for over three months to release funds for road construction because
the Reinhardt program made no provision for it, Reich finance minister
Krosigk relented to demands from both Todt and defense minister Werner
von Blomberg that road construction be financed under the Reinhardt program. An October revision of the Reinhardt program allocation scheme
included at least RM 55 million for road construction, with another RM 41
million for roads expected from an increase in automobile tax revenues.[65]

Reich officials gradually recognized that Reinhardt program projects
could not be implemented in time to avoid a sharp increase in seasonal
unemployment over the 1933–34 winter. To preserve the gains already made
in the war against unemployment and to spur a new burst of job creation,
a "second Reinhardt" program of RM 500 million in direct budget expenditures for housing repair and renovation was put in place on September
21, 1933.[66] The edifice of Nazi work creation programs was now complete.

After assuming the leadership of the German government when official
unemployment stood at about 34 percent, Hitler had devoted little time and
energy to finding a way to put Germany's unemployed back to work. There
is no indication that either he or any other top-level Nazi leader took the
initiative in developing a comprehensive scheme to alleviate the crisis. The
Nazis, however, were proud of what they considered to be their achievements in the struggle against unemployment. They rejected the criticism
of unsympathetic foreign observers, who pointed out that the Nazi "battle
for jobs" succeeded while the standard of living remained below predepression levels. Nazis such as Nonnenbruch argued that such comparisons
were invalid, because no one could produce reliable statistics showing what
the German economy would have looked like had National Socialism not
triumphed. The important question, insisted Nonnenbruch, was how the
economy would look today if the policies of Brüning or Schleicher had been
continued. "National Socialism," claimed Nonnenbruch, "transformed the
upward movement of the unemployment figure into a downward movement.
That is the decisive fact that supersedes all comparative statistics of the

years prior to the crisis and which cannot be captured in any numerical comparison."[67]

Germany's Nazi leaders simply wanted the credit that they believed they deserved. They claimed that the economic policies of Hitler's immediate predecessors had contributed to Germany's economic catastrophe and could never have produced a recovery. Hitler's "battle for work," they asserted, had reversed the upward trend in unemployment and had made the "right to work" an effective reality for all Germans who were willing and able to work.

4

Work Creation in Action: The Conquest of Unemployment

To speak of a "National Socialist" work creation program implies a degree of consistency and centralized, systematic planning that in fact did not exist. Nazi labor market policy became a free-for-all competition among Reich, Land, Prussian provincial, and local government and Nazi party authorities vying for funds and favor with Hitler for having put the most jobless back to work in the shortest time. The result was a multitude of "plans" such as the "Erich Koch Plan" (East Prussia), the "Tapolski Plan" (Rhineland Landkreis Düsseldorf-Mettmann), the "Göring Plan" (Berlin), the "Ludwig Siebert Plan" (Bavaria), and the "Dr. Otto Hellmuth Plan" (Lower Franconia). These uncoordinated plans often lacked support from Reich authorities.

The government bureaucracy and the Nazi party shared in the conception and implementation of work creation plans. Many work creation plans were associated with personalities who wielded influence in both the NSDAP and the state bureaucracy. Dr. Otto Hellmuth, a member of the NSDAP since 1922 and Gauleiter of Unterfranken (Mainfranken) since 1927, was appointed Regierungspräsident of Unterfranken and Aschaffenburg after Hitler's assumption of power. Gauleiter Erich Koch was entrusted with the administration of the East Prussian Oberpräsidium on June 2, 1933. Hermann Göring, one of Hitler's closest associates in the Nazi party, served both as minister without portfolio in Hitler's original Reich cabinet and as Prussian minister-president. Ludwig Siebert, a relative newcomer to the Nazi party in 1930 or 1931, was appointed provisional Bavarian finance minister in March 1933, and the following month was named both finance minister and minister-president of Bavaria. Hans-Joachim Tapolski served as district president (Landrat) of the rural district (Landkreis) Düsseldorf-Mettmann in the Rhineland.

Assuming a Reich commitment to the "battle for work," influential figures in both the party and state should have been able to overcome administrative and financial roadblocks in the implementation of their work creation plans. In fact, personal influence and authority did not necessarily suffice either to overpower stubborn economic and financial realities or to suppress political and bureaucratic rivalries that impeded successful implementation of the plans.

The example of East Prussia, where authorities claimed to have conquered unemployment before the Reinhardt program could have had any impact on the economy, served as a model to be emulated by other Prussian provinces and German Länder. Already on July 16, 1933, the first East Prussian rural district, Pillkallen, was declared free of unemployment. By July 26, unemployment reportedly had been erased in thirty districts, and on August 16 Oberpräsident and Gauleiter Erich Koch informed Hitler that unemployment had been banished from the entire province. This feat "provoked astonishment and admiration throughout the Reich and far beyond Germany's borders."[1]

Although the gains made in the struggle against unemployment during July and August 1933 could not be sustained, the results were nevertheless impressive (see Appendix, Table 8). The rate of reduction of unemployment in East Prussia greatly exceeded the overall rate in the German Reich. Precisely how East Prussia achieved its extraordinary success in the battle against unemployment is not entirely clear. Nazi accounts—the only accounts available—emphasize the role of resolute, clear-sighted National Socialist leadership and close teamwork between party and state under Gauleiter Koch, who was entrusted with the direction of the Oberpräsidium on June 2, 1933.[2] Whatever their leadership qualities, the Nazis had to obtain funding for the battle for jobs and had to find work for thousands of unemployed. The private sector created work for a "considerable portion" of East Prussia's unemployed, three thousand in Königsberg alone.[3] The private sector's capacity to absorb additional labor was, nevertheless, limited, and the majority of East Prussia's unemployed had to be placed on publicly funded emergency relief projects. The Nazi labor trustee (Treuhänder der Arbeit) reduced financing costs by setting wages for the emergency relief workers below the prevailing local rate for manual labor.[4]

To wage the battle for work "in the most uncomplicated manner possible," Nazi East Prussian authorities concentrated their resources on road construction and agricultural land improvement projects, dramatically increasing activity in both areas (see Appendix, Table 9). The number of emergency relief workers on these labor-intensive projects peaked in October 1933 at 57,739. East Prussian work creation projects also employed six thousand members of the Voluntary Labor Service (freiwilliege Arbeitsdienst, FAD) and up to thirty thousand agricultural Landhilfe recruits, of whom twenty thousand were drawn from regions outside East Prussia.[5]

The financing of this Prussian work creation program remains something of a mystery. Financing arrangements are not mentioned in the official account. One unofficial account claims funding was obtained through regular channels: loans under the various work creation programs, the basic subsidy *(Grundförderung)* from the RfAA, and, for youths under age twenty-five, service in the FAD or the Landhilfe.[6] This thesis lacks credibility.

The East Prussian battle for jobs of July and the first half of August opened "after a short period of preparation" following Gauleiter Koch's assumption of the direction of the Oberpräsidium on June 2, 1933. The period of preparation must have been confined to about three weeks in June. Financing for this program could not have been arranged through regular channels within three weeks. Even if application procedures and regulations were relaxed, these channels lacked resources sufficient to finance Koch's battle for jobs, and the Reinhardt program was not yet operational.

To avoid months of negotiations with various agencies for costly work creation financing packages, local communities sought to dump their unemployed into either the FAD or the Landhilfe, a solution which had the added advantage of removing the troublesome unemployed from the cities to rural agricultural areas suffering from a shortage of labor. This appears to be one of the methods chosen in East Prussia. These organizations, however, provided work opportunities only for those up to the age of twenty-five (FAD) or twenty-one (Landhilfe), and, with limited budgets, they could accommodate only a fraction of the thousands of unemployed that local welfare authorities sought to place with them. The FAD experienced no expansion under the Nazis, as budgetary restraints forced temporary recruiting blocks during 1933 and 1934. The "nazified" FAD, moreover, viewed itself as an elite group of the best of the nation's youth, and resisted pressure to serve as a convenient dumping-ground for masses of unemployed youth.

Regulations also limited expansion of the Landhilfe. Farms larger than forty hectares were ineligible for the program. No more than two Landhelpers could be placed on any farm. Farm owners were expected to provide decent housing and board for Landhelpers, preferably in their own homes, where Landhelpers could come to appreciate the values of rural life and develop a desire to adopt farming as their own profession. Most farmers did not want strangers sharing their family life, but, on the other hand, could not afford to construct separate living quarters for Landhelpers. In such areas as the Rhineland Landkreis Aachen, where farmers or local welfare and NSDAP officials failed to meet the conditions of the program, the regional and local employment offices (the RfAA funded the program) sabotaged local work creation programs by refusing to place Landhelpers. It remains unclear how thirty thousand Landhelpers could be placed in East Prussia, while fewer than fifty of a projected one thousand could be placed in Landkreis Aachen.[7]

Gauleiter/Oberpräsident Erich Koch received credit for eradicating unemployment in East Prussia. However, before Hitler came to power, Koch's predecessor as Oberpräsident, Dr. Wilhelm Kutscher, had appealed to Berlin for a series of emergency measures, including continuation of the *Osthilfe* program; reductions in local property and business taxes; a Reich subsidy to reduce rates on first mortgages to 2 percent for a period of two years; a Reich subsidy of RM 16 million to be applied to the reduction of "social burdens" (contributions to social insurance funds); funds for the maintenance of schools; restoration of Reich funds cut from the special program of freight rebates for shipments to and from East Prussia; and funds to enable the purchase of seed and feed in areas of East Prussia, where crops suffered severe weather damage during the summer of 1932.[8]

Indifference in Berlin hampered East Prussia's economic recovery. Thirty-six representatives of the Reich and Prussian interior, finance, agriculture, labor, and economics ministries, meeting on February 24, 1933, tabled virtually all of Kutscher's requests and issued a press release aimed at "calming East Prussian public opinion." Some of those present felt that the Prussian government had unfairly shifted its responsibility to the Reich government and that it was not doing enough to assist the East Prussian province. Since 1929, the Reich government had funded East Prussian assistance and had paid for the *Osthilfe* program since 1931.[9] Reich finance minister Krosigk and Reich commissioner for the Prussian finance ministry Johannes Popitz later agreed that each would furnish RM 1 million for the procurement of seed for spring planting. But the Reich finance minister rejected Hugenberg's request for a subsidy of RM 3.8 million to reduce mortgage rates in East Prussia by 2 percent, and he vetoed Reich labor minister Seldte's appeal for a Reich subsidy to reduce East Prussian employers' contributions to insurance funds for sickness, disability, and accidents.[10] Further assistance for East Prussia seemed to be a dead issue in Berlin.

Three days after Gauleiter Koch replaced Kutscher as Oberpräsident, the German press reported plans for a "large-scale undertaking for the rescue of East Prussia." The Reich government reportedly promised East Prussian firms preferential treatment in the award of private and public contracts, and had committed itself to large agricultural and forestry projects in East Prussia.[11] It is tempting to assume that the appointment of a Nazi Gauleiter to the high presidency forced Reich finance minister Krosigk to loosen his grip on the Reich purse strings. What had been denied to Kutscher could not be denied to Koch. Appealing as it is, this explanation does not appear to reflect the facts.

The press notice exaggerated the amount of assistance promised East Prussia. A July 5, 1933, meeting of high officials chaired by Hitler (who left before the meeting ended) approved preferential treatment for East Prussia in the award of contracts but did not act on Koch's plea for a comprehensive program of agricultural and industrial development. Reich interior minister Wilhelm Frick, Reich defense minister Werner von Blomberg, and Hermann Göring (as Prussian minister-president and Prussian minister of interior) supported direct financial assistance for East Prussia, but Krosigk ruled out the use of Reich budget resources. Hitler recognized the special importance of East Prussia as a border area threatened from all sides by would-be aggressors, but rejected the use of "subventions" to save East Prussian agriculture. The goal for the next four to five years, said Hitler, was to strengthen the commitment of the East Prussian population to the German Reich by placing the economy of East Prussia on a better footing than that of neighboring Polish regions. He argued that this could be accomplished merely by diverting military, Labor Service, and work creation supply contracts to East Prussia, and by strengthening the presence of German culture by establishing a national theater and a national university in Königsberg. Only if these modest measures should fail was Hitler willing to consider the use of direct subsidies. Walther Funk, a state secretary in the Reich propaganda ministry who replaced Schacht as Reich economics minister in 1937, labeled East Prussia as "a typical case where state propaganda must be harnessed for political and economic tasks . . . the economic, cultural, and social aspects of the entire propaganda apparatus must be placed in the service of East Prussia."[12] Propaganda rather than a substantial financial investment would solve East Prussia's economic problems.

Only twenty days after Hitler had rejected any large-scale direct work creation subsidies from the Reich government to East Prussia, large sums of money began to flow from Berlin to Königsberg. Had Hitler's opinion been ignored? How and where did Koch obtain these funds? Accompanied by a civil servant from the East Prussian Oberpräsidium, Koch visited Berlin between July 22 and 24 for discussions with various Prussian and Reich officials. Fritz Reinhardt (RFM state secretary) was said to have promised Koch that henceforth, the RfAA and local East Prussian welfare offices would split the cost of subsidizing "welfare unemployed" (*Wohlfahrtser-werblose*, WE) on all types of emergency relief projects. Previously, local welfare offices had paid the full subsidy for WE placed on emergency relief projects. Moreover, these emergency relief workers would continue to be counted as WE for purposes of Reich welfare assistance payments to local welfare offices, despite the fact that the RfAA would pay two-thirds of their basic subsidy on emergency relief projects. East Prussian LAA president Gassner, who would have to find the means to pay for Reinhardt's concessions, was taken by surprise and asked for confirmation that Reinhardt had agreed to such procedures.[13]

Prussian finance minister Johannes Popitz had also made promises. Gassner reported that a "Day of National Labor" was to take place in Königsberg on July 26. This would be the occasion for the official announcement of a new work creation program designed to "cleanse" Königsberg of unemployed workers. A large, province-wide East Prussian work creation program would also be launched, for which Popitz was said to have promised financial assistance. Moreover, special transportation was to bring to East Prussia a daily average of one thousand unemployed workers from other parts of the Reich. An East Prussian official suggested that the LAA set up a night shift to handle the volume of business that this program was going to generate.[14]

This ambitious East Prussian plan would rid the province of its own unemployed and would also help Germany's large industrial centers shift their unemployed to "jobs" and possible resettlement on the land in East Prussia. It may have been the promise of relieving labor market pressure in urban industrial centers that finally convinced Reich authorities to provide financial support for a major work creation effort in rural East Prussia. But, since this plan did not quite fit into any of the "regular" Reich work creation programs, some financial problems remained to be worked out. Where would the Reich government find the funds, and how would funds be poured into East Prussia immediately, without the usual time-consuming bureaucratic red tape associated with project planning and without having to have each project be "recognized" by the RfAA as eligible for support?

The Reinhardt program originally earmarked RM 100 million for "river regulation" *(Flußregulierung)*. Reich minister for food and agriculture Darré managed to have the term "river regulation" broadened to include practically any type of land improvement associated with river regulation, and subsequent operations such as plowing, fertilizing, and seeding. The new definition created a legal basis for thousands of new land reclamation projects in agricultural regions such as East Prussia. Prussia was allocated RM 60 million of the RM 100 million "river regulation" fund. In a July 29, 1933, meeting of officials representing the concerned Reich and Prussian ministries, the East Prussian administration, and Reich and East Prussian financing institutions, the Prussian economics and labor ministry agreed to hand over to the province of East Prussia RM 20 million of its RM 60 million allocation from the river regulation fund. East Prussia would obtain these funds through an expedited loan approval process. For projects requiring up to RM 25,000, East Prussian authorities merely had to send a list of anticipated projects to a credit committee set up by the Deutsche Rentenbank-Kreditanstalt. The list could be considered approved if Koch's office received no objections within two weeks. Requests for amounts over RM 25,000 were to be processed as individual project proposals in the usual manner, though the normally required questionnaire on the financial condition of the local sponsoring authority was omitted. These proposals would be processed with all possible speed. Koch's representative, Friedrich Gisevius, denied that East Prussia was getting preferential treatment, since the measures agreed to would enable his province to employ an average of 150,000 unemployed from other parts of the Reich until July 1, 1934.[15]

How was it possible suddenly to overrule Prussian officials such as Popitz, who felt that East Prussia had not done enough to help itself out of economic crisis? How did a Prussian province with only 1.89 percent of Germany's unemployed manage to obtain a share of "river regulation" funds larger than that obtained by any of the Länder except Prussia? Koch went to the top, or as close to the top as he could get, to obtain the financial support that he could not secure by using his own influence as both Gauleiter and Oberpräsident of East Prussia. It was the intervention of Hermann Göring, who now held the powerful positions of Prussian minister-president, Prussian minister of the interior, and Reich minister without portfolio, that broke the logjam holding up Reich financial assistance for an East Prussian campaign against unemployment. Over a year later, basking in the success of his program, Koch thanked Göring for having made it all possible. In a note to Göring, Koch recalled the critical moment. "I do not know," he wrote, "whether you still remember the moment last summer. We could only begin the battle for work if a large credit requested by us were granted. But the opposition was insurmountable. Then, I was able to obtain your support. A little slip of paper that you signed on our behalf worked wonders. Doors that had been closed now opened and we obtained the necessary credit. Therewith, apart from all other measures, you have performed a service for East Prussia whose importance cannot be overestimated."[16]

With Göring's assistance, Koch obtained funding for the propaganda spectacular suggested by Funk—the overnight conquest of unemployment in East Prussia. He thus secured immediate, short-term relief for East Prussia, but failed to convince the Reich finance minister to subsidize broader measures of economic relief such as first mortgages for East Prussian agricultural property. This setback was a blow to Koch's long-range plans for terminating East Prussia's seventy-year-old agricultural crisis by totally restructuring the province's economy. Koch believed that only the industrialization of East Prussia could provide a stable market for the province's agricultural products by bringing in one to one-and-a-half million new industrial workers with substantial purchasing power. The Reich government's role was to make East Prussia cost-competitive through reductions of taxes, social contributions, and freight rates, and by granting to East Prussia "special advantages" which would make it more profitable than "in the Reich" to locate new industrial facilities in East Prussia.[17]

Propelled until the spring of 1934 by funds injected for the "battle for work," and thenceforward by special East Prussian civilian construction programs and contracts for military installations, the East Prussian economy continued its upward trend. But with the military construction scheduled to be completed by the end of 1937, East Prussia's economy threatened to slip back into stagnation and crisis. Structural change remained a dream. The "productivity gap" between East Prussia and other areas of the Reich constituted the major deterrent to industrial investment in East Prussia.

Koch hoped to close this gap by resettling skilled workers from the more industrialized regions of Germany, a totally unrealistic solution as the demands of the Four Year Plan created a shortage of skilled labor throughout the Reich. Industrialization made little progress in East Prussia during the first four years of the Third Reich. Only twenty-five new factories employing 1,700 permanent workers with total annual sales of RM 10 million had been placed in operation by the end of 1936. In the autumn of 1936, Koch sought to use Hitler's new Four Year Plan, administered by Göring, as the vehicle for a comprehensive East Prussian program for agricultural land improvement, afforestation, housing construction, and industrialization.[18]

Could the "East Prussian solution" produce instantaneous economic miracles in other parts of the German Reich? The successful East Prussian "battle for work" of July–August 1933 seems to have been a special case that owed its financing to the intervention of Hermann Göring. Even with adequate financing, however, job creation plans elsewhere in the Reich were not likely to reproduce the spectacular results achieved in East Prussia. In East Prussia, physically detached from the rest of the German Reich and far removed from the nation's great population centers, the problems associated with Koch's apparently successful program were visible only to a few insiders. The inhumane conditions and outright brutality essential to the success of Koch's plan would have been difficult to impose on the working classes of Berlin and the Rhineland's industrial centers in mid-to-late 1933. RfAA officials responsible for labor market policy doubted that Koch's East Prussian program could or should serve as the model for the rest of the nation.

Koch's work creation program involved placing the unemployed on rural and urban emergency relief projects *(Notstandsarbeiten)*, either in the Reich Land Helper (Landhilfe) program or in the East Prussian Landdienst, service on the land. Land improvement projects occupied most of these laborers. East Prussia led the way in developing rural work creation projects for both the rural and the urban unemployed. East Prussia quickly filled its quota of 28,000 young Land Helpers subsidized by the RfAA under the Reich Landhilfe program. An alternative program, the East Prussian Landdienst, was quickly set up to encompass work opportunities that could not be taken up either as emergency relief projects, or by the Labor Service or the Land Helpers. The Landdienst was similar to the Landhilfe program, but there were some significant differences. Unlike the Landhilfe, which was strictly a program to combat youth unemployment, the East Prussian

Landdienst took in men up to age thirty. Whereas Land Helpers were assigned individually to individual farmers, Landdienst recruits were assigned to farms or communities in small work groups of ten to fifteen men. Prussian officials claimed that this arrangement assured tighter discipline, more effective training and indoctrination, and a better connection of recruits with the land and people. These qualities were said to make the East Prussian Landdienst a better vehicle than the Landhilfe for getting unemployed youths out of the west German industrial centers. An estimated 100,000 men could be accommodated for the low monthly cost of RM 25 per man. Since the RfAA, which financed the Landhilfe, had granted no funds for the East Prussian Landdienst, the provincial government financed the program. To assure local authorities that their unemployed would not return after service in the Landdienst, East Prussian officials claimed that the goal of the program was to prepare participants for permanent settlement on the land. But the president of the East Prussian LAA admitted that although Landdienst recruits would be given preference for permanent settlement, participants were not guaranteed settlement in East Prussia at the end of their term of service.[19]

Another East Prussian innovation in the war against unemployment was a system of primitive work camps known as "fellowship camps" *(Kameradschaftslager)*. Unlike labor service camps, which were restricted to unmarried young men, the *Kameradschaftslager* took in married heads of families as well as single young men. There were three hundred such camps in East Prussia. Each camp had a camp leader, and the camp leaders were supervised by district camp leaders (salaried employees of the district AA office) and the Gau camp leader (a salaried employee of the East Prussian LAA). Camp leaders at all levels acted as agents of Robert Ley's German Labor Front (Deutsche Arbeitsfront, DAF). The DAF thus shared with East Prussia's political authority (Gauleiter and Oberpräsident Koch) the responsibility for carrying out the work and providing political education for the laborers. Of 56,000 emergency relief workers employed in East Prussia during the fall of 1933, some 10,000 to 15,000 (mostly from Königsberg and Elbing) were collected in the labor camps.[20]

It was never clear that the *Kameradschaftslager* were justifiable on either economic or social grounds. Productivity in these labor camps was low, in part because many of the camp personnel, employed in such tasks as record-keepers, cooks, and cooks' helpers, made no contribution to production at the construction sites. Married men were separated from their families, living under the most primitive conditions and performing hard labor on earthmoving projects for which they were often physically unfit. Such hardship, in the opinion of some bureaucrats, could be justified only if the worker and his family could eventually be settled on the land permanently. It "must be doubted," stated one report, whether such rural resettlement would be possible to any great extent.[21]

Dreadful living conditions in the *Kameradschaftslager* were bound to provoke resistance among the laborers. Two thousand unemployed laborers refused the work offered under Koch's program. The camp leaders themselves caused almost as much trouble as the rank and file workers. One-third of the three hundred camp leaders had to be dismissed because of embezzlement, falsification of camp records, drunkenness, and other offenses. Dismissed camp leaders, as well as camp laborers whose political views displeased the Nazi leadership or who refused to submit to camp discipline, were sent to a penal camp "which is operated in the form of a concentration camp." The concentration camp, which also housed ordinary criminal prisoners, was recognized by the RfAA as an "emergency relief project"! East Prussia's experience with *Kameradschaftslager* suggested that other German districts adopting the system might experience even greater problems. RfAA president Syrup eventually sought to discourage the use of East Prussian–style camps when he ruled in March 1934 that henceforth, "carrying out a [work creation] project in the form of a *Kameradschaftslager* can be grounds for rejection [as an approved project], no matter how desirable the project may be."[22]

Despite disciplinary problems and criminal activity among both the laborers and the camp leaders, labor camps on the East Prussian model appealed to some local authorities because there were so few good alternatives. Cities that either could not or did not wish to maintain their own concentration camps for uncooperative laborers and criminal camp leaders were invited by the Bavarian interior ministry to send troublemakers and the work-shy to the Dachau concentration camp soon after it opened in 1934.[23]

Party and state leaders throughout the Reich were expected to match Koch's results, and many attempted to do so. In the Rhineland, Wuppertal planned to emulate the East Prussian model by placing up to nine thousand unemployed workers on emergency relief projects in neighboring rural districts. Rhine province Oberpräsident Baron Hermann von Luninck jumped on the bandwagon and ordered that "following the East Prussian example . . . some border districts in the Rhine province, too, must be pumped empty of unemployed." He set aside about RM 3.1 million of the Rhineland's RM 45 million share of Reinhardt program funds for that purpose. By mid-August 1933, the Nazi organ *Völkischer Beobachter* could report a "competition between the Oberpräsidenten that originated in East Prussia. . . From one province after the other, it is reported how the Oberpräsidenten lift one district after the other out of unemployment."[24]

One of the work creation programs inspired by Koch's success in East Prussia sought to eliminate unemployment in the Rhineland rural district (Landkreis) Düsseldorf-Mettmann. The "Tapolski Plan" was implemented in August 1933 by the chairman of the district council, Hans-Joachim Tapolski. Tapolski sought only to find work for 6,000 jobless supported by the district welfare authority; the Reich could look after 7,466 others in his district receiving either regular unemployment insurance payments (*Arbeitslosenunterstützung,* Alu) or crisis support (*Krisenunterstützung,* Kru) from the RfAA.[25] Tapolski's quotas for the employment of jobless persons required the district's public, agricultural, and industrial sectors to add new employees equal to 6 percent of their work force as of August 1. These quotas meant about 1,000 additional workers for the public sector (employed on public works projects), 2,600 for agriculture, and at least 2,000 for industry. Tapolski claimed that the employers' association, the district peasant leader (Kreisbauernführer), and the NSDAP district leadership supported these quotas. Rhine province Oberpräsident Baron Hermann von Lüninck sought to promote an "honorable competition" among the mayors and professional associations by implementing Tapolski's program throughout the province.[26]

Financing the plan through an extended Landhilfe system involved questionable practices. Under the Reich Landhelper system, a portion of the support payment ordinarily paid to the unemployed individual was instead made available to a farmer on condition that he employ an additional worker over and above his normal work force. This scheme reduced Reich outlays for unemployment support and provided work for otherwise unproductive persons. The Rhine province's allocation of Reich Landhilfe funds sufficed to employ only thirteen thousand Landhelpers. Tapolski's plan multiplied the number of possible Landhelpers by supplementing Reich subsidies to farmers with funds from district and municipal welfare budgets. The scheme was then extended to the handicrafts and industry.[27]

The extension of agricultural wage subsidies to industrial operations violated Reich regulations and had long been rejected by the German business community as an interference with the free market system. Entrepreneurs regarded such a scheme as the first step toward a "fatal subvention-economy."[28] Oberpräsident von Lüninck cleared the Tapolski plan with the Prussian interior ministry, but Reich authorities banned the use of RfAA unemployment and crisis support payments to subsidize industrial wages of unemployed persons hired under plans such as Tapolski's. Reich authorities also refused to recognize locally financed "employment premiums" as "welfare expenditures" of local authorities eligible for reimbursement under the *Reichswohlfahrtshilfe* program.[29] When Reich regulations effective in September 1933 removed agricultural labor from the national unemployment insurance system, Landhelpers completing their service under Tapolski's plan fell back into the local welfare system if employment in the private sector was unavailable. Under these conditions, the plan provided at best temporary relief for district welfare budgets.

By the end of November 1933, Tapolski had reduced the number of locally supported welfare unemployed in Landkreis Düsseldorf-Mettmann by about 3,540—not the 6,000 originally intended. Elsewhere in the Rhineland, implementation of Tapolski's plan produced undesirable results. Some district welfare associations paid a subsidy higher than that paid by the RfAA under the Reich Landhilfe program. This subsidy differential induced some farmers to replace Landhelpers employed with RfAA subsidies with Landhelpers who brought the higher subsidy of the Tapolski plan.[30] In Landkreis Aachen, firms accepting wage subsidies replaced older heads of families with young unmarried men who lived at home and had previously received no welfare benefits. The resulting increase in the district welfare burden justified complaints from agriculture and industry that the Tapolski plan represented "only an artificial masking of unemployment and an intolerable financial burdening of the public authorities."[31]

In the Rhineland, East Prussia's overnight conquest of unemployment was unattainable. Tapolski, of course, was no Gauleiter, nor did he share Koch's access to Göring. His superior, Oberpräsident von Lüninck, like most of the Oberpräsidenten of the western Prussian provinces, had made his reputation in the non-Nazi nationalist opposition to the Weimar republic. But the slow progress of the battle for work in the Rhineland cannot be ascribed merely to the provincial leadership's lack of political influence. During 1933 and the spring of 1934, the battle for jobs failed in the densely populated industrialized areas throughout the Reich.

The most embarrassing failure of all occurred in the capital of the Third Reich, Berlin, where 11 percent of Germany's unemployed were concentrated in March 1933. One year later, 15 percent of the nation's unemployed resided in Berlin; the general improvement of the German labor market had bypassed the capital. Berlin's plight was both politically and financially embarrassing to the Hitler government. On June 28, 1933, Berlin's mayor notified the Deutsche Gesellschaft für öffentliche Arbeiten (Öffa) of the city's impending default on its work creation loans. By October 1933, the city was RM 5.4 million behind in its payments, and Öffa refused to provide Berlin any of its RM 40 million share of Reinhardt program funds until this arrears was made good.[32]

In May 1934, twenty-three Oberpräsidenten, Regierungspräsidenten, and Gauleiters from Berlin and the neighboring provinces finally approved the so-called "Göring Plan" for a concerted effort against unemployment in Berlin. The Prussian administration had taken the initiative with a proposal to create about 100,000 jobs for a period of four to five months, and to increase Berlin's contingent in the Reich Landhilfe. Citing "the political importance of a decisive success in Berlin," Prussian minister-president Göring entreated Reich officials for additional emergency public works projects for Berlin. With the Reich finance ministry's consent, the RfAA agreed to put up RM 30 million to employ 30,000 of Berlin's 400,000 unemployed on emergency public works projects. The city of Berlin would contribute another RM 1 per day for each Berliner employed on such projects.[33]

The Göring Plan failed to deliver immediate relief to Berlin. Only a few projects ready for implementation were available, funding to supplement the RfAA's basic subsidy was virtually unobtainable, but of most importance, provincial authorities refused to accept Berliners in preference to local unemployed. The plan required a level of political cooperation or coercion impossible to obtain even in Nazi Germany, at least not in 1934. The Göring Plan stipulated that at least two-thirds of those assigned to its projects had to be unemployed Berliners. Provincial leaders who had agreed to these terms at the May 15 meeting backed away as the plan became operational. After two months, only 6,000 Berliners had been selected for the program, and only 1,300 had been transported to work sites.[34]

Several factors accounted for the shortage of rural projects for unemployed Berliners. Rural authorities concerned with accommodating their own unemployed had not planned projects that could employ thousands of Berliners. In some rural districts, all available earthmoving and land-reclamation projects had already either been completed by or been assigned to labor service contingents. Many localities that were willing to take unemployed Berliners could not take them in the numbers required by the Göring Plan, two-thirds of those employed on each project. Some towns and districts offered to take on a smaller portion of Berliners—perhaps 40 percent, or only 20 percent. Such projects technically did not qualify as "Göring Plan" projects, but they contributed to whatever success the plan enjoyed. Elsewhere, local employment offices reported that "little interest is shown for employing the unemployed from Berlin and other industrial cities." Local authorities were put off by the cost and difficulty of housing and feeding large numbers of workers "imported" from Berlin. Some district forest management offices refused to hire unemployed Berliners because experience allegedly had shown them to be unsuitable for forestry work.[35]

Rural areas that did accept unemployed Berliners on work creation projects found themselves inundated with more than they could accommodate. In September 1934, Wilhelm Kube, Gauleiter of Gau Kurmark and Oberpräsident of Brandenburg and Grenzmark Posen-Westpreußen, complained to Prussia's interior minister about the 21,000 Berliners serving in his territory as Landhelpers, and about the "many more" Berliners working on "militarily important" projects, on the *Autobahnen,* and on Göring Plan relief works. He refused to take additional Berliners until the spring of 1935.[36]

Hitler's massive *Autobahnen* construction projects might have absorbed thousands of jobless Berliners. At the beginning of September 1934, *Autobahnen* construction employed 4,250 Berliners (2,710 of whom were formerly supported by municipal welfare funds), about 6 percent of the 68,000 workers then employed on Reich *Autobahnen* construction.[37] Berlin authorities seeking to place more jobless Berliners in *Autobahnen* construction were forced to negotiate terms with general inspector for German roads Fritz Todt. To maximize financial relief for Berlin, 75 percent of the Berliners placed in *Autobahnen* construction were to be city-supported unemployed, and the remainder to be recipients of RfAA unemployment compensation and crisis support. The city of Berlin agreed to pay the "Reichsautobahnen" corporation a contribution of RM 0.50 a day per worker toward the costs of employment (barracks, meals) for 75 percent of the days worked by Berlin laborers on construction sites outside the province of Brandenburg.[38]

City authorities sought to place at least 15,000 jobless Berliners in *Autobahnen* construction, but Todt's agency planned to add only 5,700 Berliners, bringing the total to 9,950. Resistance thwarted this limited objective. The president of LAA Mitteldeutschland blocked the assignment of 2,000 Berliners to the Magdeburg construction site; and Brandenburg Gauleiter and Oberpräsident Kube would accept only provincial Brandenburg unemployed, excluding Berliners, for *Autobahnen* construction in his province. The district construction headquarters (*oberste Bauleitungen*, OBK) of the "Reichsautobahnen" corporation (RAB), established by law to construct the superhighway system, refused to hire jobless Berliners so long as local unemployed were available near the construction sites.[39]

The desire to accommodate local unemployed accounted for only a portion of the refusal to accept Berliners on *Autobahnen* construction sites. The many unemployed Berliners who had voted the socialist or the communist party tickets before the Nazi takeover were considered politically unreliable. Many rebelled against what they considered to be slave wages and inhumane living and working conditions on *Autobahnen* construction sites. They received encouragement from hotheads from the Labor Front who entered work-sites without authorization.[40]

Todt accused the LAA and AA of sabotaging *Autobahnen* construction by supplying construction sites with "big-city unemployed," whom he described as unfit for heavy construction work and misinformed about the conditions of work and wages. After a few days on the job, they either left or had to be dismissed by the contractors. Todt insisted on his consent before the RfAA assigned to *Autobahnen* construction sites men who were from large cities or any area not adjacent to the construction site and thus required housing in barracks. His consent also was required for deals under which cities, towns, or districts guaranteed their own unemployed a percentage of the jobs on specified *Autobahnen* construction sites.[41]

In June 1935, RfAA president Syrup lamented the refusal of provincial authorities to initiate projects for unemployed Berliners; only 7,000 had been placed out of town, and with great difficulty.[42] Berlin defaulted on its obligation to subsidize the placement of its unemployed on *Autobahnen* construction sites outside of Brandenburg. In one OBK, the city ran up subsidy obligations of RM 48,000 without making any payments. After August 15, 1935, the city no longer subsidized the employment of jobless Berliners on new *Autobahnen* construction sites.[43] Göring's influence may have facilitated Koch's success in East Prussia, but it failed to overcome roadblocks to the "Göring Plan" for Berlin.

Some of the German Länder, wishing to demonstrate their support of the Führer's program and responding to the lack of adequate funding from Reich work creation programs, undertook their own campaigns against unemployment. In Württemberg, minister-president Christian Mergenthaler (NSDAP) recommended a special RM 11 million program of Land-financed emergency relief projects to prevent an increase in unemployment during the winter of 1933–34. Despite objections from finance minister Dr. Alfred Dellinger (Deutschnationale), who argued that it was the responsibility of the Reich government to fill the gap, the cabinet ultimately accepted Reich Governor and Gauleiter Wilhelm Murr's compromise proposal of a RM 4 million program.[44]

In Bavaria, minister-president and finance minister Ludwig Siebert launched his "Siebert Program" in the autumn of 1933. With the Papen and Gereke programs winding down and the Reinhardt program barely getting under way, Siebert expected an upturn in unemployment over the winter of 1933–34. He proposed a Bavarian work creation program to provide additional employment opportunities. To fund the program, Siebert pressured Bavarian banks and chambers of commerce and industry to lend their liquid funds to the state.[45]

Although Bavarian banks and business associations responded negatively, Siebert was not deterred.[46] The Bavarian cabinet approved Siebert's proposals, which became the September 22, 1933, "Law for fighting unemployment in Bavaria." Bavaria's finance minister was empowered to provide up to RM 60 million in work creation credits from a special off-budget fund. The plan provided for an "extended Landhilfe in Bavaria" costing RM 1.5 million to support up to 25,000 additional Landhelpers; a RM 3.5 million program to create agricultural settlements on newly cleared land; a program of work creation projects to be carried out by local communities for which the state would borrow RM 12 to 15 million at 6 percent and relend it to the local communities at 4.75 percent (cost to state = RM 180,000 in interest payments); and a scheme to set up a consortium of banks led by the Bavarian state bank, which would make loans at 5 percent interest to firms promising to use the funds to hire unemployed Bavarians. The Bavarian state government could guarantee a portion of the loans.[47]

Lacking the Reich government's financial resources and capacity for creation of credit, Siebert's Bavarian program contributed little toward maintaining employment during the fall and winter of 1933–34. Delay was inevitable, since Siebert program public works projects, which supplemented those financed under Reich programs, could be implemented only after Reich credit institutions had selected projects for funding under the Reinhardt program. Siebert failed to move 25,000 welfare recipients into the

Bavarian Landhilfe during the winter of 1933/34. About one-third of those selected for duty in the Bavarian Landhilfe opted to give up their unemployment support rather than to do hard labor on the farms. The Bavarian Landhilfe contingent dwindled from 11,061 on January 15, 1934, to only 8,865 on April 15. By May, the Bavarian government had exhausted its funds for the program. To avoid a massive influx of unemployed into district welfare systems, the RfAA agreed to transfer the entire Bavarian Landhilfe contingent into the Reich Landhilfe.[48]

Bavarian businesses responded coolly to Siebert's offer of state-guaranteed bank loans to Bavarian firms pledging to hire extra workers. In Saxony, businesses had taken up only about one-third of the amount guaranteed by the Saxon state government under a similar program. Siebert disregarded this unfavorable precedent and pressed ahead with his plan. He claimed that in return for credit assistance, Bavarian industry had pledged to take on an additional 15,000 to 20,000 workers during the 1933–34 winter.[49]

The minister-president was stretching the truth. A survey by the Bavarian section of the Reichsstand der Deutschen Industrie taken in August 1933 found only 456 of 1,590 responding industrial firms indicating that they might employ an additional 12,000 workers "given the fulfillment of appropriate conditions."[50] In September a similar survey found only 114 firms willing to add 3,500 new employees over and above the 12,000 indicated the previous month. Neither one of these surveys constituted the unconditional guaranteed pledge demanded by Siebert, and Siebert's government failed to create the "appropriate conditions."[51]

Establishing the terms of Siebert's industrial credit plan required two months of negotiations with the industrialists and bankers. Banks could grant approved firms one-year credits at 5 percent, or 1 percent above the Reichsbank discount rate. The Bavarian state government offered to guarantee up to RM 15 million of such loans. Banks were to issue credits in the form of bills *(Wechsel)*, which the Reichsbank agreed reluctantly to rediscount to enable the financing to be carried out.[52]

The goal of 15,000 extra jobs over the winter of 1933–34 was a pipedream. By February 1934, credits of only RM 700,000 had been approved for borrowers who had agreed not to lay off 617 seasonal workers and to hire 412 unemployed currently drawing welfare support. By the end of August 1934, only RM 1,870,000 (90 applications) in credits had been approved, of which RM 300,000 was not taken up. Many firms rejected state subsidies in principle. Others sought sources of credit not contingent on hiring additional workers. The application process involved too much red tape, and few firms could meet the collateral requirements. But the critical problem was the Bavarian government's attempt to reduce its risk by refusing to honor its guarantee commitment.[53]

In January and February of 1934, Siebert tried to persuade the Reich government to participate in his Bavarian credit-assistance program by either providing a secondary guarantee against losses or granting a subsidy of RM 500,000. The Reich labor, economics, and finance ministries rebuffed Siebert's advances. Siebert concluded that without Reich participation, Bavaria's assumption of additional loan guarantees could not be justified.[54]

Siebert's plan foundered because Bavaria could not finance its work creation program, and the private sector showed only marginal willingness to sacrifice its balance sheet and incur new debt to take on workers it did not need.[55] The Reich bailed Siebert out of the Bavarian Landhilfe catastrophe by taking the Landhelpers into the Reich Landhilfe. But Reich authorities, "as much as they consider the Bavarian undertaking as worthy of support and would also gladly like to assist Siebert personally," refused to pay the bill for Siebert's industrial loan guarantee program. Some public works projects under the Siebert program came to fruition, but some of the funds remained uncommitted and projects remained unfinished in October 1934, long after the winter of 1933–34.[56]

Imperfect as they were, schemes such as the Koch plan, the Tapolski plan, the Göring plan, and the Siebert program contributed to the Nazi battle against unemployment. A revival of Germany's export trade also would have meant more jobs for the unemployed. But during Germany's 1933–1936 recovery, the nation's appetite for imported raw materials and food was rising, while world demand for German manufactured exports continued to stagnate at levels far below predepression levels. Nazi persecution of Jews during 1933 and 1934 may have dampened export recovery by provoking boycotts of German goods in the United States, Britain, and some countries on the continent, such as the Netherlands. Germany faced a large trade deficit and declining reserves of foreign exchange with which to purchase increasing amounts of imports. If Hitler's government could not find a way to close the gap between supply and demand in food and raw materials, the recovery spurred on by work creation expenditures would falter.

During 1933 and 1934, the foreign exchange crisis was driven by work creation programs, not rearmament.[57] Policy choices available to deal with the crisis included increasing foreign-exchange-earning exports, reducing foreign-exchange-consuming imports, imposing direct government control over Germany's limited stock of foreign exchange, and producing more import-substituting goods in Germany. The Reich government made some use of each of these options. Germany's experience with hyperinflation during the 1920s forced both Hitler and Schacht to rule out currency devaluation in an effort to make German goods cheaper and more competitive on international markets.[58]

Before rearmament took control of the nation's economy, Schacht and Nazi party officials used exhortation and threats to encourage German businesspeople to export more. Heinrich Steubel erred when he argued that "the recognition that a country poor in raw material, lacking reserves of gold and foreign exchange, can arm itself only in conjunction with the energetic promotion of exports, came too late to responsible authorities."[59] Through a variety of techniques, the Hitler government consistently promoted an increase in exports.

Paying off foreign creditors in non-interest-bearing debt certificates *(Schuldenscheinen)*, otherwise known as "scrip," conserved Germany's supply of foreign exchange and was expected to boost German exports, since foreigners would want to unload their scrip by using it to purchase German goods. Another Reich government scheme for increasing exports *(Zusatzausfuhrverfahren)* compensated exporters for losses incurred when they lowered their prices. The program provoked complaints both abroad and within Germany. Foreign competitors charged that German exporters supported by government subsidies were dumping German goods abroad. German firms that were unable to participate in the plan complained about unfair competition.[60]

During the spring of 1934, the Reich economics ministry and the Reichsbank sought to force German exporters to increase their activities. Reichsbank branches now tracked the activity of export firms in their areas, and exporters who could not justify a decrease in their firm's exporting activity risked the loss of their bank credit and public contracts. Reich economics minister Schmitt warned firms thriving on public contracts that they would now have to fulfill their "national duty" to pursue foreign trade, even if that entailed "a certain sacrifice."[61]

In September 1934, Schacht, who had taken over Schmitt's post as Reich economics minister, introduced the so-called "New Plan," a scheme that included quotas on imports and trade agreements with countries that agreed to purchase German goods. Schacht and those working closely with him continued to push for increased exports that were needed to pay for imports required to maintain the impetus of the work creation programs. To stimulate the exports needed to pay for the imports, German businesses were to be charged an assessment, described as a "self-help measure," the proceeds of which would compensate exporters who sold below cost because of low world market prices.[62]

Schacht's promotion of a policy to balance trade by increasing exports and reducing imports is widely believed to have placed him on a collision course with Hitler, ultimately resulting in his dismissal from the leadership of both the Reich economics ministry and the Reichsbank. This interpretation reflects Schacht's destiny in the long run, but it incorrectly creates the impression that Schacht's fate was sealed from the beginning because his views on foreign trade were fundamentally incompatible with autarkic Nazi views on the subject. It was Schacht's objective to skew trade relations toward those countries that were able and willing to purchase German-made goods in return for the food and raw material that they sold to Germany. Prior to 1936, statements on the subject of foreign trade attributed to Nazi officials suggested no real disagreement with Schacht's ideas and actions.[63]

German authorities could neither coerce nor entice foreign nations to import enough German goods to support the demands of both work creation and rearmament. In 1934, foreign exchange controls, employed since 1931, were tightened, and a list of imported goods based on national priority insured that no foreign exchange would be wasted on nonessential commodities or finished goods.[64] The government concluded trade agreements with countries able to supply Germany with vital materials, with the promise to the exporting country that sufficient foreign exchange would be made available to German importers.[65]

Restrictions on imports and the use of foreign exchange contributed to shortages of raw materials that threatened to undermine efforts to reduce unemployment. Nazi regulations on the use of fibrous materials and synthetic textiles combined with raw material shortages to disrupt textile production. Anecdotal evidence suggests that the actual or impending layoff of workers attributable to the unavailability of imported raw material constituted a serious problem. Border areas such as the Rhineland were especially affected by efforts to reduce imports.[66] Statistically, however, the impact of raw material shortages on Nazi labor-market policy through the summer of 1935 seems less clear. A statistical compilation based on reports of the Reich

Trustees of Labor (Reichstreuhänder der Arbeit), showed that from October 1934 through July 1935 only 9.6 percent of factory closures (either full or partial) under provisions of section twenty of the 1934 Law for the Organization of National Labor (Gesetz zur Ordnung der nationalen Arbeit, AOG), and only 6.6 percent of the layoffs of workers affected by these closures, were directly caused by the lack of raw material. Hardest hit by raw material shortages was the textile industry.[67] Although the statistics provided in the report do not include all plant closings, they are sufficiently complete to indicate that, up to the middle of 1935, raw material shortages did not cause a general disturbance in Germany's labor market.

It was possible to compensate for import restrictions through the domestic production of normally imported raw materials and foodstuffs. The substitution of domestically produced materials for imported materials not only conserved scarce foreign exchange but also created new jobs for unemployed German workers. The "war against imports" could be integrated into the "battle for jobs." Because of this job creation aspect, the financial resources of the RfAA could be called into play. RfAA funds had been used for the subsidization of private enterprise under the agricultural Landhilfe program, but RfAA president Friedrich Syrup and others in the Reich government had consistently opposed the use of RfAA unemployment support funds as subsidies to private industrial firms hiring "additional" workers. But in September 1934, more or less coincident with the launching of Schacht's New Plan, Syrup recommended the granting of RfAA support funds to private firms that intended to use them for producing domestic materials as substitutes for imported materials and products. Syrup's suggestion was approved two months later, with conditions that firms seeking subsidization had to demonstrate that they intended to create additional jobs for the unemployed by substituting domestic production for foreign imports, that there was a preponderant public interest in the domestic production of the goods in question, and that domestic production of the goods in question represented a special risk for the firm, the reduction of which risk at public expense—without affecting domestic competition—was necessary.[68]

The measure was controversial, since it threatened to create two classes of firms within the private sector: those receiving public subsidies, and those not receiving public subsidies. Surely the former would have a competitive advantage over the latter. An argument developed over who would decide which firms were to be subsidized. Since the RfAA was to provide the funds, logic seemed to dictate that the RfAA president should review the applications and award the subsidies. But on this point, the difficulties inherent in attempting to combine work creation and import substitution in a single program became evident. Whereas Syrup viewed the subsidies as a work creation measure that could also serve to reduce Germany's import dependence, others such as Wilhelm Keppler, Hitler's economic adviser and since July 1933 the Führer's economic representative in the Reich chancellery, viewed the subsidy program as an import substitution measure that might create a few additional jobs. Keppler hoped to carve out for himself a niche in the Nazi power structure, and control over Germany's raw material supply was his chosen road to power.[69] Hoping to ensure Nazi party control over yet another form of patronage, Keppler wanted to place the authority to approve subsidy applications in the hands of either the party's district economic leaders or the economic advisors to the Gauleiters. Recognizing that he would not get his way in this matter, Keppler suggested the scheme that was finally adopted. Applications would be processed by a committee including the RfAA president, representatives of interested Reich ministries, the Reich economics ministry's raw materials commissioner, and Hitler's economic adviser, Keppler.[70]

Keppler discovered that Reich finance minister Krosigk could be counted upon to interpret the raw material committee's mandate in the narrowest terms possible—even in cases involving raw material considered vital to military production. One case involved a suggestion, backed by the Reich forest master (Göring), that the German leather industry be given an RfAA subsidy to increase domestic production of vegetable tannin. Krosigk rejected the proposal, even though he recognized that excessive dependence of Germany's leather industry on foreign countries was "risky from the point of view of both military policy and foreign exchange policy." Germany consumed 50,000 tons of vegetable tannin annually, only 3,000 to 5,000 tons of which was produced domestically. The remainder was imported largely from Argentina, with lesser amounts coming from Hungary, Czechoslovakia, and Luxemburg. But Krosigk considered the tannin situation to be a price problem rather than a production problem. An increase in the price of domestically produced tannin would call forth more domestic output. Krosigk's argument convinced the committee on subsidies to reject subsidies for the leather industry.[71] The rules would not be bent and the economy disrupted merely to ensure an adequate supply of shiny new jackboots for the Fatherland's expanding army and SS corps.

The tannin case would seem to tell us much about the priorities of the Nazi state even as Hitler was announcing an expansion of the military in violation of the Versailles Treaty. It was not, as some might argue, an isolated case. A request for financial assistance in developing a new, fast, lightweight diesel engine which, according to the developer, could be used in automobiles and aircraft as well as in boats, was turned down by the committee at its fourth meeting on May 14, 1935. The committee's negative decision was based on "consideration of the possible disturbance in competitive relationships [among firms in the industry]." The presence at this meeting of a representative from the Reich defense ministry, who stated that the military was interested in the project, did not help the applicant firm.[72]

The case of the diesel engine illustrates some of the economic and organizational problems associated with the early stages of German rearmament, and also demonstrates that projects of interest to the military did not have automatic access to work creation funds. Since 1921, Michel-Motor G. m. b. H., Hamburg, had been developing a new diesel engine, for which it had a patent. A small firm, unable to finance the development on its own, the company had sought to conclude licensing agreements with foreign firms. Interest in the project was strongest in the Soviet Union and England. Upon learning of these conversations with foreign firms, the Reich economics ministry first recommended caution, but in April 1934, the Reich defense minister ruled out licensing of foreign production by Michel-Motor. With the assistance of the Reich economics ministry, the firm then obtained contracts to construct engines for the Reichsbahn (three motors for locomotives), the German navy (two engines for motor launches), and the army ordnance department of the Reich defense ministry (two engines).

When production of these seven diesel engines proved to be more than the firm could handle in its own facilities, the work, to be paid for by Michel-Motor, was transferred to the Deutsche Werft AG in Kiel. When Michel-Motor was unable to produce the funds needed to complete production of the engines, Deutsche Werft stopped working on them. Then, apparently in March 1935 (the account provides no date), Michel-Motor received a trial order for a boat engine from the British admiralty. This order was also given over to Deutsche Werft for production, and Deutsche Werft indicated that it was prepared to resume work on the engines for Michel-Motor as soon as it received full payment for the first seven. On April 17, 1935, Michel-Motor applied for a six-year credit of RM 265,000 under the RfAA subsidy program for private firms. The funds were to be used to repay the firm's most pressing debts, and to pay for the production of the eight motors for which the firm had contracts. It was this grant application that the committee chaired by RfAA president Syrup turned down on May 14, 1935. It is understandable that the defense ministry did not want German firms to license foreign production of products having the potential for military application. It is much less understandable that the German government, in May 1935, did not wish to commit RM 265,000 to the development of a diesel engine in which the defense establishment had an interest.[73]

Private firms engaged in the production of raw materials stood a better chance of obtaining subsidies from work creation funds. In September 1933, a Rhineland manganese ore mining firm received Reich finance ministry approval for a RM 800,000 Öffa loan under the Reinhardt program. At the time, there was no shortage of manganese ore; demand had collapsed during the depression, and processing plants in Rhineland-Westphalia and the Saar had in recent years purchased large amounts of cheaper Russian ore, large stocks of which were still on hand. Any additional ore mined in Germany would have to be piled up and stored somewhere. Still, the plight of nearly 400 workers laid off from the Manganerzbergwerk Gewerkschaft Dr. Geyer in Waldalgesheim bei Bingen caught the attention of Gottfried Feder, then a state secretary in the Reich economics ministry. Feder asked Reinhardt in the finance ministry if it were not possible, in the interests of work creation, to provide the firm a subsidy of RM 55,000 per month. Talks between the finance ministry and the defense ministry yielded an agreement that, until July 1, 1934, the defense ministry would contract for an additional 5,000 tons of manganese ore per month, to be mined by the Waldalgesheim firm and stored in northern and central Germany. Despite the huge reserves already on hand, this arrangement was deemed justifiable, since the armed forces had a special interest in a sufficient stock of manganese ore. An Öffa loan of RM 800,000 would enable the firm to mine the ore. In this case, the Reich finance ministry seemed unconcerned that there was at this time no provision for public subsidies to private firms under either the Reinhardt program or RfAA "productive unemployment support" regulations. The problem was circumvented by asking the provincial government of Rhein-provinz to serve as the project's sponsor, even though the funds were to go to the Gewerkschaft Dr. Geyer.[74]

The provision of Reinhardt program funds and RfAA subsidies to private ore-mining firms violated the fundamental premise of the "productive unemployment support" program. Persons hired with RfAA funds were supposed to be previously unemployed, and the RfAA funds used to employ them were supposed to be balanced by corresponding savings of unemployment support payments. Partly because of the skills required of workers in the ore extraction business, few of the employees added by private firms with RfAA subsidies were publicly supported unemployed recruited through RfAA placement offices. In some cases, persons already employed by firms receiving subsidies were transferred to new jobs created with RfAA funds, and unemployed labor was subsequently hired to fill the slots vacated by those transferred.[75]

In September 1935, Keppler's office asked that RfAA subsidies to private ore mining and extraction firms be continued and that regulations be changed to permit the employment of a wider range of persons on such projects. The Reich defense minister supported Keppler, arguing that the "decisive importance of the German mining industry for the armed forces" made it "absolutely necessary" to maintain ore mining projects. Until a special fund for this purpose could be created, the only funds available, he noted, were RfAA subsidies to private firms. The defense minister feared that a large number of mining operations would be shut down "through strict adherence to the guidelines for unemployment assistance, particularly with respect to the selection of workers," and urged a looser interpretation of regulations on the use of productive unemployment support funds.[76]

As Keppler stepped up his demands for RfAA stockpiling subsidies for privately owned mining operations, the Reich finance ministry was determined to put an end to RfAA support for private firms as soon as possible. Keppler, not satisfied with a temporary compromise that permitted subsidized private firms to retain ineligible workers hired with RfAA funds until December 31, 1935, wanted RfAA funds transferred to his office (referred to as the Büro Keppler), where he could control expenditures on subsidies to private firms. For the remainder of the 1935 budget year (ending April 30, 1936), he wanted RM 2.5 million, and an additional RM 4 million for mining operations during fiscal year 1936. According to Keppler, RfAA president Syrup agreed to hand over some RfAA funds.[77]

Reich labor minister Seldte supervised the RfAA and had to sanction any arrangements made between Syrup and Keppler. Seldte agreed to shift responsibility for the subsidization of private firms from the RfAA to "the office responsible for raw materials policy," but stipulated that the funds for the subsidies must come out of the Reich budget rather than the RfAA budget. Reich finance minister Krosigk supported Seldte. Where in the

Reich budget Krosigk would find the RM 4 million sought by Keppler for 1936 was unclear.[78]

By April 1, 1936, Keppler had won control over the subsidy program for private firms engaged in the exploitation of domestic raw materials. Funding was to come from the Reich budget. At least 70 percent of those employed on subsidized projects had to be former recipients of unemployment support. The Reich finance ministry sought to explain this shift in procedure and jurisdiction as the natural result of the development of the German economy and the needs of the national state since the program's inception in the fall of 1934. When the RfAA began to subsidize private firms, reduction of unemployment was the primary concern, and the broadening of the stock of raw materials was only a secondary concern. By the spring of 1936, however, the relationship had reversed itself; the procurement of domestic raw materials had become more important than the additional employment associated with it. Thus, it was logical that responsibility for subsidization of private firms was shifted from the RfAA to Keppler's office and that funding for the operation be provided out of the Reich budget rather than the RfAA budget.[79]

Subsidizing private firms for the purpose of inducing additional production of raw materials created jobs, conserved Germany's small stock of foreign exchange, and served Hitler's strategic purposes, but it also strengthened inflationary forces during the economic upswing. As a result of comparative advantage and unusually depressed world markets at the time, imported commodities were often less expensive than commodities produced in Germany. Reich officials were willing to pay the added cost. Reich economics minister Hugenberg's directive ordering a "preference for German labor and German products" in publicly financed projects stipulated that "all of the important factors relating to the national economy, social policy, labor policy, etc., will be considered, so that, in individual cases, higher prices can be justified, without speaking about an uneconomic use of funds."[80] This regulation hit border areas such as Aachen particularly hard. Work creation projects were threatened when local officials ordered that cement produced by the German cement syndicate priced at RM 2.35 per sack be used instead of cement imported from Maastricht at RM 1.55 per sack.[81] Reich food and agriculture minister Richard Darré convinced Reich finance minister Krosigk to provide Reich treasury funds to pay the difference in cost between less expensive imported food and raw materials and their domestically produced counterparts, "on the condition that the demand remains within the bounds of what is financially possible."[82] On the other hand, Schacht and the Reichsbank, which ultimately financed the budget deficits, supported public subsidies for the production of synthetic materials only when it was economically justified—when the projected output would not be more expensive than imported raw material.[83] In other cases, strict control and allocation of scarce foreign exchange seemed preferable to higher budget deficits.

Policies designed to create jobs through either the promotion of exports or the subsidization of import-substitution production by their very nature required initiatives by the Reich government. On the other hand, initiatives for the concrete "plans" that formed the bulk of the Reich government's "battle for jobs" came from regional and local party and state officials. With the exception of Koch's scheme for East Prussia, the plans analyzed here were implemented slowly, inefficiently, haphazardly, and incompletely. Scarcity of financial resources contributed to the inefficiencies in the implementation of Nazi work creation policy. Reich officials often tried to block regional and local work creation schemes that threatened their conservative fiscal policy. They were not going to allow Nazi Gauleiters and minister-presidents to enhance their reputations at the expense of the Reich treasury.

Funding was not necessarily the most important factor in determining the success or failure of a particular initiative. Conflicts within the NSDAP as well as party-state conflicts contributed to the chaotic implementation of Nazi work creation programs. These conflicts sometimes involved jurisdictional disputes, but frequently they centered on policy issues. Dedicated Nazis sought to ingratiate themselves with Hitler by disregarding legality and cost in order to achieve a swift, striking success in the battle against unemployment. They often met resistance from Reich, Land, and RfAA officials who were either unable or unwilling to raise the requested funds, and who insisted upon honoring regulations governing the use of public funds and the assignment of jobless persons to work creation projects.

The process by which Germany waged the battle for jobs during the early years of Hitler's regime is now better understood. This can hardly be called Hitler's war, because the hand of the Führer is seldom seen. On the other hand, the compulsion and intimidation found in other areas of Nazi activity played a significant role in the success of the work creation programs. Unemployed persons who refused hard manual labor at near-slave wages under inhumane conditions in work camps were threatened with incarceration in a concentration camp.

5

Race Policy, Agricultural Policy, and Work Creation: The Hellmuth Plan for the Rhön

German work creation projects during the 1930s generally represented temporary public measures designed to provide short-term labor market relief until an inherently healthy private sector recovered and provided jobs for the German people. In certain regions of Germany, however, the private economy was not inherently healthy. In such cases, temporary, one-time public works projects offered no hope of durable economic recovery. One such area was the Rhön and Spessart, a large region lying largely within Bavaria but stretching into Prussia and Thuringia as well. Here, Gauleiter of Unterfranken and Regierungspräsident of Unterfranken and Aschaffenburg Dr. Otto Hellmuth and his economic adviser (Wirtschaftsberater der Gauleitung) Kurt Hasslinger, conceived the "Dr. Hellmuth Plan." As originally conceived, this plan proposed to reconstruct the economic and social fabric of the Rhön and Spessart under a comprehensive program addressing the problems of transportation, agriculture, and industry. The heart of Hellmuth's plan envisioned the resettlement of a substantial portion of the Rhön's population in order to make way for the creation of larger, economically viable, productive, hereditary farms *(Erbhöfe)* operated by racially sound proprietors.[1]

Despite a propaganda campaign designed to portray his plan as a "model" example of Nazi policy at its best, Hellmuth's proposals remained, for the most part, unfulfilled dreams. Perhaps Thuringian minister-president Wilhelm Marschler was correct when he characterized Hellmuth's plans as "fantasy."[2] Yet, Hellmuth's Rhön program cannot be dismissed as mere Nazi propaganda and fantasy. The Hellmuth Plan seemed to offer the

NSDAP leadership a perfect vehicle for the implementation of their professed ideas concerning race, agricultural policy, settlement policy, and work creation. Why was so little use made of such a promising opportunity? The fate of Hellmuth's ambitious project provides insight into the implementation of nearly all of the fundamental Nazi concepts and policies during the early years of Hitler's reign.[3] It also demonstrates the limits of the power of Nazi Gauleiters.

Rhön and Spessart comprise an area thirty to forty kilometers wide stretching eastward from a line between Aschaffenburg and Fulda. A parallel line drawn on the region's eastern boundary would lie approximately thirty to forty kilometers west of Würzburg. Within this area lived a population estimated at 250,000. Even in the best of times, this region could not support its population.[4] The glass and lumber industries had died out by the end of the nineteenth century, and sheep raising and agriculture, once important economic activities in the region, no longer produced enough to feed the local population. Excessive lumbering had left denuded hillsides that could no longer support either crops or sheep grazing. The inheritance law prevailing in Rhön and Spessart, which created widely separated small plots, further contributed to low agricultural productivity.

The land could not support the population, and industrial development had bypassed this region. Road and rail transportation was virtually nonexistent; only two dead-end rail lines served the region, and most of the roads were nothing more than forest trails incapable of handling automobile and truck traffic. Long before the depression hit Germany, most of the area's male population had sought work as unskilled laborers in the Rhineland and Ruhr areas. Others emigrated to America. As jobs in the Rhineland and the Ruhr dried up in the collapse of 1929–1933, thousands of laborers returned home to an area whose decayed agricultural infrastructure could not provide a minimal standard of living.

Hasslinger characterized the situation in the Rhön and Spessart as a "disgrace to civilization" *(Kulturschande)*.[5] He and Hellmuth proposed to open up the region through the construction of a network of railways and roads; consolidate scattered farm plots and serve them with farm access roads; and improve the land to "make every piece of land usable" for sheep raising, food crops, or afforestation. The creation of a viable transportation and agricultural base would lure back industrial establishments, "which presently in this region are as good as dead."[6]

On the surface, the Hellmuth plan appeared to be nothing more than a collection of traditional types of work creation projects of the sort already in progress under the Gereke *Sofortprogramm* and the Reinhardt program. There was nothing peculiarly "National Socialist" about the plan. But Hellmuth was determined to go beyond the treatment of symptoms in order to achieve what one local newspaper later referred to as a "final solution of the Rhön question." Hellmuth and Hasslinger claimed that this was "a case of rectifying centuries of mistakes."[7]

Hellmuth and Hasslinger shared the opinion of many other officials in Lower Franconia (Unterfranken) that Rhön and Spessart suffered from "overpopulation." The Hellmuth Plan foresaw the forced removal of the "excess" population, a massive involuntary migration. Those who could feed themselves on the land that they owned could stay; the rest would be "transferred to settlement sites or somewhere else, where they will find the possibility of sustaining themselves."[8] Land vacated by those forced to leave would be combined with other plots to create large, viable, entailed farms. Insofar as it involved the involuntary migration of a large segment of the region's population to some unspecified (because they did not yet exist) "settlement sites" or to an even less reassuring "somewhere else," the Hellmuth plan could have been carried out only in the context of the demise of Weimar democracy. This was a "National Socialist" program advanced not by professional government bureaucrats, but by a Nazi "old fighter."[9]

Given the extent of disease, poverty, and general social disintegration and degeneration (including incest) discovered by Hellmuth during his October 1933 tour of the Rhön, Nazi race ideology might have suggested that this population was racially unfit to live in the Third Reich and should have been subjected to a systematic policy of sterilization and euthanasia rather than rehabilitation or resettlement.[10] This possibility was taken into account. "To begin with," wrote Hasslinger, "it was established through random sampling that the Rhön population is one of the most valuable parts of the entire German people. This determination was then confirmed in its correctness through systematic investigations of the Gau Race Policy Office. Using the method of the president [of the Thuringian Health Office] Professor Dr. [Karl] Astel, Weimar, the entire genealogical structure of the population was ascertained."[11]

Professors and doctoral students at Würzburg university conducted detailed field studies of the racial composition of nearly every village in the Rhön.[12] These pseudoscientific investigations, which included taking physical measurements and photographs of thousands of individuals, allegedly demonstrated that most Rhöners were indeed of "Nordic blood." Through decades or even centuries of neglect, through misguided agricultural policy, and through the practice of subdividing farms through inheritance, an inherently healthy people had been reduced to extreme physical and spiritual destitution. The Hellmuth plan would construct a sound economic base for the Rhön and would remove the minority of the population deemed to be racially or biologically unfit.

Hellmuth expected a warm welcome from Reich government and Nazi party officials for a program that incorporated important elements of the 1933 work creation programs—agricultural improvement, land reclamation, and settlements—as well as "racial cleansing." He soon discovered that the plan's close alignment with professed Nazi ideology and policy did not guarantee funding from Reich officials in Berlin for a project that carried a very large price tag. Mounting an intense advertising campaign to sell the plan to the Hitler government, Hellmuth organized a tour of the Rhön region, so that Reich officials could see for themselves the poverty and misery his plan would alleviate.[13] Hellmuth also organized a special exhibition designed to demonstrate the need to rehabilitate this culturally valuable area of the Reich. The exhibition, which opened in Berlin, was to be shown in Hamburg, Cologne, Düsseldorf, Munich, and other major German cities.[14]

The Rhön tour convinced RfAA officials and Reich food and agriculture minister Richard Walther Darré's special deputy for land cultivation, state minister Hans-Joachim Riecke, that the area's population indeed lived in misery and near starvation. On the basis of Riecke's report, Darré conceded that "the need is clear," and he agreed that the remedial actions proposed by Hellmuth were "applicable." But he refused to commit himself and his resources to a full-scale execution of Hellmuth's plan, because the tour had not clarified "to what extent" Hellmuth's measures could be implemented, what funds were required, and how much land could be gotten from present holders of small plots for purposes of amalgamation and resettlement.[15]

Darré's attitude toward the Hellmuth plan was critical to its success or failure. As Reich peasant leader (Reichsbauernführer) and Reich minister for food and agriculture, Darré could claim that Hellmuth's contemplated program of land reclamation and settlement lay completely within his jurisdiction. Hellmuth's proposal seemed to be a perfect vehicle for the implementation of Darré's "blood and soil" racial ideas, agricultural policy, and settlement policy. But despite the match between Darré's ideology and Hellmuth's plan, Darré never gave Hellmuth's plan his unconditional support. Darré's reluctance spelled trouble for Hellmuth.[16]

Hellmuth's plan failed to live up to the inflated Nazi rhetoric with which it was introduced. The projected cost of the program, the skepticism of Reich authorities in Berlin, resistance from Thuringian minister-president Wilhelm Marschler, and opposition from the local population combined to scale down Hellmuth's grandiose plans. The fate of the Hellmuth plan demonstrates that not even a dedicated Nazi Gauleiter could convince or force thousands of people to give up their homes (no matter how squalid), convince authorities in other areas already struggling with widespread unemployment to take in thousands of involuntary migrants, convince the Reich government to finance a gigantic resettlement and reconstruction program, and coax or force a myriad of NSDAP, Reich, Land, and municipal authorities to cooperate in the implementation of his plan.[17]

The Hellmuth plan was both ambitious and costly—exactly how costly, nobody knew. RfAA president Syrup and general inspector for German roads Fritz Todt agreed that Hellmuth's plan deserved support. They asked Hellmuth for an exact cost projection for his plan.[18] Hellmuth and Hasslinger came up with a figure of RM 135 million for the Rhön project alone, not including Spessart. Adding to this RM 18 million needed to acquire land, the total for the Rhön project came to RM 153 million. Hasslinger believed that obtaining the credits through the issue of annuity bonds, mortgage bonds, or work creation bills would be "easy to render possible," because the funds borrowed would be repaid through an increase in productivity and output of agricultural products.[19]

Reich officials meeting March 28, 1934, considered a "Working scheme for the Dr. Hellmuth Plan. Part I Rhön," which, for the Rhön without Spessart, projected a five-year program with a price tag of RM 184.55 million. Included in the plan were projects to correct the flow of rivers and streams, improve wasteland, construct access roads for farms and businesses, clear land for cultivation, improve land already under cultivation, create two hundred new farms, construct new farm buildings, repair old farm buildings, resettle households within the region, and transfer three thousand households to "other areas." Hellmuth and Hasslinger requested an additional RM 500,000 to cover costs of planning, including the creation of a special Board of Works (Bauamt) with a staff of eighty. Reich government officials rejected the use of Reich funds to cover the cost of planning, and decided that, initially, improvement projects would be limited to interior

Rhön (defined as Zone 1), with projects in Zone 2 to be taken up later. Building repair projects were removed from the plan; property owners would have to provide their own funds. Provision for the resettlement of families to other areas was also provisionally deleted from the program, on the assumption that the contemplated improvement and enlargement of agricultural acreage would increase farm income by an average of RM 200 per year per hectare. Much of the work was to be carried out by the Voluntary Labor Service, which already had five camps available in the area and planned to have three more operational in the near future.[20]

Following the March 28 meeting, Hasslinger submitted a revised proposal for the improvement of an area limited to interior Rhön at a cost of RM 61.7 million over five years. The largest saving was on settlement and resettlement, the allotment for which was reduced by RM 65 million. Despite the expressed opposition of Reich officials, Hellmuth and Hasslinger had not yet given up on their plan for the physical removal of part of the Rhön population. Hasslinger now argued that the cost of resettling Rhön families in north Germany should be charged to "other settlement measures" rather than to the Hellmuth plan. Hellmuth, in what later proved to be a very misleading statement, indicated that financing for the project, insofar as it involved loans, could be "considered as assured." Moreover, he claimed industry had promised permanent employment in other parts of Germany for some 1,800 workers from the Rhön area. The departing workers and their families would free up small plots that could be consolidated into larger farms.[21]

Under pressure from the Reich government, Hellmuth had scaled down his plan to cover only a portion of the Rhön encompassing an area of about 51,700 hectares. The estimated cost of projects in this limited area came to less than RM 70 million. But the process of shrinking the Hellmuth plan, at least in its initial stage, had not yet ended. Agreeing with a Bavarian agricultural official's opinion that "we have to begin where no failures are to be expected," Hellmuth and Hasslinger decided to launch the program with seven relatively small land-improvement projects, all on state-owned property, thus avoiding difficulties and delays in persuading or coercing private property owners to participate. Seeking to turn defeat into a virtue, Hellmuth described this cautious approach as an opportunity "to obtain new material for propaganda . . . then, it will be easier to have further projects financed," after an initial small-scale success.[22] A modest beginning would minimize the risk of failure.

Reich food and agriculture minister Darré, uneasy about Hellmuth's proposal to expropriate and resettle the small landowners, further modified Hellmuth's plan in August 1934. He ordered "as a first step" the selection of an area comprising several small Bavarian Rhön towns and the preparation of a plan for both the restructuring of land ownership and the improvement of land in this limited area. While Hellmuth was to oversee the preparation of the plan, Darré himself would handle questions dealing with settlement or resettlement. Darré opposed the expropriation of a large number of peasant smallholders. If new industries could be enticed to the Rhön, sufficient work opportunities could be created and no one would have to be resettled.[23]

Darré's reluctant attitude toward the plan, motivated largely by his skepticism about the resettlement proposals, contrasted sharply with the enthusiasm for the Hellmuth plan exhibited by Gottfried Feder, whom Hitler had appointed Reich Commissioner for Settlement Affairs on March 29, 1934. On the very day Darré was approving a miniaturized version of the Hellmuth Plan, covering only a few selected communities, Feder was telling Bavarian government officials that "a speedy implementation of the Rhön plan is necessary to alleviate the unique distress in the region." Feder informed the Bavarian government that he had created a project staff to work on the Rhön plan.[24] Had Hellmuth found a powerful ally in his struggle to bring his Rhön program to fruition? Probably not, in view of the circumstances under which Feder had received his appointment as Reich commissioner for settlement affairs, and of his relationship, as Reich commissioner, to Reich agriculture minister Darré, who also had a settlement department under his jurisdiction.

Feder, recognized as the chief theoretician of the Nazi party as Hitler assumed the chancellorship, had been rewarded with a state secretary's post in the Reich economics ministry, with responsibilities in the areas of housing and settlements. His impact on policy seems to have been negligible, and his influence in general seems to have been declining. His appointment as Reich commissioner for settlement affairs in March 1934 might indicate Feder's newfound favor with Hitler, but more likely it represented to Hitler a way of settling a troublesome jurisdictional dispute while simultaneously finding a suitable, but relatively powerless, position for Feder.

The jurisdictional problem arose out of an attempt by Robert Ley's Deutsche Arbeitsfront (DAF) to gain control over all matters pertaining to housing and settlements.[25] The DAF established a homestead office (Heimstättenamt) headed by J. Wilhelm Ludovici, who also served on Deputy Führer Rudolf Hess's staff as an assistant for settlement matters. On March 8, 1934, Hess named Ludovici "plenipotentiary for settlement questions," with vaguely defined authority that seemed to threaten and encroach upon the jurisdiction over settlement policy claimed by the economics ministry, the labor ministry, and especially Darré's agriculture ministry.

Darré vigorously protested Ludovici's attempts to take over settlement policy. To resolve jurisdictional conflicts and allay fears of unlimited expansion of the DAF and its homestead office, Hitler created the position of Reich commissioner for settlement affairs on March 29, 1934, and appointed Feder to the post. Feder, however, was a weak commissioner. According to Hitler's appointment decree, he functioned "under the direction of the Reich economics minister, in cooperation and agreement with the Reich labor minister."[26] To satisfy Darré, Hitler stipulated in Feder's appointment that "the rural settlements handled by the Reich minister for food and agriculture remain unaffected by this decree." Feder's authority thus did not appear to extend to any settlements that might be developed under the Hellmuth plan. Feder's appointment as settlement commissioner, however, did not put an end to the DAF's role in such matters. Hitler appointed the former head of the Heimstättenamt, Ludovici, as Feder's deputy commissioner. Feder was relieved of his positions and put into retirement in November 1934.[27]

In its new configuration, the once-grandiose Hellmuth plan was little more than an experimental, small-scale pilot program. If the first stage worked, additional funding to extend the plan might be made available. High-level discussions on the feasibility of implementing the Hellmuth plan that were held in Berlin on February 12 and 13, 1935, produced little hope that significant funding would ever materialize. The housing and settlement division of the Reich labor ministry indicated that there was "no possibility" it could supply any funds for the reconstruction of the Rhön. The small business division of the Reich economics ministry also indicated that funds were unavailable for a large-scale Hellmuth plan and argued that "trade in the Rhön cannot be significantly improved without disturbance to other areas." Initiatives to improve the economy apparently comprised a zero-sum game in which any effort to build up industry and trade in the Rhön must inevitably be done at the expense of some other region.[28]

Prospects for improving transportation facilities in the Rhön were dimmed when the Reich transportation ministry indicated that, because "the Führer desires the 'motorization' of Germany," the Reichsbahn would neither construct nor extend secondary lines. Such construction would probably only create large, economically unjustified costs without improving the region's economy.[29] Most agricultural experts doubted the feasibility of Hellmuth's plan to make the Rhön's wastelands suitable for agriculture. The area was climatically unsuited for agriculture. Before any significant agricultural activity could be carried out here, it was necessary to erect a crop-protecting wind barrier by means of a major afforestation project in the 20,000-hectare wasteland area. It would be at least thirty years before the trees were large enough to permit agriculture on any significant scale.[30] Discussion of the whole project began to appear academic when the Reich finance ministry reported that no funds for the Hellmuth plan were available from the various work creation programs, and rejected Hasslinger's suggestion that the plan be funded directly from the regular Reich budget.[31]

On the basis of the February 12–13, 1935, discussions, Reich agriculture minister Darré authorized a "partial project" to be carried out in Prussian Rhön under the supervision of the Oberpräsident in Kassel. In November 1935 Darré authorized Bavarian and Thuringian officials to work with Prussian officials to develop a coordinated "general plan" encompassing land improvement, settlement of farmers on reclaimed land, and road-building projects in the three Länder. But Darré remained unconvinced that small farmers should be evicted so that their land could be consolidated into large, viable hereditary farms.[32]

With his plan for Rhön and Spessart, Hellmuth had set off an interagency free-for-all in Berlin and had stirred up trouble with his Thuringian neighbors. Hellmuth originally envisaged that he would either head a central coordinating office or be appointed Reich Commissioner for the "distressed area" Rhön and Spessart. Berlin authorities never vested him with authority beyond that which he already exercised as Regierungspräsident and Gauleiter in Unterfranken and Aschaffenburg.[33] Darré sought to establish a definitive administrative structure for the Hellmuth plan in December 1934. A group of Reich, Land, and NSDAP representatives accepted a proposal drawn up in Darré's ministry that created a committee including representatives from no fewer than thirty-two Reich, Land, and Nazi party authorities to implement the Hellmuth plan. Hans-Joachim Riecke, Darré's special plenipotentiary deputy for land cultivation, was to chair this central committee. Four "expert committees" dealing with land improvement, resettlement, and property transfer; forestry projects; transportation; and industry, trade, home work, and tourism, would assist the main committee. Overall responsibility for the Hellmuth plan would reside with Darré's Reich food and agriculture ministry.[34]

Hellmuth had lost control over the implementation of his own plan, which was now hopelessly mired in an administrative morass.[35] He also needed to obtain the cooperation of several Land governments. Although most of the Rhön and Spessart lay in Bavaria, portions of the region came under the jurisdiction of Prussia, Thuringia, electoral Hesse, and Baden. Attempts to coordinate projects in these Länder under the umbrella of the Hellmuth plan proved futile. The Prussian and Bavarian governments supported Hellmuth's plan with strong reservations, particularly concerning the land redistribution and resettlement scheme.[36] In Thuringia, Hellmuth's program stirred up opposition and resentment. Fritz Sauckel claimed that since August 1932, Thuringia under Nazi leadership had already expended RM 17 million for the Thuringian Rhön. Thuringia's economics ministry pointed out that Hellmuth would have known about this remedial action had he contacted Thuringian authorities prior to launching his plan.[37]

Thuringian minister-president Wilhelm Marschler charged that Hellmuth's plan proceeded from false assumptions and as a result came to false conclusions and impractical recommendations for action. Marschler estimated the cost of Hellmuth's Rhön-Spessart program to be between 300 million and 350 million Reichsmarks. He claimed Hellmuth's economic advisor, Hasslinger, knew nothing about conditions in the Thuringian Rhön.[38] Darré attempted to minimize the conflict between Hellmuth and Marschler. It was mainly a Bavarian matter, Darré pointed out, since most of the region in question lay within Bavaria. Thuringia's immediate role in the program would be quite limited, since Hellmuth's plan was, at least in the beginning, to be confined to only a small portion of the Rhön region. The Prussian and Bavarian governments, noted Darré, had already promised their "full support" for the plan.[39]

A defensive Hellmuth now explained that his memorandum had sought to portray the distress in the Bavarian Rhön, and he denied any intent to minimize the important work of the Thuringian government in the Thuringian Rhön. He argued that this progress could best be protected by the creation of large entailed estates that could not be legally divided among heirs upon the death of the owner. Hellmuth continued to insist that there was insufficient good land to support the Rhön's population and create the required entailed estates. Resettlement of a portion of the region's population to northern Germany remained a vital part of the plan. Undeterred by the bitter opposition that his resettlement plan had evoked among the Rhön population, Hellmuth was certain that the Rhöners would agree to resettlement once they saw the prospect of jobs and land in northern Germany, especially if the entire Nazi party apparatus were set in motion to "enlighten" the affected population. All that would be required was a special Reich law on expropriation.[40]

The response of Thuringian Ministerialdirektor Roloff (Thuringian economics ministry) was largely dishonest. The Thuringian government, he claimed, hailed the proposed measures of assistance for the Rhön, "and does not wish to exercise any criticism of the basic features of the Hellmuth plan."[41] This statement was outright misrepresentation, since Thuringian minister-president Marschler had already ripped Hellmuth's plan to shreds in his memorandum of March 19, 1934. Roloff pointed out that three of the five Thuringian towns affected by Hellmuth's plan already enjoyed relatively good economic conditions, and the remaining two had shown marked improvement since the advent of a National Socialist government. He promised the "cooperation" of Thuringian authorities, but rejected any special law for the creation of a Reich commissioner for the entire Rhön. In this he was supported by minister of state Riecke, Darré's special agent for the Hellmuth plan, who indicated that the Reich cabinet would never agree to a special Reich law for the Rhön, especially one granting a Reich commissioner far-reaching authority for expropriation.[42]

Hellmuth and the Thuringian government were on a collision course. In July 1934, Hellmuth complained to the NSDAP Reichsleitung that Marschler was "sabotaging" his plan with defamatory statements to the press charging that the Hellmuth plan proposed unrealizable solutions to problems that did not exist. Describing Marschler's attacks as "motivated not by technical considerations but rather by personal considerations, because they fear that their own measures for the Rhön to date will not receive appropriate recognition," Hellmuth asked the party leadership to order Marschler to cease his interference and public denunciations.[43] Marschler in turn continued to maintain that Hellmuth's plan was inappropriate for the Thuringian Rhön, and asked propaganda minister Joseph Goebbels to block Hellmuth's press releases "judging the actions of the Thuringian government in the Rhön unfavorably and arousing unrest and exaggerated hopes in the population of Thuringian Rhön."[44] Marschler charged that Hellmuth's program amounted to nothing more than "fantastic plans that extend far beyond the area of the Gau and infringe upon the responsibility of a [Thuringian] government" appointed by the Führer himself. Marschler asked that Hellmuth be ordered to stay within his jurisdiction and desist from disturbing the Thuringian government's own reconstruction work in the Rhön.[45]

The conflict between Hellmuth and Marschler represents an excellent example of the complexity of power relationships in the Third Reich, and also illustrates the pitfalls of a system in which all power supposedly emanated from the Führer himself. Hitler was pressured to choose between two of his lieutenants, both of whom owed their authority directly to him. His response to this dilemma was typical of his approach in such cases; he refused to choose between them. Hitler ruled that "the resolution of this dispute before the highest Party court must at all cost be avoided," and ordered Marschler and Hellmuth to settle the matter between themselves.[46] Criticism of Hellmuth's plan, however, continued. In October 1936, the Thuringian newspaper *Meininger Kreisanzeiger* praised Nazi achievements in the Thuringian Rhön and commented that in Thuringia, "they didn't talk about resettlement, they didn't plan projects that could be realized only after decades—they went to work immediately," setting up work camps, clearing fields, and building roads.[47]

Not until December 1935 did the Thuringian government finally provide the Reich food and agriculture ministry with proposals for improvement of the Thuringian Rhön. It amounted to a comprehensive plan for RM 20.7 million (of which RM 5.3 million was designated as "urgent projects") in land improvement, road construction, municipal water supplies, promoting tourism, and the consolidation of scattered farmland plots. By this late date, virtually all available sources of work creation assistance, with the exception of some funds controlled by general inspector for German roads Todt, had been fully committed. The Reich food and agriculture ministry could provide the Thuringian government funds only to support land consolidation "in justified cases."[48]

Opposition to the Hellmuth Plan came not only from skeptical Reich authorities and a Thuringian minister-president who rejected what he considered Hellmuth's interference in affairs outside the Gauleiter's jurisdiction, but also from the ordinary people of the Rhön, who believed they would have to bear the costs of Hellmuth's scheme. According to Joachim Hohmann, racial studies of Rhön villages conducted by faculty and students at Würzburg University, coordinated by the NSDAP race policy office of

Hellmuth's Gau, led to the sterilization of "degenerate" families, relatives of these families, and even entire villages believed to have been corrupted through incest. In a predominantly Roman Catholic region, where Nazi ideology had never excited the population, Hellmuth's program of "racial cleansing" through sterilization and forced migration simply incited the opposition of the Roman Catholic bishops of Würzburg and Fulda and their devoted followers. Many recalcitrant inhabitants of the Rhön apparently ended up in Nazi concentration camps at Dachau and Buchenwald.[49]

Compulsory relocation was the cornerstone of Hellmuth's plan. The plan assumed that approximately 85 percent of the Rhön's farms were not viable. Those living on parcels earmarked for improvement rebelled against the notion that many of them would have to give up their land and resettle so that the remaining population could feed and shelter itself at a decent standard of living. At high-level meetings on the Hellmuth plan held in Berlin on February 12 and 13, 1935, Hellmuth, facing strong opposition from the potential victims, softened the compulsory mass resettlement aspect of his plan because it was "not practicable." Hasslinger conceded that since few people would resettle willingly, little land would be freed up for the creation of larger farms without compulsion. An official from the Reich food and agriculture ministry advised that "it is risky to proceed with coercion." Giving up large-scale resettlement narrowed the original plan significantly, "but [by narrowing the plan] the immediate task thereby stands out more clearly."[50]

Rhön farmers, with good reason, as it turned out, remained skeptical of assurances that the revised Hellmuth plan sought only "a voluntary alteration of the structure of ownership according to the expression of the will of the people themselves." Authorities attributed the "false interpretation" (compulsory resettlement) to "irresponsible elements who wish to sabotage the Gauleiter's plan." The continuing fear of resettlement ironically undermined Hellmuth's program to make the region self-sufficient in food, as farmers who believed that they were earmarked for resettlement ignored Nazi exhortations to work harder and produce more.[51]

Failing to obtain support for other elements of his program, Hellmuth turned to the construction of roads to open up the Rhön to tourism and economic growth. The centerpiece of his road construction program was the Rhönstraße, a twenty-kilometer road connecting Fladungen and Bischofsheim. In May 1934 he sought priority status for the project after a fire destroyed forty homes and business establishments in a small town in the

Rhön. In a telegram to RfAA president Syrup, Hellmuth claimed that the Rhön had been "severely afflicted" by the fire, and he asked for "urgent approval of the Bischofsheim-Fladungen project for the people of the Rhön."[52]

Because of technical and financial problems, construction on the road did not begin until 1935, and it was finally completed in 1937. Discussions concerning construction of the Rhönstraße began in May 1934 and lasted until the end of May 1935, when Hasslinger finally announced the completion of a "final" financing package of RM 708,000. The package consisted of a RfAA basic subsidy of RM 330,000 (approved in installments as work on the road progressed), a subsidy of RM 62,000 paid by the Bavarian state government out of its share of Reich automobile tax funds, a RM 216,000 credit from the Deutsche Rentenbank-Kreditanstalt, and a special subsidy of RM 100,000 that the Reich ministry for food and agriculture had agreed to provide.[53] Throughout the preparations for construction of the Rhönstraße, Hellmuth's economic adviser Hasslinger handled negotiations for financing the project. This intervention of Nazi party authorities does not seem to have expedited the process. Despite energetic support for and continual involvement in the Rhönstraße project by the Gauleitung in Würzburg, it had taken an entire year to put together the financing for twenty kilometers of secondary road construction.[54]

Until 1937, the Rhönstraße remained one of the few tangible achievements of the Hellmuth plan. Having encountered firm resistance to their original plan to relocate large numbers of Rhön families in northern Germany, Hellmuth and Hasslinger now hoped that Germany's rearmament program could solve the Rhön's problems of poverty and overpopulation. The "excess" Rhön population would provide a labor force for industries desperately trying to keep pace with the insatiable demands of the 1936 Four Year Plan. Resettlement of impoverished Rhöners in "workers' settlements" in the vicinity of factories had been an element of Hellmuth's plan from the outset. There were, unfortunately, virtually no suitable industrial plants in the Rhön. Hitler's rearmament program brought minimal benefits to the Rhön. Many local firms were small-scale artisan operations poorly equipped with machinery and unable to meet the short delivery schedule normally required in military contracts. Some of the Rhön's few thriving businesses were destroyed in the Nazi "aryanization" campaign designed to place firms in "German" hands. In Mellrichstadt, for example, of three Jewish-owned firms in the iron business, which, until 1937, "were going very well," two were undergoing aryanization, and one had "completely disappeared." An out-of-town party seeking to purchase the firms was unable to obtain credit.[55]

Industrial development became the key to the success of the Hellmuth plan, the prerequisite for resettlement of the rural poor in workers' settlements in and around the towns. Hellmuth and Hasslinger sought to convince established outside firms to set up branch factories in the area. Given the unskilled labor force and the inherent unattractiveness of this area, few major corporations were anxious to locate or relocate operations in the Rhön. Hasslinger, assisted by the Reich DAF leadership and the Rhön's leading electric utility, Überlandwerk Oberfranken, succeeded in bringing only one major firm into the Rhön region. In December 1936 Siemens-Schuckert-Werke of Berlin agreed to establish a plant for the production of electrical cable in Bad-Neustadt an der Saale.[56]

At first, employing between 300 and 500 workers, the Siemens-Schuckert plant was projected to provide jobs for up to 1,000 workers. It was unclear, however, how many of these jobs would go to impoverished inhabitants of the Rhön. Most of these destitute people lacked the skills required by the Siemens-Schuckert operation. Hasslinger presumably solved this problem by convincing Siemens-Schuckert to open a training workshop in Bad Neustadt in January 1937. But the overriding question remained whether Bad Neustadt was the most suitable (or even suitable at all) location for a new factory designed to alleviate the misery of the Rhön. The town was located not in the heartland of the Rhön, but on the outer fringe. How would workers from relatively distant points reach the factory? The fourteen-kilometer round-trip from Mellrichstadt, for example, cost forty Pfennige.[57]

With DAF assistance, Mellrichstadt authorities had initiated their own campaign to attract major firms to their town. The chief administrative officer of the Mellrichstadt district, Unger, spent a good part of December 1936 and January 1937 in Berlin, seeking out firms willing to locate plants in the town of Mellrichstadt. Unger portrayed Mellrichstadt as a potential industrial paradise; only the factories were lacking. Mellrichstadt, Unger emphasized, did not want to be left behind in Germany's economic upswing. The town authorities would do whatever was necessary to enable industrial firms to locate there.[58]

Unger's contacts with industrial firms in Berlin were not encouraging. But after discussions with Siemens-Schuckert-Werke, he had counted on the factory's coming to Mellrichstadt. News that the plant would go to Bad Neustadt rather than Mellrichstadt produced "a certain ill-humor" among Mellrichstadt's labor force.[59] Exactly how and why the factory went to Bad Neustadt remains something of a mystery. Bad Neustadt already had several large plants. Mellrichstadt, on the other hand, one of the region's oldest towns and seat of the district administration since around 1800, was, according to its own officials, becoming a "dead city."[60] Memoranda from the Bavarian economics ministry indicate that Hasslinger, concerned about labor market policy, had made every effort to have the plant located "deeper in the Rhön," in Mellrichstadt. But, since Siemens-Schuckert expressed a particular interest in Bad Neustadt, Hasslinger felt it best to stop promoting Mellrichstadt for fear of turning the firm against locating in the area at all.[61]

Bad Neustadt's Nazi Kreisleiter believed that Mellrichstadt had the potential to become an "agricultural model town." Especially now, argued the Kreisleiter, when the Four Year Plan sought to create a strong foundation for Germany's food supply as well as its industrial base, "it would be an error to try to convert a typical rural town into an industrial city." The task of assuring the food supply of the German people "offers Mellrichstadt a wonderful field of action" in rehabilitating its local economy. In an apparent condemnation of Hellmuth's plan, Bad Neustadt's Kreisleiter cautioned that "one cannot and must not consider forcible interventions which would only mean an uprooting of the overwhelmingly agrarian population." The transfer of industrial plants to Bad Neustadt would provide relief for Mellrichstadt because those factories, claimed the Kreisleiter, would hire most of their workers from the Mellrichstadt area. Siemens-Schuckert, he asserted, had agreed to secure most of its labor from the Rhön.[62]

The Siemens-Schuckert plant represented to Hasslinger a gigantic step toward realization of the Hellmuth plan. He envisioned the retraining of small farmers and their relocation to settlements in the vicinity of the new plant as the first step toward the creation of the large entailed farms that formed the core of his agricultural reconstruction plan. After completing the training course provided by Siemens-Schuckert, owners of small plots would sell them to Munich-based Bayerische Bauernsiedlung, which in turn would resell the property to another small farmer, who, by adding the newly acquired land to his holdings, would create a larger, viable entailed farm. The newly skilled laborers would receive a small home with garden plot, or, if they preferred, an apartment, in a settlement near the new Siemens-Schuckert plant. Hasslinger apparently believed that the enlightened self-interest of these uneducated, destitute small farmers would lead them to cooperate with his grandiose plan. Force, he said, would not be used; the people would do everything voluntarily.[63]

Hasslinger estimated that 500 of the 1,000 workers to be hired by Siemens-Schuckert could be drawn from the Rhön. These small farmers would each give up an average of four hectares of land, thus producing about 1,875 usable hectares. Since a viable entailed farm would require 11 hectares, Hasslinger calculated that he could create 170 such farms. At 6 persons per family, the 500 families transferred to industrial work and the 170 families now settled on newly created farms would account for a total of 4,020 persons placed in a viable economic existence under this single Hellmuth plan project.[64]

Hasslinger presumed that new businesses, accounting for 50 households, would spring up to serve the needs of those 4,020 people who now had money to spend. Assuming that these 50 families also gave up 4 hectares of land, Hasslinger now had land for another 17 entailed farms, and a total of 4,320 persons given economic life through the opening of the Siemens-Schuckert operation in Bad Neustadt. The Preh radio works in Bad Neustadt intended to hire an additional 500 workers. Assuming that they were drawn from the Rhön, Hasslinger calculated that the Preh workers, added to those already taken care of through the Siemens-Schuckert plant, would bring the total of persons economically rehabilitated to 8,640. Once Siemens-Schuckert had developed an adequate contingent of skilled labor, claimed Hasslinger, they planned to expand operations in Bad Neustadt and hire an additional 1,000 workers. In the long run, then, hiring by Siemens-Schuckert and Preh would free up 9,375 hectares and provide a secure economic existence, in either agriculture or industry, for 21,690 persons. Hasslinger seemed to cast doubt upon his own optimistic projections when he wrote that "even if only a portion of the goal can be reached, the task is still so immense that even a seventy–per cent implementation is worth striving for."[65]

By late 1936 and early 1937, with minimal assistance from the Hellmuth plan, Germany's general economic upswing had already put a substantial number of the Rhön's workforce back to work, although not necessarily in the Rhön. Some had found employment in factories in Schweinfurt, which Hellmuth regarded as a less-than-optimal solution, since it required costly out-of-town lodging and meals for Rhön workers. A number of others had found jobs in mining operations outside the Rhön. The employment pattern was returning to its predepression configuration, when most Rhön workers employed in nonagricultural work had held mining and factory jobs outside the region.[66]

In April 1937, the Bavarian economics ministry reported that the establishment of the Siemens-Schuckert plant in Bad Neustadt had already produced "a certain relief" for the Rhön, although it continued to characterize the region as a "distress area" that still required "further attention."[67] By the end of 1938, some parts of the Rhön were experiencing labor shortages. It had become impossible to distinguish between measures taken under the Hellmuth plan and those attributable to the Four Year Plan for preparing Germany for war. The *Völkischer Beobachter* described a "Four Year Plan settlement in Bad Neustadt," which "became necessary as a result of the relocation of industry, and simultaneously realized an essential part of the Dr. Hellmuth Plan." According to the press report, "hundreds" of Rhön inhabitants had given up their small holdings and found work in Bad Neustadt, while the plots they gave up had been used to create larger, viable farms.[68]

In the spring of 1938, still unable to obtain significant Reich financial support for a large-scale resettlement program in the Rhön, Hellmuth sought to incorporate his resettlement plan into settlement and housing construction programs run by Robert Ley's Labor Front. With Hitler's sanction, the DAF was creating settlements for factory workers. As Gauleiter of Mainfranken, Hellmuth ordered that the "Siedlungs-Bau-Programm 1938" set up by the DAF be carried out in his district, and directed Gau authorities to support the DAF program with all available means.[69]

The Reich government could not afford to overlook possible sources of labor for Germany's armaments plants, but it remained unconvinced that displacing poor Rhön peasants was a good way to achieve that end. Many Reich officials continued to view the conversion of Rhön wasteland to productive agricultural land as a crackpot idea. Aside from ethical and legal objections to expropriation, the cost of new agricultural settlements was prohibitive. As a result of local deforestation, most of the necessary construction materials would have to be brought into the Rhön. The cost of each farm, including structures and animals, was estimated minimally at RM 23,000 and at least RM 36,750 when costs of water provision, schools, and other public facilities were factored in.[70]

Bavarian minister-president Siebert admitted that the Hellmuth Plan could not be justified on the basis of cost-benefit analysis, "since the expenditure does not return a profit"; nevertheless, he favored carrying out the plan and the expenditure of public funds to create additional arable land in the Rhön. The Rhön provided an ideal field of action for the Reich labor service, which was now compulsory and needed suitable projects to keep its units occupied. Decisive for Siebert, however, was Hitler's Four Year Plan. Only within the context of the Four Year Plan's goal of self-sufficiency in food could the Hellmuth plan be justified and implemented, "even if this is tied to disproportionately high costs."[71]

Precisely how much of the Hellmuth plan ever came to fruition is unclear. Ten towns in which 5,453 landowners occupied 9,343 hectares (an average holding of only 1.7 hectares) had been targeted for improvements in the first phase of the Hellmuth plan. By the end of 1937, afforestation had been completed on about 1,000 hectares of high plateau between Fladungen and Bischofsheim; another 180 hectares of trees for wind protection strips had been planted in the Höhe Rhön, the crest of a ridge stretching fifteen kilometers between Bischofsheim and Frankenheim. By utilizing locally produced crushed basalt in road construction, employment in the Rhön's quarries had reached levels fluctuating between 85 percent and 95 percent of "normal," while output of the quarries averaged 70 percent of capacity during 1937.[72]

The year 1938 seems to have been the most fruitful for the plan. Prior to 1938, funding for major projects had been delayed, and after 1938, the onset of war diverted financial and material resources away from programs such as the Hellmuth plan. An unofficial preliminary accounting of the plan's achievements appeared in December 1938. It claimed that 870 kilometers of roads had been constructed at a cost of more than RM 13 million. One hundred eighty-five land improvement projects (removal of tree stumps, removal of rocks, afforestation, drainage, and irrigation) had been completed at a cost of over RM 4 million, and another 133 projects costing more than RM 11 million were in progress. Significant progress was claimed in the consolidation of small, unprofitable plots into larger, economically viable units. Of 218 planned land-consolidation projects involving 99,776 hectares, 69 projects, encompassing 28,736 hectares, had been completed. The land-register for the area, which formerly contained 230,048 plan numbers (plots), now showed only 90,000. Harvest output had risen by 25 percent. The Siemens-Schuckert plant in Bad Neustadt represented the only success in bringing new production facilities into the area.[73]

As Hitler's preparations for war neared their climax, assuring Germany's combat-readiness took precedence over all other considerations. In May 1939, Reich labor service units working on land improvement projects in the Rhön were withdrawn and put to work planting and harvesting crops on land that was already under cultivation. Funds were available for planting trees for wind protection, but no labor was available.[74] With the onset of war, the agricultural labor shortage in the Rhön worsened. In the fall of 1939, crops were harvested only with the deployment of labor from the army, the labor service, the Hitler Youth, and the League of German Girls, as well as volunteers from all walks of life.[75]

Ironically, it was the drive toward war that finally assured the Rhön a role in Germany's revival as a Great Power. Precisely because it was a wasteland, the Rhön attracted the attention of the military. By 1938, the army had taken over several labor service camps and established an area for Fourth Panzer division maneuvers. Bavarian authorities feared that the army planned to take over more territory, including the hotels and the cloister in Kreuzberg, and that the Luftwaffe also planned to carry out exercises (presumably bombing practice) in the area between Fladungen and Bischofsheim, where the Rhönstraße had just been completed. "If that is the case," warned an official in the Bavarian economics ministry, "then there is really nothing more left of the Rhön."[76]

Hellmuth was able to postpone but not prevent the takeover of extensive areas of the Rhön for military purposes after 1936. The development of large military installations and training areas, such as the Wildflecken base, devoured massive stretches of Rhön territory and often required the demolition of entire villages. A significant portion of the resettlement that took place in the Rhön between 1936 and 1945 can be attributed to military requirements rather than the Hellmuth plan. The development of military bases in the Rhön was not part of the Hellmuth plan. On the contrary, such development represented competition between the military and Hellmuth for the scarce physical and human resources of the region.[77]

The Rhön survived the onslaught of Hitler's armies, and at least until the reversals suffered in the Russian campaign, some work on Hellmuth plan projects continued during the war in 1940 and 1941. Labor for Hellmuth plan projects was supplied by Polish, Belgian, Spanish, Jewish, Greek, and Russian conscripts and prisoners of war. However, requests for additional vehicles and fuel produced no results, because large-scale projects in the Rhön were never declared "essential to the war effort."[78] On the other hand, efforts to relocate industrial plants in the Rhön, which had failed so miserably during 1936 and 1937, suddenly began to succeed only days after Hitler's armies attacked Poland on Sept. 1, 1939. Firms located along Germany's western border moved (sometimes with their workers), or considered moving, to Hellmuth's Gau of Mainfranken and the Rhön area.[79]

Why did Hellmuth's program, so compatible with Nazi ideas and programs on agricultural improvement, land reclamation, resettlement, and race policy, receive so little support from Reich officials? It might be argued that attempts to scratch out a little more agricultural output from desolate regions such as the Rhön constituted a waste of scarce resources for a nation bent on conquering rich and fertile *Lebensraum* in the east. This argument, however, is not entirely persuasive. Prior to the late summer of 1936, there was no concrete "plan" for war on which officials of either the Nazi party or the various levels of government could base domestic policy decisions. In August 1936, Hitler wrote a lengthy memorandum on rearmament and economic policy, in which he asserted that definitive solutions for Germany's economic problems could be found only in the acquisition of greater living space for its population. Both the economy and the army were to be prepared for war in four years. But the content of this memorandum, the Four Year Plan, had been shared with only Göring and defense minister Blomberg, and was not announced to the public until the Nuremberg party rally on Sept. 9, 1936. Thus, the Reichsstatthalter in Bavaria, retired general Franz Ritter von Epp, spoke as if war and the conquest of additional living space were not realistic options for Germany when he addressed the first meeting of the Bavarian land-use planning association on Aug. 18, 1936. Epp told officials from the Reich government, the Bavarian government, the NSDAP, and organizations representing Bavarian industry, commerce, and agriculture that "German living space was indeed considerably too small, but not capable of being increased, so that it was of even greater economic and political importance to concentrate and array all powers, so that this space will be used for the duration in the most suitable manner, and that this arrangement will be set in place as soon as possible."[80]

Plans for the conquest of living space in eastern Europe do not account for the lack of support for Hellmuth's program during 1934, 1935, and 1936. Other factors held up progress on the plan. The fact that the area originally targeted for reconstruction was large and lay in several Länder prompted exceptionally fierce jurisdictional rivalry. The extremely unfavorable cost-benefit ratio also worked against the program. Land reclamation projects were expected to generate increased production of food as well as jobs for the unemployed. The Nazis could not wait thirty years until afforestation rendered the Rhön suitable for productive agriculture; they needed near-term results. Moreover, the fact that agricultural settlement and resettlement formed the core of Hellmuth's program proved to be a difficult obstacle to its implementation. Settling experienced farmers on large, viable farms that were newly created by improving untillable land or by combining unprofitable, scattered small plots into larger units, had never received top priority in German work creation programs. More often, the aim was to afford relief to unemployed workers on small garden plots on the outskirts of large industrial cities.

Rural resettlement may have fit well with Nazi "blood and soil" ideology, but the reality of settlement activity failed to meet expectations. Of the RM 1 billion Reinhardt work creation program of June 1, 1933, RM 270 million was set aside for settlement designed to get the "necessary internal German migration" started. But it was used mostly to relieve large industrial centers of the financial burden created by mass unemployment. There was a particular interest in settlements for short-time workers. Only RM 50 million was earmarked for true agricultural settlement.[81] Because the RM 50 million had not been allocated completely by the beginning of December, the Reich finance minister cut RM 5 million out of the amount available, and ordered that funds originally earmarked for projects incidental to agriculture, as well as settlements on the outskirts of cities for short-time workers, be shifted to other, more pressing projects. Any need for true agricultural settlements was to be satisfied out of the remaining RM 45 million.[82]

The Hellmuth plan was nearly derailed and certainly circumscribed in scope and delayed in its implementation by interagency disputes over whether it should be undertaken, and, if so, by whom. The plan became a prisoner of the organizational chaos that characterized the Nazi regime from beginning to end. State and party authorities and agencies claiming a direct share of jurisdiction over "settlement" included the Reich agriculture, economics, and labor ministries; the Reich commissioner for settlement affairs; the DAF (including the Heimstättenamt); the agriculture policy office of the NSDAP; and the race and settlement office of the SS.

Efforts to claim credit for the Hellmuth plan's limited achievements degenerated into jurisdictional disputes. An evaluation of the Hellmuth plan's progress appearing in the special issue of the *Münchner Neuste Nachrichten* on Dec. 18, 1938, gave full credit to Nazi party leaders, and left the impression that the Bavarian state government had played no role. Bavarian minister-president Siebert took exception to this oversight. He pointed out that "a great many projects which come into question (including projects in the Rhön) were conceived, prepared, and carried out by *state* authorities." The Bavarian finance minister, claimed Siebert, assumed the obligation of finding the money for these projects. "Perhaps that is the most difficult job," he wrote, and "the public ought occasionally to hear about that, too."[83]

Along with factors already discussed, unfortunate timing may have played an important role in generating the difficulties encountered by Hellmuth in promoting his Rhön plan. Hellmuth announced the broad outline of his program on Nov. 15, 1933, and was still developing the details during 1934. On Dec. 6, 1933, Reich officials decided to reduce funding for new work creation projects and allow existing programs to play themselves out during 1934.[84] Hellmuth had missed the narrow window of opportunity.

The importance of timing is reinforced by a comparison of Hellmuth's plan for Lower Franconia with Koch's plan for East Prussia. Two Nazi Gauleiters developed programs for the economic rehabilitation of their respective districts. Koch struck early and obtained funding during July 1933. Koch's more favorable timing, however, may not have been his most important advantage over Hellmuth. Koch's apparent success and Hellmuth's apparent failure in obtaining backing and funding from the Reich government could be taken as an indication that not all Gauleiters were created equal. Koch's greatest asset as Gauleiter and Oberpräsident of East Prussia proved to be his access to a very powerful figure, Prussian minister-president and Reich minister without portfolio Hermann Göring, one of Hitler's closest associates. It was Göring who apparently opened the doors for the funding of Koch's work creation program. Such an asset was not available to Hellmuth, the Gauleiter and Regierungspräsident of the Bavarian district of Lower Franconia.

Obvious differences in their development should not obscure some important similarities in the fate of the Hellmuth plan and of the Koch plan. Hitler's government did not support either program with enthusiasm. Göring was able to salvage only a portion of Koch's program, the short-term blitz to put East Prussia's unemployed back to work on emergency relief projects. Hellmuth's program had no short-term blitz component. The other, more important portion of Koch's program, a long-term effort to reconstruct and rehabilitate the East Prussian economy by completely restructuring agricultural debt, creating new agricultural settlements, and bringing industry into the province, received no support in Berlin and made virtually no headway. This long-term component of Koch's program was similar in many respects to Hellmuth's plan. Had Hellmuth developed a short-term program for quickly putting the Rhön's unemployed back to work in June or July of 1933, perhaps he would have received more support both locally and in Berlin. Whether such a plan could have worked, given the conditions in the Rhön, is doubtful.

Perhaps the most important lesson to be learned from the fate of both the Koch plan and the Hellmuth plan is that Hitler's government was not prepared to support long-term regional economic reconstruction programs between 1933 and 1936. Hitler needed short-term propaganda spectaculars that would help the Nazis consolidate their political power and that would put the people back to work on temporary emergency relief projects until a rearmament program could provide permanent employment.

6

Local and Regional Efforts in the "Battle for Work"

Adolf Hitler received most of the credit for the conquest of unemployment, but it was the dedication and sacrifice of the "frontline troops," the local communities, that spelled success or failure for the Nazi "battle for work." Local authorities would commit local resources and increase communal debt for job creation purposes only if they were convinced of the fairness of the scheme and the certainty that participation would directly and immediately reduce the communal welfare burden.[1] Communal authorities often complained of inadequate support from the Reich government and Reich financing institutions, but local governments nevertheless contributed significantly to the war against unemployment during the first three years of Nazi rule.[2] They did so by participating in Reich work creation programs and by pursuing local initiatives for creating temporary work for the unemployed.

The scope and type of work creation program adopted by any particular local authority depended on the size and location of the city or town, its financial condition, and the type of unemployed on which local authorities wished to focus attention. Some Reich work creation programs were unavailable or only minimally available in certain areas. Labor Service projects, for example, were restricted to communes of less than 100,000 people. In border areas considered easy prey for invading armies, such as the Rhineland prior to its remilitarization in March 1936, public investment in job creation was severely restricted. Before the Nazi takeover, the criteria determining where and how Reich work creation funds would be spent were rather loose. Under the Nazis, however, construction of public swimming pools gave way to projects that met three fundamental tests: they had to contribute directly to the health and productivity of the national economy, they had to contribute to the task of making Germany less dependent on imported food and raw materials, and they had to contribute to the ultimate goal of German rearmament. Local communities offering to undertake projects meeting these criteria stood the best chance of receiving indispensable Reich financial support.

Debt burdens created by years of economic crisis and welfare outlays prevented many local authorities from taking out additional loans for work creation projects promoted by the Hitler government. The Nazis sent mixed signals. On the one hand, they cautioned against a repetition of the "irresponsible" borrowing by local authorities during the Weimar era. On the other hand, Hitler's government pressured local authorities to apply for loans under Gereke's *Sofortprogramm* and the Reinhardt program. Quite often, cities and towns in the best position to finance work creation projects were those that needed them the least.[3] The chief official in Münster concluded that strict application of the rules of creditworthiness would have produced the "downright grotesque situation" that the centers of greatest unemployment would be shut out entirely from work creation programs.[4]

No Reich work creation program could succeed until Hitler's government took steps to reduce the financial burden crushing Germany's cities. Through the debt-restructuring legislation of September 21, 1933, short-term municipal obligations were to be converted to medium- and long-term obligations at lower interest rates.[5] The importance of the Reich government's debt rescheduling program in the recovery of municipal finances is clear, but it cannot be estimated precisely.[6] Local governments also were to be limited in the amount that they could spend on welfare subsidies, the greatest source of municipal debt. Hitler and other Reich government officials promoted these schemes as measures to restore municipal finances to good health. Their practical effect, however, was to expand the borrowing capacity of financially distressed cities so that they could borrow additional hundreds of millions of Reich marks for the implementation of Nazi work creation projects. In 1933–34, nearly 60 percent of the work creation expenditure of municipalities or municipal organizations was financed by the assumption of new debt.[7] In other words, local authorities increased the financial burden on local taxpayers in order to make possible Hitler's "economic miracle."

Some Reich policies actually contributed to a short-term deterioration of municipal finances. Regulations of September 22, 1933, for example, changed the basis for calculation and payment of Reich welfare assistance *(Reichswohlfahrtshilfe)*. The regulations also released local authorities from the obligation to contribute one-fifth (the so-called *"Krisenfünftel"*) of the "crisis relief" payments made by the RfAA. Instead of contributing a fluctuating amount, depending on the movement of unemployment (which was just now becoming favorable to local welfare authorities!), local authorities were obligated to pay a fixed monthly sum as their share of welfare support, with Reich welfare assistance furnishing the remainder required to satisfy the need. As Birgit Wulff has noted, this arrangement permitted the Reich treasury to benefit from declining unemployment figures, while local welfare authorities were faced with fixed payments. In some cases, reduced Reich welfare assistance and increased local expenditures on unemployment support substantially nullified benefits derived from the restructuring of municipal debt and expenditures on work creation.[8]

The Reich government concentrated a significant portion of its 1933–34 work creation resources on the improvement of agricultural land and agricultural output, rather than on urban reconstruction and development projects. This decision slowed urban economic recovery during 1933. Large cities found it necessary to "export" many of their unemployed to areas experiencing a shortage of agricultural labor, to rural land reclamation projects, to highway construction projects in the countryside, and, in some cases, to other urban centers where revival of armaments-related industries created a strong demand for skilled labor. Aside from the financial benefit of relieving local welfare rolls, getting the unemployed out of major urban centers reduced the likelihood of political unrest among large concentrations of the unemployed.

From both a social and financial standpoint, it was easiest and least expensive to assign young, unmarried males to agricultural labor, land-reclamation projects, and road construction in areas removed from their hometowns. It made more sense to reserve any available industrial jobs in the cities for older, married heads of households. Local authorities thus made a particular effort to enroll unemployed youths in the two major rural service organizations, the Voluntary Labor Service (FAD) and the Landhelpers (Landhilfe). These efforts were not entirely successful. Limited Reich funding and the nazified FAD's reluctance to become a dumping ground for the urban unemployed restricted the number of unemployed that cities could assign to the FAD and the Landhilfe. Because the work was strenuous and living conditions were primitive and isolated, urban authorities induced young men and women to volunteer for agricultural service only with great difficulty. Urban youths did not wish to exchange the urban lifestyle for that of the farm. Farmers, on the other hand, were reluctant to take on transplants from the cities who possessed neither interest in nor aptitude for farm labor. Many rural communes feared that upon completion of their Landhilfe duty, urban youths unable to find jobs in their hometowns would stay on and join the local welfare rolls.[9]

Some German Länder and provincial administrations, such as Bavaria and the Prussian province of East Prussia, established regional agricultural service organizations that provided a potential outlet for the urban unemployed. East Prussia recruited volunteers in the Rhineland's urban centers of high unemployment. Flyers from East Prussia proclaiming "Seeking Young Settlers" were posted in Duisburg. They urged that youths age 19 to 25 who wished to become farmers and who were interested in attending a "settlers' school" in East Prussia to report for a special "agricultural placement" at the Duisburg employment office on July 17, 1933. It was the understanding of the Duisburg employment office that financing of the settlers' school was to be provided under the Reich Law on Housing and Settlement Affairs of February 18, 1933. Seven days later, eighty "settlement candidates" *(Siedlungsanwärter)*, including fifty welfare recipients, left Duisburg for East Prussia. The Duisburg welfare office provided work clothing and shoes for those who could not provide their own.[10]

Once in East Prussia, the recruits were placed in the East Prussian Landdienst, where they worked as temporary farm laborers rather than as potential permanent settlers. In October, East Prussian Oberpräsident and Gauleiter Erich Koch demanded that the Duisburg employment office make the "agreed upon" payment of RM 20 for each Duisburg Landdienst volunteer by the end of the month. Receipt of the payment would guarantee places for the Duisburg volunteers until April 1, 1934; if the payment was not made, the volunteers would be sent back to Duisburg. The Duisburg AA denied agreeing to any such payment and accused East Prussian authorities of deceiving both the volunteers and Duisburg authorities by promising training for potential settlers at special schools. Koch responded by raising his demand to RM 30 per volunteer, claiming that East Prussian authorities had meanwhile spent RM 56 on each volunteer's winter clothing. He threatened to dismiss the Duisburg contingent by Christmas if payment was not received.[11]

Given the scarcity of farm labor during 1933 and 1934, urban authorities should have experienced little difficulty in placing their unemployed youths in the countryside. LAA Ostpreußen reported in the summer of 1934 that it needed another 15,000 Landhelpers; other areas in central and southern Germany could use another 5,000. The president of LAA Rheinland estimated that his district alone could furnish 27,600 males and females age 17 to 25 who were suitable for agricultural labor, and he urged communes to send them out even if they had to pay transportation costs. The Duisburg welfare office claimed in July 1934 that it had sent "thousands upon thousands" of youths to the East Prussian Landdienst, the Reich Landhilfe, and the FAD during the summer of 1933. Very few youths age 17 to 25 could be found in the city, and some of these were either committed to the Sturmabteilung (SA) or SS, or unfit for agricultural labor.[12] Despite such notable successes, placement of unemployed youths in agricultural labor remained problematic. It remains unclear how 30,000 Landhelpers could be placed in East Prussia, while fewer than 50 of a projected 1,000 could be placed in Landkreis (rural) Aachen.[13] The welfare authority of Stadtkreis (city) Aachen reported a total saving of only RM 650 from the placement of welfare recipients in the Reich Landhilfe between December 1, 1933, and March 31, 1934. On April 10 only 7 Aachen welfare recipients were serving as agricultural Landhelpers.[14]

Some Länder and cities sought to put their unemployed to work by supplementing the Reich Landhilfe with state or local Landhilfe programs. These efforts sometimes proved too ambitious for the sponsoring agency. In Bavaria, the "Siebert Plan" implemented by minister-president Ludwig Siebert provided for an "extended Landhilfe in Bavaria" costing RM 1.5 million to support up to 25,000 welfare recipients as Landhelpers. About one-third of those selected for duty in the Bavarian Landhilfe opted to give up their unemployment support rather than do hard labor on the farms. The Bavarian Landhilfe contingent dwindled from 11,061 on Jan. 15, 1934, to only 8,865 on April 15. By May, the Bavarian government had exhausted its funds for the program. To avoid a massive influx of unemployed into district welfare systems, the RfAA agreed to transfer the entire Bavarian Landhilfe contingent into the Reich Landhilfe.[15]

An attempt to promote a "Stuttgarter Landhilfe" also fell short of expectations, despite the vigorous leadership of Stuttgart's Nazi mayor, Dr. Karl Strölin. This local Landhilfe aimed at employing unemployed Stuttgarters who were too old or otherwise ineligible for service in the Reich Landhilfe. The program, administered by the Stuttgart AA and paid for by the city of

Stuttgart, funded 1,000 Landhelpers from November 1933 to the end of March 1934. Despite an estimated shortage of 10,000 agricultural laborers in the region, only 524 Landhelpers (514 male, 10 female) had been placed in the Stuttgart Landhilfe by the beginning of April 1934. Faced with the failure of the program, the Stuttgart welfare office opened the local Landhilfe to persons over age 40, married unemployed, and even unemployed not receiving public support. With these relaxed criteria, the number enrolled in the Stuttgart Landhilfe stood at 977 on December 31, 1934.[16]

Besides agricultural service, road construction projects provided work opportunities for the urban unemployed. Competition for workplaces on highway construction sites was keen, and municipal authorities made special efforts and even paid for the privilege of placing their unemployed on *Autobahnen* stretches passing close to their cities.[17] Bavaria paid for the privilege of placing some of its unemployed on Deutsche Reichsbahn railway electrification projects. During the autumn of 1933, Nuremberg officials placed 182 of the city's unemployed (106 of whom were locally supported "welfare-unemployed," *Wohlfahrtserwerbslose*, WE) on a Deutsche Reichsbahn project to electrify the stretch between Augsburg and Nürnberg. Additional placements were expected during the ensuing winter and spring.[18] Nuremberg's success in placing these unemployed rested on the efforts of Bavaria's provisional finance minister (and later minister-president) Ludwig Siebert. Because electrification of this particular stretch stood in sixteenth place in the overall Reich program, prospects for funding by either the Reich government or the Reich railway corporation itself appeared dim at best. Siebert convinced Reich and railway officials to accept a Bavarian loan of RM 5 million as the price for moving ahead with the Augsburg-Nuremberg electrification project. The railway corporation rejected another offer of a Bavarian subsidy for electrification of the Munich-Augsburg-Lindau line, but it agreed in July 1935 to continue with the electrification of the Nuremberg-Halle stretch with the assistance of another Bavarian contribution. The Bavarian economics ministry sought to sabotage this deal because the Reichsbahn bypassed a local Nuremberg firm and awarded the contracts to large electro-technical firms outside the region. Siebert forced the economics ministry to back down, arguing that he could not jeopardize economic benefits for all of Bavaria merely to protect the interests of one local firm.[19]

Work in agriculture, on the *Autobahnen*, and on the railways soaked up unskilled labor. As Germany's economy began to recover, cities found opportunities to employ some of their jobless in industrial sectors experi-

Local and Regional Efforts in the "Battle for Work"

127

encing shortages of skilled labor. Metalworkers were already in short supply before the end of 1934. To meet the demand and simultaneously to reduce the number of "compulsory laborers" (*Pflichtarbeiter*, about whom more will be said later), Stuttgart inaugurated job retraining courses in metalworking at two trade schools. Between 1935 and 1938, this program retrained 3,200 unemployed for the metalworking trade.[20] Some cities, however, refused to spend funds to retrain their unemployed for skilled jobs, even when the terms appeared quite advantageous. When Dornier-Metallbauten G.m.b.H established a large aircraft construction facility in Lindau (Bodensee) early in 1934 (with the help of subsidies from the city of Lindau and the Bavarian state government), the firm was unable to obtain a sufficient number of trained skilled workers locally. Dornier asked the Augsburg and Nuremberg welfare offices to send several hundred young (under age 35) skilled workers to a six-week training course in Lindau prior to their employment at the new facility. Dornier expected the cities supplying the trainees to pay their travel and living expenses during the training period, as well as to subsidize a portion of the cost of construction of a barracks to house the workers. After preliminary negotiations had apparently settled the terms, Nuremberg's welfare office agreed to pay travel expenses for the trainees but refused to contribute anything toward their support during the training course. Nuremberg authorities argued that Dornier, which needed the skilled workers, would be the sole beneficiary of the deal and should therefore pay the entire cost. Dornier argued more logically that Nuremberg's temporary training expense would be more than offset by a permanent reduction in its welfare rolls. Nuremberg's welfare office held to its intransigent position and thus lost the opportunity to send 120 skilled workers to the Dornier plant.[21]

When local welfare officials could find no work opportunities for their unemployed either in rural areas or in other cities, they were forced to accommodate them in local programs financed by local funds. Given the onerous debt burden faced by most German cities in 1933, purely local work creation programs were bound to be rather modest. Since local authorities generally provided up to a quarter of the funding when they participated in Reich-sponsored projects, few financial resources remained available for purely local projects. Many of the locally sponsored programs looked more like holding actions rather than "productive work creation" designed to bring permanent benefits to Germany's national economy. They were designed primarily to accommodate the welfare unemployed (WE), persons without a livelihood, supported by the local welfare system because they were either ineligible for or had used up Reich unemployment benefits (Alu) and crisis benefits (Kru). In the first quarter of 1933, 41.1 percent of all registered unemployed depended on local welfare support, only 12.2 percent received Reich unemployment insurance benefits, 26.4 percent received crisis benefits paid out of Reich funds, and 20.3 percent of the registered unemployed received no public support at all.[22]

Before Hitler came to power, local provision of welfare for the WE had increasingly taken the form of "labor welfare," support through the provision of work rather than cash benefits, characterized by the slogan "work not welfare." Public employment of WE in labor welfare took two forms: "welfare work" *(Fürsorgearbeit)* and "compulsory labor" *(Pflichtarbeit)*. Both types of labor welfare were compulsory in the sense that local welfare officials could cut off welfare cash benefits to those who refused either type of work. But the legal and practical differences between welfare work and compulsory labor were significant to both the providers and the recipients of local welfare. Welfare work provided full-time employment with regular pay in jobs carrying insurance obligations under a regular legal employer-employee relationship. Compulsory labor, on the other hand, involved no regular employment status, no regular wage, and limited part-time work hours.[23] The immediate cost to the commune for welfare work far exceeded that for compulsory work, but in the long run, communal welfare authorities derived a much larger benefit from welfare work. Completion of six months of welfare work established renewed eligibility for Reich unemployment insurance benefits, and, later, for crisis benefits. Cities could thus shift a portion of their welfare burden back to the Reich by providing welfare work for their WE. Because compulsory labor established no regular employment relationship and provided no jobs insured under the unemployment compensation system, compulsory labor service established no claim to either unemployment benefits or crisis benefits. As Duisburg welfare work officials explained it, "welfare work creates value."[24]

It is difficult to estimate the extent to which compulsory labor in the legal sense was used by German cities during the early years of the Nazi era. As Heidrun Homburg has noted, "there are no [Reich] statistics on the number of compulsory labourers. They can only be produced by case studies of particular areas."[25] The use of compulsory labor was probably not nearly so intense under the Nazi regime as one might have supposed. Each city developed its own policy on the use of compulsory labor, and these policies often changed over time. Local welfare authorities regarded compulsory labor as a punitive last resort against suspected "work-shy" welfare recipients and illicit workers *(Schwarzarbeiter)* collecting welfare benefits while holding down unreported jobs. Groups persecuted by the Nazis were particularly susceptible to conscription into local compulsory welfare labor programs. Duisburg welfare officials directed that "since in the case of Jews it is difficult to ascertain [the existence of] illicit work or business on the side, they are to be handled severely and assigned to compulsory labor to the fullest extent possible. Gypsies are to be dealt with in the same manner."[26] On the other hand, Nazi organizations hoping to exploit compulsory laborers for their own interests often met resistance from local welfare officials determined to employ compulsory laborers only on projects deemed socially useful to the general public.[27]

Compulsory labor schemes often produced organized resistance. Duisburg's welfare office had good reason to comment in February 1933 that "as opposed to [welfare workers], our experience with compulsory workers cannot be characterized as good."[28] Between 1930 and 1933, Duisburg compulsory laborers complained about being passed over for better relief jobs by the local employment office, petitioned municipal authorities for the prevailing wage on the local free labor market, distributed a flyer titled "Down With Punitive Labor," which called the head of the Duisburg welfare office a "social fascist," and demanded that the law on compulsory labor be repealed.[29]

The extent to which welfare unemployed were forced into compulsory labor varied widely from city to city. In March 1933, Hamburg's welfare authorities registered 2,319 compulsory laborers, or 2.4 percent of all welfare unemployed. Birgit Wulff has argued that "the explanation for the small percentage lay not in a liberal handling of the regulations, but rather in Hamburg's catastrophic financial condition." Nonetheless, after a year under Hitler's National Socialist regime, the city was somehow able to engage 7.3 percent (5,277) of its welfare unemployed in compulsory labor. In September 1934, Berlin registered less than 1 percent of its welfare unemployed as compulsory workers, while Düsseldorf required nearly 60 percent of its welfare unemployed to perform compulsory labor.[30] These statistics provide an incomplete picture of the effort made by individual cities to force their unemployed into virtually unpaid work as a condition for the receipt of welfare benefits. Those who gave up their welfare benefits rather than submit to forced labor naturally do not show up in the statistics on compulsory labor. Yet, insofar as municipal welfare costs were reduced by those rejecting compulsory labor, the scheme served its purpose.[31] There are also reports of WE volunteering for compulsory labor in order to collect the small premium on top of their welfare benefit. These "volunteers" presumably were included in counts of *Pflichtarbeiter.*[32]

At the end of March 1934, 29 percent of Germany's welfare unemployed were "employed" on "value-creating unemployment support" projects *(wertschaffenden Arbeitslösenfürsorge),* partially supported by funds from various Reich work creation programs. Most of Germany's cities apparently placed fewer than 20 percent of their WE in compulsory labor paid for out of local funds.[33] This does not necessarily indicate an aversion to the assignment of the unemployed to forced labor. Other alternatives, such as the Reich "voluntary" Labor Service seemed to offer local authorities a cost-free means of ridding their cities of unemployed youths. Local officials preferred to place as many of their WE as possible on Reich-funded projects outside the cities, thereby reducing their own welfare burden and ridding the cities of potentially troublesome unemployed.[34]

Some local job creation initiatives targeted specific segments of the unemployed population, such as women. Between 1929 and November 1933, the number of domestic servants employed in the Stuttgart area declined by 3,600. The Reich unemployment insurance system dropped domestic servants from its coverage in May 1933, hoping that potential employers relieved of contributing to the unemployment insurance fund would hire more domestic help. On November 13, 1933, Stuttgart's Nazi city council approved the creation of a "Stuttgarter Haushilfe," under which the city would pay a monthly subsidy of up to RM 15 to any local household hiring an additional domestic servant on a live-in basis. The welfare office identified a relatively large number of households willing to take on additional household help, but found a "surprisingly small" number of women "suitable" for such employment. On December 4 the city council ordered unemployed women over age 25 to take compulsory training courses, whereas those under 25 were to perform compulsory work *(Pflichtarbeit)* for three hours daily while taking compulsory training courses. The program was discontinued at the end of March 1934, when it was considered superfluous in view of the improvement in the female labor market.[35]

Local and regional work creation efforts often involved close cooperation between municipal government authorities, local and regional NSDAP offices, and private industrial and commercial firms and financial institutions. Duisburg's battle against unemployment represented one example of a joint venture of local government, the local Nazi party apparatus, and the private sector. The organization of the city's work creation effort openly took advantage of the power of the Nazi party. The city administration and the NSDAP Kreisleitung cooperated to establish a committee of four "particularly competent" members to coordinate all work creation matters. A municipal work creation office was then set up as a technical advisory body to the committee of four. This apparatus, in conjunction with the local employment office, conducted what were termed "successful" negotiations with local industries leading to the hiring of additional workers. In its efforts to secure larger public works projects, such as new Rhine bridges and an airport project, Duisburg's work creation office obtained assistance from the Essen Gauleiter's work creation staff.[36]

Cooperation between the NSDAP Gauleiter, the Kreisleiter, and Duisburg's city officials produced the Duisburg-Hamborn Work creation Corporation (Arbeitsbeschaffungs-G.m.b.H. Duisburg-Hamborn) in September 1933. This public-service organization loaned funds for the partial financing of projects such as house repairs and remodeling, which could not have been undertaken without special support. The scheme was capitalized with RM 200,000, half of which was put up by the gas, water, and electricity works owned by the city of Duisburg, and the other half by the Duisburg-Ruhrort port authority. The city claimed that its own financial risk was negligible, since major local businesses and banks had signed obligations *(Verpflichtungsscheine)* valued at RM 434,000 as a guarantee against defaults on repayment of loans from the fund. The Regierungspräsident in Düsseldorf, fearing a financial catastrophe for a city whose financial situation already forced it to rely heavily on state assistance, limited the amount that the organization could lend out to RM 250,000. As the scheme proved to be reliable, the Regierungspräsident increased the society's credit-granting limit to RM 350,000. By the spring of 1934, demand for credits from the society declined, possibly because potential borrowers found the nonrepayable subsidies under the second Reinhardt program of September 1933 to be more attractive.[37]

Duisburg's initiative evoked widespread interest and was duplicated elsewhere. In the Frankfurt-Wiesbaden area, regional Nazi party leadership seized the opportunity presented by the change of leadership in Berlin and launched initiatives to promote rapid economic recovery. In this instance, Nazi organizational skills and forceful leadership created a more economically viable, rational, regional economy, the Rhein-Main-Gebiet. In creating the Rhine-Main economic district, the Nazis, as was so often the case, appropriated an old idea originated by sources totally unconnected with the Nazi movement. The advantages of systematically integrating the economic activities of this region were first stressed in a 1925 memorandum drawn up by the economic affairs office of the city of Frankfurt.[38] The memorandum provoked intense discussion, but no action followed until the Nazi party adapted the configuration of its Gau Nassau-Sud-Hessen to the Rhine-Main economic region. This step, which was taken prior to Hitler's appointment to the chancellorship and dealt only with the organization of the Nazi party, opened the way for "true cooperation" in the region after the Nazi takeover. After the takeover, some of the Gaue of the NSDAP were realigned, and Jakob Sprenger was appointed both Gauleiter for Gau Hesse-Nassau, and Reichsstatthalter in Hesse. Sprenger used his authority to break down barriers to the "organic construction" of a Rhine-Main economic district.

The most critical task facing the Rhine-Main region in 1933 was the battle against unemployment. Success in this campaign required the development of an institutional structure capable of rational regional planning. Between June and December 1933, the area's agencies representing the state, the NSDAP, industrial and trade organizations, and agricultural interests were consolidated on a regional basis. In June 1933 Gauleiter Sprenger set up in his own staff office a "Control Office for Work Creation" for his district. Sprenger then named as labor trustee for Hesse a Nazi, Dr. Carl Lüer, who had just been installed as president of the Frankfurt–Main chamber of industry and commerce. Lüer was given responsibility for managing a special commission for implementing and supervising work creation measures in the economic districts of Rhine-Main and Hesse. A Rhine-Main planning agency, headed by Reichsstatthalter Sprenger, with jurisdiction over settlements, road construction, and travel, was established in September. Industry, commerce, transportation, the press, and foreign trade were reorganized into regional organizations representing the Rhine-Main economic district. In the same month, the Rhein-Mainische Garantie-Verband was established. Its job was to facilitate financing for public and private work creation projects in the Rhine-Main region. This agency soon accumulated RM 1,864,000 in "guarantee capital" raised from the regions banks, savings institutions, credit unions, private businesses, local governments, and community organizations. By the end of February 1936, the association had handled 1,375 credit applications and had guaranteed over RM 2.5 million in loans.[39]

Sprenger's efforts seemed to produce regional economic recovery and undoubtedly won praise and admiration for the Gauleiter. But large infusions of Reich funds supported Sprenger's regional recovery programs. In 1933–34, Öffa and the Deutsche Rentenbank-Kreditanstalt poured over RM 40 million into the region. The RfAA contributed an additional RM 12 million in basic subsidies *(Grundförderung)* for work creation projects in the Rhine-Main area. Additional state funding provided work in house repair and renovation. Economic activity generated by public funds induced the region's private industry to invest RM 32 million of its own funds.[40]

The region's automobile factories (Opel in Rüsselsheim, Adler in Frankfurt–Main) showed particularly strong growth, with employment doubling between 1932 and 1933 (from around 8,000 to over 16,000), and production increasing from about 26,500 units to about 81,500. Some important sectors of the regional economy, however, began to falter in 1934–35, as the impact of public spending on work creation began to fade. With the end of the housing repair and renovation subsidies, sales of heavy iron products such as heating furnaces and radiators declined. Iron foundries and heating equipment firms avoided large-scale layoffs only by producing for inventory, soon reaching the point where "production no longer bears a correct relationship to shipments."[41]

Excessive stimulus generated by the Hitler government caused problems in at least one sector of the Rhine-Main economy. Iron-ore mining in the Lahn, Dill, and Oberhessen areas picked up at a very fast pace. But, as labor trustee Carl Lüer cautioned, the increased output and employment came at a heavy price. Hitler's government was determined to exploit every ounce of iron ore in German territory. Economic considerations no longer drove the mining industry; production at any cost was the new slogan. Government subsidies now supported renewed prospecting and discovery operations, which had ceased in 1932. In 1935, the industry drilled ninety exploratory bore holes, of which about 30 percent produced findings of ore. Between the end of 1932 and the end of 1935, regional ore production rose by over 370 percent, and employment in the mines rose by 290 percent, increases, Lüer observed, that were "tied to a very substantial monetary sacrifice." As less accessible and less rich deposits were mined, production costs per ton rose significantly, while prices remained controlled. The state had demanded the increased output, but the firms were paying the price in the form of a cost-price squeeze. Further increases in production would lead only to a further deterioration of the mining companies' financial condition.[42]

The second phase of the Rhine-Main region's economic recovery extended from March 1935 to the spring of 1936. The Rhine-Main area benefited far less than did central, southern, and eastern Germany from the introduction of universal military conscription and the beginning of open rearmament in March 1935. Because it was a border region perceived as vulnerable to a French invasion, the area did not receive the same flood of public military contracts that now stimulated economic activity in other parts of the Reich. Not until the "recovery of military sovereignty on the Rhine" with the remilitarization of the Rhineland in the spring of 1936 did the Rhine-Main region participate fully in Germany's rearmament program. The value of public contracts brought to the region by the district contract equalization office quadrupled between 1936 and 1937. The labor trustee for Hesse appropriately referred to the "militarization" of the Rhine-Main region after March 1936.[43]

Cities that lacked the potential for wider regional or national ties bolstered local employment with programs designed to increase consumption of locally produced goods and services. During the winters of 1933–34 and 1934–35, Aachen conducted an "electric offensive" (Elektro-Angriff), offering price reductions and installment payments (up to thirty-six months) for new electrical hookups. Aggressive advertising stressed the wonders of new household appliances. The 1933–34 program proved very successful; four thousand new hookups employed the entire mechanical staff of the Elektro-Gemeinschaft Aachen for half a year. Reich subsidies for housing improvements financed much of the work, and as the subsidies were phased out, the intensity of installation activity declined.[44]

Aachen's program was part of a general nationwide drive to enlist municipal gas, water, and electricity utilities in the battle for jobs. Although officially it adopted no formal work creation program, Duisburg's gas, water, and electricity works carried out a number of projects that "otherwise for the most part would not have been undertaken and which for the most part can be counted as a direct contribution to work creation." Between April 1 and November 30, 1933, Duisburg's municipal G.W.E.-Werke reported RM 1,089,900 of such projects either completed or in progress, with projects worth another RM 1,021,500 planned for the immediate future. Another RM 1,880,000 in projects designed to increase retail consumption of electricity was to be carried out in 1934 "should the occasion arise." Production of the equipment and material used in such projects created jobs, but not necessarily in Duisburg. Moreover, the projected G.W.E.-Werke expenditures for 1934 were highly capital-intensive and would have produced few new jobs.[45]

The success or failure of local work creation initiatives depended heavily on the enthusiastic support and participation of the general public as well as of the private firms in the area. To achieve this cooperation, local government and Nazi party officials resorted to a combination of inducements, propaganda, pressure, and outright threats. In the Düsseldorf area, the labor trustee for Westphalia established and directed a "work creation front" (Arbeitsbeschaffungsfront) whose purpose was to "make every German countryman an active comrade in arms in the battle for work, so as to strengthen the feeling of solidarity with both the government that leads the struggle and with unemployed countrymen."[46] Included in the front were local industrial, commercial, and handicraft chambers, guild organizations, the German Labor Front, and municipal gas, water, and electricity utilities. The activities of the work creation front were to be coordinated with the Gau's Nazi political leadership.

The aim of the work creation front was to utilize solicitation, publicity, special concessions, price reductions, and subsidies in order to obtain additional business for handicraftsmen and to prolong work through the normally slow winter months. The primary target was local homeowners, who were to be subjected to a propaganda blitz in newspapers, in the cinemas, and over the radio. Assisted by expert guidance from the NSDAP Gau propaganda office and the German Labor Front, handicraftsmen armed with Labor Front identification cards made house-to-house visits. Homeowners were urged to take advantage of the house-repair subsidies offered under the second Reinhardt plan of September 21, 1933. But since such subsidies covered no more than a quarter of the cost of any project, with the homeowner expected to provide the remainder, local utility companies were pressed to provide additional price reductions. Local handicrafts organizations negotiated with utility firms for special rates for installation of services. If negotiations proved unsuccessful, the labor trustee and the Nazi Gau leadership stood ready to take the "necessary measures."[47]

Local and regional Nazi party officials often created their own "fighting organizations" whose connection with legal government authorities was minimal or nonexistent. Organizations such as the Working Committee for the Elimination of Unemployment in the City and District of Schwabach, and the Fighting Organization Against Unemployment in Lippe, were not legally constituted public agencies empowered with decision-making authority. Lippe's Fighting Organization, though established "in close association with the Land government of Lippe and at the direction of state minister Riecke," was in fact an "approved fighting organization of the

NSDAP." Kreisleiters were to direct the work of local groups of reliable persons recommended by local Nazi leaders.[48]

As a creation of the Land's Nazi party apparatus, Lippe's Fighting Organization, like similar formations, encroached on the jurisdiction and responsibilities of the legally constituted labor market authorities, the local RfAA offices. This potentially troublesome dualism was short-lived. Established in September 1933, the Fighting Organization was dissolved at the beginning of November, and its activities were taken over by placement experts in the employment offices. During its brief existence, the fighting organization seems to have contributed significantly to shoring up Lippe's labor market. The organization negotiated credits from Lippe's Landesbank, which permitted factories to remain open, thereby preserving jobs for several hundred workers. It uncovered eighty cases of "double-earning" *(Doppelverdienertum)* and thirty-seven cases of "illicit work" *(Schwarzarbeit)*, and facilitated the replacement of twenty-one female workers with males.[49]

Local efforts to increase employment were limited by the Reich government's insistence in 1933 that local work creation programs were not to increase unemployment and add to welfare costs in another region. At least until it became clear that Germany's economic recovery was real and irreversible, many Reich officials viewed the situation as a zero-sum game; any improvement in one region came at the cost of jobs somewhere else. On such grounds, Reich labor minister Seldte rejected a plan in the Rhineland district of Düsseldorf-Mettmann, where district council chairman Joachim Tapolski sought to use local welfare funds to subsidize the wages of additional workers hired by local businesses. The employer received the worker's former welfare support payment as a contribution towards his wage. At the urging of the province's Oberpräsident, other Rhineland districts adopted Tapolski's plan. Although similar subsidies were already used to facilitate the hiring of additional agricultural labor, Reich and Prussian officials opposed the subsidizing of nonagricultural private-sector wages out of public funds. Seldte argued that subsidizing industrial wages in one area simply took jobs away from the same types of business in some other part of the Reich. The district offering subsidies reduced its welfare burden, but only by increasing the welfare burden in some other city.[50]

Decisions on public subsidies for the opening of new plants or the reopening of existing plants also raised the zero-sum issue. The RfAA rejected a request from the Nazi party district leadership in Kirchheimbolanden-Pfalz for a basic subsidy grant to assist in the opening of a new cement plant. RM

800,000 was needed to supplement the RM 1.5 million raised from private sources. The RfAA pointed out that regulations prohibited the use of basic subsidy funds *(Grundförderung)* for the establishment or operation of private works. Promotion of the cement plant with unemployment support funds would interfere with the competitive relationships within Germany's free enterprise system, and marketing the output of the projected plant would harm the sales of existing plants.[51] Essentially, the RfAA was arguing that, in October 1933, the German economy was not growing fast enough to absorb the output of an additional cement plant.

Similar considerations entered into decisions on reopening plants that had been closed down during the crisis years after 1929. Every German city had its share of such plants, and every city looked for assistance in putting workers back on the job in those plants. The case of the Ruhrort-Meiderich steelworks in Duisburg illustrates both the technical and the political questions associated with the closing and attempted reopening of a large industrial operation.

Part of the giant Vereinigte Stahlwerke concern, the Ruhrort-Meiderich steelworks was partially closed down in May 1930 and was shut down completely in February 1931. Nine thousand workers and salaried employees were thrown out of work. The closure seems to have resulted from a combination of company policy and labor intransigence. Although the facility met modern standards of production, its shutdown was part of a long-range rationalization program begun by heavy industry in 1926. The plant's trade union leadership allegedly rejected a company offer in February 1931 to keep the operation running an additional eight months if the workforce would accept a 20 percent reduction in pay.[52]

On the occasion of the national celebration of labor on May 1, 1933, the Reich chancellor's office was inundated with telegrams from various Duisburg organizations, asking for the reopening of the steelworks. In response, a working committee to study the possibility of reopening the Ruhrort-Meiderich works was set up in the Reich labor ministry. Vereinigte Stahlwerke director Dr. Albert Vögler argued that there was no market for the steel produced by a reopened plant. Reopening Ruhrort-Meiderich, he asserted, would simply shift employment and production to the reopened plant, at the expense of currently profitable operations elsewhere. Chairman of Vereinigte Stahlwerke's board of directors, Dr. Fritz Thyssen, also emphasized the zero-sum argument. Orders generated by Reich government work creation programs could possibly provide enough work to keep the Ruhrort-Meiderich plant in operation; however, there would be no net gain in output. A large portion of the total quota for Germany's steel cartel would have to be shifted to the reopened plant. Ruhrort-Meiderich would gain, but every other German steelworks would lose part of its production quota.

Vögler and Thyssen were acting in the interest of their firm by arguing against reopening the plant. They were joined by others, such as the Dortmund city administration, which petitioned the Westfalen-Süd Gauleiter to try to stop the Ruhrort-Meiderich reopening. In September 1933, Dortmund's leaders argued that the reopening of a large plant such as the Meiderich works would endanger currently operating mills such as the Hörder Verein in Dortmund. The Oberpräsident of Westphalia province, Ferdinand Freiherr von Lüninck, added his opinion that "it does not seem to be admissible to purchase the opening of a plant with the closing or reduction of work of another plant."[53]

Reich economics minister Schmitt, tacitly accepting the zero-sum argument, told the industrialists that Vereinigte Stahlwerke and the rest of the steel industry "should make a sacrifice" in the Ruhrort-Meiderich question. The Vereinigte Stahlwerke did eventually agree to rehire workers, but only after the Gauleiter in Essen, Josef Terboven, intervened and discussed the situation with Vögler in August. It was agreed that recalled Ruhrort-Meiderich workers would be assigned to Vereinigte Stahlwerke's August-Thyssen plant, rather than to Ruhrort-Meiderich. This arrangement presumably avoided the creation of additional capacity in the steel industry and averted the need to adjust production quotas. In fact, however, of the 2,084 Ruhrort-Meiderich workers recalled on February 4, 1934, only 530 were placed at the August-Thyssen works. In April 1934, 1,167 workers and 54 salaried employees were operating the Ruhrort-Meiderich works.[54]

The reluctance to enhance the economic prospects of one local economy at the expense of another reflected the Hitler government's determination to maintain Germany's integrity as a single national economic unit. Thus, the Reich economics ministry strongly opposed one method popular among local officials and business associations as a means of reviving the local economy, namely, "buy locally" *(Kauf am Ort)* propaganda campaigns. The "buy locally" campaigns represented a complex phenomenon. Superficially, they seemed to represent a reasonable attempt to support local businesses. The alternative to patronizing local establishments was to purchase from or contract with large, out-of-town firms that conducted business in markets throughout Germany. Some self-styled patriots regarded such firms as a threat to Germany's *"mittelständische Gewerbe,"* the handicraftsmen and small businesspeople who supposedly formed the backbone of a healthy German nation. "Buy locally" campaigns also may have been thinly disguised efforts to organize boycotts of large, capitalistic, possibly "Jewish" firms. Whatever the motivation behind "buy locally" campaigns, the Reich economics ministry denounced "local economic protectionism." Attempts to create "closed economic circles" in various sections of the Reich, warned the Reich economics ministry, "seriously threaten the general economic recovery."[55]

When financial incentives, propaganda campaigns, and the application of pressure on a scale consistent with civilized human behavior failed to produce the desired results in the labor market, local government and Nazi party officials resorted to threats, intimidation, and police action. The extent to which violence or the threat of violence by government or Nazi party officials contributed to the recovery of Germany's labor market defies accurate estimation, but anecdotal evidence suggests that this could have been a significant factor in Hitler's "economic miracle." The intimidation was directed against everyone who was in a position to influence the success or failure of the Nazi battle for work: public officials, employers, and the unemployed workers themselves. The degree of intimidation ranged from relatively benign to life-threatening. In a scheme tried successfully in the Rhineland district of Grevesmühlen, each farmer received a form letter signed by the chairman of the district council (Landrat) and the NSDAP Kreisleiter, listing by name the unemployed laborers whom each farmer was expected to hire at the current legal wage. The Regierungspräsident in Aachen rejected advice to institute the same system in his district. Instead, he "invited" all employers in his jurisdiction to attend meetings, where they listened to speeches from the NSDAP Kreisleiter and the Landrat detailing the importance of avoiding layoffs and hiring additional workers. Employers agreeing to hire additional workers were to be named in local newspapers and awarded a certificate of honor. Such gentility was unusual. More characteristic was the threat of the county administration (Bezirksamt) of Hilpolstein (Bavaria) to dismiss any mayor who failed to rid his town of unemployed workers within ten days. In Landkreis Aachen, the chairman of the district council virtually threatened mob action against employers who refused to hire additional workers.[56] But the most severe treatment of all was reserved for the unemployed workers themselves. SA units conducted unofficial purges of municipal welfare rolls, removing those unemployed persons whom they considered unworthy of assistance, usually because they allegedly had refused work.[57] This was a relatively benign action. Other adult males accused of refusing work or of allowing their dependents to fall into the welfare system because they had refused work were sent to concentration camps. When the Dachau concentration camp was ready for occupancy, the Bavarian interior ministry notified local officials throughout Germany that "with the possibility of placement in the concentration camp, welfare authorities are provided with a new, effective disciplinary measure against asocial persons." Local welfare authorities were invited to select the victims, who would be confined for a minimum of three months to a maximum of three years. During their stay in Dachau, inmates would develop the discipline needed for effective workplace performance.[58]

As the war against unemployment intensified, the line between "economic" actions and "police" actions became increasingly imperceptible. Interference of the political police in economic and social matters eventually provoked complaints from a dedicated Nazi, Hermann Esser, then serving as Bavarian economics minister. The Reich president's February 28, 1933, decree on the Protection of the People and the State, issued in the aftermath of the Reichstag fire, had opened up the possibility of police interference in the economy without requiring evidence that any particular law had been violated. Political police, claimed Esser, were making arrests in order to enforce general economic and social policies, "so that over time, in effect, a real economic police built itself up, which maintained no contact with state authorities in charge of the economy." Esser argued that Reich interior ministry guidelines on arrests issued April 12, 1934, and a May 2, 1934, decree concerning arrests issued by the Bavarian interior ministry, ruled out arrests by political police in matters concerning economic questions such as wages and dismissal of workers. But Esser seems to have understood that even if he had the law on his side, there was no way he could control the actions of Germany's political police. He suggested that the "economic police" and those responsible for the economy work "hand in hand" to make joint decisions in matters affecting the total economy. The police, he proposed, could at least contact economic authorities before making their arrests.[59]

In the battle for work, local officials utilized financial incentives, propaganda campaigns, and coercion. But local efforts eventually encountered limits imposed by each city's financial situation, geographical location, and market orientation, as well as the impact of Reich government policies on these factors. Adverse factors virtually ruled out significant economic recovery for some regions prior to 1936. Cities heavily dependent on foreign trade were seriously affected by Reich controls on exports, imports, and foreign exchange. The attempt to achieve autarky in foodstuffs and raw materials, the allocation of resources to industries connected with Germany's rearmament, and restrictions on the flow of foreign exchange under the 1934 "Schacht plan" only exacerbated the distress of some cities already hard hit by the collapse of international trade after 1929. Most affected were Germany's shipping and shipbuilding centers on the North Sea and the Rhine River. Work creation programs had little impact in Hamburg, where (as in other large cities) there were few opportunities for the large-scale earth-moving and land-reclamation projects favored by the Reich government in 1933. Any favorable impact that work creation programs may have had on Hamburg's labor market were nullified by the Reich government's fatalistic attitude toward the recovery of foreign trade and its decision to cut Germany off from international markets.[60]

Rhine ports such as Duisburg suffered from Reich trade and foreign exchange policies, as well as from the Reichsbahn's rate policy, which allegedly discriminated against goods destined for transport on inland navigation routes. Duisburg's industry and trade chamber criticized both the Reichsbahn and the Reich transportation minister for their refusal to equalize rates for rail and inland navigation transportation. Southern, southwestern, and especially western Germany felt very much disadvantaged by the economic policy of the Hansa cities. Reich authorities allegedly gave Hansa importers preferential treatment in the allocation of foreign exchange used to finance imports. International boycotts of German trade in protest against Germany's anti-Jewish policies also hurt cities such as Duisburg. Holland, with which Duisburg had extensive commercial ties, was particularly strong in its enforcement of the boycott.[61]

Duisburg suffered from economic disadvantages shared with other cities located in Germany's Rhineland industrial region. This was a border area, until March 1936 a vulnerable demilitarized zone. In border areas that were less exposed to attack by one of the "Great Powers," Hitler's government poured in work creation funds to impress those on the other side of the border.[62] The propaganda value of such investments probably outweighed any economic or social value. Investment in the Rhineland, however, faced unique obstacles. Separatist movements, years of foreign occupation, economic sanctions, and the 1923 Franco-Belgian occupation of the Ruhr, had taken their toll on the Rhineland's economic development. Military garrisons, a direct source of income, were not permitted in the demilitarized zone under terms of the Treaty of Versailles. Public contracts, especially those that had any military significance, were awarded to firms well removed from Germany's unprotected western border. Rhineland firms, which were expected to contribute capital to defense-related industrial projects in Germany's heartland, were prohibited from constructing such installations in the Rhineland itself.[63]

Allocations of scarce raw materials were diverted away from Rhineland manufacturing firms, and when those firms offered to switch to other less critical metals, they were told by Hitler's economic advisor Wilhelm Keppler that "nearly all metals are strategically important."[64] As military contracts under the Nazi rearmament program became a more significant form of government spending, the Rhineland found itself virtually excluded from this most promising source of economic recovery. The introduction of universal military conscription in March 1935 failed to give the Rhineland the same economic boost that it gave to other regions of Germany.[65]

With Hitler's government reluctant to commit large sums to work creation projects in areas open to French "aggression," the Rhineland's cities, which included some of the largest centers of industrial unemployment, tended to lag behind Germany's general economic recovery. Because Reich *Autobahnen* routes were chosen with national security in mind, the Rhineland was seriously disadvantaged. The situation was particularly difficult for areas lying on the west bank of the Rhine, such as the Bavarian Palatinate. Here the Reich defense ministry exercised veto power over the construction of new superhighways and the location of defense-related industries so long as Germany remained defenseless. Talks involving Bavarian officials, the chief of the army Truppenamt (head of the Office of Troops, a disguised Chief of the General Staff) Lieutenant General Ludwig Beck, and the *Autobahnen* expert in the Reich defense ministry, a Major Zorn, failed to break the defense ministry's opposition to the construction of *Reichsautobahnen* west of the Rhine. The military argued that modern highways would only make it easier for the French army to secure the Rhine bridgeheads quickly and invade interior Germany. The defense ministry used similar reasoning to veto the reopening of an IG Farben chemical plant in the Palatinate.[66]

National security considerations emphasized by the defense ministry often overrode extremely important economic and political considerations.

The political stakes could be very high. In the January 1935 plebiscite, the people of the Saarland were to choose their national home—France or Germany. Starving the adjacent Rhineland of work creation funds was not the best way to convince the Saarlanders that Germany would protect their economic interests. Nevertheless, political capital was squandered (as it turned out, with no fatal consequences so far as the plebiscite was concerned) in favor of upholding Germany's perceived national security interest. Rhinelanders referred to the process as "the sinking of the Rhineland."[67]

One of the cities in the western border area hardest hit by the Reich government's refusal to invest in the region was Aachen. Aachen's registered unemployed stood at 16,174 when Hitler came to power. Two years of National Socialism left the city with 11,807 unemployed. The 27 percent decline in Aachen's unemployed compared very unfavorably with the 51 percent decline in unemployment in the Reich as a whole. The roots of this unwholesome situation were, according to Aachen's Regierungspräsident, numerous and deep. Postwar border and tariff problems between Germany and its neighbors contributed to Aachen's economic troubles. Many German miners worked in nearby coal mines across the border in Holland, and the first to be laid off were the Germans. Locally, mills, mines, glassworks, a railway car factory, and a wire factory had either closed down or drastically reduced their labor force. The remaining industries lacked the capacity to take on any new workers, even when hiring incentives were offered. Local government cooperation with the local NSDAP leadership and the district leader of the NSBO (National Socialist Factory Cells Organization) produced meager results. Factories employing a total of 7,830 workers were able to add only 69 additional employees. The final blow to Aachen's economy came when a German coal syndicate agreement negotiated during September and October 1933 proposed to limit Aachen's coal production to its average output between 1928 and 1932. Reich economics minister Schacht claimed that Aachen's miners "would hardly be able to notice" the small reduction in output required by the agreement. The Regierungspräsident saw things differently. The agreement meant additional mine layoffs, and the local coal industry would be denied the benefit from any future improvement in the German economy.[68]

Regierungspräsident Eggert Reeder wanted a massive public work creation program for his district. Believing that Landkreis Aachen, where the mines were located, could contribute nothing toward the financing of work creation projects, he argued that such projects were feasible only if Aachen could obtain "special financing" that required no borrowing. Reeder was looking for Reich government subsidies, and he expected the Prussian government to make up 75 percent of the expected loss of Reich welfare assistance *(Reichswohlfahrtshilfe)* as Aachen put its welfare unemployed back to work.[69]

Reeder's hopes for assistance from the Reich and Prussian governments clashed with Reich government policy for the area. The Reich labor trustee for the Rhineland district assured Reeder that Hitler himself was aware of the situation in Aachen. When Hitler's economic adviser Wilhelm Keppler met with Aachen's NSDAP Gau economic advisory council in May 1934, Keppler only added to the desperation of local leaders. Keppler suggested that in areas where unemployment persisted after the implementation of government countermeasures, "migration from the border to the interior could be appropriate." In other words, the unemployed should move to the jobs. The Reich government would not sacrifice national security interests in order to bring jobs to the unemployed in western border regions. After the formal meeting, Keppler stated his position more bluntly. "With all goodwill towards the border," he told the gathered officials, "the shifting of essential industries away from the endangered border into the interior of the country must be striven for, and the implications for population policy stemming from this [transfer of industry] must be accepted."[70] Western border regions could expect no help from Berlin, at least not while the region remained demilitarized and defenseless.

In the battle for jobs during the first three years of the Nazi era, local and regional authorities made a substantial effort at considerable financial cost. One may discard any notion that the Reich government under Hitler's charismatic, visionary leadership quickly stepped in with massive work creation programs financed from Berlin. The portion of German work creation projects that was locally financed varied from one municipality to another. Duisburg, a Rhineland industrial city hard hit by the ravages of unemployment, seems to have invested a great deal of effort and financial resources in the struggle to handle an overwhelming tide of unemployed. Reich statistics purporting to demonstrate the depression bottoming out and beginning to recover during the last quarter of 1932—before Hitler came to power—mask the horrendous suffering that continued to plague many of Germany's largest cities long after the alleged recovery had begun. On January 31, 1933, Duisburg's welfare office supported 64,971 cases involving

147,934 persons including dependents. The Duisburg AA supported another 15,451 cases involving a total of 38,372 individuals including dependents. Thus, over 42 percent of Duisburg's population was being supported by either the local welfare office or the AA as Hitler assumed the chancellorship. Duisburg's situation became more desperate before it began to improve. Duisburg's Nazi mayor, Dr. Ernest Kelter, characterized February and March 1933 as "a previously unknown low point in all areas of the [city's] economy."[71] By April 1, 1933, the number of cases handled by the welfare office had declined by only 257, while the number of cases supported by the AA had increased by 113. No economic miracle was evident in Duisburg.

Duisburg's situation had improved markedly by April 1935, but, of all the Rhineland industrial cities, it still claimed the highest ratio of unemployed per 1,000 population receiving cash support from the welfare office.[72] Although total employment had increased from 88,969 at the end of December 1932 to 103,118 by the end of March 1935, Kelter sought to have the city declared an economically distressed area *(Notstandsgebiet)* in October 1934. Though Reich officials refused to classify Duisburg as a distressed area, Kelter's efforts finally obtained recognition of the city's dire situation. In March 1935, Duisburg's treasurer reported that the Reich government had finally acknowledged the city's distress by channeling RM 2 million in assistance funds into Duisburg during the preceding few months.[73]

The availability of Reich loans and RfAA basic subsidy grants under the Reinhardt program should not obscure the fact that cities made substantial financial sacrifices in order to provide work for their unemployed. Duisburg carried out RM 25.25 million in direct work creation projects in the belief that the expenditure was cost-effective. Nonrepayable subsidies from the Reich government covered only RM 3.27 million of the total. The RfAA contributed RM 4.4 million in nonrepayable basic subsidies *(Grundförderung)*, and loaned the city another RM 182,000. Loans from Öffa under the Gereke *Sofortprogramm* and the Reinhardt program totaled RM 4.95 million. Credits obtained by contractors accounted for another RM 2.5 million of the financing. By far the largest contributor, however, was the city of Duisburg itself, which provided over RM 9.4 million for work creation projects between 1933 and 1936. Over RM 6 million of Duisburg's contribution financed the city's own work creation program, while the other RM 3 million represented the city's share for projects under various Reich programs.[74]

Duisburg's work creation effort was matched throughout Germany. Sixty-nine percent of the RM 911,437 spent by the city of Düsseldorf for canal and waterway projects during the period 1933 through 1935 came from the city's own funds and local private sources.[75] Stuttgart's effort was equally impressive. The city carried out work creation projects valued at RM 18.5 million between 1929 and 1934, about a third of the total expenditure coming in 1933. RfAA subsidies covered about RM 2 million of the cost, and the city took out loans for another RM 3.5 million. The remaining RM 13 million came out of Stuttgart's welfare budget and other local resources.[76]

Local governments, local taxpayers, and local workers made great sacrifices in order to make Hitler's battle for work a success. Millions of people were put back to work between 1933 and 1936. The Reich government and leading Nazi officials in Berlin may have provided some of the "leadership," and Hitler received the credit; but it was the regional and local leaders of both the party and the state who took most of the initiative in developing concrete programs to put people back to work. They did not wait for orders from Berlin before taking action to combat unemployment during 1933. And it was the ordinary people at the local level who provided much of the money and all of the coerced labor that made Hitler's "economic miracle" possible.

7

Road Building: "Motorization," Work Creation, and Preparation for War

Hitler's promotion of the "motorization" *(Motorisierung)* of Germany, his special interest in the development of the automobile industry and the construction of *Autobahnen* to meet the requirements of modern civilian and military transportation, is well known and has been described elsewhere in some detail.[1] Less fully chronicled is the role of road and highway construction in Nazi work creation programs, the manner in which work on Germany's network of roads and superhighways was organized, and the problems of labor supply and labor performance inherent in this ambitious construction program. These matters merit attention in any general study of Nazi work creation programs.

In Nazi Germany, all roads were *not* created equal. Authorities concerned with road construction made a distinction between what might be termed "ordinary" roads, and the ultramodern superhighways, the *Autobahnen*, that figured so prominently in Hitler's thinking. Of course, there was a connection (both conceptually and physically) between the two types of roads; without a rational network of feeder roads, the *Autobahnen* would be little more than showcase highways with relatively little economic or military significance. Thus, in terms of route planning and the allocation of funds, the two types of roads had to be coordinated. The appointment of Fritz Todt as General Inspector for German Roads *(Generalinspektor für das deutsche Straßenwesen)* on June 30, 1933, was designed to assure this coordination.

A professional engineer, Todt had already developed a clear and detailed view of the future role of road construction before Hitler came to power. In

December 1932, Todt drew up a forty-nine-page memorandum on "Road construction and road administration," in which he provided an historical overview of how Germany's road network had deteriorated during the Weimar years, and explained the steps needed to give Germany a technically advanced road system capable of meeting the requirements of modern automobile and truck traffic.[2]

From 1926 to 1930, relatively large sums (an average of RM 1 billion per year spent by national, Land, district, and municipal authorities) were made available for reconstructing roads. Much of this expenditure, argued Todt, had been wasted on unproved construction techniques and incompetent work. Planners had no concept of a unified road network. Despite these shortcomings, road construction had created jobs. Between 1927 and 1932, road construction, renovation, repair, regular maintenance, and the provision of the necessary materials had provided direct employment for 600,000 to 800,000 workers. About one-third were employed for the entire year, and two-thirds for the nine-month "high season." Financing during that period came from Reich automobile tax receipts placed at the disposal of the Länder according to a set formula, road construction subsidies granted by the Länder out of general tax revenues, and loans taken out by various authorities responsible for the upkeep of Land, Kreis, or municipal roads.

Todt viewed road construction as a key element in the reconstruction and rehabilitation of the German Reich. "The roads of a country," he wrote, "are the lifeline of the nation." The "lifeline" to which Todt referred was the nation's military lifeline, and had nothing to do with Germany's economic well-being. Trade and commerce were simply coincidental to the primary use of facilitating the movement of troops and administrative units. Todt envisioned a network of "strictly automobile roads" *(reine Automobilstraßen)*, serving only motor vehicle traffic.

These highways would serve primarily strategic purposes, though "economic usage by passenger and freight traffic is permitted." With the *Autobahnen* network contemplated by Todt, an army of 300,000 troops carrying their most urgently needed equipment could be transported in 100,000 requisitioned automobiles from Germany's eastern border to the western border in two nights. As a first step, Todt estimated, a limited system of five to six thousand kilometers could be considered sufficient.[3]

The *Autobahnen* would be supplemented by a network of secondary "general traffic roads" based on Germany's existing network of through roads. Most of these roads would have to be reconstructed considerably to meet military standards, assuring rapid long-distance transit on roads strong enough and wide enough to handle heavy military vehicles. Finally, there would be access roads, the country lanes, field paths, and so-called communal connecting roads. Often unpaved and impassable, they would have to be improved and incorporated into the larger road network. Todt estimated that it would take five years to complete the entire network of *Autobahnen*, secondary roads, and access roads. To administer this elaborate national system of roads, he proposed to create a special Reich "Commissariat for Road Construction" headed by a specially empowered commissioner, preferably an expert with experience in the road construction industry.

Todt estimated the total cost of his five-year road construction program (including all three classes of roads) at RM 5 billion. He was thus proposing a program five times the size of the Hitler government's June 1933 Reinhardt work creation program. Financing, he thought, could be secured through a combination of tax revenues and credit creation. "Experts in finance," Todt wrote, "have opened up possibilities in the way of productive credit creation." But only half of the RM 5 billion would have to be financed through credits; the remainder could be covered by revenues from the automobile tax and various taxes on fuel and oil. To relieve some of the financial burden, the Reich government would have to provide interest-free road construction funds.

Although Todt stressed the strategic and military significance of his proposed road construction program, he also recognized the importance of road construction in the battle against unemployment. He believed that road construction projects could be started up quickly without much preparation, providing jobs in all parts of the Reich for vast numbers of the unemployed. Housing and caring for workers, a major drawback in other types of work creation projects, constituted, in Todt's view, no problem, "since no large centrally concentrated mass of workers is needed; rather, small troops of workers could be distributed all over Germany."[4] The employment effect of spending for road construction could be enhanced by at least temporarily limiting the use of machinery at construction sites. Todt estimated that an expenditure of RM 1 billion per year, with proper organization, the limited use of machinery, and the preferential selection of the most labor-intensive projects, would provide nine months' employment for approximately 600,000 workers. Simple earthmoving jobs might be performed by Labor Service units, but the actual construction of the roads would be reserved for skilled labor employed by private construction contractors.

Todt's road construction scheme closely resembled the road policy and administrative organization adopted by Hitler's government in September 1933. As inspector general for German roads, Todt became the "commissioner" envisaged in his plan. Hitler embraced Todt's scheme largely because he shared Todt's assessment of the military and strategic importance of a modern road network. But other aspects of Todt's argument for road construction, such as its work creation potential, also impressed Hitler. Perhaps, in the final analysis, it was Todt's emphasis on the propaganda value of road construction that convinced Hitler to promote Todt's scheme. Given the high visibility of road construction and the fact that construction would be spread throughout the Reich, every German would be able to see that the Führer was putting his people back to work. Experts and tourists alike would come from all parts of the world to witness Hitler's marvel, the construction of the *Autobahnen*.

The absence of any provision for funding of road construction in the original Reinhardt program might be explained by the belief that Hitler intended to implement the *Autobahnen* program within a few months. Nevertheless, Hitler's support for Todt's program did not necessarily assure its immediate implementation, and certainly not in the precise form advocated by Todt. Some members of Hitler's first cabinet opposed Reich expenditure for any road construction program, while others objected to degrading the authority of the Reich transportation minister by creating a special Reich commissioner for roads. Although road construction ultimately figured heavily in Nazi work creation programs, the RM 1 billion Reinhardt program of June 1933 originally included no funds whatsoever specifically earmarked for that purpose. The omission of road construction projects from the Reinhardt program seems to have reflected the Reich finance minister's feeling that road building had received generous funding in earlier work creation schemes, and also the belief held by many representatives of heavy industry that road building would do little to stimulate their sector of the economy.

Further complicating the allocation of funds for road construction were "certain differences of opinion" between Hitler and his Reich transportation minister, Peter Paul Freiherr von Eltz-Rübenach. Hitler favored new superhighways *(nur-Autostraßen)*, while Eltz-Rübenach supported the extension of Germany's existing road network as the only financially responsible option.[5] Funding for "luxury roads" *(nur-Autostraßen)* was expressly prohibited under the Gereke *Sofortprogramm* of early January 1933. State and local governments lacked funds for the maintenance of new roads of any sort. One agency estimated the annual cost of maintaining existing through-traffic roads at RM 500 million, a sum equal to the entire *Sofortprogramm!*[6]

While Hitler and Eltz-Rübenach debated the relative merits of *Autobahnen* construction or extension of Germany's network of ordinary roads, conflicting interests also set supporters of new superhighways against advocates of the extension, modernization, and electrification of Germany's railway system. Additional investment in railway extension and modernization would have made more sense than development of a form of transportation that depended on imported oil for which Germany could not pay with its limited supply of foreign exchange. This was more than a theoretical debate. The German national railway corporation, the Deutsche Reichsbahn, stood to lose investment opportunities, current business, and potential profits if significant resources were channeled into the construction and operation of a network of superhighways.

Before the government could commit significant financial resources to road construction, philosophical differences, conflicts of interest, and jurisdictional disputes had to be ironed out. This task could be accomplished either by the assertion of Hitler's will in support of one side or another, or through some sort of compromise solution that enabled Hitler to have his *Autobahnen* while avoiding an "either-or" choice that would have provoked a messy confrontation with powerful interests. Hitler chose the latter, less confrontational route.

On April 10, 1933, Hitler told Reichsbahn general director Julius Dorpmüller that the German national railway corporation would have to undertake the construction of an *Autobahnen* network. He assured Dorpmüller that the railway's interests would be protected and that "the railway would not be destroyed." In Hitler's mind, the issue seemed to be settled. The Reich transportation ministry objected, but Hitler dismissed their arguments and demanded new roads capable of withstanding both the relentless pounding of heavy traffic and aircraft bombing.[7]

Hitler again spoke with Dorpmüller on May 30, one day after the Reich cabinet approved the Reinhardt program without earmarking any funds for road construction. Dorpmüller offered to make available RM 50 million of Reichsbahn funds for *Autobahnen* construction. Hitler asked Dorpmüller to collaborate with Reich transportation minister Eltz-Rübenach on the drafting of a law to create a special corporation charged with construction of the new roads. The corporation would be a division of the Reichsbahn.[8]

Eltz-Rübenach tried unsuccessfully to retain a role for the Reich transportation ministry in the new highway program. The Länder, too, raised serious concern about a new Reich superagency that would control Land road projects.[9] The Law on the Creation of a "Reichsautobahnen" Corporation of June 27, 1933, together with the Decree on the General Inspector for German Roads of June 30, 1933, clearly placed dominant authority over both *Landstraßen* and *Reichsautobahnen* in the hands of the General Inspector, Todt, to the detriment of both the Reich transportation minister and the RAB corporation.[10] This legislation resolved the competition between rails and superhighways and initiated the transfer of most of the Reich transportation minister's jurisdiction over roads to Todt. Legally, the RAB corporation functioned as a branch of the German railway corporation, the Deutsche Reichsbahn-Gesellschaft, an arrangement designed to reduce the risk of destructive competition between road and rail. The railway company immediately provided the RAB corporation with RM 50 million in capital, so that work on the superhighways could begin before definitive financing had been arranged.

Todt, the new general inspector for German roads, found himself with no funds for ordinary roads and only RM 50 million to finance *Autobahnen* construction. No less frustrated were local officials looking for worthwhile work creation projects, as well as military authorities hoping to capitalize on "work creation" as a means of procuring roads of alleged significant military value. Many regional and local officials, including Prussian interior minister Hermann Göring, had assumed Reinhardt program funds could be used for road construction, at least in cases in which local authorities had no alternative sources of funding.[11] Reinhardt program regulations issued on June 28 described "excavation and earth-moving projects" *(Tiefbauarbeiten [Erdarbeiten])* as "hydraulic structures" (*Wasserbauarbeiten*, dams, canals). The Reich finance minister, who approved the release or reallocation of Reinhardt program funds, insisted that if road construction was not mentioned explicitly, then no Reinhardt program funds could be spent for that purpose. Reich transportation minister Eltz-Rübenach joined forces with Reich defense minister Blomberg to secure construction of some general-purpose roads that were considered important for national defense.[12] Nevertheless, up to the end of August 1933, Reich finance minister Krosigk continued to insist that road construction had already been supported "on a most considerable scale" under the Papen and Gereke work creation programs, and he approved Reinhardt program funds for "road construction" only for some purely agricultural roads (not public thoroughfares) providing farmers access to their fields.[13]

Fearing soaring unemployment during the winter of 1933–34, Todt sought funds for an emergency "winter program" that would keep normally laid-off workers employed over the 1933–34 winter.[14] In September, he was promised RM 25 million from the automobile tax fund and RM 25 million from the Reinhardt program. The Deutsche Rentenbank-Kreditanstalt later agreed to make available to Todt RM 1.25 million in unused credits from the Gereke *Sofortprogramm*.[15] Late in October, Krosigk supplemented the original RM 25 million with an additional RM 30 million, raising Reinhardt program funding for road construction to RM 55 million.[16] The promised funds represented no new money for road construction but simply shifted funds from one use to another. The RM 55 million in Reinhardt program funds was to come out of a fund originally set up to redeem coupons for the purchase of basic necessities *(Bedarfsdeckungsscheine)*, issued in lieu of wages to laborers on earthmoving projects.[17] Moreover, Todt and Öffa "raided" credits originally allocated to Länder and provinces for purposes other than road construction. Work creation credits available for the entire Reich were neither increased nor reduced, but merely rearranged.[18] Todt's 1933–34 winter road construction program represented a bailout for the especially depressed German stone industry. The emergency funds were to be used for the advanced ordering of construction materials to be used during the following spring and summer. When the expected new orders for the crushed stone produced during the winter failed to materialize, many workers who had been kept on over the 1933–34 winter were laid off in July 1934.[19]

The allocation of RM 55 million out of a RM 1 billion work creation program for road construction, repair, and extension hardly represented a total commitment to the "motorization" of Germany. In November 1933, Todt himself described the amount of funds available for roadwork as "comparatively very small."[20] By February 1934, as the RM 55 million for the 1933–34 emergency winter program was running out, Todt was again forced to search for funds to finance work on the network of ordinary roads. The total road requirement (excluding *Autobahnen*) for the entire Reich was estimated at RM 300 million for the year. About RM 105 million of this would come from automobile tax revenues, leaving a sum of RM 200 million to be financed somehow.[21] Todt needed to find a regular source of funding for ordinary road construction.

Reich finance minister Krosigk told Todt that he would get no Reich budget funds for ordinary road construction until at least 1935, and, possibly, not even then. He suggested that Todt "bridge the gap" by borrowing for road construction and maintenance, by shifting funds from *Autobahnen* construction to construction of ordinary roads, or by using an advance from the Reichsbank.[22] For 1934–35, the Reichsbank was willing to provide the RAB RM 500 million, financed through the issue of bills, repayable within three years. The RAB could turn over to Todt RM 200 million of the RM 500 million for the construction of ordinary roads. The RAB's lawyers objected to handing over funds for construction of ordinary roads. The Reich finance ministry argued that the RAB's charter obligated it to carry out any business connected with or necessitated by the construction of the *Autobahnen*. After it was agreed that the phrase "business thereby necessitated" could be understood to mean the temporary financing of feeder roads, the Reich finance ministry authorized the RAB to transfer RM 200 million to Todt for 1934–35.[23] In August 1934, Todt still complained that "up to now, the road construction work creation programs have brought desirable, but only relatively small, improvements to the road construction situation."[24] He wanted a new work creation program that would stress construction of more bridges, detours around congested cities, and feeder roads leading to the *Autobahnen*, with less emphasis on the extension of existing roads. Hitler's government, however, had no plans for a new work creation program.[25]

Todt's attempts to establish permanent funding for *Autobahnen* construction proved no less frustrating than his search for reliable funding for ordinary road construction. Despite Hitler's great interest in the *Autobahnen*, no stable, permanent funding system was ever established to ensure their construction. The RAB, apparently unaware of the scale and pace of construction envisioned by Hitler and Todt, scheduled a September 19, 1933, meeting to consider an estimated expenditure of RM 4.7 million for the remainder of 1933, and RM 40.75 million for 1934. But, on the preceding day, these figures had been superseded as a result of a meeting between Hitler and the leading officials concerned with the *Autobahnen* program. Here it was agreed that, in the initial stage, 1,000 kilometers of *Autobahnen* would be constructed annually, up to a total of 6,500 kilometers. Estimates of the construction cost per kilometer varied between RM 350,000 and RM 500,000. Using the lower figure, construction of 6,500 kilometers of *Autobahnen* would cost over RM 2.25 billion, or an annual requirement of RM

350 million. The higher figure gives a total cost of RM 3.25 billion, or an annual requirement of RM 500 million.[26]

The projected cost of Hitler's first 6,500 kilometers of *Autobahnen* dwarfed the RM 1 billion spent on the June 1933 Reinhardt work creation program, the financing of which had already posed serious problems for Reich finance minister Krosigk and Reichsbank president Schacht. Where would they possibly find another RM 350 million to RM 500 million each year to finance *Autobahnen* construction? Krosigk made it clear in September 1933 that the Reich budget could provide no funds for *Autobahnen* construction, and he and Schacht suggested that *Autobahnen* construction could and should be financed by cutting back other work creation programs and projects.[27] Claiming recent Reichsbahn work creation expenditures of nearly RM 1 billion on equipment that the railway did not need, Reichsbahn and RAB director Dorpmüller left the impression that little more could be expected of Germany's national railway.[28]

On October 20, 1933, Schacht promised Dorpmüller that the Reichsbank would provide the entire RM 3.6 billion needed for the first 6,500 kilometers of *Autobahnen*. Todt, skeptical that Reichsbank funding would materialize when needed, continued to seek funding elsewhere.[29] In October 1933, he convinced the RfAA to support construction of the *Autobahnen* as "emergency projects" *(Notstandsunternehmen)*, an arrangement that lasted until May 15, 1934, after which the RfAA no longer recognized *Autobahnen* construction as emergency projects and discontinued basic support *(Grundförderung)* payments.[30] Todt tried and failed in February 1934 to persuade Öffa to shift Reinhardt program funds originally earmarked for the financing of communal roads to *Autobahnen* construction.[31] On March 6, 1934, Todt requested RM 44 to 48 million in RfAA basic subsidies, enough to pay about 13 percent of the estimated cost of *Autobahnen* construction from April 1, 1934, to March 31, 1935.[32] Feeling confident by the end of April that "financing of the Reichsautobahnen poses no particular difficulties, because Reichsbank credits are available for that purpose," Todt now suggested that the RfAA basic support subsidy requested for the *Autobahnen* be used instead to carry out the general road construction program.[33]

Contrary to Schacht's assurance, the Reichsbank did not provide the entire RM 3.6 billion for financing *Autobahnen* construction.[34] By 1942, *Autobahnen* construction had ceased. Between 1934 and 1941, Todt had to scrape up construction funds from a variety of sources. The Reichsbank seems to have frozen its financial contribution in 1936, at which time the

RfAA and the Reichsbahn stepped in with loans amounting to RM 550 million. RfAA loans increased each year until 1941 and were supplemented by loans from the Reich insurance institution, the German insurance industry, the Reich finance ministry, and other sources (see Appendix, Table 10). Debt service on *Autobahnen* construction loans became an ever-growing burden. Eventually, the debt was supposed to be paid off by a combination of Reichsbahn earnings, tolls and fees on automobile owners, profits from the gas station monopoly on the *Autobahnen*, and from taxes on properties adjoining the *Autobahnen*, whose value would increase. Meanwhile, Todt indicated, service on the debt would be provided out of the construction capital.[35] Karl Lärmer's judgment that "monopoly capital" wanted the *Autobahnen* but was not prepared to finance them seems correct in spirit, especially if one substitutes "most Germans" for "monopoly capital."[36]

Viewed from the perspective of road construction, as distinct from automobile production, the Nazi commitment to the "motorization" of Germany appears quite tentative, at best. R. J. Overy has estimated Germany's public investment in roads, both local and national, at "more than RM 3,500m. from 1933 to 1936, RM 800m. in 1933 and RM 1,200m. in 1934. Most of this expenditure was on the ordinary roads, and not on the *Autobahnen*, the new highways authorized in 1933, which did not become a significant element until 1935."[37] These raw statistics fail to convey the difficulty with which Todt obtained any Reich funds at all for ordinary road construction during 1933 and 1934. The Reinhardt work creation program made a small contribution to road construction during 1933 and 1934. The largest contributions to the funding of road construction came from the automobile tax and RfAA funds collected from workers' contributions, both of which had a deflationary effect, as well as from Reichsbank advances, which had an inflationary effect. Whether the net effect on economic activity was stimulating or simply neutral is debatable. In any event, at least RM 200 million that was diverted to ordinary roads during 1934–35 represented funds originally earmarked for the *Autobahnen*. In the absence of the *Autobahnen*, the Reichsbank probably would not have made this RM 200 million available for ordinary roads. Moreover, the sums spent on roads, RM 800 million in 1933 and RM 1,200 million in 1934, assuming that they are accurate, look far less impressive when placed against the estimated annual cost of RM 500 million merely to maintain existing through-traffic roads in Germany.[38] Given the cost of ordinary road maintenance, the figures cited by Overy suggest that there were modest sums of new money for new roads and that the largest portion of it went to the *Autobahnen.*

The "motorization" of Germany must be considered within the context of German rearmament. This requirement holds true even for the period 1933–1935, when military spending as such was rather modest. A portion of the ordinary road construction during that period was carried out only because the Reich defense ministry certified that the roads in question were important to the military. For the 1933–34 budget year, the Reich defense ministry requested RM 9 million for road improvement in East Prussia alone.[39] Military considerations influenced the selection of *Autobahnen* routes, notwithstanding Todt's attempts to create the impression that he, and he alone, held the authority to decide where the *Autobahnen* would be built.[40] The Reich defense ministry had its own "expert for Reichsauto-bahnen," a Major Zorn. He and his superiors held a virtual veto on *Autobahnen* routes, especially proposed routes in militarily sensitive border areas. Thus, planned routes such as Cologne-Aachen, Frankfurt/Main-Mainz-Saarbrücken, Ludwigshafen-Kaiserslautern-Saarbrücken, and Saar-brücken-Stuttgart were dropped or significantly delayed, even though social, political, and labor market considerations indicated a strong need for such projects.[41]

The production of motor vehicles may also have been linked to military requirements long before military expenditures became the driving force in the German economy. Overy seems to rule out this possibility with his statement that "some of the orders for vehicles came of course from the armed forces, but this was a tiny percentage before 1936."[42] This rather narrow view of the "military demand" for motor vehicles might lead to the unwarranted conclusion that Hitler sought to stimulate motor vehicle pro-duction out of his desire to see Germany "motorized," when in fact he and the military leadership wanted private vehicles available to commandeer as troop and supply transports in the event of a military emergency. The idea of the "motorization" of Germany certainly did not originate with Hitler. Germany's motor vehicle industry had promoted motor vehicle production prior to Hitler's appointment to the chancellorship, stressing the military value of developing a privately owned fleet of modern vehicles capable of being adapted to military use.

In August 1932, the Reichsverband der Automobilindustrie e. V. had proposed to Papen's government a "work creation" program based on the revival of Germany's motor vehicle industry. Hitler later implemented virtually every suggestion contained in this proposal. The automobile industry emphasized the desirability of having available a large fleet of modern trucks and other motor vehicles that could be pressed into service quickly during a military emergency. In the course of the long economic depression, Germany's stock of vehicles had become obsolete and run-down. In an emergency, this stock could never satisfy the nation's military, economic, and civilian demand for transportation. Germany's motor vehicle industry had to be put in a position to "fulfill its military-policy tasks" by following the motor vehicle program adopted in Italy.[43]

In the "Italian system" as described by the German automobile manufacturers' association, certain types of vehicles produced in Italy were free of any vehicle tax for three years. To promote the general deployment of vehicles of modern design and construction, especially heavy trucks, the Italian military was permitted to sell its trucks to the public, granting large subsidies and accepting payment on the installment plan. Trucks purchased from the military by private firms were free of all taxes. With this system, the Italian war ministry had been able "to periodically renew the trucks in service, and to replace them with vehicles that meet the current requirements of the military administration."[44]

The German automobile industry plan gathered dust until Hitler came to power because most public authorities considered it just one more plea from a "special interest" group for assistance from the government. During the course of the Depression, every industry in Germany had proposed some sort of publicly assisted program designed to provide employment and restore profitability. Such proposals were answered politely by Reich officials and placed in the drawer, to be discovered decades later by historians. The automobile industry's 1932 proposal failed to enlist support from public officials in Germany, including local authorities who would have benefited directly from additional production and employment. Although urged by BMW (Bayerische Motorenwerke A.G.) to back the industry proposal, Munich's municipal council refused to lend its full support because the proposal's economic value was "limited to a narrow circle of interest." The council suggested that road construction and tourism would provide a better solution to the unemployment problem.[45]

Prior to Hitler's chancellorship, public authorities were not yet prepared to embark openly on an "economic" program in which military objectives were so apparent as they were in the automobile industry's proposal. Much the same situation existed with respect to *Autobahnen* construction. One did not have to be a Nazi to recognize the military value of these roads. The push for construction of modern superhighways had begun well before Hitler assumed the chancellorship. Since the 1920s, the Society for the Preparation of an Automobile Road Hansa Cities-Frankfurt-Basel (Verein zur Vorbereitung der Autostraße Hansastädte-Frankfurt-Basel, HAFRABA), had led the campaign for construction of the new roads. What changed after January 30, 1933, was not the goal but the spirit and organization with which construction of the *Autobahnen* was pursued. HAFRABA changed its name to the "Association for the Preparation of the Reichsautobahnen" (Gesellschaft zur Vorbereitung der Reichsautobahnen, "Gezuvor") and adopted the Führer principle. Germany was divided into eleven sections, each led by a "section leader" drawn from the ranks of the Gezuvor board of directors. Gezuvor was entrusted with responsibility for directing work on all technical, economic, transportation policy, and propaganda matters connected with the preparation and support of the construction of the *Autobahnen*.[46] In keeping with the new National Socialist spirit, associations representing "special interests" were no longer permitted to influence the selection of routes for the proposed highways. That responsibility, as noted before, was now reserved for Todt and the military authorities.

Responsibility for the actual construction of the superhighways lay with the RAB, created as a branch of the Deutsche Reichsbahn. This agency established fifteen construction districts charged with supervising and carrying out the construction of the highway network. The German national railway administration strongly influenced the administrative structure and personnel of the RAB. The railway corporation had bought and paid for this influence by providing RM 50 million for the founding capital of the new *Autobahnen* administration. The RAB's board of directors consisted of the chairman of the Reichsbahn board, Julius Dorpmüller, and two other Reichsbahn directors, Willy Hof and Karl Rudolphi. A seven-member administrative council, also chaired by Dorpmüller, supervised such operations as preparing the RAB budgets, keeping the accounts, approving the assumption of debt and expenditures, and maintaining the organization's liquid assets at a comfortable level.[47]

Todt's relationship to the RAB was tenuous. Though he was not a member of either the board of directors or the administrative council of the RAB, the general inspector for German roads was to be invited to all meetings of the administrative council. He had the right to speak on all matters before the council but could neither propose motions nor vote on motions. He also had the right to request (in writing) special meetings of the administrative council.[48] As general inspector for German roads, Todt was responsible for selecting *Autobahnen* routes and determining the appearance and technical specifications of the new highways. The Reich government held supervisory rights over the RAB until 1935, when these rights were entrusted to Todt. Not until June 1938 was Todt named chairman of the board of directors of the RAB.[49] The timely and efficient completion of the *Autobahnen* network required cooperation between the RAB and the general inspector for German roads.

With great fanfare and much attention to the propaganda opportunity offered by the beginning of work on the *Autobahnen*, construction on the first stretch, the Frankfurt/Main-Darmstadt section of the Frankfurt/Main-Mannheim-Heidelberg route, began on September 23, 1933. Gauleiter Jakob Sprenger personally handed out shovels to seven hundred unemployed laborers and led their march to the work site. Hitler turned the first official shovelful of dirt and later led the ceremonies opening this first completed stretch of the *Autobahnen* network on May 19, 1935.[50] A second stretch connecting Munich and Holzkirchen was opened on June 29, 1935. The opening of the first two thousand kilometers was celebrated on December 17, 1937. A year later, on December 15, 1938, the opening of the first three thousand kilometers was celebrated.[51] The employment effect of *Autobahnen* construction mounted steadily until the middle of 1936. In October 1933, construction work was limited to a nineteen-kilometer portion of the Frankfurt/Main-Mannheim-Heidelberg stretch, employing 1,000 laborers.[52] Direct employment on *Autobahnen* construction peaked at 121,668 in June 1936 (see Appendix, Table 11).

Behind these raw employment statistics lies the story of the way in which the land and labor needed for this vast undertaking were acquired and of the conditions under which German men labored at the construction sites. Hitler and Todt were dedicated to the rapid and efficient completion of the *Autobahnen*, but the process took place within a complex process of negotiation among a myriad of Reich, Land, provincial, and municipal authorities representing both the state and the Nazi party. The process of planning the *Autobahnen* and finding and mobilizing the necessary financial, physical, and human resources for the projects was a gargantuan task.

Autobahnen construction was carried out by private firms that had submitted successful bids for the work. Nazi ideology and interests dictated that public contracts be awarded only to good German or good Nazi private firms, especially small businesses. In 1933 and 1934, the Hitler government and Todt set aside Nazi ideology and interests, and placed *Autobahnen* contracts with firms that seemed able to carry out the work quickly and efficiently. The awarding of public contracts to private firms followed guidelines set down in Reich regulations supplemented by Reich cabinet guidelines of July 14, 1933.[53] Contracts for work on the *Autobahnen* represented a much-sought-after prize. Groups representing special interests or claiming to represent the national interest constantly complained about the distribution of contracts. To address these complaints and insure uniform procedures in the awarding of *Autobahnen* construction contracts, Todt issued a set of "Guidelines for the Award of Contracts for the Construction of Reichsautobahnen" on February 22, 1934.[54]

Guided by his desire to promote the most efficient, expeditious, and competent construction of superhighways, Todt voted for the status quo and came down on the side of large, established firms with expertise and experience in road construction and a good record of completing public contracts in a timely and competent manner. Although the Nazis had represented themselves as the champions of the struggling handicraftsmen and small firms against the powerful, organized, industrial capitalists, Todt refused to let his *Autobahnen* construction projects become a welfare program for these downtrodden groups. The first projects for 1934 were to be given only to firms that had already carried out similar projects in the particular economic region in question, so as to avoid the intrusion of new competition from "outside" firms. Small firms might participate in *Autobahnen* construction as members of subcontracting working groups *(Arbeitsgemeinschaften)* including smaller contractors, in which the primary contractor would perform work amounting to no more than half the total value of the contract. Not until July 1935 was an effort made to steer more public contracts to the handicrafts *(Handwerk)* sector.[55]

Competition for *Autobahnen* construction contracts was fierce. Nazi party officials and Reich government officials in Berlin found it difficult to check efforts by municipal authorities and unofficial organizations such as the Kampfbund für den gewerblichen Mittelstand to purge "Jewish firms" representing "foreign capital" from the list of approved suppliers of goods and services. Keeping public contracts out of the hands of "non-Aryans" was not a high-priority matter for the Hitler government during 1933 and 1934. Not until December 1934 did the RAB put out a strong warning against the employment of Jewish firms on *Autobahnen* construction projects.[56] Work creation and the "absolutely necessary stabilization of the economic situation" were not to be disrupted by ruthless hunts for "non-Aryan" capital. More important was the extent to which a firm contributed to work creation by employing "German" workers, using "German" machinery, and processing "German" raw materials. The Reich government wanted an environment in which "serious foreign capital looking for investment opportunities" would "retain its confidence in the security of the German economy and legal security in the new [Nazi] state."[57] Reich government law and regulations on this matter were to be obeyed by local party and government leaders, even "if they perhaps do not seem to completely conform to national socialist concepts."[58] This was a difficult order for many Nazi party faithful to accept. Observing that many public authorities were still doing business with Jewish firms, an NSDAP economic expert wrote that "it is difficult to understand that such things happen in our national socialist state. It's not right that Aryan firms are still disadvantaged for the benefit of Jewish firms."[59] Despite repeated warnings from Reich officials, guidelines prohibiting actions against "Jewish capital" were violated openly and seem to have become totally obsolete.

Just as construction contractors competed fiercely for *Autobahnen* contracts, local government and welfare authorities contested vigorously for the opportunity to place their unemployed, especially "welfare unemployed" supported by local welfare funds, on *Autobahnen* construction projects. Beyond the immediate employment effect, there were long-term benefits associated with *Autobahnen* construction. Cities linked to new markets and raw material sources would experience economic growth. The development of tourism would stimulate local business.

The selection of *Autobahnen* routes could determine which cities would derive the greatest immediate benefit from construction projects. But local and regional unemployment rates were not necessarily the decisive factors in determining the first *Autobahnen* routes, and local unemployed did not always receive priority in placement on the work sites. Early route plans, for example, left Duisburg out of consideration. At 132.6 per thousand of population at the end of January 1933, Duisburg's ratio of supported unemployed was one of the highest in Germany, and higher than that of neighboring cities in Germany's depressed industrial heartland.[60] Duisburg officials attributed the city's omission from early *Autobahnen* plans to pressure brought by the North Sea Hansa ports (Hamburg, Bremen, Lübeck), which feared that revitalization of the great Rhine port would hamper the recovery of Germany's northern ports. During July and August 1933, Duisburg's industries and port authority waged a press campaign and lobbied Todt to tie Duisburg into the planned *Autobahnen* network. In September, Todt agreed in principle to connect Emmerich and Frankfurt/Main, by way of Duisburg. It took another ten months, however, to resolve arguments over the route through Duisburg. *Autobahnen* authorities proposed a route that would have demolished most of the Duisburg Woods and required moving the newly built Duisburg zoo, while city officials hoped to save the woods and the zoo by cutting through built-up areas of the city. *Autobahnen* authorities rejected that option because of the added cost of digging up and relocating gas, water, and electric lines, tramway lines, and railway lines, and military authorities objected that the route favored by city officials placed the road too close to railway lines and the Wedau railway station. Duisburg officials accepted the route proposed by *Autobahnen* engineers only after *Autobahnen* authorities threatened to turn the matter over to a state police investigation in July 1934, and after the Essen OBK agreed to give special consideration to local firms in contracting for steel to be used in bridge construction.[61]

The city of Duisburg eventually placed about 3,000 laborers on *Autobahnen* work sites in the area. But other cities discovered that the location of an *Autobahnen* route nearby or even within the city limits did not assure the placement of local unemployed workers on the construction sites. Of the 200 laborers originally employed on the first stretch of the Frankfurt/Main-Heidelberg-Mannheim route, only about 25 percent came from the ranks of supported unemployed. Another 15 percent represented regular employees of private construction firms, and 60 percent were members of the SS, SA, and Stahlhelm, or persons brought in by Hitler to celebrate the Führer's turning of the first shovel of dirt.[62] Heidelberg is a good example of a city that failed to gain substantial employment from nearby *Autobahnen* projects. On the Heidelberg-Mannheim stretch from January through July 1934, Heidelberg placed an average of only 28 Heidelberg workers in a group of nearly 2,700 laborers from the Heidelberg and Mannheim areas. Because the Heidelberg AA had been assigned 10 percent of the employment quota on the Heidelberg-Mannheim stretch (raised to 20 percent after Heidelberg's mayor petitioned the LAA Südwestdeutschland), Heidelberg's mayor figured that the city's 2,275 "welfare unemployed" entitled it to about 250 workers. The Heidelberg AA, whose district included rural communities near the city, apparently favored the rural areas in assigning workers to construction sites, even though about twelve kilometers of the highway lay within Heidelberg's city limits.[63]

Heidelberg's experience highlights the difficulty in reconciling the various purposes that were supposed to be served by construction of Germany's superhighways. The *Autobahnen* were to promote the general economic interests of the nation by providing a rational network of roads suitable to the requirements of a modern transportation system. They were to improve the military's capacity to transport troops and supplies quickly and efficiently. And, from 1934, they were to constitute Germany's largest work creation program. Depending on which purpose was considered, criteria for the selection of routes, the assignment of priorities for the construction of the various routes, and the selection of labor for the construction sites differed. Todt and the military authorities were most interested in the rapid and efficient construction of a modern highway system that would move people and material quickly from one place to another. They, along with the firms holding *Autobahnen* construction contracts, wanted an experienced, healthy, politically reliable labor force that was used to hard physical labor. On the other hand, the Reich labor ministry, the RfAA, and local welfare officials hoped to use the *Autobahnen* projects to put tens of thousands of unemployed Germans back to work, without much regard for their suitability for the work.

In 1934, Reich labor minister Seldte sought to promote *Autobahnen* construction where most of the unemployed were concentrated—the Rhine-Westphalia industrial region, industrial areas of Saxony, lower Silesia, upper Silesia, a portion of the Rhine-Main economic region, Berlin, and the Hansa cities, especially Hamburg. In suggesting the Berlin-Stettin route, which could draw its labor force from the tens of thousands of Berlin unemployed, he urged Todt to consider "the urgent requirements of labor market policy," without prejudicing national economic goals, "even if, in some cases, this should make things a bit more difficult technically." Todt seems to have waited three months before promising Seldte that, to the extent permitted by the requirements of transportation policy, labor market policy considerations would determine the selection of new stretches for construction. Todt informed the directors of the RAB that Seldte's "viewpoint coincides completely with mine," and he urged them to put as many unemployed as possible to work on *Autobahnen* construction. The RAB directors passed the word to district construction headquarters that it was a "duty of honor" to employ as many unemployed as they could, and as quickly as possible. But neither Todt nor the RAB leadership provided quotas, guidelines, or suggested priorities in selecting routes near large pockets of urban unemployment. The RAB considered Seldte's pleas for more employment of the jobless on the *Autobahnen* as "suggestions," and urged district headquarters to comply "wherever it is possible and justifiable."[64]

Jobs for the Germany's urban unemployed could be provided either by locating *Autobahnen* construction sites near the largest cities or by transporting the urban unemployed to distant construction sites. Since the bulk of the new *Autobahnen* network was not going to be located in the immediate vicinity of Germany's largest centers of urban unemployment, thousands of urban laborers had to be assigned to distant rural work sites. Accomplishing this mass movement of labor posed formidable organizational and logistical problems. Where it was achieved, it was done only after much haggling among RAB officials, Todt's office, the RfAA, and city officials anxious to clear their welfare rolls of as many unemployed as possible.

Private contractors constructing the *Autobahnen* resented the complex system under which they were required to obtain their laborers through the local RfAA employment offices (Arbeitsämter, AA). If a single AA was unable to supply the entire labor force needed for construction of a particular stretch, or if a construction site was staffed with unemployed laborers from a number of distant cities, more than one AA was involved.[65] In such cases, one of the AA was designated by the supervising Landesarbeitsamt (LAA) as an "equalization office." After contractors had notified the equalization offices of their labor requirements, each AA received its quota, which was based on its proximity to the construction site and the number of unemployed in its district. Members of the SS, SA, and the Stahlhelm received preferential treatment. When stretches under construction lay within the boundaries of two adjoining LAA districts, construction firms had to deal with two equalization offices.

Until the RfAA ceased providing basic subsidies for *Autobahnen* construction on May 15, 1934, the LAA set work rules and financing regulations. After May 15, 1934, Todt agreed to continue to honor most of the RfAA's regulations for employment and working conditions. He insisted, however, that members of the SS, SA, and Stahlhelm, heads of large households, and Nazi comrades in dire economic situations, should be able to work on the *Autobahnen* even if they had no claim to unemployment benefits or any other type of public support. He also insisted on dropping the work-stretching requirement that the workforce be replaced every thirteen weeks, because private firms could not operate efficiently under such conditions. Finally, Todt demanded that since the RfAA was no longer contributing financially, the decision on how many costly unemployed from large cities should be assigned to distant work sites should rest with his office, rather than with the LAA. The RfAA forced Todt to compromise. Todt would have to list by name individuals in a "dire economic situation" if he wanted them declared eligible for assignment to *Autobahnen* construction, and he would have to negotiate agreements with the LAA on the number of urban unemployed to be assigned to *Autobahnen* construction.[66]

Preferential placement of the urban unemployed on *Autobahnen* construction sites raised ethical and logistical problems. Rural areas had their own unemployed. Was it fair, or politically wise, to ask these rural unemployed and the local welfare authorities who supported them to defer to "outside" laborers brought in to take "their" jobs? Moreover, the OBK and construction firms preferred rural, agricultural workers who were used to hard, backbreaking work. Many urban unemployed assigned to *Autobahnen* construction sites were physically unfit. Others were considered "politically unfit," having been infected with the socialist or communist urban virus. Construction costs rose considerably when urban unemployed were assigned to rural construction sites. Since they could not live at home, barracks had to be built. Such building cost money and delayed the start of highway construction until the barracks were completed. Then there were travel costs, as workers' visits to their families had to be subsidized.[67] As the rearmament program and military conscription began to soak up more of the unemployed by the end of 1935, Todt and RfAA president Syrup ordered that first priority be given to the hiring of local unemployed on Reich construction projects, including the *Autobahnen*. In view of the added costs of housing, food, and travel for family visits, the importation of non-local labor was to be avoided whenever possible.[68]

From the beginning, placement of the urban unemployed on *Autobahnen* construction projects had been a selective, competitive process. Todt had always considered the *Autobahnen* as a modern transportation system rather than as a gigantic work creation project. Because construction of the *Autobahnen* was carried out by private firms expecting to earn a profit on public contracts, there was never any possibility that the big cities could simply dump their hundreds of thousands of unemployed into the *Autobahnen* construction projects. Private firms hired only the labor that they needed to complete the work for which they had bid. They were not in the welfare business. How, then, did cities compete in the race to place a maximum number of their unemployed on *Autobahnen* work sites? Why were some cities more successful than others?

German cities paid for the privilege of placing their unemployed on *Autobahnen* construction sites. Stuttgart was asked to pay about one-fifth of the land-acquisition costs for the Stuttgart-Ulm stretch, a sum of RM 400,000 payable in two installments of RM 200,000 each. For the Stuttgart-Heilbronn stretch, Heilbronn and Stuttgart each gave subsidies of RM 250,000 in cash for land acquisition, in addition to which Stuttgart was required to provide a RM 2.5 million loan at 4 percent. In return for these "contributions," Stuttgart was assured 30 percent of the workplaces on the Stuttgart-Ulm stretch and an undetermined number on the Stuttgart-Heilbronn stretch. Beyond the immediate employment effect of these "investments," Stuttgart's economy stood to benefit long-term from an improved transportation network giving better access to markets in Germany and Italy.[69]

Nuremberg, burdened with a larger number of unemployed, obtained better terms than Stuttgart in securing work for its jobless on *Autobahnen* construction sites. Claiming that the city had exhausted its own work creation possibilities (a dubious claim, as indicated by the city's refusal to provide training for skilled metalworkers needed in aircraft production, described in Chapter 6), Nuremberg's city council asked LAA Bayern to guarantee the city's unemployed at least 60 percent of an estimated 9,000 to 10,000 workplaces on *Autobahnen* construction sites in Upper Franconia. City authorities made no offer of payment. The LAA allotted Nuremberg 3,980 places, 40 to 45 percent of the estimated available jobs on the specified sites. This quota, according to LAA estimates, provided work for 59 percent of Nuremberg's able-bodied males capable of hard labor.[70] Nuremberg officials struggled to supply the allotted quota of labor. An initial five-day recruitment drive was a disaster. Only 83 percent of the 1,850 males who had been called for screening actually reported. On the first day, only 47 percent of those offered work accepted it, and by the fifth day the acceptance rate was down to 27 percent. Most of those refusing cited the fifteen-month separation from their families, concerns about their children's welfare during their absence, doubts that the wages offered would support both themselves and their families back home, and apprehension about hard outdoor labor during the harsh winter months. Very few appeared to be "work-shy."[71]

Placing laborers on *Autobahnen* construction sites did not constitute a "final solution" for any city's labor market problems. As each stretch was completed, the labor force employed on it once again became unemployed. Completion of the Duisburg segment of the *Autobahnen* and the scheduled release of 2,300 laborers on November 15, 1936, produced a potential crisis for Duisburg officials. Todt's representative, AA director Carl Birkenholz, offered to reassign some of the workers to other *Autobahnen* construction sites, but Duisburg authorities refused to pay a subsidy of 0.50 RM per day per worker. Birkenholz responded that "other city administrations were paying subsidies of 1 RM, and we [Duisburg] would have to do the same if we wanted to have our workers taken care of."[72]

The price that cities had to pay for placing their unemployed on *Autobahnen* construction sites and other projects outside the cities was not as onerous as the price paid by the workers themselves. *Autobahnen* workers performed backbreaking labor in foul weather for low pay. Construction of the *Autobahnen* was carried out by profit-seeking private contractors who had every incentive to exploit their labor force to the limit. Workers were particularly at risk because construction firms were trying to recover losses incurred during the worst years of the Depression. In his speech at the 1933 May Day celebrations, Hitler had spoken of the honor and dignity of manual labor. Laborers on the *Autobahnen* discovered that National Socialism, which from its beginnings had displayed anticapitalist tendencies, failed to protect the builders of the Thousand Year Reich from exploitation by German entrepreneurs, many of whom were good Nazis.

If manual labor was ennobling, then work on the *Autobahnen*, where the use of large earthmoving machinery was at first prohibited, must have been the most ennobling work of all. As Hitler's battle for work began in 1933, Reich government regulations sought to stimulate employment by substituting manual labor for the use of machines in all sectors of Germany's economy. Karl Lärmer has suggested that the Nazis were simply trying to turn necessity—a shortage of heavy road construction machinery and the shortage of capital needed to increase the stock of heavy equipment rapidly—into a virtue, especially where *Autobahnen* construction was concerned. Fascist propaganda, argued Lärmer, put this situation to good use by creating the impression that the use of machinery had been prohibited in order to create more jobs.[73]

Records of *Autobahnen* construction authorities confirm a shortage of heavy construction equipment. But they also indicate that limitations on the use of heavy machinery were more than a propaganda ploy designed to take advantage of a shortage of machinery. At the end of November 1933, RAB headquarters in Berlin notified district offices that the employment of heavy machinery for excavation work "in consideration of the condition of the labor market is, until further notice . . . undesired." District offices were to solicit contract bids based on both machine labor and manual labor, and contracts were to be awarded on the basis of the cost of manual labor.[74] Not until July 1936 did Todt and the Reich finance minister conclude that other large construction programs (probably military construction) had improved the labor market situation to the point where "the stepped-up use of manual labor on the *Autobahnen* can be dispensed with." Todt ordered a resumption of the use of heavy machinery to its "normal extent" in earthmoving work and dropped the requirement for contract bids based on manual labor. Only on work sites near the major centers of unemployment—Altona, Berlin, and Dresden—would the emphasis on manual labor continue. During 1937, labor shortages forced the OBK to use more machinery and less manpower.[75]

Often praised by Nazi potentates as the heroes of Germany's moral and material reconstruction, the men who constructed Hitler's superhighways struggled for their existence under the most unheroic of conditions. Physically demanding work in all sorts of weather and degrading living conditions in desolate barracks far from home made jobs on the *Autobahnen* among the least desirable in Germany during the economic recovery. Conditions at *Autobahnen* work sites alarmed Nazi organizations such as Robert Ley's German Labor Front (DAF), which intervened on behalf of the *Autobahnen* laborers. Members of the DAF were eventually banned from the work sites unless authorized to enter by district construction offices.[76]

The wages and working conditions of *Autobahnen* laborers were regulated by the RfAA, the Labor Trustees (*Treuhänder der Arbeit*, TdA), and the private contractors who hired them. The DAF also sought to play a role. When the RfAA ceased the granting of basic subsidy funds for *Autobahnen* construction in May 1934, its influence on wages and working conditions declined. Dr. Carl Birkenholz, an AA director brought into Todt's staff as special expert on social questions, gradually assumed greater authority over working conditions on *Autobahnen* construction sites, while authority to set wages on *Autobahnen* construction sites (and elsewhere) shifted to the Labor Trustees.

During 1933, the Nazis began to establish a legal framework that would exclude both labor and management from the process of fixing wage rates. A May 1933 law created labor trustees, who issued wage-scale regulations and gave or withheld approval for large-scale layoffs. German businessmen by and large accepted the labor trustee system precisely because it was designed to protect the status quo and ensure that the big industrialists would not be swept away along with the labor unions. Though they were empowered to establish new wage scales, labor trustees generally sought to maintain the existing depression-level pay scales.[77]

Labor trustees tended to raise wage rates for *Autobahnen* construction workers. They did so not out of sympathy for the laborers—most of the trustees had professional ties with management rather than labor—but in order to head off labor disturbances that threatened to disrupt construction of the *Autobahnen*. The East German Marxist historian Karl Lärmer characterized *Autobahnen* workers' pay as "starvation wages."[78] In fact, wage rates on *Autobahnen* construction sites varied in accordance with prevailing local rates for unskilled workers engaged in excavation and earthmoving. Some laborers on the *Autobahnen* achieved weekly earnings comparable to those of the average German industrial worker, yet others worked for something closer to a "starvation wage." In 1934, gross weekly earnings for an industrial worker came to RM 32.36, while net pay came to RM 28.15 (official) or RM 27.45 (Hachtmann corrected figure).[79] In the interest of creating as many jobs as possible, the forty-hour week was standard until it was extended to forty-eight in May 1934. Thus, in some Bavarian districts prior to May 1934, *Autobahnen* laborers were paid between 50 and 64 Pfennige per hour (depending on location), with weekly gross earnings ranging between RM 16 and 25.60. Deductions for social contributions reduced the weekly gross by about RM 4. With the shift to a forty-eight-hour week, gross weekly earnings ranged between RM 20 and 30.72.[80] In July 1934, *Autobahnen* laborers working on stretches administered by the Frankfurt/ Main OBK received net weekly wages (after deduction of social contributions) ranging from RM 25.50 to RM 28. At the end of July, the trustee granted increases, bringing net weekly earnings up to a range of RM 28.30 to RM 31.[81]

Pressure to increase wage rates came not only from the *Autobahnen* workers themselves, but also from the DAF, AA offices, and Todt's office, which sought to preserve social peace and avoid construction delays. Because Todt did not want rebellious workers disrupting the pace of construction, he was willing to make some concessions for the sake of preserving order on the construction sites. By August 1936, laborers on the Frankfurt/Main-Limburg-Köln stretch were earning between 53 and 68 Pfennige per hour, or RM 25.44 to 32.64 per fourty-eight-hour week, compared with RM 34.40 for industrial workers during 1936.[82] Because they "endangered the financing of work creation" by adding to the cost of publicly financed projects, officials in the Reich labor ministry criticized trustee-approved "special regulations" that included "significant" wage increases. Seldte argued that lower wages would encourage additional hiring and asked labor trustees to submit contemplated wage increases to him so that he could evaluate their potential impact on work creation programs.[83] Seldte conceded that job satisfaction on the *Autobahnen* had to be maintained, but that on their side, "the workers must recognize the financial limits of their social expectations, and turn a deaf ear to the agitators who seek to run down everything that has been done by way of work creation."[84]

The most serious menace to *Autobahnen* construction workers was posed not by low wages but by the brutal working conditions and nearly subhuman living conditions that constantly threatened the health and safety of the laborers. Todt was not pleased with what he saw during a visit to a construction site near Frankfurt/Main in November 1933. He ordered the construction firm to provide him with data on the health of the workers and their original occupations. Of the 384 men at the site, 24 were master craftsmen and regular employees of the construction firm *(Stammarbeiter)*. The remaining 360 were ordinary laborers drawn from the ranks of the unemployed. On November 9, 1933, 57 laborers (16 percent) were ill and absent from work; some work crews reported as many as 30 percent ill and absent. Over a fourteen-day period, the number of ill and absent ranged between 55 and 62 laborers. On the other hand, of the 24 permanent employees, none had ever missed work because of illness. Of the laborers, 85 percent were between twenty and forty-five years of age; 12 percent were under twenty years of age; and less than 3 percent were over fifty years of age. Fifty-three occupational groups were represented among the 360 laborers, the largest being "mechanics, garage men" (62) and "unskilled workers, factory worker" (55). Only one laborer who was experienced in excavation and earthmoving *(Tiefbauarbeiter)* was employed on this work site.[85]

Laborers on this construction site, most of them in their prime working years, experienced a high incidence of physical breakdown on the job, largely because their previous work history had not prepared them for hard manual labor on *Autobahnen* construction sites. The data raise the question of whether *Autobahnen* laborers were exposed to the working and living conditions normally expected in all-season, outdoor, heavy construction work, or whether they were systematically exploited and subjected to inhumane conditions. From his Marxist viewpoint, Karl Lärmer has described the *Autobahnen* laborer as underpaid, overworked, and poorly fed, conditions that produced very high accident and illness rates. Work sites and barracks, he argued, were nothing more than "military prisons for the workers." Construction supervisors had only two concerns: insuring big profits for the construction firms and making sure that the military's highways were completed on time.[86]

Those who are disinclined to accept the words of a Marxist, as well-documented as they may be, will easily find for themselves evidence of outrageous exploitation in the records left behind. RfAA officials expressed alarm at blatant attempts by construction firms to increase their profits by exploiting laborers. The president of LAA Hessen reported one firm that was offering workers a premium of RM 0.30 for each additional cubic meter of earth moved per day after the twelfth cubic meter. This "incentive" resulted in average output of eighteen to twenty cubic meters per day per worker, well above the previous average of thirteen to fourteen cubic meters. Since the firm had won the bidding for this stretch on the Frankfurt/Main-Heidelberg route with an estimate of only nine to eleven cubic meters per day per worker, it was making a huge profit over its original cost estimate. The laborers, on the other hand, were giving "a performance exceeding human capability," resulting in highly abnormal illness and accident rates, as well as permanent injury to their health.[87]

The story was the same in Bavaria, where the director of AA Traunstein reported many complaints of *Autobahnen* and general road construction contractors making "superhuman" demands of their laborers, who, after years of near-starvation in the ranks of the unemployed, could not maintain the work pace demanded by employers whose only concern was profit. The AA director suggested that the construction firms be reminded that the purpose of public works projects was to put the unemployed back to work, not to ensure big profit margins.[88]

Concerned over the plight of *Autobahnen* laborers, DAF activists intervened directly on construction sites. Both the construction firms and the OBK complained to Todt about disruptive DAF activities. In the Leignitz area, a DAF demand for a work slowdown brought productivity on the

Breslau-Leignitz stretch to the lowest level of any *Autobahnen* construction area. In the Breslau area, DAF men complained of the "inhumane treatment" of laborers and of the unreasonable productivity demands on laborers. Todt responded by banning DAF visits to construction sites without authorization from the OBK.[89] Expressions of discontent among *Autobahnen* laborers took many forms. In one case, when arsonists set fire to the workers' barracks, only 10 percent of the laborers housed in the building responded to the barracks leader's pleas for help in extinguishing the blaze and salvaging what could be saved. Todt branded the workers politically unreliable arsonists and saboteurs.[90]

Developed by Hitler's government as a military project that provided jobs for unemployed German laborers, Germany's *Autobahnen* contributed to the nation's war effort in ways that no one could imagine in 1933. As Allied bombers were turning Germany's airfields into rubble in May 1944, Hitler approved the use of a fifteen-kilometer stretch between Munich and Rosenheim as an airstrip. Both ends of the stretch were to be barricaded to keep out general traffic; however, for their convenience, Hitler and other Nazi potentates were issued keys allowing them to open the gates and use the stretch. Their drivers were urged to reduce speed in the area in order to avoid collisions with aircraft.[91]

Hitler's *Autobahnen* have been regarded as one of the few positive legacies of the Nazi catastrophe. This view tends to discount the high financial and human cost of "motorization," and evades the question of who ultimately paid the price. A combination of construction firms anxious to recoup losses incurred during the Depression, Hitler's accession to power, and the development of a Nazi terror apparatus opened up possibilities not available to governments in the Weimar system. As the economy recovered, construction funds could be obtained by raiding the RfAA's unemployment compensation fund, the Reich treasury could make some funds available, and the Reichsbank could create some credit. But, in fact, the *Autobahnen* were "paid for" by the laborers themselves, who were given a choice between two unpleasant alternatives: either endure inhumane conditions on *Autobahnen* construction sites or lose unemployment compensation and welfare payments.

Nazi propaganda gave the impression, which unfortunately still lives, of hundreds of thousands of German men laboring happily to fulfill their Führer's dream of superhighways crisscrossing the German Fatherland. Nazi propaganda misled the public with respect to both the actual number of men directly employed in *Autobahnen* construction, and their physical well-being and state of mind. Construction of the *Autobahnen* did put some Germans back to work. It may be considered a blessing that, on average, only 81,000 of them were forced to endure barbaric working and living conditions on *Autobahnen* construction sites each month.[92]

8

The "Voluntary" Labor Service under National Socialism

Nazi propaganda from the 1930s depicted brigades of Germany's finest young men, marching happily to work, shovels instead of guns on their shoulders. Draining swamps, reclaiming land for agricultural use, tens of thousands of these young men, dedicated to their Nazi Führer, were making Germany a land fit for the heroic master race. The Voluntary Labor Service (freiwilliger Arbeitsdienst, FAD), however, was not a Nazi institution. It was a product of the Weimar system, established in 1931 by chancellor Heinrich Brüning's government as a means of creating temporary work for unemployed young men. Under National Socialist rule, the FAD, which exchanged voluntarism for compulsion, was portrayed as one of the keystones of Germany's economic and moral recovery.

Hitler set the tone for a reorganized and ennobled FAD two days after assuming the chancellorship, when he outlined a vague four-year plan designed to save Germany's farmers from ruin and put Germany's unemployed back to work. Hitler emphasized the role that compulsory labor service *(Arbeitsdienstpflicht)* was to play in this scheme. In a speech on May 1, 1933, at Tempelhof airfield, the chancellor told his audience that compulsory labor service would reestablish manual labor as "honorable work," and promised to introduce a compulsory scheme before the end of the year.[1]

Reality never quite mirrored Hitler's early grandiose plans for the FAD. As a child of the Weimar republic, the labor service never overcame the stigma attached to every institution connected with the detested Weimar system. The Labor Service struggled to find a central role in Germany's economic recovery. Hitler's government was more than two years old when

175

six months of compulsory service in the Reichsarbeitsdienst (RAD) was decreed for all young Germans.[2] By then, over two-thirds of Germany's unemployed had already been put back to work. Under the Nazis, membership in the Labor Service had declined or stagnated until compulsory service provided support for 200,000 young men. The organization survived but never found a clear functional role in Hitler's revolutionary system. What happened to Hitler's vision of a noble labor service leading Germany to national economic and moral regeneration?

As envisioned by its National Socialist proponents, the FAD was to perform several important functions in the forging of a truly National Socialist Germany. It served as a vehicle for political indoctrination, training "good Nazis," breaking down class barriers and creating a sense of national community. The FAD also provided financially distressed communities with inexpensive labor for socially useful projects. It was a living example of the Nazi slogan, "work ennobles." Ultimately, the FAD would provide premilitary training for Germany's young men.[3]

With such a wide variety of potential functions, the FAD should have been guaranteed a prominent place in the Third Reich's institutional hierarchy and should have received high priority in budgeting and staffing during the early years of the Nazi regime. But, for a number of reasons, the FAD never attained the prominence and priority promised in Nazi rhetoric. Once in power, Nazi leaders could not agree on a practical role for a "National Socialist" labor service. Hitler's government no less than its predecessors encountered Reich budget constraints and higher-ranking priorities that determined the size and function of the German labor service. Additionally, the outcome of bureaucratic jurisdictional disputes and personal rivalries within the Nazi government and party structure and within the FAD itself significantly affected the size, scope of authority, and type and amount of work allotted to the labor service.

The FAD's leadership failed to hold its own in the incessant power struggles that characterized the Nazi regime. This failure reflected more than a mere lack of expertise in the game of power politics. The FAD never convinced Nazi party and Reich authorities that it possessed either the "moral authority" needed to instill the spirit of National Socialism in Germany's youth or the technical expertise required to establish German autarky in food and raw materials by reclaiming unusable land in a cost-effective manner. Moreover, as it became clear that a revitalized German military machine was going to conquer rich farmland in eastern Europe, the reclamation of marginal land within Germany's borders could be viewed as a waste of scarce Reich resources.

The outside world viewed Germany's labor service as one of the more successful institutions developed in response to the Great Depression. President Franklin D. Roosevelt may have been influenced by the German experiment when he asked the United States Congress to authorize and fund a Civilian Conservation Corps (CCC) in March 1933.[4] Established during the latter half of 1931, the German FAD undertook agricultural land improvement and forestry projects, providing work for up to 250,000 unmarried young men aged sixteen to twenty-five. The RfAA, an agency of the Reich labor ministry, funded and administered the FAD. RfAA president Friedrich Syrup also served as Reich commissioner for the FAD. Acting as district commissioners for the FAD, presidents of the RfAA's Land labor exchange offices (Landesarbeitsämter, LAA) selected FAD work creation projects, and the local labor exchange offices (Arbeitsämter, AA) coordinated the assignment of recruits to projects and distributed support payments. Any public-service corporate entity could sponsor projects; and any organization, whether it was linked to the socialist movement, religious establishments, or paramilitary groups such as the Stahlhelm, could organize FAD labor units. Prior to the Nazi conquest of power, the FAD was a liberal, democratic, and pluralistic institution.[5]

Before Hitler's appointment to the chancellorship, the Nazi party's interest in the FAD was minimal. The Labor Service, after all, was part of the detested "Weimar system." Hitler's special deputy for labor service affairs, retired colonel Konstantin Hierl, saw no reason for Nazi involvement in an organization that he described as "the falsification of the idea of compulsory labor service." Before 1933, Nazi organizations established only a handful of FAD camps. The SA leadership positively detested the FAD and also rejected the idea of building a National Socialist labor service. For the SA, a labor service represented nothing more than unwanted competition, although a few SA leaders conceded that a Nazi labor service might provide some economic security for unemployed SA troopers.[6]

Hitler's assumption of power blurred the FAD's mission. Its role in work creation programs receded as the organization became an instrument for the nazification and militarization of Germany's youth. The organization was nazified during the 1933 *Gleichschaltung* process. Now led by Konstantin Hierl, the Nazi labor service viewed itself as an elite group of the best of the nation's youth who were sacrificing a portion of their lives for the rebuilding of the Fatherland. This new self-image rendered the labor service unsuitable for its original task of soaking up hundreds of thousands of unemployed youths. Under Hierl's leadership, the organization resisted pressure to serve as a convenient dumping-ground for masses of urban unemployed, particularly those "antisocial" elements who allegedly refused legitimate offers of physically strenuous and low-paying work.[7] Nevertheless, Hierl and other enthusiasts argued for compulsory labor service *(Arbeitsdienstpflicht)* as a means of revitalizing Germany. A Nazi labor service, then, might be either an elite organization of young Nazi heroes or a mass organization based on compulsory service. These seemingly contradictory views, sometimes held by one and the same person, undoubtedly impeded the development of the FAD during the Third Reich's early years.

The wholesale revamping of the objectives and operation of the FAD was expedited by the Nazi gains in the March 5, 1933, Reichstag elections, the March 23 Enabling Act, and Nazi takeovers in the Länder and Prussian provinces during February and March. Nazi authorities had no intention of leaving the labor service in the hands of the RfAA, a Reich agency that they considered to be infested with socialists, communists, and Jews. Friedrich Syrup, RfAA president and Reich commissioner for the FAD, was a career civil servant who joined the NSDAP only in 1937. Nazification substantially altered the RfAA's personnel, but purges alone could not create a labor service that was "Nazi" in organization, mission, and spirit.[8]

As Reich labor minister in the last pre-Hitler government of General Kurt von Schleicher, Syrup had temporarily given up his positions as RfAA president and FAD Reich commissioner. When Stahlhelm leader Franz Seldte became Reich labor minister in the first Hitler cabinet, Syrup's position had to be clarified. On February 2, 1933, Seldte obtained the Reich cabinet's consent to reappoint Syrup as president of the RfAA, and informed the cabinet that he wanted the post of FAD Reich commissioner for himself, thereby breaking the personal union between the FAD and the RfAA. The cabinet expressed no objections.[9] Seldte seems to have had little interest in administering the FAD. He demanded the Reich commissioner's post largely to protect the Stahlhelm's interests against the influence of both Syrup and Alfred Hugenberg, who headed the Reich economics ministry as well as the food and agriculture ministry in Hitler's original cabinet.

Hugenberg, who claimed jurisdiction over every organization that had anything to do with economic policy or economic recovery, threatened to curtail Seldte's sphere of authority. Syrup had already annoyed Seldte prior to the Nazi takeover by resisting attempts by Seldte's Stahlhelm and other reactionary forces to take control of the labor service. Syrup believed that the economic impact of the FAD had been "greatly overestimated," and he sought to restrict the FAD to small, experimental projects until the efficacy of the scheme could be proven. This resriction ruled out FAD participation in large road construction, canal-building, and land reclamation projects. Syrup also opposed universal compulsory labor service, estimating the annual cost at one billion RM to support one million recruits. He saw no prospect of finding projects to occupy this massive army of laborers, particularly during the winter months.[10]

Hitler's appointment of Seldte as Reich commissioner for the FAD threatened Hierl's influence and created the possibility that the FAD might soon become a tool of the Stahlhelm rather than an organ of the NSDAP.[11] Hierl responded with a proposal for a National Socialist labor service, calling for universal compulsory labor service beginning with a call-up of the first contingent during the winter of 1933–34. The existing state-subsidized FAD would be transformed "immediately" into a "state labor service on a voluntary basis." The FAD's ties with the RfAA and the LAA would be severed and replaced with a new Reich organization based on a military model. Qualified personnel from the Nazi party and Stahlhelm would have equal access to FAD leadership positions. Faced with Hitler's wish to have Seldte as Reich commissioner for the FAD, Hierl demanded a post as state secretary in the Reich labor ministry and deputy Reich commissioner for the FAD, thus assuring himself a place "at his [Seldte's] side as number two leader" of the FAD. Hierl envisioned his duties, authority, and relationship to the Reich labor minister as analogous to those of the head of the army high command in his relationship to the defense minister.[12] Hierl was appointed state secretary on May 4, 1933.

As state secretary for the FAD in the Reich labor ministry, Hierl immediately pressed for an ambitious four-year program of agricultural and forestry projects requiring an FAD budget of at least RM 200 million for fiscal 1933–34, RM 360 million for 1934–35, and RM 425 million each for 1935–36 and 1936–37.[13] Hierl based his budget estimates on the widely held assumption of an early introduction of compulsory labor service. Heinrich Mahnken, who had led the Stahlhelm's labor service and represented Seldte in FAD matters prior to Hierl's appointment as RAM state secretary, had indicated in April that a law on compulsory labor service was imminent. Its precise timing "depended essentially on the foreign policy situation" and might have to be delayed until the fall of 1933 or spring of 1934. League of Nations criticism of German plans for the labor service forced Hierl to "camouflage" the military aspects of the new FAD.[14]

The foreign policy situation—international objections to anything resembling German remilitarization—was only one of several roadblocks to the introduction of compulsory labor service. Hierl's inability to obtain a firm FAD budget during 1933 and 1934 delayed introduction of compulsory service, which in turn compounded Hierl's difficulties in obtaining a satisfactory budget. The FAD's budget problems had developed steadily after the relaxation of eligibility regulations in July 1932. Enrollment mushroomed from 74,517 (end of June) to 254,000 (end of October). Funding failed to keep pace with the FAD's explosive growth. In November 1932, funds for fiscal year 1932 (ending March 31, 1933) were exhausted. Thousands of enlistees were dismissed, labor camps were closed, and by the end of January 1933 only 175,000 remained in active service. The RfAA contributed an additional RM 25 million to keep a limited number of FAD projects going until the end of the fiscal year.[15]

Those who hoped that the Nazi takeover would resolve the FAD's financial crisis were disappointed. Hierl entertained visions of annual FAD budgets of RM 450 million from 1934 to 1937, with enrollment rising to 700,000 by July 1934. Such expectations were unrealistic, since Hitler had already characterized Seldte's FAD request of RM 374.6 million for the 1933–34 budget year as "extraordinarily high." Hitler suggested that the FAD could manage with RM 200 million if it economized on administration and provided a Spartan existence for the volunteers. He indicated on June 16, 1933, that the introduction of compulsory labor service had to be postponed until at least April 1, 1934, and ruled out any significant changes in FAD organization and operations. Reich finance minister Krosigk held to the RM 200 million figure suggested by Hitler. The Reich finance ministry and the FAD argued over the FAD budget for months. When he submitted his 1934–35 request for RM 260 million in February 1934, Hierl claimed that his 1933 budget had not yet received formal approval. For 1933–34, he apparently received only RM 195 million of the finance minister's original allocation of RM 200 million.[16]

Discussions concerning the FAD budget were complicated by a controversy over the proper place for the FAD in the Reich's organizational structure. Should the FAD become an independent Reich agency, or should it remain a department of the Reich labor ministry under Seldte's supervision?

Several inconclusive meetings failed to resolve the matter. A high-level September 27, 1933, meeting chaired by Hitler appeared to settle the issue. The FAD was to remain formally under Reich labor minister Seldte's jurisdiction, but Hierl was to administer the organization "completely independent" of the RAM.[17] Seldte later concluded such a system was "out of the question." If the FAD was to be "independent," it should be detached from any ministry and led by someone with authority similar to that once held by the Reich Commissioner for Work Creation. Objections from defense minister Blomberg and Reich interior minister Wilhelm Frick ruled out the immediate appointment of a special Reich commissioner. Blomberg wanted Seldte to retain ultimate control over the FAD, while Frick promoted a scheme to create a new government ministry for the SA. The SA minister would supervise the FAD, and the SA and FAD could share the RM 200 million set aside for the FAD for fiscal year 1933–34.[18]

Three days after Hitler tamed the SA during the "Night of the Long Knives" (June 30, 1934), Hierl received the title "Reichskommissar f. den freiwilligen Arbeitsdienst." Technically satisfying Frick's objections to the "splintering" of Reich authority, the decree placed the new Reich commissioner under the authority of Reich interior minister Wilhelm Frick, rather than directly under Hitler. Frick, however, proposed to give Hierl "the most independence possible."[19]

Although Frick's scheme to merge the FAD into an SA Reich ministry never came to fruition, the idea influenced Reich finance minister Krosigk when he allocated funds for fiscal year 1934–35. Krosigk countered Hierl's request for RM 260 million with an offer of RM 108 million. RM 108 million was to be the FAD's share of a single appropriation of RM 250 million covering both the SA and the FAD. The argument that SA expenditures were "unproductive" compared with those of the FAD made no impression on the Reich finance minister, who remained unrelenting in his efforts to curb FAD spending. He indicated that if the matter remained in dispute, Hitler would have to make the final decision on the level of FAD funding.[20]

In the absence of a budget capable of financing its hoped-for expansion, the FAD acquired funds from other sources. Cities in the Rhineland straining under heavy welfare expenditures gave FAD recruitment offices a one-time payment of RM 25 for each locally supported "welfare unemployed" young man taken into the FAD. The president of the Rhineland LAA and the head of the employment office in Essen sought to stop this practice, as it disadvantaged the RfAA in its attempts to place the unemployed whom it supported in the limited number of FAD places available. Hierl ultimately appealed directly to Hitler, who instructed the Reich finance minister to reexamine the possibility of increasing FAD funding. Hierl's persistent complaining eventually paid dividends. In three successive stages between June and December 1934, the finance minister increased the FAD's 1934–35 allotment to RM 160 million, 180 million, and finally to 195 million.[21] This increase still left Hierl with no more than he had received in 1933–34, and far less than the RM 260 million that he had requested. Inadequate funding and a shortage of approved labor projects ruled out any expansion of the FAD during 1933 and 1934. Krosigk's miserly approach to the FAD reflected Hitler's priorities, which downplayed the FAD in favor of rearmament and other vehicles for work creation.[22]

Budgetary problems did not slow the nazification of the FAD during 1933. As Hierl explained to the Reich chancellery, "it was necessary to remove the large numbers of parasites who were on hand from the earlier so-called labor service."[23] Seldte set up a Reich Leadership of the Labor Service (Reichsleitung des Arbeitsdienstes) headed by Hierl. During March and April 1933, administrative responsibilities relating to the FAD were transferred from the RfAA's Land labor exchange offices to district commissioners and district leaders loyal to the new regime. These new leaders were responsible for the development of a core of 216-man labor camps, formation of a cadre of camp leaders, the indoctrination and physical training of FAD enrollees, the planning of work projects, and other administrative tasks. Although it was clear that the responsibilities of the new FAD leaders "could be more or less compared to those of military commanders and intendants," Hierl denied charges in a committee report from the Geneva disarmament conference that labeled the reorganized FAD as a disguised military formation.[24]

The creation of an administrative structure based on the Führer principle represented a first step toward the nazification of the FAD. To complete the nazification process, the NSDAP had to force non-Nazi organizations out of the business of organizing and supporting FAD units. Phasing out "open" labor camps in favor of "closed" camps, a move begun before Hitler came to power, helped to establish a Nazi monopoly on FAD units. The systematic process of closing down or taking over non-Nazi FAD units began earnestly in March 1933. Some disbanded "voluntarily," others were shut down by the SA auxiliary police. In June, the FAD directorate barred all but the

NSDAP and the Stahlhelm from operating FAD units. Other organizations were to turn over their camps to one of these authorized groups by June 20.[25] Because such a rapid reorganization would have disrupted work creation projects being carried out by the labor service, this deadline was not enforced rigidly.

The Stahlhelm itself was dissolved and its members incorporated into the SA in July 1933. The National Socialist Reichsverband Deutscher Arbeitsdienstvereine e.V. (R.D.A.) now became the sole legal organizer of FAD labor units. This umbrella organization supervised the activities of thirty district organizations (Arbeitsgauvereine). Non-Nazi FAD organizations were ordered to turn over their labor camps to the appropriate district organization by August 10, 1933. The Arbeitsgauvereine were "semiofficial" agencies of the NSDAP. They provided an organizational structure for the FAD labor camps but did not actually control their operations. This control was reserved for new Reich state authorities, the FAD Gau directorates headed by Arbeitsgauführer appointed technically by the Reich labor minister but in fact by Hierl as RAM state secretary for the FAD. Within each district, a number of Gruppenführer supervised work creation projects and FAD barracks. From December 1933, FAD enlistment offices handled recruitment as well as placement of recruits completing their term of service. The RfAA's only remaining role in the FAD was the provision of the enlistees' support payments.[26]

Leading a reorganized and nazified FAD, Hierl still could not convince either Reich or local officials of the value of his organization. Desperate for financial and moral support, Hierl appealed directly to Hitler in September 1933. He stressed the role that a strong labor service could play in Germany's economic rehabilitation and drive toward self-sufficiency by underlining the organization's "great economic mission of improving harvests through land improvements, protecting harvests from destruction by flooding, repairing rural agricultural roads, and creating new farmland through the reclamation of swamps and wasteland." Land reclamation could create 10,000 new farms. Within one year, the "proper utilization" of a half-million young men in the labor service could provide enough food to support at least 250,000 additional Germans. Within four years, Germany would be able to support at least one million more people. The FAD could not perform its economic mission because of the absence of any systematic Reich work creation plan, the Reinhardt program's failure either to earmark funds for the FAD or to permit FAD input in the allocation of project funds, a shortage of technical expertise at the Land level, an inadequate supply of ready-to-go projects suitable for FAD units, and the absence of funds for the provision of permanent barracks. Unsympathetic officials entrusted with administering Reinhardt program funds discriminated against the FAD. Hierl asked Hitler for a new work creation program that would accommodate the FAD's requirements, enable the Länder to hire expert planning personnel, and increase the amount of available work creation funds.[27]

Hierl's assessment of the FAD's problems was valid but incomplete. It was mistaken to attribute the FAD's ineffectiveness to a few hostile bureaucrats in Berlin and inadequate funding. Employment of the FAD was only one of several means of financing and carrying out work creation projects. The FAD's failure to get its share of work creation funds reflected a general lack of confidence in the organization's competence, efficiency, cost-effectiveness, reliability, and integrity. Local and regional officials looking for the best way to carry out work creation projects often turned away from the FAD.

Potential sponsors of work creation projects suitable for labor service participation were often put off by the cost of providing camps for FAD units. With the closure of all "open" labor camps, it became mandatory to construct permanent camps with barracks, each capable of meeting the material and spiritual needs of 216 young men. Communities had to guarantee work for 174 men for at least four years in order to qualify for a FAD unit. The work sites had to lie within six kilometers of the barracks to avoid long hikes to and from work. The Reinhardt program made no specific provision for the construction of FAD camps. The cost of FAD barracks construction could be included in the cost estimate for Reinhardt program projects, up to a limit of 10 percent of the total project cost or RM 50,000.[28] But funding agencies preferred projects that could get under way immediately and discouraged those that would be delayed and made more costly by the construction of FAD camps.

Hoping to lure an FAD detachment that would soak up local unemployed youths, many communities rushed to construct expensive camps and barracks, often with borrowed funds, before approved work creation projects had been secured. The FAD encouraged this practice, in some cases offering to pay rent on barracks before they were constructed.[29] This approach got priorities backwards; permanent camps should have been built only after viable work creation projects had been identified and approved. The Deutsche Gemeindetag, an organization representing German municipal administrations, advised local officials against committing public funds for construction of FAD camps that might never be occupied.[30] This was sound advice, but it reduced the likelihood that sponsors of local work creation projects would employ FAD units.

To justify the construction of permanent camps, the FAD had to identify long-term projects capable of employing large numbers of young, unskilled workers. Theoretically, this posed no problem. During 1933, the FAD compiled an inventory of projects suitable for the labor service. By September 1933, this inventory included sufficient work to occupy an FAD force twice its current size of 234,000 for nearly three decades.[31] These theoretical projects never materialized. Local authorities could not finance most of these projects, and the priorities of local welfare officials generally placed the reemployment of older heads of families ahead of jobs for unemployed, unmarried young men. This preference favored emergency relief projects *(Notstandsarbeiten)*, from which young unmarried males were technically excluded. The closing down of "open" FAD camps often forced local officials to convert FAD projects into emergency relief projects. Still without a firm budget during the autumn of 1933, the FAD made its projects more expensive and unattractive by demanding that project sponsors pay a special cash subsidy of RM 0.30 for each day worked by each FAD volunteer.[32]

Whereas the number of RfAA-supported emergency relief workers hovered between 300,000 and 400,000 early in December 1933, membership in the FAD barely exceeded 230,000. The FAD was locked in a struggle with the RfAA. They were competing for limited financial resources and a limited stock of worthwhile, technically prepared work creation projects. Access to the seemingly unlimited supply of unemployed labor was in fact restricted by widely varying needs and capabilities defined by age, sex, marital status, and the number of dependents. Hierl claimed that many RfAA emergency relief workers were ineligible unmarried youths who shied away from labor service discipline and preferred the higher pay received by emergency relief workers. While these young men occupied places on local emergency relief projects, many older, married emergency relief workers were separated from their families by assignments to projects far from their homes. Hierl claimed that FAD units could have carried out many of these distant projects and that the older men could have been assigned to sites close to their families. Moreover, he termed conditions in the emergency relief barracks "ethically and socially intolerable." The barracks lacked discipline and leadership and provided fertile ground for Marxist and communist agitators. Concluding that emergency relief projects were "conceivably unsuitable as a means to

[Germany's] economic reconstruction," Hierl proposed that a third of funds for RfAA emergency relief projects be placed at the FAD's disposal.[33]

The RfAA had its own demands. During 1934, the RfAA sought to move older, married, unemployed urban males with dependents into work creation projects outside the cities, but close enough to permit the workers to live at home and commute to their work sites. The actual distribution of work creation projects during 1933 had followed no rational plan with respect to geographical distribution. Many RfAA-supported projects were located in rural areas far from the homes of the urban workers employed on them, while many FAD camps, barracks, and work-sites lay on the outskirts of cities. The RfAA demanded that FAD projects near large cities be turned over to the RfAA for conversion to emergency relief projects.

Hierl in turn insisted that the RfAA turn its rural projects over to the FAD and provide the FAD with funds to construct new camps as needed. Hierl also demanded strict enforcement of the rule that assignment to emergency relief work be restricted to men who were either married or over age twenty-five if single. He further stipulated that the RfAA change its regulations to permit men leaving FAD service to be assigned to emergency relief projects, even if they did not qualify for unemployment support.

In December 1934, RfAA president Syrup and Hierl finally agreed on a suitable division of projects. Hierl agreed to allow the conversion of FAD projects near large cities into emergency relief projects. Syrup agreed to provide Hierl with funds to construct new camps in rural areas. Reich finance minister Krosigk approved the plan to turn over FAD projects to the RfAA but directed Syrup not to provide Hierl with funds for construction of camps. Hierl, he claimed, already had sufficient funds in his budget to cover any new construction arising from the agreement with Syrup.[34]

Hierl devised other strategies for expanding the FAD's role in the Nazi state by broadening the scope of projects within the FAD's purview. Just days after the Reich cabinet had approved the Reinhardt program, the FAD requested that the category "regulation of rivers and streams" (Flußregulierung) be broadened to include the FAD's main type of activity, the improvement of agricultural land; that the amount originally earmarked for river regulation be raised from RM 100 million to RM 120 million; and that the FAD be explicitly recognized as eligible for carrying out such projects. In June 1934, Hierl's "Regulation of the Employment of the Labor Service" sought to establish the FAD's right to carry out certain types of projects. The labor service would focus on land reclamation projects, forest improvement projects, settlement projects (both farm and suburban), and rural roads and paths dedicated to the movement of crops and farm equipment. But Hierl claimed certain additional "works of secondary importance" *(Nebenarbeitsaufgaben)* within the FAD's legitimate sphere of activity. These included participation in the construction of airports, arenas for national festivals, ponds for fire-fighting purposes, air raid shelters, protection from natural catastrophes, harvest assistance, and participation in the construction of the *Autobahnen*.[35]

Success in winning a major role in the construction of Germany's *Autobahnen* network would have assured the FAD's future, and Hierl would have become one of the most powerful figures in the Nazi hierarchy. But every agency involved in the construction of the *Autobahnen* resisted Hierl's bid for a large share of the work. Hierl needed the support of Fritz Todt, who as general inspector for German roads wielded immense authority and bore responsibility for building Hitler's *Autobahnen*. Todt first considered Hierl's request for a share of the construction work at the beginning of 1934. He avoided a confrontation by approving some sort of FAD participation in construction of the *Autobahnen*, but he was determined to limit participation to tasks that would neither increase costs nor jeopardize construction schedules. Todt ruled that only subsidiary projects, independent of the main work of the primary contractors and having no bearing on a project's completion date, could be considered for assignment to the FAD. He advised FAD district leaders to discuss with the RAB's regional construction headquarters (OBK) "whether and how" participation of the FAD might be "possible and useful"; he cautioned the RAB against increasing construction costs by utilizing FAD units; and he still claimed that it was necessary on the grounds of popular education and propaganda that the FAD participate in an undertaking of such fundamental importance as the Reichsautobahnen.[36]

When approached by the FAD, *Autobahnen* regional construction headquarters typically found that employment of FAD units was "neither possible nor useful." The OBK had a limitless number of reasons why FAD units could not be utilized on *Autobahnen* construction sites: most of the work had already been contracted out to private firms, some of the work required the use of heavy equipment for which FAD units were untrained and unqualified, work sites were too distant from FAD camps, some of the projects were too small to occupy a full FAD unit, work had to be completed within short deadlines to avoid disruption of traffic, and high unemployment rates in towns adjacent to *Autobahnen* work sites ruled out the use of FAD units from outside the region.[37]

Hierl continued to press his case. In September 1934, the RAB notified the OBK that "the labor service has once again expressed its desire to be employed in the construction of Reichsautobahnen. This desire ought to be complied with." The OBK were asked again to identify projects that could be carried out by FAD units without disrupting the work of private contractors. Renewed discussions between OBK and FAD district leaders produced virtually no *Autobahnen* construction work for the FAD. Hierl finally secured the RAB's agreement to some "Principles for the Employment of the Labor Service on the Reichsautobahnen." Although the document began with the imperative that "the labor service must be put to use in the construction of the Reichsautobahnen,"[38] this directive produced only minimal FAD participation in *Autobahnen* construction.

Hierl's failure to gain a strong role for the FAD in *Autobahnen* construction reflected three fundamental problems. Nazi labor market policy and the technicalities of Nazi labor market statistics, the method of determining the number of "unemployed" and "employed," virtually ruled out the large-scale use of FAD units for *Autobahnen* construction. Moreover, the demand for FAD services was limited by the widespread perceptions of FAD leadership as incompetent in technical matters, and the employment of FAD units as an inefficient, costly means of completing public works projects. Finally, Hierl lacked influence in the Nazi hierarchy sufficient to win preferential treatment for the FAD.

Access to employment in *Autobahnen* construction was strictly regulated by a number of directives issued by various agencies. The "Special Regulation on Manpower Requirements for the *Autobahnen*," issued during the autumn of 1933, began with the stipulation that "through the construction of the highways, a significant reduction in unemployment must be achieved." All labor, with the exception of a small core of professionals, was to be recruited through the local AA from the ranks of unemployed persons receiving unemployment support or crisis relief. An exception to this rule was made in a "Reich agreement on the preferential placement of fighters for the national revolution," under which the AA were to give preferential placement to members of the SA, SS, and Stahlhelm who had joined prior to January 30, 1933, and Nazi party comrades with membership numbers below 500,000.[39]

Under these regulations, which were reinforced by the "Social-policy requirements for work on the Reichsautobahnen" drawn up in Todt's office during the autumn of 1934, it was virtually impossible to accommodate the employment of FAD units in *Autobahnen* construction, since most FAD recruits failed to meet the required tests.[40] Beginning with official labor market statistics for July 31, 1933, Land Helpers, emergency relief workers *(Notstandsarbeiter)*, public relief workers, and members of the FAD were removed from the "unemployed" category, and, with the exception of FAD recruits, counted as "employed." Counted as neither "unemployed" nor "employed," FAD recruits disappeared from official German labor force statistics, though they were counted as insured by the national workers' health insurance service until April 30, 1935.[41] In a statistical sense (and Hitler wanted rapid statistical results for propaganda purposes), employment of FAD units could not meet the stipulation that "through the construction of the highways, a significant reduction in unemployment must be achieved." Hierl's best hope of securing a significant role for the FAD in *Autobahnen* construction was to obtain the same preferential treatment granted to certain members of the SA, SS, Stahlhelm, and NSDAP. Unfortunately for Hierl, preferred status for the FAD remained beyond his reach.

Both Todt and Hitler desired the completion of the *Autobahnen* network in the most expeditious and cost-effective manner. The FAD could play only an indirect role in achieving these objectives. Laborers assigned by AA to *Autobahnen* construction often proved to be unreliable troublemakers. Unwilling to do backbreaking work at near-slave wages, disgusted by the wretched housing and inadequate food provided on the work sites, workers either left their jobs or had to be dismissed. Some burned down their barracks in protest. Todt needed disciplined labor. Under the regulations outlined before, the FAD itself could not provide this labor. But FAD volunteers who could find no regular employment upon completing their enlistment period could be assigned by the AA to work on the *Autobahnen*. These young men could provide Todt with a disciplined, physically fit labor force. A December 1934 arrangement between Todt and RfAA president Syrup stipulated that 3 percent of the total *Autobahnen* labor force was to consist of recently released FAD men.[42]

Had Todt seriously desired the FAD as a partner on the *Autobahnen* construction team, he could have used his direct access to Hitler (which Hierl did not command) to overcome any technical roadblocks. Todt had to concede some participation to the FAD but sought to keep it to a minimum.

Todt's desire to avoid adding to Hierl's influence was only one of several considerations shaping his attitude toward the FAD. The FAD suffered from its reputation as an inefficient, corrupt, organization led by incompetent quasi-military leaders who knew little and cared less about the technical aspects of work creation projects. Years later, the historian Henning Köhler wrote that the labor service's main contribution to work creation was the creation of 25,000 jobs for FAD *Führer*.[43]

Theoretically, employment of the FAD should have been one of the least expensive means of completing work creation projects. But the FAD developed a reputation as one of the least cost-effective alternatives. FAD specifications for barracks for its young national heroes resulted in lodging costs much higher than those incurred by private contractors providing minimal shelter for laborers. The miserly compensation given labor service "volunteers," often unskilled youths who faced the loss of welfare support if they refused FAD service, translated into low productivity. Employment of FAD units often resulted in higher costs than the use of either emergency relief workers or labor hired on the free market.

The FAD Reich directorate estimated that the average FAD volunteer achieved in a six-hour day (the remainder being reserved for instruction and sports) half the output of a wageworker in an eight-hour day. Some FAD volunteers exceeded this average productivity standard, but some matched only 20 percent of the output of free-market labor. The Bavarian economics ministry estimated that even when FAD labor met the average output standard, free-market wage labor was still less expensive. The daily support per FAD volunteer came to RM 2.14. Added to this was the cost to project sponsors for debt service on barracks construction loans, and costs of utilities, all of which came to about RM 2.80 per worker per day. "Unproductive" days for which projects sponsors had to pay—Sundays, holidays, sick days, vacation days, days spent on barracks maintenance, days lost to bad weather—all of which generally accounted for a quarter of the total project days, brought the total cost for each productive day to RM 3.50. Assuming that FAD volunteers produced half the output of free-market wageworkers and that the market rate for wage labor was RM 5 per day (including social insurance contribution), FAD volunteers cost more—much more if they produced only one-third or one-fifth as much as the wage laborer.[44]

The variation of FAD productivity estimates between 20 and 50 percent of free-market levels made it nearly impossible to estimate the cost of FAD work creation projects with reasonable accuracy. Sponsoring and funding agencies thus favored projects planned for execution in some other manner. The FAD Reich directorate sought to mollify critics by measuring and certifying the performance of its units more adequately. In August 1933, Hierl ordered camp leaders to keep a record of each unit's productivity. To assure credibility, the chief of the appropriate Land technical authority (Landeskulturamt, Forstamt, Siedlungsamt) was to verify the information in the record. Some Land authorities welcomed this regulation, but others refused to tie up state technical personnel in the oversight of FAD projects.[45]

The FAD's low productivity simply added weight to other charges, including bloated organization, excessive time spent on indoctrination and premilitary training at the expense of work, technical incompetence, corruption, and even disloyalty to Nazi ideals. Although most of the criticism was directed against Hierl and other FAD leaders, much of the trouble had been caused by the fruitless discussions concerning the FAD's organization and status and the lack of a firm budget. The FAD's precarious situation prevented rational planning and investment in barracks, machinery, and clothing. Moreover, as Benz has observed, the Reinhardt work creation program had "pushed the FAD off into meaningless projects."[46]

Besieged with complaints about the FAD's activities in Bavaria, minister-president Ludwig Siebert ordered an investigation by the state economics ministry's labor and welfare department during the winter of 1933–34. The report found the FAD's huge administrative apparatus "unjustified," given the fact that the number of FAD recruits had not grown since January 1933. The Reichsverband der Arbeitsdienstvereine and the thirty district organizations absorbed 20 percent of the RfAA support payments for administrative costs and compensation of leadership personnel. The new FAD recruiting offices *(Meldeämter)* seemed particularly wasteful, since the AA previously handled recruitment at no cost to Land governments. While the report noted a predominance of incompetent military men in the FAD's top leadership and administrative positions, the FAD Reich directorate, itself heavily laden with former military officers, claimed that retired officers held "only" 43 percent of the top posts. The report found significant levels of incompetence among nonmilitary FAD leaders as well. Rounding out the report were complaints about the high cost of FAD barracks, the unreliability of FAD units (units assigned to a project were often commandeered without notice for other uses), the low productivity of FAD volunteers, and the refusal of FAD leaders to cooperate with state officials in planning and executing public works projects.[47]

Indoctrination of FAD volunteers with Nazi values was no substitute for expertise in the planning and execution of public works projects. The FAD lacked an adequate staff of qualified, technically trained engineering experts. Even though there was no shortage of unemployed technical experts in 1933, the FAD made no effort to add them to its permanent staff. In May 1933, Hierl created the Office for Project Planning and Development of the Labor Service Leadership, a central planning office entrusted with developing projects and technical expertise for the FAD. The appointment of retired corvette captain Hermann Tholens as director of this office added little in the way of technical competence. Hierl planned to obtain the necessary expertise by borrowing technical officials from Land governments and assigning them to each FAD district headquarters. Each "borrowed" official would in turn bring in one or two additional technical experts to constitute a planing staff in each FAD district.[48] The permanent cadre of retired military officers would not have to be diluted.

One of the experts loaned to the FAD was Gustav Zahnow, a graduate engineer with extensive Prussian state service experience in forestry, agriculture, and the construction of canals and roads. He was a member of the NSDAP and a founding member of the National Socialist FAD in 1932. Zahnow spent much of the next decade trying to transform the FAD into a technically competent organization capable of being developed into a central Reich planning authority. When prospects for this goal faded, he tried to convince Reich authorities of the need for a new national planning superagency, a "Generalstab der Arbeit," that would develop, coordinate, and execute all types of public projects, including those that did not then fall under FAD jurisdiction. Zahnow's efforts in both directions were frustrated by the complacency, indifference, and rivalry of Reich officials who had a vested interest in the status quo.[49]

Zahnow scorned Hierl's plan to assign one or two borrowed technicians to each FAD district. To achieve what he considered a proper ratio of one technical expert for each hundred FAD volunteers would have required three to four thousand engineers, a number Zahnow admitted that neither the technical staffs of the Länder nor the free market could supply. Zahnow considered Tholens's leadership of the FAD technical planning section a disaster. "Tholens placed no value on expert personnel," wrote Zahnow, "and openly asserted that a graduate engineer really cannot feel happy in the Reichsarbeitsdienst." Tholens preferred unskilled persons whom he could train in a few months and dominate more easily than trained engineers. Tholens, claimed Zahnow, believed that planning was a matter for state authorities, not the FAD.[50]

Gottfried Feder pointed out to Zahnow in 1940 that his critique of the FAD and proposal for the total reorganization of Germany's planning and development apparatus "could be viewed as criticism of the highest Reich leadership," Adolf Hitler.[51] Other Nazis had criticized the FAD's leadership in violent terms. Josef Schmidt, head of the Munich office of Gauleiter Julius Streicher's infamous anti-Semitic newspaper, *Der Stürmer,* had composed a stinging memorandum on the FAD that found its way to the desk of Bavarian minister-president Ludwig Siebert. Schmidt accused Hierl of turning the German labor service into an institution in which Germany's youth is "extorted, tormented, and educated in communist ways of thinking." For this disgraceful state of affairs, Schmidt blamed Seldte, Hierl, and Tholens. Tholens, "who is accustomed to seeing people only as numbers," had "turned the labor camps into bone-crushing mills and penitentiaries" by ordering that productivity be doubled from three cubic meters of earth moved per day to six cubic meters. After a few months of this slave labor, claimed Schmidt, young men routinely complained that they had "entered the labor service as a Nazi and came out a communist."[52]

Schmidt traced the FAD's problems to former Stahlhelm leader Seldte and to Hierl. They had packed the FAD with dedicated Stahlhelm men, one of whom, the FAD deputy chief of personnel, allegedly had written an anti-Hitler tract in 1932. Those who resisted these "reactionary elements," such as Hellmuth Stellrecht (head of the office for organizational matters) and retired major Otto Lancelle (inspector of the instructional department, responsible for training of FAD leaders) sought to have Hierl removed from FAD leadership, but they themselves were forced out by Hierl. Having "cleaned house," Hierl appointed to his inner circle more "old, fossilized officers," men with old ties to the non-Nazi right, the Stahlhelm, and even the communist party, men estranged from the young and the working people. Schmidt suggested that Hitler be informed of the FAD's calamitous situation and that Hierl be replaced with a leader raised in the ranks of the FAD itself.[53]

Hierl's position was precarious.[54] Threatening the FAD's very existence during 1934 were a foreign exchange crisis caused by rising imports during

Germany's economic recovery and a growing shortage of agricultural labor caused by renewed "flight from the land" as economic recovery opened up better-paying factory jobs. These crises directly affected the type of projects that the FAD could undertake and the amount of young labor that it could absorb into its ranks. The answer to the trade balance problem was the "New Plan" implemented in September 1934 by Reichsbank president and Reich economics minister Schacht. Schacht demanded a reduction of "unnecessary" food and raw material imports and the substitution of domestic supplies where possible. The plan's success required a substantial increase in Germany's agricultural output, to be achieved through additional inputs of land and labor. The FAD expected to provide the labor, but in the end, the labor service played a surprisingly small role in achieving the New Plan's goals.

Wolfgang Benz has argued that Hierl, the FAD leadership cadres, and the recruits had lost their "fighting spirit," that they no longer represented a cause, that they had no goal toward which to struggle, such as German self-sufficiency in food.[55] This judgment may not be entirely justified. On July 28, 1934, Arbeitsgauführer Fritz Schinnerer proclaimed that "the FAD serves the economic goal of achieving self-sufficiency in food [Brotfreiheit]." A few months later, Hierl ordered that FAD units be placed only on projects that contributed to increasing food production and easing the foreign exchange crisis.[56] The will to help the nation out of its dilemma clearly existed. But just as the FAD geared up for the "battle for food," its supply of unemployed young men was threatened. Catastrophic economic collapse and massive unemployment had brought the FAD into existence. But as Germany's economic recovery began to soak up the unemployed during 1934, some FAD recruiting offices were discovering that there were no more young unemployed available in the cities. Those who were available shunned rural agricultural labor, since better jobs in nearby factories were opening up. "Advertising campaigns" seeking to entice new recruits into the FAD failed miserably. Many volunteers with at least six months of service were leaving to take up better industrial jobs.[57]

As industrial recovery drained off "surplus," low-wage agricultural labor, the growing scarcity of agricultural labor threatened the plan to reduce food imports by increasing agricultural output. Hoping to check the "flight from the land," FAD Reich commissioner Seldte ordered the AA to place in farm jobs all FAD recruits who had served six months by March 31, 1934. FAD volunteers could be dismissed prior to completion of six months' service if they consented to take up agricultural jobs. The Reich finance ministry not only supported Seldte's initiative because it promised budgetary savings but also suggested the mandatory dismissal of all FAD recruits with at least twenty weeks of service.[58]

Hierl correctly perceived the initiatives of Seldte and Krosigk as the latest and most serious of ongoing efforts by what he often referred to as "conservative forces" and "the bureaucracy" to undermine the FAD. He thought that Hitler might dissolve the labor service if opponents could demonstrate that the FAD's manpower requirements siphoned off precious agricultural labor. Hierl countered that agricultural labor could not be provided simply by taking it from the FAD, whose 250,000 young recruits equaled only 8 percent of the registered unemployed. Any sudden reduction in FAD manpower would disrupt ongoing projects. The agricultural sector's labor requirement, argued Hierl, must be secured from industry, the emergency relief workers, the remaining unemployed, and only as a last resort from the FAD. Any compulsion required should be directed not against FAD volunteers who were willing to sacrifice for their Fatherland but against the unemployed who preferred to collect welfare support rather than to work. The ultimate cause of the farm labor shortage, "flight from the land," could be stemmed only in two ways: first, by blocking rural migration to the cities, and second, by permitting industry to hire away agricultural workers only if agriculture's labor requirement was already satisfied.[59]

To save the FAD from annihilation by predators from within the Hitler government, Hierl proposed two labor market regulations, both of which were implemented. In addition to blocking rural migration to the cities, Hierl suggested an *Arbeitsplatzaustausch,* an exchange of work places requiring young unmarried factory workers to give up their jobs in favor of older married heads of families. Displaced factory workers who originally came from farms would be placed in agricultural labor. The remainder would be assigned to the FAD, which, for its part, would release its former farm workers, who would "voluntarily" return to the farms. Former farm laborers working on emergency relief projects were to be released and returned to the farms. In principle, no young worker was to be forced into involuntary unemployment under the exchange program. RfAA president Syrup later admitted that practice did not always conform to principle.[60]

Hierl hoped these regulations would assure both agriculture and the FAD an adequate supply of manpower. Ultimately, however, only universal, compulsory labor service *(Arbeitsdienstpflicht)* could assure Hierl and the FAD a secure position in the National Socialist system. As he outlined the proposed *Arbeitsplatzaustausch*, Hierl again called for the introduction of compulsory labor service. Because Hitler was preparing for the introduction of universal, compulsory military service, and it was not clear how the manpower requirements of both the military and the FAD could be satisfied if service in both was made compulsory. Hierl viewed compulsory service in both organizations as complementary rather than competitive. He rejected the notion that service in the FAD was nothing more than a substitute for universal military service, prohibited under the Treaty of Versailles. The FAD, emphasized Hierl, was not an army in disguise—it had legitimate functions in its own right. The army protected Germany from external enemies; the labor service protected Germany from the chaos of internal class struggle. Compulsory military service would not make service in the labor service superfluous; compulsory labor service would not make military service unnecessary.[61]

Compulsory service in the renamed Reichsarbeitsdienst (RAD) was introduced on June 26, 1935. After newspaper reports of weapons found in RAD barracks strengthened the widespread suspicion that service in the RAD represented disguised military training, Reich interior minister Wilhelm Frick ordered that nothing was to appear either in reports directed to the public or in official notices "from which it might be concluded that military training took place in the labor service camps." Hierl also sent out a directive stressing that "the labor service is an economic, social, political, and educational institution that has nothing to do with military objectives." Any behavior that might connect the RAD with military or police activities, including the carrying of weapons and the wearing of steel helmets, was to cease. Reich minister for public enlightenment and propaganda Joseph Goebbels ordered that "nothing may be spoken and written that could connect the labor service with the defense of the country."[62]

Shortly after the introduction of compulsory military service in March 1935, the Reich cabinet discussed a draft law for compulsory, universal labor service. Economics minister Schacht and labor minister Seldte strongly opposed the proposal. While denying any "fundamental objections" to the "basic idea of compulsory labor service," Schacht argued that "the time for its introduction by law has not yet arrived." The military had not yet determined its annual manpower requirements, and Schacht feared mandatory service in both the labor service and the military would disrupt the economy and make it difficult to satisfy the demand for skilled labor. Reich financial resources, already strained by demands "in other vital areas," could not provide for compulsory labor service. Seldte recognized "the very noble, lofty moral and educational value of the idea of labor service" but questioned whether the present moment was "appropriate" for the introduction of compulsory service. The simultaneous demands of both the military and the compulsory labor service threatened to create shortages of agricultural labor, skilled labor, and artisans. Seldte wished to defer discussion of compulsory labor service until the labor market impact of compulsory military service could be assessed.[63]

Schacht and Seldte delayed the Reich cabinet's formal consideration of compulsory labor service until interior minister Frick requested on May 13, 1935, that the draft proposal be considered at the next meeting. Concerned about funding this gigantic undertaking, the cabinet nevertheless approved the June 26 Reichsarbeitsdienstgesetz. It was left to Hitler to set the RAD's manpower quota and duration of service. Hitler decided that the compulsory labor service should cost the Reich no more than its voluntary predecessor. Hierl grudgingly accepted Hitler's decision limiting the RAD temporarily to 200,000 men serving six months.[64]

Hierl had finally won his battle for universal compulsory labor service. But the manpower and financial resources consumed by Hitler's program of rearmament and conquest prevented Hierl from developing the RAD into a great empire within the Nazi structure. Hierl had spent the years since Hitler's accession to power trying to convince his party comrades that the labor service could and should play a fundamental role in transforming Germany into a "National Socialist" society. Although the logic of his argument was sound, Hierl failed to break into the inner power structure of the Nazi movement, and the labor service never gained equal status with the SA and SS as an exemplar and protector of the "National Socialist spirit." Viewing the FAD as a remnant of the detested Weimar system, many Nazis remained unconvinced that the organization had anything at all to do with the National Socialist movement.

Given the fundamental indifference or even antipathy of much of the Nazi party's leadership toward the FAD, Hierl's persistent efforts to transform his organization into an independent organ of the state were probably counterproductive. In pursuing this goal, Hierl was by implication denying that his organization was an affiliate of the Nazi party. Such an assertion by Hierl could only alienate the Nazi hierarchy, especially those who had no interest in a labor service in any form. "Hierl's intention to develop the labor service as much as possible as an independent state organization," observed Benz, "was interpreted as an attempt to evade the Party's claim of total control."[65]

The Reichsarbeitsdienstgesetz of June 26, 1935, which transformed the formerly "voluntary" organization into a state institution, threatened to move Hierl and the new RAD farther from the mainstream of the National Socialist party. Hoping to forestall this potentially fatal development, Hierl argued that transforming the labor service into a state institution in no way implied the disconnection or removal of the labor service from the National Socialist movement or party. On the contrary, he asserted, "with the nationalization of the voluntary National Socialist Labor Service, the National Socialist movement has once again conquered a piece of the state." The new RAD law, claimed Hierl, did not alter the labor service's "inner bond" with the NSDAP.[66] In fact, the essential "inner bond" between the labor service and the National Socialist movement had never existed. Hierl's incessant demands for independence and the implementation of compulsory labor service embedded in the state rather than in the Nazi party merely widened a gap that had existed when Hitler came to power.

The lack of an inner bond between the FAD and the NSDAP—the absence of a strong traditional connection between the FAD and the Nazi movement prior to Hitler's ascent to power—goes a long way toward explaining Hierl's apparent lack of authority and influence in the Nazi power structure. Shortly after his appointment to the chancellorship, Hitler emphasized the central role that compulsory labor service would play in the economic and moral rehabilitation of the German nation. Two-and-one-half years elapsed before Hitler's government made labor service compulsory— for no more than 200,000 young men. Meanwhile, the FAD led a shadowy existence, struggling for a suitable budget, resisting attempts to remove its top leadership, and fending off schemes to merge it with organizations such as the SA. In this case, Hitler's rhetoric did not become reality. The Nazi Führer's words did not represent a "blueprint for action."

In 1933 and 1934, German labor market policy, out of political and economic necessity, focused on providing work for older, married heads of families, and sought to assure agricultural interests an adequate supply of young, unmarried laborers. These policy goals worked against Hierl's attempts to shift human and financial resources to the labor service. By 1935, the demands of compulsory military service, combined with the continuing shortage of agricultural labor, obliged Hitler to restrict the size and cost of Germany's new, "compulsory" Reichsarbeitsdienst. The implementation of Hitler's professed vision of labor service was limited by Nazi party historical tradition, by the indifference or opposition to a labor service among other Nazi leaders, and by the hard economic and political realities involved in the conquest of unemployment, the provision of an agricultural labor force, and preparation for war.

9

From Creating Jobs to Allocating Labor

A nation preparing for war must control its labor supply and direct it into those sectors of the economy most essential to military preparedness. In the long run, Hitler's government was preparing Germany for war. At some point during the economic recovery, work creation had to give way to efforts to control and allocate the existing labor supply *(Arbeitseinsatz)* and expand the total active labor force. Signs of the transition from work creation to the control and allocation of labor were visible by the spring of 1934.[1]

Those who see Hitler's early "work creation" programs as nothing more than disguised rearmament would argue that there was no transition at all in National Socialist labor market policy. And some who concede the existence of a distinct period of work creation during 1933–34 nevertheless argue that the conquest of unemployment, never an end in itself for Hitler's government, was merely a stage in a planned long-range process leading to war. Thus, Frieda Wunderlich has written that "it would be too narrow to characterize the policy of the first two or three years of the [National Socialist] régime as designed to reduce unemployment. In fact, the aim was more far-reaching from the very beginning. Labor as an important factor of warfare . . . was to be regulated in its distribution in accordance with the 'defense' objectives of a directed economy. Centralization and tightening of control of labor allocation was aimed at during the whole period."[1]

Perhaps Hitler's government contemplated labor market control and labor allocation from the beginning, but the first Law on the Allocation of Labor (Gesetz zur Regelung des Arbeitseinsatzes) was not issued until May 15, 1934.[2] Hitler's government enacted systematic labor market controls only after it became clear that the 1933–34 work creation programs were leaving behind masses of unemployed labor in the large cities and that the programs had failed to halt the migration of agricultural labor into urban industrial areas. Initial Nazi labor market controls were designed to rectify these deficiencies.

Creating jobs through public works programs effectively provided "work and bread" for Germany's unemployed, but this expensive approach was opposed by conservatives both within the government (most notably Reich economics minister Hugenberg) and among Germany's business and banking leadership. Because public works programs took time to plan and implement, the Nazis would reap no significant political benefits from work creation until spring or summer 1934. The government thus looked for ways to reduce statistical unemployment as quickly as possible, without necessarily creating a corresponding number of new jobs.[3] Changes in registration procedures, incentives to workers, especially women, to leave the labor force, and the use of the state's police powers to control the labor market all provided less expensive, fast-working supplements to direct work creation programs.[4]

During 1934, government policy shifted from the creation of work to the steering, regulation, and control of the labor market. The RfAA played a critical role in both developing and implementing specific control measures. The growing importance of this role marked the final transformation of the RfAA's primary mission. In the depths of the Depression from 1930 to 1933, the RfAA's principal role was to pay out unemployment compensation and crisis support to qualified applicants. The six million unemployed strained the RfAA's financial and human resources to the limit. "The economic crisis," observed Andreas Kranig fifty years later, "was also a crisis of the RfAA."[5]

During 1933, as direct work creation began to play a larger role in the "battle for work," the RfAA's focus began to shift. As "unemployment" began to decline, the provision of support payments diminished in importance as an increasing share of the RfAA's financial resources went to the provision of basic assistance *(Grundförderung)* for emergency work creation projects carried out under the Gereke *Sofortprogramm* and the Reinhardt program. Job placement and the assignment of the unemployed to work creation projects now occupied personnel in the local RfAA employment offices.

When the Hitler government decided in December 1933 not to fund new work creation programs and to allow existing programs to wind down, four million Germans remained officially unemployed. The 1933 "battle for work," combined with a "natural" turnaround in the business cycle, had reduced official unemployment by two million. As great as this achievement was, it was not enough, and it had operated very unevenly with respect to the location, age, and sex of the unemployed. Recovery of the labor market had largely bypassed large urban industrial areas and older male heads of households. To address these anomalies in Germany's economic recovery, the RfAA's attention in 1934 turned increasingly toward the allocation of labor *(Arbeitseinsatz)*. The allocation and regulation of labor now became the major instrument in the pursuit of full employment.

As understood by RfAA president Friedrich Syrup, labor allocation policy involved the systematic management of the labor force in a manner that would promote the economic and social policies of the German national state. The RfAA was to design and administer labor market measures designed to reduce the massing of unemployed in large cities, to reverse the "flight from the land" and alleviate the scarcity of labor in the agricultural sector, and to promote German social goals by providing jobs for unemployed older male heads of households. The pursuit of such aims required gradually increasing compulsion and coercion against individuals, restriction of individual freedom of movement and choice of occupation, and an extension of the RfAA's legal authority over the labor market. The 1927 law establishing the RfAA had given the agency power to regulate the labor market insofar as the unemployed were concerned. The Nazis gave the RfAA the authority to intervene and regulate conditions where an employment relationship between workers and employers already existed. By the end of 1934, the RfAA could give jobs to the unemployed and take jobs away from the employed. During the following years, labor was mobilized and organized for war. By the end of 1935, the RfAA had a total monopoly on all placement activities. "Within only two years," concluded Wunderlich, "the placement system had been transformed into a planned system of labor allocation."[6]

Of the Nazi efforts to influence the development of the labor market, one of the best known is the marriage loan program.[7] The postwar "impoverishment" of Germany, and particularly the effects of inflation, forced many younger women into the labor force during the 1920s. One breadwinner in the family no longer sufficed. Hitler's Reich labor minister, Franz Seldte, echoed the popular claim that the marked expansion in the female labor force since the Great War had driven male workers into unemployment. Seldte regarded the replacement of male workers by females as bad labor market policy and unacceptable on psychological and ethical grounds. Females in the labor force had to be put back into the housekeeping role for which they were especially suited, and male heads of families had to receive highest priority for employment.[8]

Seldte's views reflected broad-based attacks on women in the labor force and a widespread notion that women who had jobs during a period of catastrophic unemployment should be replaced by unemployed men—the "real" breadwinners in a "normal" household.[9] Because they were generally thought of as "double earners" *(Doppelverdiener)*, persons earning income that merely supplemented that of the male primary income-earner, married women became particular targets of those seeking to force women out of the labor market. Seldte shared the view of many NSDAP and state officials that working women and so-called "double earners," families with two sources of income, constituted a single problem calling for a single solution. Unlike many Nazi party activists, however, Seldte opposed the regulation of female labor and double earning by means of laws and decrees. He preferred to rely on his ability to influence, convince, and pressure public and private employers to replace women with unemployed male heads of households.[10]

Hitler's government adopted Seldte's approach. Women were not simply ordered out of the active labor force. Although local Nazi party leaders and SA men did not hesitate to take illegal action to rid the workplace of women and double earners, leading Nazi party figures and the Reich government were not willing to alienate either the business community or the general public by forcing women and double earners out of the labor force during 1933. The government was more interested in steering women into certain types of work, such as domestic service and agricultural work, rather than rooting them out of the labor force altogether.[11] Women were given incentives to give up occupations and jobs that were suitable for males. The June 1, 1933, work creation program provided for government marriage loans for women (the loan was actually paid to the bridegroom!) who agreed to leave the industrial labor force. Theoretically, unemployed male heads of families could then be put back to work as replacements for the women. Marriage loans insured that women displaced from industrial jobs would not end up as additions to the unemployment statistics. Hitler's government could reduce unemployment without creating new jobs.

Physical examinations of couples applying for marriage loans provided municipal health officials an opportunity to assess the biological, hereditary, and racial quality of the applicants, thereby laying the foundation for the subsequent racial classification of the entire population.[12] The marriage loan program represented more than an element of Nazi labor market policy. Its purpose was to increase the number of marriages and raise Germany's birth rate, free up jobs for men, and increase orders for factories producing furniture and household goods.[13]

The marriage loans were to cost the government nothing, since they were initially financed by a special tax on unmarried wage earners and other unmarried persons subject to income tax.[14] The interest-free loans were to be repaid over an eight-year period. The Reich government marriage loan program was supplemented by the activities of a number of employers who gave "marriage subsidies" *(Heiratzuschüße)* to females leaving their jobs for marriage.[15]

High demand for marriage loans and contribution receipts below expectations forced the Reich government to reduce the average size of its loans from the original RM 730 in August 1933 to RM 560 in February 1934. Beginning with 8,346 loans in August 1933, the number reached 40,981 by December 1933. By January 31, 1935, the government had issued 379,000 marriage loans at a total cost of RM 206 million. At the end of 1935, a total of 523,000 loans had cost RM 300 million, averaging about RM 575 per loan. Between August 1933 and January 1937, some 700,000 couples, about one quarter of those who were married during that period, benefited from marriage loans. In 1932, 28 percent of wage workers and 38 percent of salaried employees in firms employing more than five persons were women; for 1934, the respective numbers had fallen to 24 percent and 36 percent. In January 1933, women comprised 18.76 percent of the official unemployed; by January 1935, they accounted for only 13.79 percent of the unemployed.[16]

Statistically, the marriage loan program seems to have worked. Females did leave the labor force, and women as a percentage of the unemployed did decline. The extent to which marriage loans contributed to the declining proportion of females in the industrial labor force and among the unemployed is difficult to judge. Mason has argued that very slow growth of the insured female labor force during the first three years of Nazi rule "was only to a very limited extent a reflection of policies towards women." It was, rather, an unintended result of emphasis on stimulation of rearmament-related investment goods industries, where female employment was traditionally low.[17]

There is no reliable way to distinguish between "additional" marriages prompted by the loans, and marriages that would have taken place without the loans. The number of marriages increased as a natural result of Germany's economic recovery. Utilizing Reich Statistical Office marriage statistics for fifty-one large cities, accounting for one-third of all German marriages in 1932, the *Nürnberger Zeitung* reported that 88 percent of the increase in marriages in 1933 was "made possible" by marriage loans. The Reich finance ministry assumed that 80 percent of an estimated 250,000 marriage loans to be paid out in 1934 would represent "additional" marriages that otherwise would not have taken place. But even without loans, many women normally gave up their jobs upon marrying. In Britain and Belgium, where no marriage loans were offered, "retirement through marriage" was apparently common during the 1930s.[18]

Whatever the effect of marriage loans, it is not valid to attribute the decline of women in the labor force solely to marriage. Marriage, with or without loans, was not the only reason that German women left the labor force in 1933 and 1934. As Overy has noted, many women had taken relatively low-paying jobs in the first place only because male family members had lost relatively high-paying jobs during the depression. Overy believed it was "likely" that, as males found employment during the recovery, many women would leave jobs that they had taken only out of necessity.[19] The RfAA considered women who had replaced men in the workforce during the Depression as temporary employees. With the recovery well under way by late summer 1933, the RfAA undertook a deliberate policy to "replace female labor with male unemployed above all in those occupational sectors in which male workers were replaced by female labor during the years of declining economic activity."[20]

Women leaving jobs, for whatever reason, were not always replaced by men. Realistically, a general replacement of female labor by males was not possible. In certain occupations and branches of industry, female labor was considered indispensable.[21] The experience of Duisburg's municipal administration provides a small-scale example of the manner and extent to which the reduction of female labor was accomplished in the public sector. Between July 1 and October 20, 1933, thirty-one female salaried employees left municipal employment. Only eight left as a result of marriage. Eighteen (unmarried) left employment "because of their economic situation"—their parents now had a secure income. Three simply retired, and two were forced to leave under provisions of the Reich "Law for the Restoration of the German Civil Service," which provided for termination of those found to be politically unreliable or racially unsuitable. Twenty-three unemployed male salaried employees were hired as replacements. They were members of the SA, SS, and the Stahlhelm. Although it is reasonable to assume that among Duisburg's fifty thousand unemployed there were more than twenty-three SA, SS, and Stahlhelm men available for these vacant positions, the city hired eight women as replacements for the remaining open slots.[22]

Marriage loans enabled the Reich government to remove employed females from the labor force without forcing them into the ranks of the officially counted unemployed. But what could be done about unemployed females who appeared in the unemployment statistics and drew unemployment compensation, crisis relief, or municipal welfare? Since Nazi labor market policy favored the hiring of male heads of households, the outlook for clearing women from the unemployment rolls appeared bleak. Yet, ways were found to remove women from the unemployment statistics and keep them off. Most of the unemployed women in Duisburg, for example, held occupations that the local RfAA placement office reserved almost exclusively for males. The solution, suggested local Nazi party officials, was a "special action" for the retraining of unemployed women as domestic servants. A special propaganda blitz, accompanied by a monthly subsidy of RM 8, would convince reluctant households to hire these women. Stuttgart established a similar program, the Stuttgarter Haushilfe, with the aim of training and placing "a few hundred" unemployed females by the end of March 1934.[23] In April 1933, the Reich government had already exempted domestic servants and their employers from contributions to (and payments from) the RfAA unemployment compensation fund. This exemption not only made it less expensive for households to hire domestic servants but also effectively removed unemployed domestic servants from the unemployment statistics. From the standpoint of official unemployment statistics, there was a distinct incentive to "retrain" and reclassify as many women as possible as "domestic servants."

In the long run, Nazi efforts to remove women from the workforce failed. "Most women who were registered as unemployed in 1932," observed Overy, "found their way back into the workforce after 1933, not into the kitchen."[24] There were 3.4 million more women in the active German labor force in 1939 than there had been in 1933. In September 1937, full employment in many sectors of the German economy, as well as the need to insure an adequate supply of labor for the fulfillment of the Four Year Plan, occasioned a shift in the government's marriage loan policy. Following Reich finance minister Krosigk's proposal, the government dropped the requirement that female recipients of marriage loans leave the active labor force. Women who continued to work or resumed work, however, would have to add interest payments to the normally interest-free loan repayment.[25]

Another target of authorities intent upon reducing statistical unemployment quickly and inexpensively during 1933 were the "double earners" *(Doppelverdiener)*, two-income families or individuals receiving income from more than one source.[26] Although many of those alleged to be "double earners" were married women with jobs, the rather ill-defined concept included employed children of a working adult, an individual working short hours who needed two jobs to make ends meet, retirees who supplemented meager retirement benefits with part-time work, and families that received both earned and unearned income.

Was it fair that some households enjoyed two incomes while millions of unemployed, willing workers could not put food on the table for their families? For many, justice seemed to dictate that double earning be halted. During 1933, local Nazi party zealots took matters into their own hands. They waged an unauthorized war not only against double earners but also against families whose total income, no matter how earned, exceeded amounts deemed appropriate by local Nazi party officials. As one step toward weeding out alleged double earners, local NSDAP leaders sought to compel Reichsbank branch personnel to complete a questionnaire about the economic and employment status of each employee and his or her family.[27] In Kassel, NSDAP officials set the maximum monthly income for a husband and wife in Hesse at RM 110 per month, with an additional RM 20 permitted for each child.[28] Policy on double earners became embroiled in jurisdictional disputes between Nazi party officials and Reich government authorities. Resolving the double earner question involved an assertion of power as well as an assertion of the principle of social justice.

Random, uncoordinated actions against double earners by local Nazi party officials prompted counteraction by the Reich labor ministry and the Reich economics ministry in October 1933. Seldte and Schmitt argued that spontaneous local actions against double earners lacked any legal basis, threatened the authority of the state, and encouraged denunciations of alleged violators. Regulations prohibiting double earning, they argued, penalized performance and achievement—the most productive workers were most often the ones seeking a second job. The preservation of "family values" and the promotion of a sound national population policy also played a large role in shaping the government's attitude toward double earning. Two-income families, argued Seldte and Schmitt, almost always needed the additional income; without it, they could not support their children, and many marriages would break up. The two Reich ministers condemned unauthorized activities against double earners.[29]

Having convinced the Reich government to adopt their position, Seldte and Schmitt sought to establish firm guidelines and halt unauthorized attacks on double earners. In a joint memorandum on the subject issued November 20, 1933, they stressed that there was no basis in law for requiring employees to furnish sworn statements of family income and property or for dismissing alleged double earners from jobs. They pointed to the irrational results of attempts to define "double earners." A worker employed for only thirty-six hours each week who supplemented his income by working a couple of additional hours in a second job would be classified as a "double earner," whereas another worker employed for a normal forty-eight-hour week would be considered a "single earner" even though he earned more than the "double earner." It was equally irrational to classify as a "double-earner" a married father working short ours, whose wife or child had to work in order to make ends meet. The only reasonable means of distinguishing between "single" and "double" earners would have been to establish a "permitted" income level for each individual worker and every job category, a gargantuan task "whose absurdity is obvious."[30]

A prohibition of double earning would endanger many social policy goals of the Reich government. Marriages and the formation of new families would be discouraged, many existing families would disintegrate under economic pressure, families would be discouraged from seeking a higher standard of living, and youths would be denied the opportunity to get valuable work experience if their parents had a job. Moreover, persons in certain occupations, such as scholars, writers, and artists, could survive only with the help of supplementary income from some other job.[31]

How, then, did the government intend to deal with the perceived problem of double earning? Seldte and Schmitt argued that a general law or administrative order as to what constituted "unjustified double earning" would be both harmful and "impossible." Only case-by-case consideration could determine whether double earning was "justified" or "unjustified." All relevant circumstances, especially social considerations, would have to be taken into account. Only in "particularly crass cases" were workers to be dismissed and replaced. Authority to make such decisions rested with the proprietor and director of each establishment, not with local Nazi party officials. A generally accepted definition of double earning proved elusive, no general law or decree on the matter was promulgated, and the regulations on double earning issued in the joint memorandum of November 20, 1933, remained the most definitive statement on the matter issued by Reich authorities.[32]

Government policy on marriage loans and double earners might suggest that Hitler's government, in contrast to Nazi party activists, opposed compulsory, coercive measures to control the labor market. If this was indeed the government's position in 1933, it did not last long. During 1934, the government relied increasingly on coercive control measures to achieve its aims in the labor market. This shift to a more coercive approach to resolving labor market problems resulted in the first instance from the partial failure of the 1933 work creation programs. These programs were proving ineffective against some of the most stubborn urban concentrations of unemployed workers. Moreover, by 1934, the Hitler government's desire to prepare Germany's labor market for rearmament was becoming incompatible with a free-market labor policy.

Two factors in particular pointed to increased control over the labor market through the use of coercion. First was the Reich government's decision in December 1933 that no new work creation programs would be initiated in 1934, and that existing programs would be allowed to play themselves out and die.[33] The amount of RfAA funding available for subsidizing work creation projects was to be cut. The number of unemployed had fallen by about two million since Hitler's appointment to the chancellorship. But, with nearly 3.8 million German workers still officially counted as unemployed, the "battle for work" was far from won, and the decision to wind down work creation programs that had begun only a few months earlier may have been premature. Eventually, open rearmament and the reintroduction of compulsory military conscription would soak up many of the remaining unemployed. In the meantime, coercive controls on the labor market might take up some of the slack left by declining work creation expenditures and reduce the number of officially counted unemployed. The use of the state's police powers to control the labor market provided a less expensive substitute for direct work creation programs.

The second factor inviting greater reliance on government control and coercion in the labor market was the geographic and demographic uneven-ness of the government's success in reducing unemployment during 1933. Although the disappearance of unemployed labor produced labor shortages in some rural agricultural areas, unemployment in Germany's major cities remained intractable at rates far above the national average. Overy has observed that the Reich government provided "selective help for particular regions" by locating work creation projects in economically backward, pri-marily agrarian regions; by placing government contracts in depressed areas; and by encouraging the relocation of industries (for strategic reasons) to central and southern Germany. "The result of these initiatives," he con-cluded, "was that unemployment declined in all major regions at a more or less equal pace between 1933 and 1937, falling furthest in central Germany and East Prussia and least in Saxony and Silesia."[34] (See Appendix, Tables 12 and 13.)

Overy's analysis can be fine-tuned to provide greater precision with respect to both timing and geography. A clearer and somewhat different picture emerges if the "regional" view is supplemented by statistics on the development of unemployment in cities with over 100,000 inhabitants and if the focus is concentrated on 1933–34. During 1933 and the first part of 1934, Germany's large cities struggling with the largest concentrations of unemployed labor did not benefit substantially precisely because the work creation programs favored land reclamation projects in rural areas. Attempts to assign masses of urban unemployed to these rural projects during 1933–34 were not very successful. The case that most shocked and disturbed Reich officials was Berlin, where 11 percent of Germany's unemployed were concentrated in March 1933. One year later, 15 percent of the nation's unemployed resided in Berlin. The general improvement in the national labor market had bypassed the nation's capital. It was this situation that the Reich government was determined to address during 1934.

At the beginning of 1934, unemployment ratios varied considerably according to the size of the city: large cities over 100,000 averaged 103 unem-ployed per 1,000 inhabitants; medium-size cities, 80 per 1,000; and small towns, 42 per 1,000.[35] The battle for work had produced equally uneven results among various age groups. Among males between the ages of eighteen and twenty-five, work creation measures reduced official unemployment by two-thirds during the first eighteen months of Hitler's government. But, despite lip service paid to the urgency of finding employment for older married heads of families, two-thirds of the unemployed over forty found no employment under work creation measures (see Appendix, Table 14).[36]

The relative ineffectiveness of 1933 work creation programs in dramatically reducing big-city unemployment rates appeared to reflect a basic structural defect in the distribution of Germany's population with respect to both space and occupation. During the four-year economic crisis as well as the early recovery during 1933, many rural Germans in search of work migrated to cities. Many experts believed that economic recovery could never correct a perceived population imbalance that originated in massive internal population migrations during Germany's industrialization between 1871 and 1914 and that persisted after the Great War. While rural areas had become depopulated, overcrowded cities had spawned nothing but misery and contributed to the physical and moral decay of the German people. Germany's agriculture, handicrafts, and reputation for high-quality industrial production had all suffered; there was a chronic surplus of salaried employees and academics; small retailers could no longer make a living; unskilled laborers had flooded the industrial regions; and young women were no longer being prepared for their "natural occupations as housewives and mothers." It seemed clear to both experts and ordinary people that "the spatial and occupational distribution of the population in Germany is unhealthy."[37]

A "correct" labor market policy could reverse all of these unhealthy developments. Syrup implied that RfAA policy under the Nazis was not a knee-jerk reaction to a particular economic crisis but rather was part of a carefully considered long-term program to correct a fundamental structural problem. The RfAA, said Syrup, had been doing its part since 1933 to reverse decades of dangerous population development. During 1933, RfAA strategy was based on the assumptions that rural work creation projects should take precedence over urban projects and that the urban unemployed should be moved out of the cities and assigned to rural land reclamation projects.[38] But results showed that the 1933 battle for work "had in no way fully engaged the strongholds of unemployment, the big cities and industrial regions."[39] Government control over the allocation of labor seemed to offer the only hope of halting the influx of job-seekers into large cities.

Syrup's initiative produced the May 15, 1934, Law on the Allocation of Labor, under which persons seeking employment could move to a district with higher unemployment only with the permission of the RfAA. The law also empowered the RfAA to regulate and restrict the movement of agricultural laborers into industrial occupations. Local AA were to prevent the movement of agricultural labor to urban industrial jobs and were to pressure industrial employers to dismiss workers with agricultural origins so that they could be assigned to agricultural employment.[40]

This addition to the RfAA's authority, admitted Syrup, represented "a great interference with freedom of movement," although Syrup and others have maintained that the new powers were used sparingly and reasonably.[41] Syrup first made use of his new authority by barring migration of workers to Berlin, with dramatic results. From more than a half million at the beginning of 1934, the number of Berlin unemployed fell to less than 200,000 by the autumn of 1935.[42] Despite its apparent utility, Syrup imposed the migration block only on Berlin, Hamburg, Bremen, and the Saarland (after the January 1935 plebiscite reestablishing full German jurisdiction over the area), even though a number of other cities suffering under higher unemployment rates asked that migration be blocked. The migration block served political purposes as well. Migration into Hamburg and Bremen was blocked in an attempt to prevent Germans from using those cities as points of departure for overseas destinations. In the Saarland, the Reich government wanted to demonstrate to the Saarlanders, as well as to the rest of the world, that they had made the right decision in the plebiscite. The government would cement their allegiance to the Third Reich by wiping out unemployment quickly.[43]

Why did the RfAA make such limited use of its authority to regulate or ban certain types of internal migration, when so many large cities were swamped with unemployed workers? The government's expressed desire to interfere as little as possible with individuals' job and career decisions and prospects, noted by Syrup at the time and later by Tim Mason, seems out of character for the Nazi government. More revealing was Syrup's remark that the government wished to help especially endangered regions of Germany by blocking migration but that it also sought to avoid creating "autonomous economic regions" by erecting too many "blocking walls and barriers."[44] The Reich government sought to avoid the breakup of Germany's national economy into a patchwork of autarkic local economic units. Local interests had to be subordinated to the national interest.

Finding jobs for unemployed older married male heads of households also required coercive controls on the labor market. The proposed solution was quite simple; single workers under age twenty-five would be compelled to give up their jobs to older unemployed heads of households. This "exchange of workplaces" *(Arbeitsplatzaustausch)* was to be accomplished under the August 10, 1934, Decree on Manpower Distribution and the August 28, 1934, Directive on Manpower Distribution.[45] In addition to the exchange program, when vacancies occurred in a "natural way" as younger workers "voluntarily" left jobs, employers were obligated to give preference to older applicants. Younger workers could be hired only with the consent of the local AA. The element of compulsion in the workplace exchange program was somewhat muted by the fact that the new regulations recognized management's traditional authority to make decisions vital to the operation of the firm, by allowing each firm to decide how many, if any, young workers were to be exchanged for older workers. The technical and economic requirements of the individual firm would determine how many young workers could be replaced without harming the interests of the firm. Syrup explicitly declined to set any general quota. "Norms or principles concerning the correct age distribution of the employees of a firm," wrote Syrup, "do not exist and cannot be established."[46]

Employers, as Mason has observed, did not embrace the program enthusiastically. In the LAA Westfalen district, two-thirds of the 5,250 large firms or independently reporting branch factories indicated that they would not be able to undertake any job exchanges. Economic self-interest provided reason enough to withhold cooperation. Younger workers were stronger, commanded lower wages (if under age twenty-one), and tended to be less indoctrinated with trade union and socialist ideas. The exchange of younger workers for older ones created higher wage bills. In some cases, higher quality work from the more experienced older workers offset the higher wages, but as one AA report observed, "quality is unfortunately less in demand." In any case, replacing younger workers with older ones at higher cost violated "pure capitalistic thought." Another AA observed that industrial employers believed job exchanges interfered with the smooth flow of operations. Though the AA report cited no open complaints, it noted that factory managers readily agreed to the dismissal of young workers, but then refused to replace them. In such cases, management was using the workplace exchange system as an opportunity to get rid of excess labor. Both workers and employers seeking to circumvent the job exchange directive received support from the DAF, which refused to cooperate in enforcing the edict. This refusal may have reflected the organization's concern for the welfare of younger workers, but it more likely stemmed from the DAF's rivalry with the RfAA in the struggle for control of labor market policy. The DAF pointed to the job exchange directive as an example of what it considered to be the RfAA's antisocial labor market policies.[47]

According to Syrup, 130,000 workplaces were freed up through the workplace exchange program between October 1934 and October 1935.[48] The government itself did not want wholesale dismissals of young workers who would simply replace older workers on the unemployment rolls. Management was urged to consider its social obligations in deciding how many young workers to release; that is, the number released should be no more than agriculture, domestic service, the labor service, and the Landhilfe "actually needed."[49] The job exchange program did not get under way until the late autumn of 1934, when opportunities to place dismissed youths in regular agricultural employment, the Landhilfe, or the labor service were limited.[50]

Cost factors and logistical problems often conspired to prevent a matchup of supply and demand for young workers. LAA Ostpreußen reportedly needed 15,000 additional Land Helpers, and LAA Mitteldeutschland needed 5,000 additional Land Helpers. The president of LAA Rheinland estimated that he had available 27,600 unemployed young males and 5,000 unemployed young females suitable for agricultural work. But the large surplus of cheap, willing, youthful labor encouraged industrial employers to hire young workers and would continue to do so in the absence of a government order to stop the practice. Equally important, however, was the expense incurred by large cities that sought to place their young unemployed in agricultural work. Many cities refused to pay the required travel and support costs for young, locally supported welfare recipients who were sent to remote agricultural areas. RfAA officials urged the cities to bear these "not insignificant" costs, arguing that the pressing social problem of unemployed youth could not be ignored and that the effort would ultimately more than pay for itself as local welfare expenditures decreased.[51]

Though the proclaimed purpose of the workplace exchange program was to replace unmarried workers under age twenty-five with older married heads of families, it is clear that political goals as well as social goals dictated the manner in which the program was implemented. On the basis of information provided in a questionnaire administered to all unmarried male and female employees who had not reached age twenty-five by September 30, 1934, preferential treatment was to be given to early joiners of the SA, SS,

Stahlhelm, and NSDAP, and those who had held positions of leadership in the Nazi party and its affiliated organizations.

Young workers who had belonged to a "national organization" prior to January 30, 1933, would be the last to be dismissed. Some authorities argued that a young worker who was "a tested fighter in the national movement" should retain his job if the prospective replacement was an older man with family obligations whom the Nazis believed to be an "asocial element."[52]

Unemployed older heads of families stood the best chance of being selected as replacements under the job exchange system if they had joined the SA, SS, or Stahlhelm prior to January 30, 1933, or had held a Nazi party membership number below 300,000. These Nazi "Old Fighters" had received preferential treatment from the earliest days of Hitler's government. The RfAA's local offices had participated in special drives designed to reward Hitler's faithful with jobs, while the rest of the unemployed would have to await their turn for bread and work.[53] Although these drives were remarkably successful and certainly help to explain the precipitous decline in registered unemployment during the Hitler government's first eighteen months, their very success produced a reaction among industrial employers by May 1934. The campaigns to employ veteran Nazis had left many firms bloated with excess labor; they simply could not absorb additional workers without jeopardizing the profitability of the firms. Moreover, many of the Old Fighters given jobs in these special employment drives had either lost most of their skills in the course of long-term unemployment or never had the skills required for their new jobs. Under pressure from Nazi party activists, firms had hired many of these unproductive Old Fighters, only to lay them off later, claiming that there was insufficient work to keep them occupied. To protect themselves from pressure to hire more Nazi deadwood, firms eventually began requesting by name those individuals who were known to possess the skills and stamina required for the available jobs.[54] By the autumn of 1935, an economy now stimulated by increasing rearmament expenditures had absorbed most of the unemployed Old Fighters. Many had found jobs with Nazi party organizations or with the Reich, Land, and local governments.

Until 1935, the Hitler government initiated only piecemeal and sporadic efforts to control the labor market. The systematic and comprehensive regulation of the allocation of labor began with the introduction of the workbook (*Arbeitsbuch*) for workers and salaried employees under the law of February

26, 1935. The books were introduced in stages, beginning with the armaments and construction industries. Once the system was in place, employment could be secured only upon presentation of a workbook in proper order, listing vital information such as age, health, marital status, place of residence, training and education, skills, previous positions held, present position, and familiarity with agriculture. The employer held each worker's book, returning it to the employee when he or she left the job. Workers and employers were required to keep the books current by registering any changes in status as they occurred. Local AA registered all workbooks and copied information from each book into a card file. The AA card index thus provided authorities with a complete record of all persons in the labor force in any given area and of their availability for assignment and allocation to various trades and jobs. By 1936, "the workbook made the worker a complete tool of the authority." RfAA president Syrup also noted that the workbooks would play a large role "in the event we should be drawn into a warlike entanglement."[55]

It was expected that the distribution of workbooks, begun in June 1935, would be completed during the autumn of 1936. The task, in fact, was completed only in the spring of 1939.[56] As the Four Year Plan got under way in 1936, the resulting labor shortage made it attractive for employees to leave undesirable jobs for better-paying employment in armament-related industries. The RfAA countered this threat to its control over the movement of labor by giving employers the right to retain the workbook of any worker who, without justification, "prematurely" tried to terminate his employment and move to another job.[57]

Both the introduction of compulsory military service and compulsory labor service in 1935, and the acceleration of Hitler's rearmament program under the 1936 Four Year Plan, strained Germany's labor market to its limits. Shortages of labor, especially skilled labor, which had already affected certain critical industries in 1934, now became endemic. Armed with the instruments of control developed since 1934, the government and RfAA struggled to manage Germany's labor market and to provide adequate supplies of labor for industry, agriculture, and the military. These controls quickly proved inadequate, and the November/December 1936 and February 1937 decrees implementing the Four Year Plan contained many new restrictions on labor mobility.[58] To soften employers' resistance to state regulation of their labor force, Syrup explained the new 1936–37 labor market regulations as "not so much prohibitions as orders" designed to appeal to the individual employer's sense of duty and responsibility. On the other hand, Syrup counseled against an overly inflexible implementation of the latest labor market regulations, since that would give workers the impression that the AA were unfairly protecting the interests of the firms. A conscious attempt was made, argues Hachtmann, to keep the 1936–37 labor market regulations sufficiently elastic to preserve employers' freedom of action.[59]

As Hitler's drive to prepare Germany for war moved ahead at a feverish pace after 1936, the most draconian labor market measures could no longer assure enough workers to staff the armaments industries. Either by means of incentives or coercion, more people had to be brought into the active industrial labor force. In 1937, married women with marriage loans were permitted to reenter the labor force. In 1939, there were 14.8 million women in Germany's total active labor force, compared with 11.4 million in 1933. Men over age 65 were also encouraged to take jobs, an initiative that produced meager results. Only 21.2 percent of the employed in 1939 were males 65 years or older, well under the figure of 30.8 percent reached in 1925.[60] On the other hand, the government's attempts to shift labor from handicrafts to industrial production by tightening qualifications for master artisans seemed to bear fruit. Much of this decline, however, was registered by one-person firms that had been established as a desperate last resort during the economic crisis by unemployed persons who were not trained as handicraftsmen. Most of these people shifted willingly to industrial jobs once they became available during the recovery. Similar government attempts to "proletarianize" persons engaged in the retail trades failed to mobilize significant numbers of new workers for the industrial sector. Here, too, the government succeeded only in removing distortions to the national economy caused by the Great Depression.[61]

In the search for the manpower required to keep Hitler's armament industries running at peak capacity, the government did not overlook even the most "undesirable" elements. By 1938, attempts to draw back into the active labor force the trade union, social democratic, and communist workers who had been forced out in 1933 promised few rewards. Most of these people had been rehired by industry since 1934, without any incentive or pressure from the government. Persons previously classified as "asocial elements" were now actively recruited for jobs; a May 10, 1939, decree from the Reich justice ministry made it easier to transfer imprisoned criminals to the labor force. At the end of 1938, RfAA president Syrup authorized the expedited employment of all unemployed Jews capable of work.[62]

The "natural" flow of labor, guided by a minimal amount of coercion, seemed to benefit the politically favored armaments industries. Only when the development of the labor market threatened to slow the tempo of rearmament in 1938 did the Nazi state intervene with the most draconian measures. Construction of the West Wall would require a workforce of 400,000, far more than the free labor market steered by a few regulations could provide. To meet this demand for labor, the government decreed on June 22, 1938, that every German citizen could be ordered by the RfAA president to work for a limited period of time on a designated project. A decree of February 13, 1939, abolished limitations on compulsory labor service. Factories could be ordered to turn over entire sections of their staffs to the state for work on armament projects. A March 10, 1939, order subjected all workplace moves to approval by the responsible AA.[63]

After 1933, Hitler's government shifted its focus from work creation to control of the labor force and labor allocation. Compared with what followed in 1938 and 1939, government intervention in the labor market in the years 1933–1935 was "not very substantial." But before the Second World War had begun, Nazi authorities had completed the "open militarization of the conditions of labor." From the point of view of labor market policy, Hitler's invasion of Poland denoted merely the transition from an "as-if-it-were-war" situation to an actual war situation.[64]

10

The Nazi Economic Achievement: A Comparative Evaluation

Hitler's government and the Nazi party credited themselves with an economic miracle without questioning its veracity or probing too deeply into its origins. In 1977, the historian Timothy W. Mason described the sharp reduction in unemployment during 1933 and 1934 as a propaganda masterpiece and optical illusion achieved largely by statistical manipulation.[1] The wide discrepancy between the Nazi view of their own achievements in combatting unemployment and the verdict of some historians forty years later requires an explanation and evaluation. How successful was the "battle for work" between 1933 and 1936, and to what extent did the Hitler government's direct work creation programs contribute to that success?

Mason's interpretation implies that the Nazi leadership understood the "fraudulent" nature of its claims for reducing unemployment and merely sought political gain for themselves by misleading the public. Although this charge of chicanery and deception is entirely consistent with the "Big Lie" technique widely attributed to the Nazis, it must be verified by an examination of the basis for official claims for an economic miracle attributable to Hitler's policies. Did state and party leaders understand that they were simply churning out false propaganda for the masses, or did they sincerely believe that legitimate statistical evidence demonstrated a clear connection between Germany's economic recovery and Nazi initiatives under Hitler's leadership?

Because the Hitler government had no work creation policy until the enactment of the June 1 Reinhardt program, very little of the sharp decline in unemployment during the first three-quarters of 1933 could have resulted from Nazi policies and programs. Most of the improvement in the labor market during this period of 1933 must be attributed to other factors, including an incipient "natural" economic upswing, seasonal improvement, a modest impact from the Papen and Gereke programs, and any improvement in market psychology that may have accompanied Hitler's assumption of the chancellorship. Hitler's work creation programs were barely operational when RfAA president Syrup drew up a September 30, 1933, memorandum, "Concerning the Relief of the Labor Market in the Winter of 1933–34." With modifications and additions, Reich labor minister Seldte forwarded Syrup's report to leading Reich officials a month later under the title "The Status of the German Battle for Work."[2]

The purpose of the Syrup-Seldte status report was to evaluate what had been achieved so far in the campaign against unemployment and to clarify the measures needed over the winter to avoid a reversal of the progress already made. Trends in labor market statistics convinced Seldte that the fight against unemployment had produced "great results" during 1933. By mid-October 1933, the number of unemployed stood at 1,300,000 (25.2 percent) below the previous year's level and 630,000 below the level of October 1931.[3]

Seldte counted seasonal relief of the labor market and a temporary boom in the textile industry among the leading factors in Germany's labor market recovery to the October 1933 levels. "Decisive support" from measures of the Reich governments of Papen, Schleicher, and Hitler, argued Seldte, had contributed to the outcome. Seldte described the Reich government's direct work creation effort as "a concentrated attack on the frozen economy such as no central authority has ever undertaken before." He estimated that these public works projects had put a half-million unemployed workers back on the job. RfAA basic support funds for emergency relief projects provided work for another 700,000 (as of September 30, 1933) who, in the absence of such support, would most probably have found themselves unemployed. "Public labor market policy" was "an essential source for the increase in employment over the previous year."[4]

When he again reviewed the results of the battle for jobs in December 1934, Seldte still believed that state action through the Papen program, the Gereke *Sofortprogramm*, and the Reinhardt program had contributed "to a not insignificant degree" to Germany's economic revival. "If the desired result was to be achieved," he wrote, "it was necessary to expand the volume of additional public orders as far as it seemed possible from the point of view of financial policy, because an economy as large as the German could be broken loose from its petrification only by a very powerful impulse."[5]

Seldte argued that government measures had succeeded not simply because they were "correct" but because they had fostered "the creation of a public opinion for the conquest of unemployment." Public policy had transformed the apathetic resignation of the crisis years into the general conviction that every endeavor, every act of will, was worth the effort. The long-term unemployed renewed their efforts to find work, and employers were more willing to retain workers during periods of slack orders.[6] In short, the Hitler government's success in the battle for work represented more than a victory for technical labor market policy. It marked a triumph in psychological and spiritual reconstruction.

In the final analysis, Seldte attributed the recovery of the labor market in 1933 to the "Nazi revolution," the triumph of National Socialist principles, and the Nazi Führer's leadership qualities. This explanation could be used to support the argument that expensive public works programs were unnecessary. This was precisely the direction taken by Hitler's adviser on economic matters, Gottfried Feder. Upon learning in December 1933 that most of the funds earmarked for work creation since 1932 remained unspent, Feder drew the seemingly logical conclusion that "the improvement in the economy was attributable not to the impact of work creation programs, but to the reestablishing of trust in the political leadership of the Reich." What the country needed was not more work creation projects in 1934, but rather increases in purchasing power and the private sector's investment capacity, to be achieved by means of lower taxes, lower interest rates, and reduced contributions to unemployment insurance.[7]

Most of the individuals and institutions responsible for German economic policy attributed some portion of the 1933–1934 recovery to measures of the government, but they consistently avoided any estimation of the size of that portion.[8] One of the few specific estimates of the importance of government activities in the 1933 recovery came from Reich economics minister Kurt Schmitt, formerly a leading figure in Germany's insurance industry. Schmitt estimated that up to a third of the improvement during 1933 resulted from public measures. More important had been a real, broad-based improvement originating in the economy itself. This modest estimate of the portion of the recovery attributable to government programs reflected Schmitt's background in the private sector and his conviction that "artificial work creation" alone could not eradicate unemployment. Schmitt seems to have subscribed to the "initial spark" theory of economic recovery, whereby government action merely touches off a natural upswing. "One cannot wait until a natural healing [of the economy] comes spontaneously," asserted Schmitt. The entire economy had to be "taken hold of, resuscitated, and set into motion, so that the result was a natural upswing and a natural upward development."[9]

Few Nazis would have conceded that two-thirds of the 1933 recovery had been produced by a spontaneous cyclical upswing. Such a conclusion would have been unthinkable to Fritz Reinhardt, the Reich finance ministry state secretary whose name was attached to the Hitler government's direct work creation program. In June 1934, Reinhardt, whose Nazi credentials were impeccable, gave a progress report on the battle for work. He claimed that "within a year we have succeeded in eliminating half of the unemployment" and asserted that unemployment would be eliminated entirely within two years at most.[10] Given the date of his speech, "within a year" meant that the war against unemployment had begun only with the June 1, 1933, Reinhardt program. Reinhardt ignored the significant reduction in unemployment between January and June 1933, implying that the Papen program and the Gereke *Sofortprogramm* had contributed nothing to the astonishing decline in unemployment during the previous eighteen months. How did Reinhardt explain such miraculous results up to June 1934, and on what basis did he predict a miracle of equivalent proportions during the coming year?

Reinhardt's analysis rested on the assumption that politics drives economics. "The reduction of unemployment," he asserted, "can be attributed primarily to the replacement of the party-state by the Adolf Hitler–state."[11] National consolidation behind a strong, focused program capable of dealing with a catastrophic situation was possible only in the Führer-state led by Adolf Hitler. The Nazi Führer's vision, will, and capacity to lead was the key to Germany's economic recovery. Most of the economic recovery measures that were enumerated and discussed by Reinhardt seem remarkably tame and traditional for a movement that claimed to have revolutionized politics and transvalued values. He merely mentioned the *Autobahnen* construction program in a list of other measures being taken to combat unemployment, most of which were tax breaks designed to stimulate consumption. Reinhardt spoke about the public works program that bore his name, but he spoke at greatest length about RfAA basic assistance for emergency relief projects, which had nothing to do with "Nazi" policy, and the marriage loan program, which only indirectly created new jobs. According to Reinhardt, the marriage loan program revolutionized the function of women in German society and played a central role in Germany's economic recovery.

Reinhardt predicted that government programs would reduce registered unemployment by one million during the following six months and put the remaining unemployed back to work within a year. Of this reduction, at least 300,000 would come from additional emergency relief employment supported by RfAA basic assistance grants, and another 300,000 from a sharp increase in Landhilfe enrollment.[12] Labor market developments fell far short of Reinhardt's expectations. Registered unemployment had declined by nearly 2.4 million between June 1933 and June 1934. It fell by another 254,200 during the next three months before beginning to rise again. After January 1935, the decline in unemployment resumed, but there were still nearly 1.9 million unemployed at the end of June 1935.

Where had Reinhardt's predictions gone wrong? Reinhardt's projected increases in the number of RfAA-supported emergency relief workers and Land Helpers never materialized. The number of emergency relief workers had already peaked in March 1934 at 630,163. By June the number had fallen to 392,433 and continued to decline to a 1934 low of 292,000 in August. Efforts to pump up the labor market for the winter of 1934–35 brought the number of emergency relief workers back up to 354,000 in December 1934, still fewer than the level of June 1934. Moreover, the number of Land Helpers, limited by financial constraints imposed by the Reich finance minister, had already peaked at 163,000 in April 1934. Between June and December 1934, the number enrolled in the program declined from 140,000 to 66,000.

Why did Reinhardt publicly project significant increases in the numbers of emergency relief workers and Land Helpers, when he certainly must have known that the Reich government had already decided in December 1933 that existing work creation programs would be allowed to play themselves out in 1934, and that the RfAA had been directed to cut its funding for basic assistance grants in 1934? RfAA president Syrup had warned Reinhardt that the number of emergency relief workers had to be reduced by a third and that "interference with ongoing [work creation] measures is unavoidable."[13] It cannot be assumed that Reinhardt knew in June 1934 that Germany's economy was to be placed on a fast track to war. Even if he did understand that rearmament and military conscription would put the remaining unemployed back to work, he could not have publicly stated this probability in June 1934. Perhaps that is why Reinhardt spoke of hundreds of thousands of additional emergency relief workers and Land Helpers who would most certainly never materialize. In any case, the transition to a rearmament economy came too late to fulfill Reinhardt's prediction that unemployment would be eradicated by June 1935.

In April 1935, Reich interior minister Frick ordered a halt to all work creation expenditures by cities and towns whose fiscal year 1935 budget would not be balanced. Frick's order signified the virtual prohibition of local work creation spending. The Nazi war against unemployment had not yet been won, as two-and-a-quarter-million Germans remained out of work. But Germany's forthcoming rearmament effort, announced in March, would require the mobilization of a significant portion of the nation's financial resources. Local governments could not be allowed to spend precious financial resources on work creation just as rearmament was about to soak up the remaining unemployed labor.

Frick's decree probably had little practical impact on the availability of Reich work creation programs to cities and towns. By the spring of 1935, meaningful Reich assistance for work creation was no longer available to most cities; and by the end of 1935, the German economy had absorbed virtually all of the economic stimulus generated by the work creation programs of 1932 and 1933. This stimulus does not appear to have set Germany's economy on a path of self-sustained natural growth. At 2,507,955 on December 31, 1935, registered unemployment was only 96,745 less than the level of December 1934. Even more disturbing was the fact that unemployment increased by 26.4 percent between November and December 1935, whereas the seasonal increase between November and December 1934 had been only 10.7 percent.

The other side of the coin offered no comfort, either. Employment, which had slipped by 3.9 percent in the November–December period in 1934, fell by 5.5 percent in the corresponding months of 1935. But the new year 1936 brought a miraculous statistical turnabout. Registered unemployment rose by only .5 percent, and employment rose by .5 percent in January 1936, compared with a 14 percent increase in unemployment and a 3 percent decline in employment a year earlier. Were the forces of rearmament and economic preparation for war taking hold of the German economy?

Japan's military attaché in Berlin, General Hiroshi Oshima, reported at the end of 1935 that the focal point of the German government's economic policy had shifted from work creation to the creation of a new German military force and the construction of *Autobahnen*. "Today," wrote Oshima, "the national policy goal of arming the German people dominates a large portion of [Germany's] economic life."[14] General Oshima ventured no opinion on whether Germany's economic recovery would have been sustained without this rapid transition to a rearmament economy, but he did note one troubling aspect of Germany's recovery. After rapid increases during the first months of 1935, industrial production had not risen further since May. The number of employed, on the other hand, had continued to increase until August. On balance, Oshima considered Germany's economy to be strong.

The failure of industrial production to rise above its May 1935 level for the remainder of the year, however, signaled that Germany's economic recovery was not yet complete. Work creation was winding down, but the rearmament program was not yet taking up all of the slack. The introduction of compulsory labor service and compulsory military service may have contributed to the reduction of unemployment without a corresponding increase in output.

Moreover, Germany's need to import foodstuffs and raw materials could not be met with the limited amount of foreign exchange available to German importers. Schacht's attempts to limit imports of foodstuffs and raw materials in 1935 failed to restrain either the demands of Reich food and agricultural minister Darré for additional imports of fats, or of Göring's insistence on additional resources for the expansion of the military air force. Germany's economy was heading toward an impasse, but, in June and July 1935, many of the nation's economic leaders expressed optimism for Germany's future.

The Reichsbank, which had risked its integrity by providing discount facilities for work creation bills, seemed pleased in July 1935 with the results produced by Reich government economic policy since January 30, 1933. For Reichsbank director Dr. Franz Döring, the real economic miracle was the noninflationary economic recovery that had resurrected Germany's capital market, healing wounds inflicted by the 1931 banking collapse. It was a sure sign of recovery when, at the beginning of 1935, the Reich government was able to issue a RM 10 billion conversion loan at 4.5 percent. Döring conceded that effective work creation programs had contributed to this result.[15]

There was no sign of inflation; currency in circulation had increased only slightly from the level of May 1933; Reichsbank lending had increased only to the extent that it was necessary to accommodate the modest increase in currency in circulation and to compensate for the loss of gold and foreign exchange and the accumulation of blocked foreign accounts; and the redemption of work creation bills would pose no problems. Germany's economic recovery had boosted Reich tax and tariff revenues from RM 6.65 billion in 1932–33 to RM 8.22 billion in 1934–35.[16]

Döring seems to have believed that Hitler's government planned to halt massive expenditures on work creation and make a seamless transition to a self-sustaining market economy. "A repetition of work creation programs on the scale of 1933–34," he wrote, "is not planned and not necessary. The German economy has found its way back to its own sources of strength."[17] Germany's own capital markets, Döring believed, could once again provide adequate resources for the private investment required to retain and expand on the gains made in the battle against unemployment. He was betting that Germany's economic recovery had reached the point at which self-sustained "natural" growth could replace a steady diet of public work creation programs, without fear of a relapse into higher rates of unemployment. Had the rearmament program not shifted into high gear at the end of 1935, Döring might well have lost his wager.

If Germany's economy remained incapable of self-sustained growth after two-and-a-half years of stimulus from direct and indirect work creation measures, was national socialist economic policy flawed? Not necessarily. The alleged achievements of Nazi economic policy during the first three years of Hitler's rule need to be evaluated within the context of the experience of other advanced industrial nations. Württemberg's economics minister boasted that, compared with more advantaged industrial countries possessing "great riches and inexhaustible sources of raw materials," Germany's record of economic recovery was enviable. In the course of two years, Germany had put over 60 percent of its unemployed back to work. During the same time span, England reduced unemployment by only a little more than 15 percent, from 2.7 million to 2.3 million. In the United States, "despite even the strongest credit expansion and the extraordinarily energetic use of state funds," unemployment barely declined from 11.9 million in March 1934 to 11.7 million in March 1935.[18]

Germany's economic recovery during 1933, 1934, and 1935 appeared statistically much stronger than that of Britain and of the United States, and suggested that Germany under Hitler's leadership was doing something different. If that was the case, then in what respects did economic recovery policies and programs in Germany differ from those in Britain and the

United States? Did the Germans simply throw much larger sums of public funds at the problem of unemployment, or did they finance work creation expenditures in a more "expansionary" manner?

British and American fiscal and monetary policy during the 1930s can best be described as traditional, conservative, even timid. Both the British Treasury and the American President Franklin D. Roosevelt were devoted to the balanced budget, even if they did not always achieve such a balance in practice. Hoping to retain the confidence of the financial and industrial community both at home and abroad, British authorities refused to breach the dikes of orthodox finance. Relatively high levels of British government expenditure in 1931 and 1932 represented increased outlays on relief and other transfer payments rather than the capital investment that might have helped Britain out of the crisis.[19] The substantial budget surplus of fiscal year 1933–34 resulted, in large measure, from sharp reductions in government expenditure well beyond the government's savings on unemployment relief. The British government's "inherently deflationary" fiscal policy during 1931–32 justifies the conclusion that "the direct contribution of fiscal policy to [British] recovery was extremely limited."[20]

Reducing expenditures and increasing taxation would seem to be counterproductive in the midst of a depression, but contemporary sources indicate that balancing the 1931–32 budget in this fashion boosted the confidence of businesspeople and investors and provided a "psychological stimulus" to the economy. Whether such a psychological boost was sufficient to overcome the deflationary policies of the government is not statistically verifiable. Neither Richardson nor others explain how domestic policies in Britain (balancing the budget) and Germany (smashing organized labor, an alleged confidence-builder for Hitler's government) could have overcome deep investor pessimism induced by chaotic financial conditions abroad and the depressed state of international trade. In any case, the British government persisted in its balanced-budget policy long after the restoration of confidence had been achieved.[21] And yet, there was a recovery. How complete was that recovery, and how did it develop in the absence of a supportive fiscal policy?

The lower turning point in Britain's depression came in August or September 1932. The year 1933 witnessed a vigorous recovery. The recovery continued in 1934, but at a slower pace. An increase in international trade and international investment counterbalanced a portion of the 1934 slowdown in domestic demand. When domestic demand recovered in 1935, it was accompanied by an upswing in Britain's foreign trade. The traditional explanation for the turning point in late 1932 and the subsequent upswing, stresses Britain's departure from the gold standard in September 1931, a move that opened the way for the depreciation of the pound and an expansionist monetary policy.[22] A plentiful supply of cheap money facilitated a construction boom in housing and stimulated consumption spending. Thus, devaluation and cheap money were the keys to Britain's recovery.

Devaluation produced a significant short-term competitive advantage for British exports in 1932, but it provided only "a small competitive boost" for the longer period 1932–1937. Devaluation and tariffs significantly increased the competitiveness of British manufactures with imports but had relatively little effect on export competitiveness. Britain's share of world trade continued to fall in the 1930s, but at a slower rate. The current balance showed an average deficit of £37 million between 1932 and 1938, compared with an average surplus of £22 million between 1925 and 1929.[23]

The primary benefit to Britain from leaving the gold standard was the government's freedom to pursue an expansionary, cheap money policy after 1932. Bank rate declined from 6 percent in February 1932 to 2 percent by June, where it remained until the beginning of World War II. Long-term rates declined as well, helping to balance the budget by enabling the government to convert the 5 percent War Loan to 3.5 percent in the summer of 1932. Housing construction benefited most from lower interest rates. Mortgage rates declined, the average length of mortgages increased, the portion of the total purchase price covered by mortgages increased, and the cost of working capital to builders fell. These changes pushed down the weekly cost of purchasing a house by 5.2 percent in 1932 and another 7.5 percent in 1933.[24]

Aside from its "cheap money" policy, the government played no role in the housing boom. Virtually all of the increment in home building during the 1930s represented unsubsidized private construction that was financed by the building societies. While housing accounted for only 3 percent of gross domestic product, it accounted for 17 percent of the change in gross domestic product between 1932 and 1934. Building accounted for only 7.5 percent of total employment but accounted for up to 30 percent of the increase in employment between 1932 and 1935.[25]

If private construction fueled the housing boom, was Britain's recovery largely "natural" and spontaneous? Could the recovery beginning late in 1932 be attributed to the "normal recuperative powers of a market economy"? Factors that might explain a spontaneous recovery seem inapplicable in the British case. Declining interest rates, a key factor in the recovery, resulted from a conscious policy decision. There was nothing natural or spontaneous about the government's decision to abandon the gold standard. Declining real wages might have made it more attractive to hire more labor, but average wages in manufacturing deflated by retail prices steadily increased from 1924 to 1935, and did not decline until 1936. Although Britain's economy may have been "catching up," closing a large technological gap that had developed between 1899 and 1929, it is not apparent why such a gap should have started to close in 1932. An autonomous structural shift toward modern new industries such as motor cars, precision instruments, dyestuffs, synthetic chemicals, and consumer durables could have sparked a spontaneous recovery. But the new industries accounted for less than 20 percent of all manufacturing output in 1935, and traditional industries accounted for most of the acceleration of growth in the 1930s.[26]

On balance, it seems reasonable to conclude that in the British recovery, the role of government policy was greater than that of spontaneous forces. Some supply conditions were indeed favorable to growth—there was a potential available to be tapped. But policy decisions, such as getting off gold, devaluation, protection, and the shift to a "cheap money" policy, transformed potential into the reality of a five-year recovery at an average growth rate of 4 percent a year.[27] Had British fiscal policy been less stringent, the recovery might have been more robust than it was.

Direct work creation through public works expenditure played virtually no role in Britain's economic recovery. Planned public works expenditures between 1920 and 1932 were in fact curtailed. Schemes that were supported by the Unemployment Grants Committee (UGC) provided minuscule amounts of employment for the large army of unemployed. Direct employment on UGC-financed projects peaked at 59,000 in March 1931. After the UGC was dissolved in 1932, work continued on projects that were already approved, but direct employment on these projects fell from 23,975 in 1932 to only 6,779 in 1934. Separate road programs employed no more than 16,000 in fiscal year 1931, and only about 2,000 in 1934–1935. In other words, the British government had no labor market policy at all. Unlike Germany's recovery, the most notable feature of which was a sharp and rapid decline in statistical unemployment, Britain's economic "recovery" seems to have bypassed most of the unemployed. Between 1932 and 1935, unemployment fell by only 28 percent, far short of Germany's achievement.[28]

Could a massive public works program have induced a labor market recovery comparable to that of Germany? Counterfactual speculation produces inconclusive results. In 1929, the Liberal leader David Lloyd George proposed a £250 million emergency public works program of road and bridge construction, housing development, land drainage, and expanded telephone and electricity services. Some economists at the time, including J. M. Keynes, supported such a loan-financed program. The Treasury refused to consider it, arguing that it would destroy Britain's finances without improving the labor market picture in any substantial way.

Within the past twenty years, analysts have employed econometric models in an effort to declare a winner in the debate between Keynes and the Treasury. These models predict that a very large deficit-financed public works program either would have reduced unemployment substantially with little or no adverse effect on Britain's capital markets, or would have totally undermined confidence in British finance and touched off a catastrophic flight of capital, without alleviating unemployment to any appreciable degree. Middleton has suggested that a large loan-financed public works program would have required a Nazi-style controlled economy, an option that was "inconceivable" in Britain. Glynn and Howells have estimated that it would have required a £537 million public works program to mop up the unemployed in 1932. Such a sum, they argue, lay in the realm of "political and economic fantasy." But the gradual transition to a war economy after 1936 suggests that a more vigorous program of reflation might have been possible without placing too much of a strain on the system.[29]

Britain experienced a "recovery" of sorts, but in the absence of a large public works program, there were still over two million unemployed in 1938. This defect in Britain's recovery may help to confirm that Germany's "spontaneous recovery" was immeasurably assisted by public works expenditure financed by the Reichsbank. It may still be argued, however, that the British and German situations are not comparable. During the peak year 1932, the rate of unemployment among insured British workers was 22.1 percent, and 17 percent among all workers. These rates are far below those experienced by German workers. Moreover, because British unemployment rates had hovered above 10 percent prior to 1929, the "collapse" from 1929 to 1932 was not nearly so catastrophic as it was in Germany. Alan Booth has argued that the slump "neither devastated the British economy nor upset the balance of interest-group power."[30] He uses this argument to explain why the British government did not offer and the British public did not demand a massive public works program. The same argument might explain why the recovery of Britain's labor market was less spectacular than that of Germany. If the collapse of the labor market was less catastrophic, then one could expect its recovery to pre-1929 levels to be less spectacular. The first six years of President Franklin D. Roosevelt's New Deal offered a sharp contrast to both Germany's economic miracle and Britain's more modest recovery. The unemployment rate, which peaked in 1933 at 24.9 percent, remained high at 17 percent when Roosevelt was reelected in 1936, fell to 14.3 percent in 1937, and climbed back to 19 percent during the recession of 1938. Roosevelt's continued electoral success casts doubt on the assumption that Hitler's government would not have survived had it failed to eradicate statistical unemployment quickly. As Peter Fearon has observed, "the curiosity of the New Deal is that so much political benefit was derived from policies which, with the benefit of hindsight, can be criticized as ambiguous and counter-productive. . . Although an understandable economic disappointment, the New Deal was a successful political balancing act."[31]

In a recent comparative study of the Great Depression, John A. Garraty argued that both the Nazis and the New Dealers "reacted to the depression in similar ways, distinct from those of other industrial nations." Roosevelt's Civilian Conservation Corps had its counterpart in Germany's Labor Service. Roosevelt's industrial organization under the National Industrial Recovery Act reflected Hitler's organization of thirteen "estates" governing all branches of Germany's economy. Both Hitler and Roosevelt promoted rural resettlement programs. "Of the two," admitted Garraty, "the Nazis were the more successful in curing the economic ills of the 1930s. They reduced unemployment and stimulated industrial production faster." Garraty attributed the dissimilar results of similar programs to Germany's employment of deficit spending on a larger scale, and to the superiority of the Nazi system in mobilizing society, "both by force and by persuasion." Thus, the Nazis were able to launch "a huge public works program," while American work creation programs were "relatively smaller," but "nonetheless impressive."[32]

The use of such vague terms as "huge," "relatively smaller," and "impressive" to describe German and American public works programs is uninformative at best and misleading at worst. Germany spent between 1 and 2.5 percent of its gross national product on direct work creation measures between 1932 and 1935, an effort best described as "not a substantial stimulus."[33] The stimulus from the New Deal's "relatively smaller" direct work creation program must have been less impressive yet. Judged by the sheer magnitude of the direct work creation effort, neither program should have produced astonishing results. Although Garraty noted that American work creation programs at no time enrolled more than one-third of the unemployed, he overlooked the fact that Germany's programs were not remarkably better in this respect. At the peak during March and April 1934, approximately 37 percent of Germany's unemployed were working as emergency relief workers, "welfare workers," Land Helpers, and Labor Service recruits. Garraty's emphasis on the role of deficit spending for work creation is not supported by his observation that between 1933 and 1939, the German national debt nearly quadrupled, while the American rose by less than 50 percent. In the period 1936–1939, the German national debt exploded in response to a rearmament program that had nothing to do with "work creation."

During the Roosevelt administration, public works projects similar to those in Germany were carried out in the United States by the Public Works Administration (PWA) established under the National Industrial Recovery Act (NIRA) of June 1933, and by the Works Progress Administration (WPA) after 1935. The PWA had its own Housing Division, entrusted with the promotion of housing construction and slum clearance. The Federal Housing Administration (FHA) guaranteed mortgage loans and facilitated reduced interest rates for prospective homeowners. But none of these initiatives produced results comparable to those produced by similar programs in Germany, and the British government obtained better results without any direct intervention or funding by government agencies. Whereas "cheap money" for the private sector produced a "housing boom" in Britain, the PWA's Housing Division managed to get only 21,000 new housing units built and 10,000 slum dwellings cleared between 1933 and 1937, creating relatively few jobs in the process.[34]

Mutually contradictory New Deal policies may have reduced or slowed the potential for economic recovery. Between 1933 and 1935, National Industrial Recovery Act codes generated a 14 percent rate of inflation, which nullified the expansionary impact of a 14 percent increase in nominal money supply.[35] Roosevelt remained uncommitted to any large-scale work creation program financed by deficit spending. The New Deal hoped that direct emergency relief payments could keep the unemployed going until a natural recovery put them back to work. Private and local relief efforts, however, could not indefinitely support twelve million unemployed and their families.

In May 1933, the Roosevelt administration established the Federal Emergency Relief Administration (FERA), authorized to provide to the states outright grants for purposes of relief. The more than $3 billion in Federal funds granted to the states through FERA financed the major portion of all relief given to the unemployed and their families between May 1933 and December 1935, when FERA was ordered to liquidate its affairs.[36]

FERA was a relief agency, not a public works program. Title II of the 1933 National Industrial Recovery Act, however, appropriated $3.3 billion for the Public Works Administration. PWA projects were slow to leave the drawing board, as they became enmeshed in Interior Secretary Harold L. Ickes's "penchant for meticulous planning and zeal against the pork barrel."[37] Moreover, PWA contracts went to private firms, which were not obligated to hire from relief rolls. Thus, PWA public works projects offered little immediate relief to the nation's swelling direct relief rolls. With winter approaching, Roosevelt created the Civil Works Administration (CWA) by executive order on November 9, 1933, and shifted $400 million from the PWA budget to finance short-term, light construction projects that could be started up almost immediately. The CWA was a stopgap measure designed to create jobs until large-scale public works programs could take up the slack. The $400 million was supposed to provide jobs for 4 million workers within thirty days.[38]

By January 18, 1934, Roosevelt's CWA projects employed 4.2 million workers. Moreover, by paying PWA wage rates, CWA employment provided average wages nearly comparable to those of private industry, the only New Deal work relief program to do so. Considering the number of unemployed accommodated at relatively high wage rates, the CWA appears as a brilliant success when measured against Hitler's achievement in labor market policy. Had the momentum continued, historians might be analyzing the basis for Roosevelt's "economic miracle" as well as Hitler's. The CWA, however, was disbanded as quickly as it had been created. After January 18, 1934, working hours were reduced, wage rates were slashed, and construction crews were laid off. Except for residual activities, the CWA was out of business by the end of March. In a sense, success killed the CWA. The employment of over 4 million workers at relatively high wages quickly used up the agency's $400 million budget. Roosevelt refused to spend $200 million a month on public works employment when FERA could provide relief for only $60 million a month. The president acted under great pressure when he ordered the phaseout of the CWA by the end of spring 1934. Businesses complained that the CWA took potential work away from them. Agricultural interests, particularly in the South, complained that high CWA wage rates siphoned off their labor force. Social workers complained that engineers had taken over their traditional role as caretakers of the poor and disadvantaged.[39]

The Hitler government's commitment to long-term, large-scale expenditure on direct work creation was barely greater than that of the Roosevelt administration. In Germany's case, however, the recovery was kept alive by increasing spending on rearmament. In isolationist America, rearmament was not a politically viable economic option for Roosevelt. In April 1935, with recovery no more imminent than it had been when Roosevelt took office in 1933, the U.S. Congress approved a $4.8 billion public works program to be carried out by the Works Progress Administration (WPA). Between July 1935 and June 1941, expenditures on WPA projects totaled approximately $11.4 billion. Fiscal conservatives considered this an outrageous sum, but compared with the size of the American economy and the employment deficit that needed to be addressed, WPA expenditures were rather modest. In 1936, earnings of workers enrolled in WPA projects, the Civilian Conservation Corps, and the National Youth Administration combined amounted to only 2.6 percent of the national income.[40] At no time did the WPA employ more than one-third of the unemployed. An average of 2,060,000 persons received WPA employment monthly from 1936 through 1941, ranging from a low of 1,136,000 in 1941 to a peak of 2,717,000 in 1938. The mix of WPA projects closely resembled that of German work creation projects—construction and engineering projects; highway, road, and street construction and improvement; water supply, sewage disposal, and other public utility projects; and construction of public buildings.[41]

Six years of Roosevelt's New Deal and the expenditure of over $21 billion on various public relief and federal work programs left the United States in 1939 with nearly 9.5 million unemployed, 17.2 percent of the civilian labor force. The WPA could not conquer unemployment, because "a combination of Roosevelt's personal fiscal conservatism, a persistent optimism about imminent economic recovery, and congressional hostility to the WPA would always prevent adequate funding."[42] Roosevelt's battle for work required a larger long-term investment of financial resources. WPA funds were allocated to state offices on a month-by-month basis, making long-term project planning impossible, restricting the type of projects that could be undertaken, and preventing the completion of other projects. Perhaps the introduction of a truly massive public works program financed by deficit spending could have quickly brought America's labor market crisis under control. But few economists advocated such a program, and political support for expenditures on such a scale in peacetime was lacking.[43]

The economic situation that Hitler and the Nazis faced in Germany on January 30, 1933, was probably more catastrophic than the calamity faced by Roosevelt. Yet, with rather modest work creation programs financed by relatively modest deficit spending, Germany managed to put a very substantial portion of its unemployed back to work before rearmament took hold of the economy. Roosevelt's failure and Hitler's success cannot be explained by different levels of tolerance for reckless deficit spending on huge public works programs, because neither leader spent recklessly on public works. Perhaps the psychological and political climate created by the economic policies of each of these leaders contributed as much to the different outcomes as did the economic policies themselves.

It is widely agreed that Hitler's political and economic policies helped to revive a feeling of confidence among Germany's businesspeople and bankers. Roosevelt failed to inspire such confidence among American business and financial leaders, because his policies were perceived as inimical to the free enterprise system. Some of the interests that Roosevelt sought to regulate during the 1930s accused him of conducting a "war against business," charges that some historians continue to accept uncritically today. The government's alleged prolabor policy is supposed to have destroyed businesses, shattered business confidence, and dashed any opportunity for recovery that might have arisen. Roosevelt and his cohorts, according to this view, were not even interested in promoting economic recovery. They sought to smash big business and "carry out their own agendas for radical change of the economic system even at the expense of delaying recovery." Recovery finally came after 1940 not because massive government spending during the Second World War produced a "Keynesian" revival, but because Roosevelt finally "repudiated the early policies of his administration," abandoned his "war against business," and cooperated with business in fighting and winning a multifront war.[44]

Inadequate as such analysis may be, the issue of business "confidence" continues to play a role in discussions of economic developments in Germany, Britain, and the United States during the 1930s. The British government's stringent fiscal policy and rejection of any sort of deficit-financed public works program supposedly strengthened business confidence and contributed to Britain's recovery. Once Hitler's government dismantled a "socialist" republic, smashed Germany's trade unions, eliminated some of the "social costs" that had allegedly made German business uncompetitive, and demonstrated that it planned no radical experiments with either the currency or the budget, it secured allegiance from Germany's business and financial leadership. On the other hand, Roosevelt was promoting a New Deal under which "Brain Trusters" would regulate business, trade unions would gain collective bargaining rights, and social costs would soar. Under these conditions, business "confidence" may have been greater in Britain and Germany than it was in the United States. This confidence is presumed to have induced businesspeople to invest in additional productive capacity and labor. Is this presumption warranted?

Businesspeople generally invest and employ additional labor because they have orders to fill, or at least the fairly certain prospect of orders. The difference between Germany's economic recovery under Hitler and America's relative stagnation under Roosevelt may lie in the relative probability of new orders for goods, especially heavy durable goods and producer goods. Roosevelt set out to raise both prices and consumer purchasing power, believing that such measures would revive both investment and the demand for goods. This indirect approach failed to ignite significant investment in durable goods and producer goods. Hitler, on the other hand, made it clear that in the near future, a major rearmament program would make heavy demands on the nation's durable goods and producer goods industries. There was no mystery as to where the demand would come from or whether it would be sustained over a period of time. With that assurance, German firms could reopen factories and recall workers with "confidence." Roosevelt had nothing similar to offer America's business community. America's isolationist posture, strongly supported by business and finance, ruled out any significant rearmament program. Thus, even though rearmament expenditures did not put Germany back to work between 1933 and the middle of 1935, the prospect of such expenditures certainly contributed to business "confidence" during that period.

Explanations of success and failure that focus on the economic policies of the Nazis and of the New Deal tend to overlook structural factors that may have influenced the rate of recovery in Germany and the United States. Especially important in this respect is the recent work of Michael A. Bernstein, who has argued that the depth and persistence of the slump in the United States resulted from a conjunction of a crisis in financial markets with a long-run transformation in the kinds of goods and services demanded by firms and households. The share of consumer spending devoted to traditional goods such as housing and standard clothing fell, while the share going to processed food products, tobacco, household appliances, medical care, recreation, and education rose. Important traditional industries such as textiles, iron and steel, and lumber experienced weakening markets, while "new" industries including appliances, chemicals, and processed foods found new opportunities for expansion. This shift in consumption patterns called for a realignment of investment patterns. The share of total investment increased for consumer nondurable goods, and for durable products such as appliances, automobiles, and communications equipment. Investment in such industries continued during the depression. Firms in the newer industries, argued Bernstein, were young and vigorous, but were not yet sufficiently strong or numerous to ensure recovery in the event of an economic crisis. Had the crash occurred at a time when the newer industries were more fully established, the crisis would have been shorter, business expectations would have been less depressed, and net investment would have increased at an earlier date.[45]

Armed with this theory of an incomplete structural transformation, Bernstein reexamined the role of the National Recovery Administration (NRA), which set the restrictive industrial codes that evoked much of the wrath of the business community against the New Deal. Shortcomings in these codes, argued Bernstein, did not result from the New Deal's economic ignorance or any willful attack on the free enterprise system. Because NRA code authorities were dominated by older firms within the older industries, there was an inherent bias toward helping slow-growth sectors, and little assistance for the new industries that could have led a recovery. NRA policies that restricted output and artificially supported prices hampered efforts of firms in newer industries, or new firms in older industries, to compete and penetrate the market. A constellation of powerful material interests "made effective government intervention problematic" during the 1930s.[46]

Bernstein's structural analysis of the absence of a real recovery of the American economy in the 1930s may be applicable to Germany's situation. In 1981, David Abraham argued that a split between modern, dynamic export-oriented, capital-intensive industries and traditional domestically oriented heavy industries (coal, iron, and steel producers) prevented Germany's industrial class from imposing its own conservative stamp on German politics during the last years of the Weimar republic. Fragmented material interests ruled out the solidification of an industrial bloc and may have contributed to the collapse of the Weimar republic.[47]

Abraham's argument fared badly with many reviewers, some arguing that Abraham's industrial "fractions" were imaginary (Turner, Feldman), others arguing that the divisions among branches of industry were even more complex than Abraham had imagined (Maier, Mason).[48] The divisions within Germany's industrial community during the late Weimar and the Nazi eras cannot be expressed as a simple dichotomy between dynamic new industries and stagnant old industries. Moreover, as dynamic as they were, Germany's new industries were not numerous enough or economically powerful enough either to determine political decisions or to lead Germany out of economic depression—"value-added economic dynamism could not ensure political clout."[49] There is a parallel here with Bernstein's thesis that America's dynamic new industries were too young and too weak to pull America out of the depression, and lacked the political clout to influence NRA policies.

It is quite possible that Hitler and Roosevelt faced similar structural configurations in the industrial sector in 1933. Much depended on how they responded to similar challenges. Bernstein has argued that NRA policies tended to assist traditional, slow-growth heavy industrial sectors. In Germany, too, Hitler's long-range political and strategic goals made some industries more important to him than others. Hitler's government provided special treatment and opportunities for some industrial sectors and some firms within sectors. This differentiation may have become more pronounced with Hitler's move to all-out rearmament and autarky in 1936, but some industrial sectors and firms were indulged by Hitler's government from the beginning. Were these favored industries or firms the type that could have led Germany out of the depression? Did they represent the new dynamic sector, or the traditional heavy industries?

Among the industries showing the most rapid recovery from 1933 to the end of 1935 were automobiles and aircraft. Investment and output in these industries rose at a rate higher than that of overall economic growth. Why did these industries in particular experience above-average recovery rates during the first two or three years of the Nazi era? How important were government policies in the recovery of these industries?

Harold James has argued that Germany's recovery had little to do with Nazi economic policy, which he has described as "rather unadventurous and conservative." He discounts the role of agricultural price supports, the "motorization" program, and public spending on building and construction in the recovery, and he doubts that the indisputable rise in automobile production and sales was a consequence of government policy. The growth of the automobile industry in the 1930s may have simply made up for a deficit in automobiles incurred during the 1920s, "although the catching-up process clearly benefitted from sympathetic government policy."[50]

James's explanation of the vitality of Germany's automobile industry during the 1930s contrasts sharply with Overy's insistence that Hitler's "motorization" policy played a critical role in Germany's economic recovery. Simon Reich's recent study of the German motor car industry indicates that Hitler's policy toward automakers in Germany was not uniformly supportive. On the basis of Reich's findings, Overy has written that "the economic nationalism of the regime brought special treatment and opportunities for German producers at the expense of the American multinationals, Opel and Ford."[51]

Reich's argument is in fact somewhat more complex than Overy implies. Reich agreed with Overy that "the Nazi regime was keen to rejuvenate the automobile industry, which it considered an economically and militarily strategic sector."[52] Because Opel accounted for half the output of Germany's auto industry, the government, argued Reich, needed Opel's cooperation in order to implement its "motorization" policy. Opel's size and market share made it a key player in Hitler's battle for jobs during the years 1933 through 1935. Employment in the automobile industry as a whole rose from an annual peak of 34,392 in 1932 to 51,036 in 1933, 80,858 in 1934, and 100,937 in 1935.[53]

It was not simply Opel's size that made the firm an attractive partner in Hitler's economic and strategic policies. Both Opel and Ford were "foreign" corporations in Germany in 1933. Its German name notwithstanding, Opel was in fact owned by General Motors, which had purchased 76 percent of the firm's stock from its German owners in 1929 for $28 million. Though both were foreign companies, Opel initially received preferential treatment from the Hitler government and held 42.8 percent of the German automobile market in 1935. Ford "fared much worse between 1930 and 1934 than its competitors," falling to ninth place among German producers, with a market share between 1.3 and 1.9 percent.[54]

If both firms represented "foreign capital," why did one fare so much better than the other under the Nazis? In contrast to Ford, Opel retained both its German name and German management. Its vehicles were "made in Germany." Opel's efficiency seemed to place the firm in the best position to produce and sell the Volkswagen for less than the RM 1,000 stipulated by Hitler. Perhaps most important, Opel's management made an especially strong effort to maintain cordial relations with the Nazi government and became "a willing and active military supplier to the German army throughout the 1930s and 1940s."[55]

Opel management's enthusiasm for the Nazi regime and eagerness to assist in Hitler's military buildup contributed significantly to that firm's economic success during the early years of the Nazi regime. Unlike Opel, the much smaller Daimler-Benz specialized in large, expensive sedans, an orientation that proved disastrous during the 1920s and early 1930s, when demand for such vehicles was modest. Although the firm's business judgment may not have been sound, the political instincts of the firm's management seem to have been well attuned to the trend in Germany. The firm's senior managers actively supported the Nazi party during the early 1930s. With Hitler's assumption of the chancellorship, Daimler-Benz participated in the formulation of state policy (arguing for the exclusion of Ford and Opel from the Volkswagen project) and became "an able and willing military producer."[56] The firm's supportive and cooperative attitude toward the Nazis paid large dividends. During the four years 1933–1936, outside investors, including the government, pumped RM 216.9 million into Daimler-Benz, whereas Opel received only RM 85 million from outside sources. Nearly 80 percent of Opel's investment came from ploughed-back profits, whereas outside investors provided over 61 percent of the investment in Daimler-Benz. Between 1933 and 1936, 42 percent of all funds provided by outside investors to six major auto manufacturing firms went to Daimler-Benz, while 16.5 percent went to Opel.[57]

The investment patterns and government-firm relationships revealed by Overy and Reich suggest that the boom in automobiles was not, as James argued, simply a catching-up process that benefited from sympathetic government policy. There seems to have been a clear government policy that directed investment to politically reliable firms willing to work toward Nazi objectives. James nevertheless concluded that in 1933 and 1934, Germany experienced "a relatively spontaneous cyclical recovery," characterized by increased consumption of consumer goods, especially automobiles. Until 1935, recovery took place within the framework of fiscal conservatism and orthodox policies developed by Hitler's predecessors. During 1935, public investment and rearmament took hold of the economy and turned the consumer goods boom into a dynamic upward swing led by producer goods industries.[58]

Interpretations of Germany's economic recovery can be placed in the context of recent historical treatments of Nazi Germany. Studies of the Nazi era have generally reflected two dominant schools: the "intentionalist" view that Hitler's ideas, translated into concrete policies and programs according to a "blueprint" for action, explain developments in Nazi Germany and much of Europe between 1933 and 1945; and the "structuralist" view, which downplays the role of Hitler's ideas and his will to implement those ideas, arguing that Hitler was merely one part of a power structure that included big business, the army, and the Nazi party as a whole. For the structuralist, the course of events reflected ad hoc solutions to immediate problems rather than the results of carefully planned initiatives.

As Peter Hayes has observed, the debate between intentionalists and structuralists has taken place without much reference to the German economy.[59] My own work on Nazi economic policy and work creation programs tends to fall into the "structuralist" category. James's argument for a relatively spontaneous cyclical recovery, though overstated, fits well with the structuralist interpretation of the Nazi era. It would be difficult to accommodate a spontaneous consumer boom into an intentionalist interpretation of Germany's economic development during the first two years of Hitler's regime.

Hayes himself has taken a more intentionalist approach to Germany's economic development after 1933. His study of IG Farben in the Nazi era, as one reviewer noted, "ultimately revolves around corporate mentalities and individual responsibilities."[60] The behavior of this corporation in Nazi Germany, argued Hayes, resulted from "the interaction of Hitler's will, the pressures of competition, the heritage of a single industry, the logic of professionalism, and the frailties of ordinary people."[61] Hayes has acknowledged that he is "taking issue somewhat with Harold James's depiction of the allegedly 'conventional' nature of the Nazi recovery." He insists that Hitler had a plan for restructuring the economy, that "the Nazi regime sought, from its outset, to engender a particular kind of economic revival, one that redistributed resources toward sectors vital to 'arms, autarky, and aggression.'" The plan worked, enabling the Nazi state to carry out "the most rapid recovery from the Depression among major industrial nations."[62]

Neither Hayes nor anyone else has been able to demonstrate conclusively a causal link between Nazi economic policies and Germany's unique recovery from the Depression. Hayes may well be justified in arguing that Hitler's policies steered the recovery in certain directions, but that argument is quite different from the claim that Hitler's policies were responsible for the recovery itself. Hayes's argument notwithstanding, then, James's case for a relatively spontaneous cyclical recovery driven by conservative, conventional policies, merits serious consideration. Nevertheless, after analysis of Germany's economic policy and labor market policy, there is still a missing piece in this puzzle. Perhaps one needs to go beyond this analysis to understand Germany's economic recovery and the role played in that recovery by Nazi work creation programs.

Although many of the economic tools utilized by the Nazis during the early years of the Third Reich represented no radical break with Weimar, the spirit in which they were used was certainly different. In her assessment of policies toward youth in the transition from Weimar to the Third Reich, Elizabeth Harvey has found both contrast and continuity. Mechanisms and policies developed in the Weimar period for dealing with young people were easily adaptable to Nazi purposes. But the means employed by the Nazis to implement their policies, "positive incentives combined with an uninhibited application of force," went far beyond the tools available to Weimar authorities. In the area of economic policy, one might note, incentives had already been tried by the Papen government, in the form of tax concessions for the employment of additional workers. The incentive did not work, and Harvey correctly observes that "with the installation of the Nazi regime, measures to organize the labour market, put the young unemployed to work, and discipline the work-shy were quickly made more comprehensive and more coercive."[63]

Nazi economic and labor-market policies may not have represented a sharp break with those of the last governments of the Weimar Republic, but the more comprehensive and often brutal implementation of those policies must have contributed significantly to Germany's singularly rapid and complete recovery from the Depression. Roosevelt, observed Bernstein, had to act in order to maintain domestic tranquility, "but the requirements for political stability (not to mention tranquility)—humane action, aggressive intervention—interfered with the requirements for economic recovery— taking steps to bolster business confidence, meeting the demands of the business community, and the like."[64] Hitler, too, had to act, but he had an advantage denied his American counterpart working within the framework of a constitutional system. In Nazi Germany, "humane action" was never a requirement for political stability or tranquillity.

Nazi work creation programs were implemented in a fragmented, decentralized fashion, with little coordination from Berlin. What those programs lost through inefficiency and lack of focus they recouped through coercion. Gauleiter Erich Koch's "concentration camp" system virtually eliminated unemployment in East Prussia during the summer of 1933. "Work-shy" unemployed from all parts of Germany could be sent to Dachau for "reeducation." Unemployed Nazi SA and SS men, whose loyalty to their Führer had earned them the right to something better than a "job" in a work camp or hard labor on the *Autobahnen,* could be given one of the hundreds of thousands of new positions created in national and local governments and the Nazi party administration. Under these conditions, it is not surprising that so many unemployed disappeared from the unemployment rolls so quickly.

R. J. Overy has argued that large-scale public investment and spending "lay at the centre of the recovery and must remain the primary explanation," and that "the first priority" was "work creation."[65] With some reservations and qualifications, Overy's judgment is reasonable, but it leaves unanswered the question of what portion of Germany's economic recovery from late 1932 to the end of 1935 was attributable to direct work creation programs. Relevant quantitative data, some of which appears in the appended statistical tables, does not provide a conclusive answer to this question.

Estimates of the employment effect of direct and indirect government support for sectors such as roads, cars, and housing between 1933 and the end of 1935 vary considerably. Many employment estimates supposedly demonstrating the impact of public spending either utilize comparative data from the 1920s, or compare 1932–1933 with the period after 1935. The years that need to be "explained," however, are 1933, 1934, and 1935, the years during which work creation expenditures might have stimulated the economy most. Overy has claimed that by the end of 1934, there were 210,000 directly working on the roads, and by 1936 there were 124,000 working on the *Autobahnen* alone. Todt's adviser on social policy, Dr. Carl Birkenholz, indicated in July 1934 that 143,000 persons were employed in "Straßenwesen." Hitler and deputy Führer Rudolf Hess claimed that about 400,000 persons were involved directly or indirectly in road construction at the end of 1934 and early 1935. Another 600,000, according to Hitler, were employed in the German automobile industry and its suppliers, in auto repair facilities, and in the construction of auto factories and garages. "Motorization" thus supposedly employed about 1 million Germans at the beginning of 1935.[66] These estimates represent selected dates, often peak periods, and exaggerate the number employed in road construction and repair and automobile production in any particular month. On monthly average, for example, only about 80,000 workers were employed in *Autobahnen* construction.

Estimates of the employment effect of spending on housing construction, remodeling, and repair are equally questionable. Overy estimated that activity in house building and repair produced a decline in registered unemployment among "building workers and labourers" from 914,425 (January 1933) to only 430,787 (October 1933). These statistics, however, refer to unemployment in *Baugewerbe,* a broad category including much beside housing construction and repair. In fact, most of the skilled and unskilled construction workers who found employment during 1933 found it in *Tiefbau,* large earthmoving projects, rather than in the housing sector. In many sectors, including metalworking, lumber, and construction, a significant portion of the 1933 decline in registered unemployment was accounted for by placement in agriculture, in the labor service, or on emergency relief projects unrelated to the workers' original profession.[67] Although the number of housing units produced annually rose, the trend of net gain in housing units was less than reassuring. The net gain in housing units in 1932, 1933, 1934, and 1935 was 141,265; 178,038; 283,995; and 238,045 respectively. The portion of this net gain achieved through reconstruction and remodeling of existing dwellings was 19.8 percent; 38.9 percent; 45.5 percent; and 20.9 percent. The portion of the net gain in housing attributable to public bodies and authorities was 8.7 percent, 9.8 percent, 13.6 percent, and 8.1 percent. The 1934 net gain in housing units fell considerably short of the 317,682 net gain in 1929.[68] These figures amply demonstrate the limited and ephemeral impact of the Reinhardt programs of June and September 1933.

In the absence of a reliable model of the German economy during the 1930s, estimates of the precise contribution of direct public work creation to Germany's economic recovery must remain largely speculative and conjectural. RfAA president Syrup and Reich labor minister Seldte, the two leading officials most directly responsible for and familiar with labor market developments, provided no such estimates. Reich economics minister Kurt Schmitt estimated that a third of the recovery during 1933 resulted from "public measures," including but not limited to direct work creation programs. Overy recently estimated that direct work creation accounted for 20 percent of the 2.8 million increase in employment during 1933–34.[69]

The recovery of Germany's labor market during 1933 and 1934 was not simply an optical illusion conjured up by statistical manipulation. It was real. Direct work creation measures sponsored by Hitler's government and its immediate predecessors reduced unemployment and raised employment well beyond levels that would have been attainable under a strictly spontaneous recovery. It seems reasonable to credit direct work creation measures with approximately 25 percent of the recovery.

Although historians cannot deny the contribution of Hitler's government and his Nazi party to Germany's economic recovery, they should not overestimate that contribution, either. Much of the initiative in creating work came from Reich officials who were not Nazis, and particularly from local and regional party and government leaders who could not and did not wait for orders from their Führer. Hitler performed no "economic miracle." Labor market statistics, housing statistics, and other indicators demonstrate that Germany's economic recovery had not become self-sustaining by 1935. Stagnation was threatening gains made during 1933 and 1934. The economic miracle was nothing more than a short-term, temporary boost to the economy, artificially joined to a modest spontaneous recovery by an infusion of public work creation funds that would not be repeated in 1934. In the absence of the transition to a "rearmament economy" during 1935 and preparation for war under the 1936 Four Year Plan, there would have been no talk of Hitler's "economic miracle."

Does the lack of a self-sustaining recovery by 1935 signify the failure of Hitler's economic policies? Overy doubts that Hitler seriously desired such a recovery. He argues that there was a difference between Nazi recovery policy and "liberal recovery policies such as those in Britain and the United States which were designed to stimulate the early stages of a recovery which would then become self-sustaining and reduce the need for state intervention."[70] This analysis does not explain Germany's economic development during the first years of the Nazi era. The early recovery policy of Hitler's government, between 1933 and 1935, was guided by an economic leadership committed to creating conditions favorable to a self-sustaining recovery. Schmitt, Krosigk, and Schacht expected deficit-financed public investment to produce a self-sustaining recovery that would then pay off the debt created by work creation programs. Their recovery program was quite similar to the "liberal" recovery policy employed in the United States, although quite different from Britain's "liberal" recovery policy, which lacked a direct work creation component. The unfortunate fact is that so-called "liberal" recovery policies failed to produce self-sustaining recoveries in either Germany or the United States. In the United States, respect for the American constitutional process, and an apparent reservoir of compassion and common decency among the public, combined to prevent the development of "illiberal" alternatives to the failed economic policies of Republican laissez-faire in the 1920s and Roosevelt's moderate government intervention during the 1930s. Germany's leadership, including those who had helped to implement moderate economic policies between 1933 and 1935, gambled that failed economic policies could be salvaged by resorting to rearmament, war, and plunder. They encountered surprisingly little resistance to such ideas.

Appendix

Notes

Sources

Index

Appendix

Table 1 Development of the German labor market, 1928–1938

Year and month	Employed	Percent change	Unemployed	Percent change	Percent unemployed
1928					
January	16,253,309		1,896,274		10.45
February	16,330,692	0.48	1,817,511	− 4.15	10.01
March	16,685,996	2.18	1,541,845	− 15.17	8.46
April	17,641,520	5.73	1,252,296	− 18.78	6.63
May	17,967,499	1.85	1,118,202	− 10.71	5.86
June	18,156,532	1.05	1,087,768	− 2.72	5.65
July	17,959,081	− 1.09	1,045,013	− 3.93	5.50
August	18,114,612	0.87	1,046,083	0.10	5.46
September	18,197,883	0.46	1,055,749	0.92	5.48
October	18,096,908	− 0.55	1,207,905	14.41	6.26
November	17,566,644	− 2.93	1,664,159	37.77	8.65
December	16,493,693	− 6.11	2,463,956	48.06	13.00
1929					
January	15,848,577	− 3.91	2,820,214	14.46	15.11
February	15,472,669	− 2.37	3,049,706	8.14	16.46
March	16,669,035	7.73	2,483,937	− 18.55	12.97
April	18,061,426	8.35	1,711,665	− 31.09	8.66
May	18,490,269	2.37	1,349,833	− 21.14	6.80
June	18,638,209	0.80	1,260,044	− 6.65	6.33
July	18,538,700	− 0.53	1,251,452	− 0.68	6.32
August	18,538,214	0.00	1,271,990	1.64	6.42
September	18,426,564	− 0.60	1,323,603	4.06	6.70
October	18,232,350	− 1.05	1,557,146	17.64	7.87

Table 1 (continued)

Year and month	Employed	Percent change	Unemployed	Percent change	Percent unemployed
November	17,713,701	−2.84	2,035,667	30.73	10.31
December	16,535,224	−6.65	2,850,849	40.04	14.71
1930					
January	16,159,052	−2.27	3,217,608	12.86	16.61
February	15,934,161	−1.39	3,365,811	4.61	17.44
March	16,292,750	2.25	3,040,797	−9.66	15.73
April	16,794,032	3.08	2,786,912	−8.35	14.23
May	17,119,940	1.94	2,634,718	−5.46	13.34
June	17,032,602	−0.51	2,640,681	0.23	13.42
July	16,842,552	−1.12	2,765,258	4.72	14.10
August	16,687,470	−0.92	2,882,531	4.24	14.73
September	16,540,443	−0.88	3,004,275	4.22	15.37
October	16,230,390	−1.87	3,252,082	8.25	16.69
November	15,692,687	−3.31	3,698,946	13.74	19.07
December	14,617,300	−6.85	4,383,843	18.52	23.07
1931					
January	13,969,776	−4.43	4,886,925	11.48	25.92
February	13,764,746	−1.47	4,971,843	1.74	26.54
March	14,092,463	2.38	4,743,931	−4.58	25.18
April	14,812,609	5.11	4,358,153	−8.13	22.73
May	15,197,016	2.60	4,052,950	−7.00	21.05
June	15,253,178	0.37	3,963,946	−2.20	20.63
July	15,019,923	−1.53	3,989,686	0.65	20.99
August	14,617,644	−2.68	4,214,765	5.64	22.38
September	14,369,597	−1.70	4,354,983	3.33	23.26
October	13,977,887	−2.73	4,623,480	6.17	24.86
November	13,433,460	−3.89	5,059,773	9.44	27.36
December	12,440,270	−7.39	5,668,187	12.02	31.30
1932					
January	12,084,599	−2.86	6,014,010	6.10	33.23
February	11,927,514	−1.30	6,128,429	1.90	33.94
March	11,974,364	0.39	6,034,100	−1.54	33.51
April	12,534,931	4.68	5,739,070	−4.89	31.41
May	12,743,882	1.67	5,582,620	−2.73	30.46
June	12,779,325	0.28	5,475,778	−1.91	30.00
July	12,755,994	−0.18	5,392,248	−1.53	29.71

Table 1 (continued)

Year and month	Employed	Percent change	Unemployed	Percent change	Percent unemployed
August	12,754,583	−0.01	5,223,810	−3.12	29.06
September	12,834,351	0.63	5,102,750	−2.32	28.45
October	12,914,536	0.62	5,109,173	0.13	28.35
November	12,698,673	−1.67	5,355,420	4.82	29.66
December	12,983,402	2.24	5,772,984	7.80	30.78
1933					
January	11,487,211	−11.52	6,013,612	4.17	34.36
February	11,532,788	0.40	6,000,958	−0.21	34.23
March	12,192,696	5.72	5,598,855	−6.70	31.47
April	12,697,620	4.14	5,331,252	−4.78	29.57
May	12,179,941	−4.08	5,038,640	−5.49	29.26
June	13,306,896	9.25	4,856,942	−3.61	26.74
July	13,435,581	0.97	4,463,841	−8.09	24.94
August	13,715,795	2.09	4,124,288	−7.61	23.12
September	13,920,977	1.50	3,849,222	−6.67	21.66
October	14,062,337	1.02	3,744,860	−2.71	21.03
November	14,020,204	−0.30	3,714,646	−0.81	20.95
December	13,287,238	−5.23	4,059,055	9.27	23.40
1934					
January	13,517,998	1.74	3,772,792	−7.05	21.82
February	13,967,253	3.32	3,372,611	−10.61	19.45
March	14,686,865	5.15	2,798,324	−17.03	16.00
April	15,322,237	4.33	2,608,621	−6.78	14.55
May	15,560,487	1.55	2,528,960	−3.05	13.98
June	15,529,683	−0.20	2,480,826	−1.90	13.77
July	15,532,793	0.02	2,426,014	−2.21	13.51
August	15,558,981	0.17	2,397,562	−1.17	13.35
September	15,621,095	0.40	2,281,800	−4.83	12.75
October	15,636,436	0.10	2,267,657	−0.62	12.67
November	15,476,144	−1.03	2,352,662	3.75	13.20
December	14,873,276	−3.90	2,604,700	10.71	14.90
1935					
January	14,409,075	−3.12	2,973,544	14.16	17.11
February	14,687,969	1.94	2,764,152	−7.04	15.84
March	15,278,651	4.02	2,401,889	−13.11	13.58
April	15,929,961	4.26	2,233,255	−7.02	12.30

Table 1 (continued)

Year and month	Employed	Percent change	Unemployed	Percent change	Percent unemployed
May	16,385,896	2.86	2,019,293	−9.58	10.97
June	16,504,322	0.72	1,876,579	−7.07	10.21
July	16,640,207	0.82	1,754,117	−6.53	9.54
August	16,689,880	0.30	1,706,230	−2.73	9.27
September	16,634,227	−0.33	1,713,912	0.45	9.34
October	16,507,509	−0.76	1,828,721	6.70	9.97
November	16,496,708	−0.07	1,984,452	8.52	10.74
December	15,581,790	−5.55	2,507,955	26.38	13.86
1936					
January	15,672,053	0.58	2,520,499	0.50	13.85
February	15,647,824	−0.15	2,514,894	−0.22	13.85
March	16,415,690	4.91	1,937,120	−22.97	10.55
April	17,038,756	3.80	1,762,774	−9.00	9.38
May	17,520,183	2.83	1,491,235	−15.40	7.84
June	17,675,483	0.89	1,314,731	−11.84	6.92
July	17,838,872	0.92	1,169,860	−11.02	6.15
August	17,895,919	0.32	1,098,498	−6.10	5.78
September	17,886,222	−0.05	1,035,237	−5.76	5.47
October	17,785,115	−0.57	1,076,469	3.98	5.71
November	17,597,812	−1.05	1,197,140	11.21	6.37
December	16,954,844	−3.65	1,478,862	23.53	8.02
1937					
January	16,599,462	−2.10	1,853,460	25.33	10.04
February	17,014,107	2.50	1,610,947	−13.08	8.65
March	17,497,362	2.84	1,245,338	−22.70	6.64
April	18,447,732	5.43	960,764	−22.85	4.95
May	18,776,446	1.78	776,321	−19.20	3.97
June	18,941,252	0.88	648,421	−16.48	3.31
July	19,094,961	0.81	562,892	−13.19	2.86
August	19,150,927	0.29	509,257	−9.53	2.59
September	19,105,121	−0.24	469,053	−7.89	2.40
October	19,128,112	0.12	501,847	6.99	2.56
November	18,964,223	−0.86	572,621	14.10	2.93
December	18,109,163	−4.51	994,784	73.72	5.21
1938					
January	18,079,083	−0.17	1,051,745	5.73	5.50
February	18,228,359	0.83	946,334	−10.02	4.94

Table 1   (continued)

Year and month	Employed	Percent change	Unemployed	Percent change	Percent unemployed
March	18,831,301	3.31	507,649	−46.36	2.63
April	19,400,663	3.02	422,530	−16.77	2.13
May	19,857,312	2.35	338,355	−19.92	1.68
June	19,997,924	0.71	292,240	−13.63	1.44
July	20,169,727	0.86	218,328	−25.29	1.07
August	20,245,329	0.37	178,762	−18.12	0.88
September	20,243,179	−0.01	155,996	−12.74	0.76
October	20,238,540	−0.02	163,941	5.09	0.80
November	20,235,915	−0.01	152,430	−7.02	0.75
December	19,266,861	−4.79	455,656	198.93	2.31

Source: Statistische Beilage zum Reichsarbeitsblatt, 1928–1939. Percentage calculations made by author.

Table 2   Quasi-unemployed ("substitute" unemployed), 1933–34 (end of month, in thousands)

Month	Notstandsarbeiter	Fürsorgearbeiter	Landhelfer	Arbeitsdienst	Total
1933					
January	23	59		175	257
February	37	59		193	289
March	88	64		213	365
April	114	67	16	235	432
May	121	69	77	242	509
June	115	70	123	252	560
July	140	71	150	263	624
August	187	70	160	257	674
September	232	66	165	234	697
October	314	59	164	220	757
November	401	56	163	227	847
December	277	50	160	232	719
1934					
January	417	45	156	225	843
February	507	43	157	241	948
March	631	43	161	240	1,075
April	602	46	163	230	1,041
May	502	48	153	228	931
June	387	53	140	229	809

Table 2 (continued)

Month	Notstandsarbeiter	Fürsorgearbeiter	Landhelfer	Arbeitsdienst	Total
July	315	56	129	229	729
August	292	56	117	226	691
September	330	55	104	225	714
October	331	55	91	212	689
November	353	52	76	234	715
December	354	53	66	233	706

Source: Willi Hemmer, *Die "unsichtbaren" Arbeitslosen. Statistische Methoden—Soziale Tatsachen* (Zeulenroda, Germany: Bernhard Sporn, 1935), p. 189.

Table 3 Official, IfK, and "corrected" estimates of employment, October 1933–December 1934 (thousands)

Month	Official (1)	IfK "substitute" (2)[a]	"Corrected" (1) minus (2) (3)	IfK "regular" (4)	Discrepancy (4) minus (3) (5)
1933					
October	14,062	750	13,312	13,590	278
November	14,020	840	13,180	13,470	290
December	13,287	710	12,577	12,860	283
1934					
January	13,518	830	12,978	12,970	−008
February	13,976	920	13,056	13,330	274
March	14,687	1,050	13,637	13,920	283
April	15,322	1,050	14,242	14,570	328
May	15,560	930	14,630	14,910	280
June	15,530	800	14,730	15,010	280
July	15,533	730	14,803	15,090	287
August	15,559	700	14,859	15,150	291
September	15,621	640	14,981	15,260	279
October	15,636	600	15,036	15,300	264
November	15,476	630	14,846	15,140	294
December	14,873	610	14,263	14,540	277

Source: Beilage zum Wochenbericht des Instituts für Konjunkturforschung, January 30, April 30, 1935; *Statistische Beilage zum Reichsarbeitsblatt,* 1934, 1935. Official *Krankenkassen* statistics and IfK estimates include workers and salaried employees (*Arbeiter* and *Angestellten*).

a. Includes Arbeitsdienst, Landhelfer, Notstandsarbeiter, Fürsorgearbeiter.

Table 4 Development of the German labor market, 1933

Months[a]	Unemployed	Employed
January–February	− 12,654	+ 45,577
February–March	− 402,103	+ 659,908
March–April	− 267,603	+ 504,924
April–May	− 292,612	+ 482,321
May–June	− 181,698	+ 126,955
June–July	− 393,101	+ 128,685
July–August	− 339,553	+ 280,212
August–September	− 275,066	+ 205,182
September–October	− 104,362	+ 141,360
October–November	− 30,214	− 42,133
November–December	344,409	− 732,966

Source: Unemployment calculated from *Statistische Beilage zum Reichsarbeitsblatt,* 1934, Nr. 7, p. 18; employment calculated from "Siebenter Bericht der RfAA" (1934–35), issued as *Beilage zum Reichsarbeitsblatt,* 1935, Nr. 35, p. 15.
a. End of month to end of month.

Table 5 Projected burden of work creation programs on Reich treasury (million RM)

Program	1934	1935	1936	1937	1938
Papen program					
Bill redemption (incl. related costs)	190	55			
Gereke *Sofortprogramm*					
Bill redemption	53	137	137	137	137
Related costs	28	25	17	8	1
First Reinhardt program					
Bill redemption	28	243	243	243	243
Related costs	35	40	25	15	50
Second Reinhardt program					
Subsidies	475	—	—	—	—
Tax reimbursement	58	58	58	58	58
Total (Papen, Reinhardt 1 and 2)	867	558	480	461	444
Tax vouchers	312	324	336	348	360

Table 5 (continued)

Program	1934	1935	1936	1937	1938
Grand total (Papen and Reinhardt programs, tax vouchers)	1,179	882	816	809	804

Source: BAK, R2/18682, RFM, in-house report, May 23, 1934, "Die öffentliche Arbeitsbeschaffung u. ihre finanziellen Auswirkungen auf den Reichshaushalt. Beitrag zum 'Finanziellen überblick über den Reichshaushalt 1934.' " "Related costs" (*Nebenkosten*) included reimbursement to participating credit institutions for costs connected with implementation of the work creation programs.

Table 6 Work creation bills in circulation, 1934–1936 (million RM)

End of month	Bills in circulation	Percentage held at Reichsbank
March 1934	854	46
June 1934	1,048	50
September 1934	1,183	58
December 1934	1,276	52
March 1935	1,307	41
June 1935	1,206	34
September 1935	1,041	30
December 1935	1,022	16
March 1936	1,046	10
April 1936	1,008	7
June 1936	929	12
August 1936	825	13

Source: BAK, R2/18701, Reichsbank-Direktorium to Reich finance minister, October 7, 1936, with enclosed report, "Die Inanspruchnahme der Reichsbank aus den Arbeitsbeschaffungsprogrammen des Reiches."

Table 7   Reich government expenditures on work creation, 1932–33 through 1935–36 (million RM)

		Amount and portion of allocation paid out								Total for period	
	Allocated	1932–33	Percent	1933–34	Percent	1934–35	Percent	1935–36	Percent	Amount	Percent
Reich budget	1,085	20.7	1.9	203.0	18.7	462.9	42.6	125.0	11.5	812.0	74.8
RfAA		40.1		233.3		276.6		214.8		764.8	
Öffa	1,257	57.9	4.6	522.7	41.6	492.3	39.2	113.5	9.0	1,186.4	94.4
Dt. Bau- u. Boden-Bank	220			77.3	35.1	102.9	46.8	24.8	11.3	205.0	93.2
Dt. Rentenbank-Kreditanstalt	338	14.3	4.2	214.2	63.4	84.6	25.0	13.2	3.9	326.3	96.5
Dt. Siedlungsbank	53			10.2	19.2	25.8	48.7	16.7	31.5	52.7	99.4
Various credit institutions	20	5.0	25.0	12.0	60.0	3.0	15.0	—		20.0	100.0
Total		138.0		1,272.0		1,448.0		508.0		3,367.0	
Total w/o RfAA	2,973	98.0	3.3	1,039.0	35.0	1,172.0	39.4	293.0	9.9	2,602.0	87.5

Source: BAK, R2/18701, RFM, "Die Arbeitsbeschaffungsmaßnahmen der Reichsregierung 1932 bis 1935," Denkschrift prepared by Reichsbankrat Düll before transferring from RFM.

Table 8   The East Prussian labor market, 1933–34

Month	Unemployed	Percentage of Reich unemployed	Employed
1933			
January	129,520	2.2	365,414
February	131,073	2.2	362,243
March	124,564	2.2	368,456
April	98,037	1.9	399,787
May	81,970	1.6	433,783
June	75,508	1.6	444,318
July	28,703	0.6	464,429
August	2,672	0.1	500,336
September	2,848	0.1	499,718
October	6,600	0.2	495,823
November	14,781	0.4	471,057
December	37,474	0.9	450,561
1934			
January	38,783	1.0	452,433
February	37,668	1.1	456,738
March	22,537	0.8	463,765
April	15,115	0.6	488,161
May	16,629	0.7	506,348
June	13,559	0.5	514,278
July	9,309	0.4	517,759
August	10,912	0.4	515,355
September	8,106	0.4	510,401
October	14,542	0.6	497,946
November	14,641	0.6	474,473
December	31,223	1.2	451,595

Source: Statistische Beilage zum Reichsarbeitsblatt, 1934, no. 7, Tables XXVII, XXX; Statistische Beilage zum Reichsarbeitsblatt, 1935, no. 7, Tables XXXII, XXXVI; Siebenter Bericht der Reichsanstalt für Arbeitsvermittlung und Arbeitslosenversicherung für die Zeit vom 1. April 1934 bis zum 31. März 1935, issued as *Beilage zum Richsarbeitsblatt,* 1935, No. 35, p. 15, Übersicht 18, "Die Entwicklung der Zahl der beschäftigten Arbeiter und Angestellten in den Landesarbeitsamtsbezirken."

Table 9   East Prussian road construction and land improvement projects, 1931–1933

Road construction in East Prussia, 1932–1934

	Days of work	Cost of construction
1932–33	50,000	RM 0.8 million
1933–34	450,000	RM 4.0 million

Agricultural land improvement in East Prussia

	Area improved	
	(1,000 hectares)	Cost
1931	12.5	RM 7.5 million
1932	10.5	RM 5.3 million
1933	64.0	RM 25.4 million

Source: Nationalsozialistische Aufbauarbeit in Ostpreussen, pp. 21–23.

Table 10 Financing *Autobahnen* construction, 1934–1941 (million RM)

Year	Akzeptkredit (Reichsbank)	Reichsbahn loan	RfAA loan	Reichsversicher-ungsanstalt loan	Reichsgruppe "Versicherungen" loan	Reich finance minister loan	Sonstige Kredite[a]	Total
1934	248							248.0
1935	780							780.0
1936	450	400	150.0				279.4	1,279.4
1937	450	400	375.0	100	237.2	300.0	33.6	1,895.8
1938	450	400	625.0	100	237.2	902.0	33.6	2,747.8
1939	450	400	1,425.0	100	237.2	980.9	37.5	3,630.6
1940	450	400	1,901.5	100	237.2	921.1		4,009.8
1941	450	400	2,925.0	100	237.2	312.6		4,424.8

Source: BHStA, MA 106949, Geschäftsbericht der Gesellschaft "Reichsautobahnen" über das 2. Geschäftsjahr 1934, and for 1935, 1936, 1939, 1940, 1941. For 1933, see Reichsstatthalter 553. For 1937, see MWi 8682. Annual reports for 1933, 1934, and 1935 are also found in GHStA 90/1718.
a. Various credits, uncovered remainder of a Reich bridge loan.

Table 11   Employment on *Autobahnen* construction, 1934–1938 (monthly averages)

Month	1934	1935	1936	1937	1938
January	5,000[a]	35,421	67,305	43,989	51,530
February	8,000[a]	47,417	61,044	44,307	70,571
March	14,500[a]	72,295	92,994	66,781	95,306
April	23,000[a]	91,733	103,750	85,222	102,499
May	29,000[a]	106,963	114,174	92,198	107,796
June	38,000[a]	111,592	121,668	93,869	114,633
July	46,000[a]	113,139	121,104	95,588	111,284
August	58,000[a]	110,772	112,483	98,042	107,140
September	68,000[a]	106,431	104,878	97,851	106,878
October	77,000[a]	96,749	93,286	94,655	107,802
November	83,863	94,074	86,616	92,327	107,534
December	80,294	66,953	69,941	76,107	91,086

Source: BHStA, MA 106949 and Reichstatthalter 553; GStAPK, 90/1718, Geschäftsberichte der Gesellschaft "Reichsautobahnen," 1933–1941.
a. Interpolated from graph in Geschäftsbericht for business year 1934, p. 35.

Table 12   Regional unemployment and percentage of total Reich unemployment by Landesarbeitsämter, 1933

Region	January	April	August	December
Ostpreussen	129,250	98,037	2,672	37,474
	2.2	1.9	0.1	0.9
Schlesien	487,649	406,277	313,348	322,632
	8.1	7.6	7.6	8.0
Brandenburg	891,855	794,438	667,489	643,275
	14.8	14.9	16.2	15.9
Pommern	141,079	104,896	51,602	50,324
	2.3	2.0	1.2	1.2
Nordmark	385,851	363,329	296,563	298,460
	6.4	6.8	7.2	7.4
Niedersachsen	357,941	308,779	212,967	255,162
	5.9	5.8	5.2	5.6
Westfalen	482,696	440,281	323,164	297,507
	8.0	8.3	7.8	7.3
Rheinland	737,021	705,329	600,225	546,981
	12.3	13.2	14.6	13.5
Hessen	332,532	300,164	248,201	225,386
	5.5	5.6	6.0	5.5
Mitteldeutschland	515,508	442,131	316,349	313,201
	8.6	8.3	7.7	7.7

Table 12 (continued)

Region	January	April	August	December
Sachsen	718,586	654,416	527,387	504,018
	12.0	12.3	12.8	12.4
Bayern (incl. Pfalz)	516,188	439,055	339,958	362,784
	8.6	8.2	8.2	8.9
S-W Deutschland	317,186	274,120	224,368	231,851
	5.3	5.1	5.4	5.7

Source: *Statistische Beilage zum Reichsarbeitsblatt,* 1934, no. 7, Table 27.

Table 13 Regional unemployment and percentage of total Reich unemployment by Landesarbeitsämter, 1934

Region	January	April	August	December
Ostpreussen	38,783	15,115	10,912	31,223
	1.0	0.6	0.4	1.2
Schlesien	314,237	190,314	194,203	242,823
	8.3	7.3	8.1	9.3
Brandenburg	617,010	455,392	354,666	342,110
	16.4	17.5	14.8	13.1
Pommern	44,760	22,636	26,951	35,466
	1.2	0.9	1.1	1.4
Nordmark	257,298	201,022	183,848	186,253
	6.8	7.7	7.7	7.1
Niedersachsen	190,987	115,557	107,131	119,434
	5.1	4.4	4.5	4.6
Westfalen	269,559	198,261	194,192	212,712
	7.1	7.6	8.1	8.2
Rheinland	509,577	412,272	384,079	404,250
	13.5	15.8	16.0	15.5
Hessen	211,755	151,845	148,782	155,893
	5.6	5.8	6.2	6.0
Mitteldeutschland	286,354	176,402	169,606	179,135
	7.6	6.7	7.1	6.9
Sachsen	474,546	336,485	320,342	354,863
	12.6	12.9	13.4	13.6
Bayern (incl. Pfalz)	347,635	208,359	187,236	222,632
	9.2	8.8	7.8	8.6
S-W Deutschland	210,291	124,961	115,614	117,906
	5.6	4.8	4.8	4.5

Source: *Statistische Beilage zum Reichsarbeitsblatt,* 1935, no. 7, Table 32.

Table 14   Unemployed by age group and sex, 1933–1935
(workers and salaried employees)

Age group	6/16/33 Number	6/16/33 Percent	6/15/34 Number	6/15/34 Percent	10/31/35 Number	10/31/35 Percent
Under 18	166,467	3.3	135,168	5.0	131,600	6.8
M	88,007	2.2	67,264	3.1	70,349	4.5
F	78,460	7.7	67,904	12.6	61,251	17.3
18 < 25	1,150,966	22.8	372,696	13.8	296,052	15.4
M	853,832	21.2	279,355	13.0	243,497	15.5
F	297,134	29.0	93,341	17.3	52,555	14.9
25 < 40	2,228,799	44.1	1,227,525	45.6	794,928	41.4
M	1,823,233	45.2	1,011,810	46.9	676,087	43.1
F	405,566	39.6	215,715	39.9	118,841	33.6
40 < 60	1,333,555	26.4	851,538	31.6	609,797	31.7
M	1,107,813	27.5	698,369	32.4	496,574	31.7
F	225,742	22.0	153,169	28.3	113,223	32.0
60 < 65	139,835	2.7	86,428	3.2	72,834	3.8
M	125,830	3.1	78,603	3.7	66,585	4.2
F	14,005	1.4	7,825	1.5	6,249	1.8
65 and older	35,980	0.7	22,840	0.8	16,616	0.9
M	32,856	0.8	20,473	0.9	15,338	1.0
F	3,124	0.3	2,367	0.4	1,278	0.4

Source: "Achter Bericht der Reichsanstalt für Arbeitsvermittlung und
Arbeitslosenversicherung" for period April 1, 1935–March 31, 1936, issued as *Beilage zur
Reichsarbeitsblatt,* 1936, no. 34, pp. 8–9.

Notes

Abbreviations

AA	Arbeitsamt (ämter); local labor office
Alu	Arbeitslosenunterstützung; Reich unemployment support
BAK	Bundesarchiv Koblenz
BAP	Bundesarchiv Potsdam
BHStA	Bayerisches Hauptstaatsarchiv
BDC	Berlin Document Center
DAF	Deutsche Arbeitsfront; German Labor Front
FAD	freiwilliger Arbeitsdienst; Voluntary Labor Service
GStAPK	Geheimes Staatsarchiv Preußischer Kulturbesitz, Berlin-Dahlem
HHStA	Hessisches Hauptstaatsarchiv, Wiesbaden
HStAS	Hauptstaatsarchiv Stuttgart
IfK	Institut für Konjunkturforschung; Economic Research Institute
Kru	Krisenunterstützung; Reich crisis support
LAA	Landesarbeitsamt (ämter); regional labor office
LRA	Landratsamt
N-WHStA	Nordrhein-Westfälisches Hauptstaatsarchiv, Düsseldorf
N-WStAD	Nordrhein-Westfälisches Staatsarchiv Detmold
N-WStAM	Nordrhein-Westfälisches Staatsarchiv Münster
NSDAP	Nationalsozialistische Deutsche Arbeiterpartei; National Socialist German Workers' Party
OBK	Oberste Bauleitung für den Bau der Kraftfahrbahn; regional *Autobahnen* construction office
Öffa	Deutsche Gesellschaft für öffentliche Arbeiten; German financial institution for public works
RAB	Reichsautobahnen corporation
RABl	*Reichsarbeitsblatt*
RAM	Reichsarbeitsminister (ium); Reich Labor Ministry

RfAA	Reichsanstalt für Arbeitsvermittlung und Arbeitslosenversicherung; Reich Institution for Placement and Unemployment Insurance
RFM	Reichsfinanzminister (ium); Reich Finance Ministry
RGBl	*Reichsgesetzblatt*
RM	Reichsmark
RWH	Reichswohlfahrtshilfe; Reich welfare assistance
RWM	Reichswirtschaftsminister (ium); Reich Economics Ministry
SA	Sturmabteilung; Nazi Stormtroopers
SS	Schutzstaffel
StAD	Stadtarchiv Duisburg
StadtAN	Stadtarchiv Nürnberg
StaDü	Stadtarchiv Düsseldorf
StAN	Staatsarchiv Nürnberg
StAS	Stadtarchiv Stuttgart
StAW	Staatsarchiv Würzburg
TdA	Treuhänder der Arbeit; labor trustees
WE	Wohlfahrtserwerbslose; welfare unemployed

Preface

1. Gerhard Kroll, *Von der Weltwirtschaftskrise zur Staatskonjunktur* (Berlin: Duncker & Humblot, 1958), p. 473.

2. BAP, 25.01, Bd. 2/6788, "Dr. Goebbels vor der ausländischen Presse am 28.2.34," Goebbels speech titled, "For World Peace."

3. Friedrich Forstmeier and Hans-Erich Volkmann, eds., *Wirtschaft und Rüstung am Vorabend des Zweiten Weltkrieges* (Düsseldorf: Droste Verlag, 1975); idem, *Kriegswirtschaft und Rüstung, 1939–1945* (Düsseldorf: Droste Verlag, 1977).

4. Jürgen Stelzner, *Arbeitsbeschaffung und Wiederaufrüstung, 1933–1936* (Tübingen: Tübingen University dissertation, 1976); Michael Wolffsohn, *Industrie und Handwerk im Konflikt mit Staatlicher Wirtschaft? Studien zur Politik der Arbeitsbeschaffung in Deutschland, 1930–1934* (Berlin: Duncker & Humblot, 1977); R. J. Overy, *The Nazi Economic Recovery, 1932–1938* (London: Macmillan, 1982; 2nd rev. ed. Cambridge: Cambridge University Press, 1996); Overy, *War and Economy in the Third Reich* (Oxford: Clarendon Press, 1994); Harold James, *The German Slump: Politics and Economics, 1924–1936* (Oxford: Clarendon Press, 1986), particularly Chapter 10, "A Nazi Recovery?"

5. Birgit Wulff, *Arbeitslosigkeit und Arbeitsbeschaffungsmaßnahmen in Hamburg, 1933–1939* (Frankfurt/Main: Peter Lang, 1987); Dieter Pfliegensdörfer, *Vom Handelszentrum zur Rüstungsschmiede: Wirtschaft, Staat und Arbeiterklasse in Bremen 1929 bis 1945* (Bremen: Universität Bremen, 1986).

Introduction

1. Charles S. Maier, *In Search of Stability: Explorations in Historical Political Economy* (Cambridge: Cambridge University Press, 1987), p. 97.

2. Harold James, "Economic Reasons for the Collapse of the Weimar Republic," in Ian Kershaw, ed., *Weimar: Why Did German Democracy Fail?* (New York: Weidenfeld & Nicolson, 1990), p. 55.

3. *Akten der Reichskanzlei: Regierung Hitler, 1933–1938,* prepared by Karl-Heinz Minuth (Boppard am Rhein: Harald Boldt Verlag, 1983), pt. 1, vol. 1, pp. 50–51, Ministerbesprechung vom 8. Februar 1933, 16:30 Uhr; Avraham Barkai, *Nazi Economics: Ideology, Theory, and Policy* (New Haven: Yale University Press, 1990), p. 160, notes Seldte's response, but does not develop the idea. For the view that work creation was rearmament, see Wolfram Fischer, *Die Wirtschaftspolitik des Nationalsozialismus* (Hanover: Gustav Peters, 1961), pp. 7, 17–21; Dieter Petzina, "Hauptprobleme der deutschen Wirtschaftspolitik 1932/33," *Vierteljahrshefte für Zeitgeschichte* 15 (1967), pp. 18–55; Wilhelm Deist, *The Wehrmacht and German Rearmament* (Toronto: University of Toronto Press, 1981), pp. 105, 110; Hans-Erich Volkmann, "Die NS-Wirtschaft in Vorbereitung des Krieges," in Wilhelm Deist et al., eds., *Ursachen und Voraussetzungen der Deutschen Kriegspolitik* (Stuttgart: Deutsche Verlags-Anstalt, 1979), pp. 232–253; Volkmann, "Aspekte der nationalsozialistischen 'Wehrwirtschaft' 1933 bis 1936," *Francia* 5 (1977), pp. 523–526. For a contrary view, see Michael Wolffsohn, "Arbeitsbeschaffung und Rüstung im nationalasozialistischen Deutschland: 1933," *Militärgeschichtliche Mitteilungen* 19 (1977), pp. 9–21; Wolffsohn, *Industrie und Handwerk im Konflikt mit Staatlicher Wirtschaft? Studien zur Politik der Arbeitsbeschaffung in Deutschland, 1930–1934* (Berlin: Duncker & Humblot, 1977), p. 112n22; Jürgen Stelzner, *Arbeitsbeschaffung und Wiederaufrüstung 1933–1936* (Tübingen: Tübingen University dissertation, 1976), pp. 235–238, 270.

4. Maier, *In Search of Stability,* p. 96; R. J. Overy, *The Nazi Economic Recovery, 1932–1938* (London: Macmillan, 1982), p. 47; Overy, "Unemployment in the Third Reich," *Business History* 29 (July 1987), p. 272; Overy, "The German Motorisierung and Rearmament: A Reply," *Economic History Review* 32 (1979), p. 113; Overy, *War and Economy in the Third Reich* (Oxford: Clarendon Press, 1994), pp. 60–61. Michael Geyer, "Zum Einfluß der nationalsozialistischen Rüstungspolitik auf der Ruhrgebiet," *Rheinische Vierteljahrsblätter* 45 (1981), p. 253, estimates expenditures on armed forces financed through both the Reich budget and "Mefo-bills" during 1933–34 and 1934–35 at approximately RM 6 billion. Taking a contrary view, Harold James argued that although German armament expenditure in the years 1933–1936 was "relatively small compared with later sums," it came to more than twice the amount spent on work creation and "represents a major stimulus given to the economy." See Harold James, *The German Slump* (Oxford: Clarendon Press,

1986), pp. 382–383. James included the 1935–36 armaments expenditure of RM 5.487 billion. The period of German economic recovery that needs to be explained, however, runs from the end of 1932 to the middle of 1935.

5. Overy, "Unemployment in the Third Reich," p. 272; Overy, *War and Economy*, pp. 60, 181. Usually overlooked is the fact that only about two-thirds of this estimated military expenditure represented "new" spending above levels already reached prior to Hitler's accession to power.

6. Direct employment in the aircraft industry rose sharply from 4,000 (Jan. 1933) to 53,865 (Jan. 1935), but the absolute numbers represent only a small fraction of the total labor market. In Oct. 1938, the aircraft industry employed 205,000. See Edward L. Homze, *Arming the Luftwaffe* (Lincoln: University of Nebraska Press, 1976), pp. 75, 93; Wilhelm Deist, "Die Aufrüstung der Wehrmacht," in Wilhelm Deist et al., eds., *Ursachen und Voraussetzungen der Deutschen Kriegspolitik*, pp. 480–481. The fact that series production of the Panzer I tank did not begin until the winter of 1934–35 suggests a modest employment effect from production of heavy equipment for the ground forces before 1935. See Deist, "Aufrüstung der Wehrmacht," p. 427. There was a significant increase in spending on both ship construction and naval infrastructure during 1933 and 1934, some of which was carried out under the Gereke *Sofortprogramm*. Statistics on the employment provided are lacking. See Jost Dülffer, *Weimar, Hitler und die Marine: Reichspolitik und Flottenbau, 1920–1939* (Düsseldorf: Droste Verlag, 1967), pp. 241–243, 563.

7. Overy, "Unemployment in the Third Reich," pp. 266–267; *War and Economy*, p. 53.

8. Helmut Marcon, *Arbeitsbeschaffungspolitik der Regierung Papen und Schleicher: Grundsteinlegung für die Beschäftigungspolitik im Dritten Reich* (Frankfurt am Main: Peter Lang, 1974), argues most forcefully that the Nazis ultimately reaped the benefits of their predecessors' programs.

9. On February 9, 1933, the Reich's share of *Sofortprogramm* funds was increased to RM 140 million by reducing the share for local communities by 10 percent. On March 17, "employment premiums" previously paid under the Papen program were terminated, and the RM 100 million thus freed up was made available to the military. In July, *Sofortprogramm* funding was increased from RM 500 million to RM 600 million to accommodate projects important to national policy. See BAK, R43II/536 and R43II/540, "Niederschrift über eine Sitzung des Ausschußes der Reichsregierung für Arbeitsbeschaffung in der Reichskanzlei," Feb. 9, 1933; *Akten der Reichskanzlei*, pt. 1, vol. 1, pp. 58–64, 237; BAK, R2/18660, RFM, Vermerk, "Finanzierung der Arbeitsbeschaffungsmaßnahmen 1933," July 8, 1933; RGBl, 1933, vol. 1, p. 464, July 13, 1933.

10. Overy, "Unemployment in the Third Reich," p. 266, and Wolffsohn, *Industrie und Handwerk*, pp. 114–115, attribute the refusal of local authorities to apply for Gereke program funds to "the poor state of municipal finances." This explanation

fails to convey the resentment of the terms of the Gereke program. Württemberg's economics minister Dr. Reinhold Maier (Deutsche Demokratische Partei) referred to the program as a "swindle" during a Feb. 7, 1933, meeting of state ministers. See HStAS, E130b, Bü3221, p. 417, excerpts from minutes of Feb. 7, 1933, meeting of state ministry. For statistics on payouts by the Deutsche Gesellschaft für öffentliche Arbeiten, the Deutsche Rentenbank-Kreditanstalt, and the Deutsche Bau- und Bodenbank A.G., see BAK, R2/18656, 18656a, 18656b.

11. Jürgen Baron von Kruedener has argued that Brüning pursued a deflationary policy because he thought that it was the best way to combat the economic crisis and ensure his political survival. See von Kruedener, "Could Brüning's Policy of Deflation Have Been Successful?" in von Kruedener, ed., *Economic Crisis and Political Collapse: The Weimar Republic, 1924–1933* (New York: Berg, 1990), p. 82.

12. Borchardt began the controversy with his publication "Zwangslagen und Handlungsspielräume in der großen Wirtschaftskrise der frühen dreißiger Jahre: Zur Revision des überlieferten Geschichtsbildes," *Bayerische Akademie der Wissenschaften, Jahrbuch 1979* (Munich, 1979), pp. 87–132.

13. Among those raising the most serious objections to Borchardt's thesis has been Carl-Ludwig Holtfrerich, beginning with his critique "Alternativen zu Brünings Wirtschaftspolitik in der Weltwirtschaftskrise?" *Historische Zeitschrift* 235 (1982), pp. 605–631, followed by Borchardt's response, "Noch einmal: Alternativen zu Brünings Wirtschaftspolitik?" *Historische Zeitschrift* 237 (1993), pp. 66–83. Harold James has generally supported Borchardt, beginning with his response to Holtfrerich, "Gab es eine Alternative zur Wirtschaftspolitik Brünings?" *Vierteljahrschrift für Sozial- und Wirtschaftsgeschichte* 70 (1983), pp. 523–541. Readers who wish to follow the "Borchardt controversy" in relatively accessible English language sources should consult Knut Borchardt, *Perspectives on Modern German Economic History and Policy* (Cambridge: Cambridge University Press, 1991); Kershaw, ed., *Weimar: Why Did German Democracy Fail?;* von Kruedener, ed., *Economic Crisis and Political Collapse.* Von Kruedener's "Introduction: The 'Borchardt Debate' on the Failure of Economic Policy at the End of the Weimar Republic," in *Economic Crisis and Political Collapse,* pp. xi–xxx, summarizes the debate up to 1986. Borchardt's contribution to that volume, "A Decade of Debate about Brüning's Economic Policy," pp. 99–151, addresses the literature published up to 1988.

14. Carl-Ludwig Holtfrerich, "Economic Policy Options and the End of the Weimar Republic," in Kershaw, ed., *Weimar: Why Did German Democracy Fail?,* p. 74.

15. Holtfrerich, "Alternativen zu Brünings Wirtschaftspolitik," p. 620; "Economic Policy Options and the End of the Weimar Republic," pp. 66, 72.

16. Borchardt, "Zwangslagen," p. 99; *Perspectives,* p. 152; Holtfrerich, "Alternativen," pp. 630–631; von Kruedener, "Introduction: The 'Borchardt Debate,' " in *Economic Crisis and Political Collapse,* p. xviii.

17. Precisely when the Reichsbank would have been willing, or was willing, to allow a significant increase in the money supply and finance large-scale work creation programs is difficult to determine with certainty. For conflicting views on this question, see James, *German Slump*, pp. 321–322, and Holtfrerich's critique of James in "Alternativen," p. 621, especially note 38.

18. Dr. Hermann Pünder, Regierungspräsident in Münster, and formerly a state secretary in the Reich chancellery, asked the same question in Jan. 1933. "Even if we can count on a sum of around one billion marks [for work creation]," wrote Pünder, "one must keep in mind that this large sum represents only one-fortieth of the German national income even in the crisis-year 1932." The June 1, 1933, "Reinhardt Program" authorized RM 1 billion for work creation. See *Vossische Zeitung*, January 10, 1933, "Von draussen gesehen: Arbeitsbeschaffung und Verwaltungsreform," by Dr. Hermann Pünder.

19. Henry A. Turner, Jr., *German Big Business and the Rise of Hitler* (New York: Oxford University Press, 1985), p. 276.

20. For a breakdown of spending under the Papen program as well as other work creation programs from 1932 to 1934, see Wolffsohn, *Industrie und Handwerk*, pp. 449–452; Birgit Wulff, *Arbeitslosigkeit und Arbeitsbeschaffungsmaßnahmen in Hamburg, 1933–1939* (Frankfurt am Main: Peter Lang, 1987), pp. 29–30. Prior to the Münster program, Papen had earmarked RM 135 million for roads, canals, and agricultural land improvement projects, bringing his total allocation for direct work creation to RM 302 million.

21. BHStA, MWi 5637, Bayerische Gesandtschaft, Berlin, to [Bavarian] Staatsministerium des Äußern, für Wirtschaft und Arbeit, Aug. 30, 1932. The words quoted are those of the Bavarian ambassador's account, not those of the Reich finance minister himself.

22. Gerald D. Feldman, "Industrialists, Bankers, and the Problem of Unemployment in the Weimar Republic," *Central European History* 25 (1992), p. 96.

23. Ibid., p. 77. Feldman cites a letter of Hjalmar Schacht to Paul Reusch dated Aug. 17, 1949.

24. Ibid., pp. 93–94.

25. James, "Economic Reasons for the Collapse of Weimar," p. 52.

26. Ibid., p. 55.

1. National Socialist Labor Market Statistics

1. Timothy W. Mason, *Sozialpolitik im Dritten Reich* (Opladen: Westdeutscher Verlag, 1977), pp. 127–128, 134, 138–139. Rüdiger Hachtmann, *Industriearbeit im "Dritten Reich": Untersuchungen zu den Lohn- und Arbeitsbedingungen in Deutschland, 1933–1945* (Göttingen: Vandenhoeck & Ruprecht, 1989), p. 37, argues that "when one subtracts these 'quasi-unemployed' from the number of employed, it becomes

obvious that a substantial reduction in unemployment set in only in 1934 . . . only from the middle of 1934 did the growth in the number of employed rise abruptly without the [inclusion of] the 'quasi-employed.' "

2. Michael Kater, *The Nazi Party: A Social Profile of Members and Leaders, 1919–1945* (Cambridge, Mass.: Harvard University Press, 1983), p. 75. Kater's use of the term "inconsistent arithmetic" needs to defined, and his claim that scholarship has shown that the Nazis resorted to "outright falsification" of labor market statistics (presumably on an important scale) does not stand up under scrutiny. There is no question that the Nazis resorted to "statistical manipulation" through the reclassification of certain categories of workers. It is not clear, however, that this manipulation was "illegitimate."

3. Harold James, *The German Slump* (Oxford: Clarendon Press, 1986), p. 371.

4. For discussions of Reich statistics in general see Wolfgang Reichardt, "Die Reichsstatistik," in Friedrich Burgdörfer, ed., *Die Statistik in Deutschland nach ihrem heutigen Stand: Ehrenabgabe für Friedrich Zahn* (Berlin: Verlag für Sozialpolitik, Wirtschaft und Statistik Paul Schmidt, 1940), vol. 1, pp. 77–88; Friedrich Facius, *Wirtschaft und Statistik: Die Entwicklung der staatlichen Wirtschaftsverwaltung in Deutschland vom 17. Jahrhundert bis 1945*, Schriften des Bundesarchivs, no. 6 (Boppard am Rhein: Harald Boldt Verlag, 1959); Alfred Jacobs, "Der Weg bis zum Ende der Reichsstatistik," offprint from *Jahrbüchern für Nationalökonomie und Statistik*, vol. 185, pt. 4 (1971), pp. 289–313.

5. Gianni Toniolo and Francesco Piva, "Unemployment in the 1930s: The Case of Italy," in Barry Eichengreen and T. J. Hatton, eds., *Interwar Unemployment in International Perspective* (Dordrecht: Kluwer Academic Publishers, 1988), pp. 227–228.

6. C. W. Guillebaud, *The Economic Recovery of Germany from 1933 to the Incorporation of Austria in March 1938* (London: Macmillan, 1939), p. vi; Gerhard Kroll, *Von der Weltwirtschaftskrise zur Staatskonjunktur* (Berlin: Duncker & Humblot, 1958), p. 473.

7. For a complete treatment of the nazification of the RfAA, see Dan P. Silverman, "Nazification of the German Bureaucracy Reconsidered: A Case Study," *The Journal of Modern History* 60 (Sept. 1988), pp. 496–539.

8. The charter of the IfK stipulated that "the current president of the Reich Statistical Office serves as head of the Institut." See BHStA, MA106718, Bavarian acting Plenipotentiary to Reichsrat, Ministerialrat Seyboth, to [Bavarian] economics ministry, June 17, 1933.

9. John A. Leopold, *Alfred Hugenberg: The Radical Nationalist Campaign against the Weimar Republic* (New Haven: Yale University Press, 1977), pp. 136–137.

10. James, *German Slump*, pp. 278, 333. In May 1933, Hugenberg proposed his own work creation scheme financed through the issue of RM 1.5 billion in "Reich treasury notes" *(Reichskassenscheine)*. He claimed the scheme was not inflationary.

See BAK, R43II/536, Reich economics minister (signed Hugenberg) to State secretary in the Reich chancellery, "Denkschrift über die Finanzierung der Arbeitsbeschaffung," May 11, 1933.

11. BHStA, MA 106718, Bavarian acting Plenipotentiary to Reichsrat, Ministerialrat Seyboth, to [Bavarian] economics ministry, June 17, 1933. Seyboth indicated that Hugenberg's dissatisfaction with Wagemann resulted both from Wagemann's leadership of the IfK and his personnel policy in the Reich statistical office.

12. *Wochenbericht des Instituts für Konjunkturforschung*, Aug. 2, 1933, front-page announcement titled "Das Ziel unserer Arbeit," signed by Wagemann.

13. Deutsche Abeitsfront, Arbeitswissenschaftliche Institut, *Jahrbuch 1938* (Berlin, 1939), vol. 2, pp. 19–22. The DAF rejected International Labor Organization statistics for the same reason. The DAF established its own Statistische Zentralstelle der DAF within its Arbeitswissenschaftlichen Institut. The DAF statistical office collected data on wages, prices, and work time, and statistics on membership in various professions. For data on national income, production, employment, and unemployment, it relied on statistics furnished by the Reich Statistical Office and the IfK.

14. BHStA, M Wi 3092, Bavarian economics ministry, Vormerkung (signed Gorter), June 8, 1937, concerning establishment of a branch of the IfK.

15. Ibid.; BHStA, M Wi 3092, president of Bayer. Statistischen Landesamt [Friedrich Zahn] to Staatsmin. f. Wirtschaft, Abt. f. Handel, Industrie u. Gewerbe, June 25, 1937; Albert Pietzsch, president of Munich chamber of industry and commerce, to Bavarian economics ministry, July 12, 1937; [Bavarian] Land Statistical Office to economics ministry, department of commerce, industry, and trade, July 23, 1937.

16. Estimates of the "invisible" unemployed ran as high as two million at the beginning of 1933. See Willi Hemmer, *Die "unsichtbaren" Arbeitslosen: Statistische Methoden—Soziale Tatsachen* (Zeulenroda, Germany: Bernhard Sporn, 1935).

17. "Sechster Bericht der Reichsanstalt für Arbeitsvermittlung und Arbeitslosenversicherung für die Zeit vom 1. April 1933 bis zum 31. März 1934," issued as *Beilage zum Reichsarbeitsblatt* (Berlin, 1935, no. 4), p. 39; Silverman, "Nazification of the German Bureaucracy," pp. 514–515; Hans Mommsen, *Beamtentum im Dritten Reich* (Stuttgart: Deutsche Verlags-Anstalt, 1966), p. 55; Oscar Weigert, *Administration of Placement and Unemployment Insurance in Germany* (New York: Industrial Relations Counselors, 1934), pp. 151–153; Weigert, a professional civil servant in the Reich labor ministry who authored the 1927 unemployment insurance law, was, like Wagemann, targeted for dismissal by Hugenberg. A list of key personnel in Reich and Prussian ministries, prepared by Hugenberg's Deutschnationale Volkspartei central office in April 1933, lists Ministerialdirektor Dr. Weigert with this notation: "SPD, muß raus." See BAK, Hugenberg/85.

18. For example, see N-WHStA (Kalkum branch), Arbeitsamt Kempen 6, report

on examination of AA Kempen by LAA Rhineland, 18.1.32–23.1.32, pp. 54–55, sent by president LAA Rheinland to director AA Kempen, June 9, 1932, complaining of "absolutely unacceptable" statistical record-keeping procedures in the Kempen (Rhineland) office.

19. BAK, R163/27, president RfAA to LAA presidents, May 15, 1934, containing Syrup's order establishing training programs; R163/28, Hagen AA director to president LAA Westfalen, September 20, 1935, containing training curriculum; R163/28, president RfAA to LAA presidents, June 28, Nov. 8, 1935, containing guidelines for examination of RfAA salaried employees.

20. Sechster Bericht der RfAA, (1933–34), p. 52; BAK, R163/53, president RfAA to LAA presidents, March 1, 1938; Weigert, *Placement and Unemployment Insurance*, pp. 57, 206. Under Syrup's March 1938 guidelines, unannounced examinations of statistical records were to be made only every second month, and the time allotted was to be sufficient only to "at least scrutinize through random samples the basis of the computations, the recording of statistics, etc. . . . Examinations of less than one hour will not do justice to their objective."

21. "Simplified" statistical procedures effective October 1, 1933, are found in BAK, R163/73, "Statistiken der Arbeitslosenversicherung und der Krisenfürsorge, hier: Neuregelung ab 1 Oktober 1933." These regulations were published in the *Reichs-Arbeitsmarkt-Anzeiger, Beilage,* no. 19, Oct. 10, 1933.

22. BAP, 39.03, no. 226, president RfAA to LAA presidents, Sept. 30, 1933, concerning "Arbeitsmarktstatistik; Wohlfahrtserwerbslose."

23. StADü, IV/1858, president RfAA to LAA and AA, Sept. 27, 1933; BAK, R163/73, "Statistik der wertschaffenden Arbeitslosenfürsorge; hier: Neuregelung ab September 1933," sent by Berlin RfAA headquarters to LAA and AA, published in *Reichs-Arbeitsmarkt-Anzeiger, Beilage,* no. 19, Oct. 10, 1933. Prior to July 1933, emergency relief workers had been counted as "unemployed." Changes in the classification system are discussed later.

24. BAK, R163/53, president RfAA to LAA presidents, May 25, 1932, and Nov. 11, 1933; president LAA Südwestdeutschland to AA directors, Nov. 14, 1933; president RfAA to LAA presidents, June 6, 1936.

25. Weigert, *Placement and Unemployment Insurance,* p. 160; RABl, 1933, for laws of May 12, 1933 (domestic workers), and Sept. 22, 1933 (agricultural, forestry, and fishery workers). The government estimated that the exemptions affected 750,000 domestic workers and 400,000 workers in agriculture, forestry, and fisheries. See *Sechster Bericht der RfAA,* (1933–34), pp. 31–32.

26. For a systematic examination of "invisible unemployment" in Germany during the 1930s, see Hemmer, *Die "unsichtbaren" Arbeitslosen.*

27. Weigert, *Placement and Unemployment Insurance,* pp. 23–24; Royal Institute of International Affairs, *Unemployment: An International Problem* (Oxford: Oxford University Press, 1935), pp. 68–70, 276. For a view accepting the validity of Ger-

man labor market statistics, see Friedrich Baerwald, "How Germany Reduced Unemployment," *American Economic Review* 24 (Dec. 1934), pp. 620–621. Baerwald argued that "German labor statistics reproduce exactly the movements and fluctuations of the labor market. They show not only the exact number of the employed but also the exact number of the unemployed."

28. *Sechster Bericht der RfAA*, (1933–34), p. 1n1; IfK, *Wochenbericht*, March 7, 1934; Mason, *Sozialpolitik*, pp. 126–128, 134, 138–139. On July 31, 1933, there were 140,126 emergency relief workers, 144,981 Land Helpers, 262,992 enrolled in the Labor Service, and 71,000 public relief workers (Fürsorgearbeiter), for a total of 619,099 affected by classification changes. When Hitler came to power on Jan. 30, 1933, these groups had numbered approximately 258,321. For statistics, see *Statistische Beilage zum Reichsarbeitsblatt* (1934, 1935); Hemmer, *Die "Unsichtbaren" Arbeitslosen*, p. 189.

29. BAK, R43II/537, Chefsbesprechung im Reichsarbeitsministerium, Dec. 6, 1933, concerning work creation measures in 1934; *Akten der Reichskanzlei*, pt. 1, vol. 2, p. 1005; StAD, 102/1687, clipping from *Mitteilungen des deutschen Städetages*, Jan. 15, 1934, "Der Arbeitsmarkt im Dezember 1933," citing Syrup's article in *Wirtschaftsring* (no date given). During the Sept. 1933 meeting of the Generalrat der Wirtschaft, Dr. Albert Vögler, general director of the Vereinigten Stahlwerke AG, vigorously disputed the interpretation of official unemployment statistics with economics minister Kurt Schmitt and labor minister Franz Seldte. See BAK R43II/321, pp. 55–57; *Akten der Reichskanzlei*, pt. 1, vol. 2, Erste Sitzung des Generalrats der Wirtschaft, Sept. 20, 1933, pp. 776–778.

30. Weigert, *Placement and Unemployment Insurance*, pp. 8–9. Weigert attributed the discrepancy in unemployment statistics to the unemployment of persons not registered with Reich employment offices ["invisible unemployment"], and "the fact that [in the census] presumably many sick persons incorrectly described themselves as unemployed."

31. See, for example, N-WHStA, Reg. Aachen, Regierungspräsident Aachen to Oberpräsident Rheinland, May 28, 1934, indicating "significant" differences between AA and local welfare authority estimates of WE; Vorsitzenden des Kreisausschußes des Landkreises Aachen, Kreiswohlfahrtsamt, to LAA Rheinland, June 25, 1934, concerning a large discrepancy in WE estimates; StADü, 102/1687, Regierungspräsident, Düsseldorf, to Bezirksfürsorgeverbände, March 1, 1934, pointing out statistical discrepancies in the counting of WE; Oberbürgermeister, Duisburg, to Regierungspräsident in Düsseldorf, March 10, 1934, explaining the source of a discrepancy of 2,238 WE. From the point of view of welfare, there were 29,110 welfare unemployed on Jan. 31, 1934, in the LAA Rheinland district. But 2,238 of these were "employed" as "welfare employed" *(Fürsorgearbeiter)* or otherwise "employed." Only 26,872 were denoted as "jobless welfare unemployed" ("arbeitslose Wohlfahrtserwerbslose").

32. Germany, Statistisches Reichsamt, *Statistisches Jahrbuch für das deutsche Reich* (1935), p. 509.

33. Ibid.

34. StADü, IV 958, Deutscher Gemeindetag *Monatlicher WE-Schnelldienst*, Sept. 30, 1933, letter of Deutscher Gemeindetag to städischen Bezirksfürsorgeverbände [BFV] mit mehr als 20,000 Einwohner, dated Sept. 20, 1933; *Monatlicher Arbeitslosen-Schnelldienst* (formerly *Monatlicher WE-Schnelldienst*), Jan. 29, 1934.

35. StADü, IV 958, *Monatlicher Arbeitslosen-Schnelldienst*, April 25, 1934.

36. For official employment statistics see *Siebenter Bericht der RfAA* (1933–34), p. 15, issued as *Beilage zum Reichsarbeitsblatt*, 1935, no. 35. For official unemployment statistics, see *Statistische Beilage zum Reichsarbeitsblatt*, 1934, no. 7, p. 18. Mason's assumption that German labor market statistics exactly mirrored changes in classification regulations was shared by many labor market experts at the time. Leo Grebler, for example, asserted that persons enrolled in the Labor Service were counted as unemployed "up to 30 July 1933, but not afterwards. At that date there were about 130,000 persons in the labor service, *so that the apparent reduction of unemployment was increased by that figure* (emphasis added)." See Leo Grebler, "Work Creation Policy in Germany, 1932–1935," *International Labour Review* 35 (1937), pp. 511–512. In fact, participants in the labor service were included in statistics for the unemployed up to and including June 30, 1933, not July 30 as Grebler indicated. Prior to June 30, members of the labor service were included in the official unemployment statistics only if they had reported to the local employment office as looking for work. After June 30, they did not appear in the official statistics on the employed, because those statistics included only those employed in occupations covered by compulsory national health insurance. See Hemmer, *Die "unsichtbaren" Arbeitslosen*, p. 55. For additional discussion of the impact of statistical changes June–July 1933, see *Sechster Bericht der RfAA*, (1933–34), p. 1n1; IfK, *Wochenbericht*, Aug. 16, 1933.

37. Hemmer, *Die "unsichtbaren" Arbeitslosen*, pp. 43, 55–56.

38. Michael R. Darby, "Three-and-a-Half Million U. S. Employees Have Been Mislaid: Or, an Explanation of Unemployment, 1934–1941," *Journal of Political Economy* 84 (1976), p. 7. Robert A. Margo has also argued that since "substitute" employment for many American emergency relief workers was long-term and stable, though poorly payed, it may be appropriate to count some fraction of long-term relief workers as employed. See Margo, "Interwar Unemployment in the United States: Evidence from the 1940 Census Sample," in Eichengreen and Hatton, eds., *Interwar Unemployment*, pp. 326–333.

39. In making any "correction," one must keep in mind an average of 265,000 workers per month who appear in IfK estimates of employment but are not accounted for in official health insurance employment statistics. For "corrections" beginning on or after July 31, 1933, one must add to official statistics on the

"employed" the appropriate number from the labor service. Monthly discrepancies that need to be accounted for in this manner are given in the Appendix, Table 3, column 5. Beginning Sept. 30, 1934, emergency relief workers employed on Reich *Autobahnen* and waterway projects were no longer counted as either *Notstandsarbeiter* nor as "looking for work," and were no longer considered as "substitute" employed. They continued to appear in the official Krankenkassen employment statistics, which made no distinction between regular and substitute employment. On Sept. 30, 1934, *Autobahnen* construction employed 64,250 workers. See Karl Lärmer, *Autobahnbau in Deutschland 1933 bis 1945-Zu den Hintergründen* (E. Berlin: Akademie-Verlag, 1975), p. 54.

40. Seldte's memorandum can be found in several locations, including BAK, R41/5; BAK, R43^{II}/534, 537; BHStA, MA106743; HHStA, Abt. 485, 824, RAM to obersten Reichsbehörden, etc., Nov. 15, 1933, with enclosed report, "Der Stand der deutschen Arbeitsschlacht," dated end of Oct. 1933. The HHStA copy is used here. Seldte's memorandum is based on Syrup's memorandum, BAK, R41/5, "Zur Entlastung des Arbeitsmarktes im Winter 1933/34," enclosed in, president RfAA to RAM, Sept. 30, 1933.

41. Jonathan R. Kesselman and N. E. Savin, "Three-and-a-half Million Workers Never Were Lost," *Economic Inquiry* 16 (1978), pp. 206–207.

42. Ibid.

43. See IfK, *Wochenbericht*, March 15, 1933, p. 208, for an explanation of the new index basis, and a monthly index of German industrial production from Jan. 1926 to Jan. 1933, calculated on the new basis. For the 1935 changes see IfK, *Wochenbericht*, June 19, 1935, pp. 97–100. The IfK claimed its new index number of monthly production (excluding foodstuffs and luxury items) "agrees almost exactly with the previously published monthly index number." The new quarterly index number (including foodstuffs and luxury items) began to take a different track beginning with 1934 statistics, exhibiting a difference of about 3 percent from the previously published index number. From time to time, but not consistently, the quarterly index number was to be seasonally adjusted.

2. Financing Germany's Economic Recovery

1. Gerhard Kroll, *Von der Weltwirtschaftskrise zur Staatskonjunktur* (Berlin: Duncker & Humblot, 1958), p. 576.

2. BAK, R43II/309a, Lehnich, "Nationalsozialistische Arbeitsbeschaffungspolitik," speech delivered in Königsberg to Tagung des Volksbundes für das Deutschtum im Ausland, June 8, 1935.

3. Although Hitler apparently dropped Schacht because of Schacht's resistance to Hitler's unlimited spending on rearmament, Schacht had praised Hitler's "dar-

ing" rearmament policy and claimed that it could not have been carried out "without a correspondingly daring economic and financial policy, among whose most important leaders and bearers is the Reichsbank." See HHStA, Abt. 483/10929, press clipping from *Frankfurter Volksblatt* (F. V.), Jan. 22, 1937, "Schacht—60 Jahre," quoting from an article (unnamed newspaper, no date) attributed to Schacht at the turn of the year, 1935–1936.

4. BAK, R42II/536, "Besprechung mit Industriellen über Arbeitsbeschaffung," May 29, 1933; BAK, R43/321, "Generalrat der Wirtschaft," meeting of Sept. 20, 1933. These documents are also found in *Akten der Reichskanzlei*, pt. 1, vol.1, pp. 506–527, and pt. 1, vol. 2, pp. 749–821.

5. BAK, R43II/536, "Vermerk über die Chefsbesprechung am 31. Mai 1933, über Arbeitsbeschaffung."

6. Among those chiefly responsible for designing Gereke's program and the mechanism of financing was Reich economics ministry Oberregierungsrat Wilhelm Lautenbach. See Willi A. Boelcke, *Die deutsche Wirtschaft, 1930–1935: Interna des Reichswirtschaftsministeriums* (Düsseldorf: Droste Verlag, 1983), p. 28; Arthur Schweitzer, *Big Business in the Third Reich* (Bloomington: Indiana University Press, 1964), p. 674, n. 4.

7. For details on prefinancing by means of work creation bills, see Otto Nathan, *The Nazi Economic System: Germany's Mobilization for War* (Durham: Duke University Press, 1944), pp. 282–283; BAK, R2/18675, RFM to Reichsschuldenverwaltung (signed Reinhardt), June 26, 1933; Deutsche Bau- und Bodenbank AG, Sekretariat, to Geheimer Regierungsrat Dr. Poerschke [RFM], June 14, 1933; R2/18676, RFM to Deutsche Rentenbank-Kreditanstalt, Aug. 4, 1933; R28/59, Reichsbank-Direktorium to all Reichsbank branches, Feb. 28, 1934, concerning "Arbeitsbeschaffungsmaßnahmen 1933 (Reinhardt-Programm)," which contains a list of all banks participating in the consortium; N-WStAD, L80ID, Gr. XVIII, 2, Nr. 6, Bd. VII, Deutsche Gesellschaft für öffentliche Arbeiten, *Bericht über das Geschäftsjahr 1932* (Berlin, 1933), pp. 5–6; StADü, IV/1858, Stadt Düsseldorf, Tiefbauamt II, memorandum, May 1933, "Durchführung des Arbeitsbeschaffungsprogramms 1933. Geschäftsverfahren innerhalb der Stadtverwaltung." Annual redemptions by the RFM were to take place between July 16 and October 15.

8. Martin Wolfe, "The Development of Nazi Monetary Policy," *Journal of Economic History* 15 (1955), p. 393.

9. Harold James, *The German Slump* (Oxford: Clarendon Press, 1986), pp. 372, 373, 378.

10. StAD, 102/1687, clipping from *Mitteilungen des deutschen Städetages*, Oct. 20, 1933, "Arbeitsbeschaffung und Steuerreform," Reinhardt speech before the Deutschen Juristentag 1933; BAK, R41/5005, Lautenbach memorandum of May 16, 1933, "Die finanzpolitischen Voraussetzungen einer aktiven Konjunkturpolitik";

memorandum of May 19, 1933, to Ministerialdirektor Dr. Reichardt; Lautenbach to State secretary Dr. Johannes Krohn, RWM, May 26, 1933, with enclosure, "Die Finanzierung der Arbeitsbeschaffung kontradiktorisch dargestellt."

11. Nathan, *Nazi Economic System*, p. 115; Samuel Lurie, *Private Investment in a Controlled Economy: Germany, 1933–1939* (New York: Columbia University Press, 1947), pp. 61, 63; Gerhard Kroll, *Von der Weltwirtschaftskrise zur Staatskonjunktur* (Berlin: Duncker & Humblot, 1958), p. 597; James, *German Slump*, p. 373.

12. Lautenbach agreed that Germany had no choice but to finance work creation programs with treasury bills rediscountable at the Reichsbank. That, he observed, would require either a change in the banking law or "a certain evasive maneuver." See BAK, R41/5005, undated, untitled Lautenbach memorandum.

13. BAP 25.01, Bd.2, Nr. 6517, Reichsbank memorandum, "Zur Finanzierung der Arbeitsbeschaffung," Dec. 6, 1935. The final version of this memorandum by Reichsbank director Franz Döring was made available to the media in Aug. 1936, under the title "Die Finanzierung der Arbeitsbeschaffung in Deutschland."

14. This expectation proved to be justified over time. For statistics on the Reichsbank's portfolio of work creation bills, see the Appendix, Table 6.

15. BAP, 39.05, Nr. 16, "Zur Finanzierung des Arbeitsbeschaffungsprogramms," notes and outline for an upcoming meeting with the bank consortium, dated Feb. 4, 1933; BAP, 39.05, Nr. 41, Reichs-Kredit-Gesellschaft to RFM (copy to Reich Commissar for Work Creation), Jan. 26, 1933, concerning "Arbeitsmaßnahme f. besondere Tiefbauten." The "intrusions" mentioned by the Reichs-Kredit-Gesellschaft undoubtedly referred to revaluation measures taken by the government during the 1924 stabilization of the mark.

16. BAP, 39.05, Nr. 41, Reichs-Kredit-Gesellschaft to RFM (copy to Reich Commissar for Work Creation), Jan. 26, 1933, concerning "Arbeitsmaßnahme f. besondere Tiefbauten."

17. BAP 25.01, Bd. 2, Nr. 6515, "Arbeitsbeschaffung und Reichsbank," Schacht speech in Jütterborg, Aug. 19, 1935. Schacht identified the fundamental error of Weimar economic policy as excessive reliance on foreign credits, which financed a "mismanaged domestic economy." Germany, he argued, should have built up capital out of its own resources.

18. Ibid.

19. BHStA, MA 106743, Der bayerische stellv. Bevollmächtigte zum Reichsrat, Ministerialdirektor Dr. [Paul] Hammer, to [Bavarian] Minister-president [Ludwig] Siebert, June 7, 1933, with enclosure, copy of Reichsbank memorandum concerning its role in financing the Reinhardt program, "Finanzielle Auswirkungen von Maßnahmen zur Beschäftigung von Arbeitslosen," 14 pages, undated (probably May 1933). Hammer had been asked to treat the memorandum as the "confidential personal work of an official expert."

20. Hjalmar Schacht, *My First Seventy-six Years: The Autobiography of Hjalmar Schacht*, trans. Diana Pyke (London: Allan Wingate, 1955), p. 317.

21. BHStA, MA 106743, May 1933 Reichsbank memorandum, "Finanzielle Auswirkungen von Maßnahmen zur Beschäftigung von Arbeitslosen." Franz von Papen's government had taken a similar gamble with its "Papen program." See BHStA, MWi 5637, Bayerische Gesandschaft, Berlin, to [Bavarian] Staatsministerium des Äussen, für Wirtschaft u. Arbeit, Aug. 30, 1932, for comments by Papen's finance minister, Krosigk.

22. BAK, R43II/758, RFM to Reich chancellor, Feb. 16, 1934. The terms of the work creation programs called for annual redemption of one-fifth of the total amount of work creation bills between 1934 and 1938. The correct 1934–35 redemption figure for work creation bills, referred to in other RFM correspondence, is RM 320 million (RM 120 million for the Gereke *Sofortprogramm*, and RM 200 million for the Reinhardt program).

23. BAK, R2/18681, RFM, Vermerk, Feb. 16, 1934, concerning "Haushaltsansätzen für die Wechseleinlösung bei der Arbeitsbeschaffungsmaßnahmen"; Vermerk, March 7, 1934, "Einlösung der zur Vorfinanzierung der Arbeitsbeschaffungsmaßnahmen dienenden Wechsel"; RFM to Reichsbank-Direktorium, March 7, 1934; Reichsbank-Direktorium to RFM, March 14, 1934; R2/18682, in-house RFM report, May 23, 1934, "Die öffentliche Arbeitsbeschaffung und ihre finanziellen Auswirkungen auf den Reichshaushalt. Beitrag zum 'Finanziellen überblick über den Reichshaushalt 1934' "; R2/18660, RFM to president of Landesfinanzamt, Berlin, March 14, 1934; R2/18686, RFM, Vermerk, Feb. 7, 1935, "Einlösung von Arbeitsbeschaffungswechseln"; RFM to vice president of Reichsbank-Direktorium [Fritz] Dreyse, Feb. 7, 1935 (draft). In budget year 1935, the RFM offered to pay the entire RM 360 million owed the Reichsbank, as well as RM 70 million owed the major credit institutions, but it sought relief from repayment of RM 200 million of a RM 500 million loan from savings banks.

24. BAK, R2/18686, RFM, Vermerk, Feb. 7, 1935, "Einlösung von Arbeitsbeschaffungswechseln."

25. For running accounts of work creation payouts by the Deutsche Gesellschaft für öffentliche Arbeiten (Öffa), see BAK, R2/18656; the Deutsche Rentenbank-Kreditanstalt (RKA), R2/18656a; the Deutsche Bau- und Bodenbank AG, the Deutsche Siedlungsbank, and the Reichs-Kredit-Gesellschaft AG, R2/18656. The rise and decline of work creation bills in circulation and the percentage held by the Reichsbank can be traced in BAK, R2/18701, Reichsbank-Direktorium to RFM, Oct. 7, 1936, with enclosure, "Die Inanspruchnahme der Reichsbank aus den Arbeitsbeschaffungsprogrammen des Reiches."

26. BAK, R2/18701, Reichsbank-Direktorium to RFM, Oct. 7, 1936, with enclosure, "Die Inanspruchnahme der Reichsbank aus den Arbeitsbeschaffungsprogram-

men des Reiches." So intense was the secrecy concerning rearmament spending that the Reich finance ministry declined to inform the Reich audit office in writing of the amount of Mefo-bills in circulation. The audit office was advised to make personal contact with the Reich finance ministry for a verbal report. See BAK, R2/13716, Rechnungshof des Deutschen Reiches to RFM, Feb. 10, 1936, concerning "Stand der Verpflichtungen u. Forderungen des Reiches aus der Arbeitsbeschaffung"; RFM to Rechnungshof, March 16, 1936 (draft).

27. BAK, R2/18701, Reichsbank-Direktorium to RFM, Oct. 7, 1936, "Die Inanspruchnahme der Reichsbank aus den Arbeitsbeschaffungsprogrammen des Reiches"; BHStA, Reichsstatthalter 504, *Verwaltungsbericht der Reichsbank für das Jahr 1935* (Berlin, 1936), pp. 3–4.

28. BAK, R2/18701, Reichsbank-Direktorium to RFM, Oct. 7, 1936, report, "Die Inanspruchnahme der Reichsbank aus den Arbeitsbeschaffungsprogrammen des Reiches."

29. Ibid.; BHStA, Reichsstatthalter 504 *Verwaltungsbericht der Reichsbank f. das Jahr 1935*, pp. 3–4; *Geschäftsbericht der Bayerischen Vereinsbank für das Geschäftsjahr vom 1. Januar bis 31. Dezember 1935* (Munich, 1936), p. 6. In 1935 excessive money-market liquidity created by work creation financing enabled the Reich treasury to place with banks, savings institutions, and insurance companies RM 1.8 billion in six-to-ten-year 4½ percent treasury bonds. This occasion marked the first time since 1929 that the Reich government had been able to float medium-and long-term loans.

30. BHStA, Reichsstatthalter 504, *Verwaltungsbericht der Reichsbank für das Jahr 1935*, pp. 3–4; BAK, R2/18701, Reichsbank-Direktorium to RFM, Oct. 7, 1936, "Die Inanspruchnahme der Reichsbank aus den Arbeitsbeschaffungsprogrammen des Reiches."

31. Öffa was established on the basis of a July 26, 1930, decree of the Reich president, RGBl, 1930, vol. 1, p. 311.

32. N-WStAD, L80ID, Gr. XVIII, 2, Nr. 3, Bd. VI, Prussian minister-president (signed Braun) to Reich chancellor, June 8, 1931, with enclosure, "Denkschrift über die Entwicklung der wertschaffenden Arbeitslosenfursorge."

33. Ibid.

34. Ibid.

35. N-WStAD, L80ID, Gr. XVIII, 2, Nr. 3, Bd. VI, Deutsche Gesellschaft f. öffentliche Arbeiten AG, *Bericht über das Geschäftsjahr 1930*, pp. 5–7.

36. N-WStAD, L80ID, Gr. XVIII, 2, Nr. 3, Bd. VI, Öffa, *Bericht über das Geschäftsjahr 1930*, p. 7; Prussian minister-president to Reich chancellor, June 8, 1931, with enclosure, "Denkschrift über die Entwicklung der wertschaffenden Arbeitslosenfürsorge"; GStAPK, 151/1339, "Niederschrift der Verhandlungen über die Frage der Finanzierung der Maßnahmen der wertschaffenden Arbeitslosenfürsorge für das Rechnungsjahr 1932 am 26. Januar 1932 im [Prussian] Finanzministerium"; Prussian finance minister, Vermerk, wertschaffenden Arbeitslosenenfürsorge in

Preußen, Feb. 19, 1932; Prussian finance minister to Prussian minister-president, Feb. 19, 1932 (draft); Prussian minister for Volkswirtschaft to Prussian finance minister, Aug. 6, 1932.

37. Figures on 1933–34 financing operations in N-WStAD, L80ID, Gr. XVIII, 2, Nr. 3, Bd. VI, Öffa, *Bericht über das Geschäftsjahr 1933* (Berlin, 1934), pp. 5–7. For the "reconstruction" of Öffa's supervisory board, see HStAS, E130b, Bü 3223, RAM (signed Seldte) to Reichsrat, May 11, 1933; Württembergische Bevollmächtigte zum Reichsrat to Württemberg economics ministry, May 18, 1933.

38. N-WStAD, L80ID, Gr. XVIII, 2, Nr.3, Bd. VI, "Richtlinien für die Gewährung von Darlehen der Deutschen Gesellschaft f. öffentliche Arbeiten AG," Beschluss der Generalversammlung vom 13. Juni 1933; BAK, R2/18701, RFM, memorandum, "Die Arbeitsbeschaffungsmaßnahmen der Reichsregierung 1932 bis 1935," April 1937, prepared by Reichsbankrat Düle before he left the RFM. According to this document, total Reich expenditures on work creation from the Reich budget, the RfAA, and all participating credit institutions such as Öffa during this four-year period came to RM 3.36 billion. R2/18606, "Nachweisung der Einnahme und Ausgaben der Reichsanstalt in Rechnungsjahr 1934" [April 1934–March 1935], Anlage IB (2) 3310/297, June 17, 1935, shows a 1934–35 expenditure of RM 255.6 million for RfAA work creation basic subsidies, compared with the RM 276.6 cited in the April 1937 document. It is possible that the 1937 calculation included RfAA expenditures for the Landhilfe and the Women's Labor Service, which came to RM 20.9 million in 1934–35.

39. StAD, 500/433, president RfAA, decree of Feb. 27, 1934, reproduced in press clippings from *Nachrichtendienst des Deutschen Gemeindetages*, March 21, 1934, and *Mitteilungen des Deutschen Städetages*, April 1, 1934; president RfAA to LAA and AA, Oct. 8, 1934, "Durchführung der Notstandsarbeiten im Winter 1934/35," explaining the purpose of the Feb. 27 reduction in the basic subsidy rate. To conserve scarce financial resources for work creation projects over the winter of 1934–35, Syrup ordered some districts to save most of their allotted funds for use after Oct. 31, 1934.

40. BAK, R2/18606, president RfAA to RFM, May 10, 1934; StAN, LRA Schwabach 1984, 4282, Bayerischer Gemeindetag to Bayerischen Arbeitsbeschaffungs-Programm mit Darlehen bedachten Gemeinden u. Bezirke, May 12, 1934; StAN, LRA Hilpoltstein, 46[II], Deutscher Gemeindetag, Landesdienststelle Bayern, to all Gemeinden, etc., July 2, 1934, announcing the lifting of the freeze; StADü, IV/1858, president LAA Rheinland to AA, June 26, 1934, indicating that the freeze on project approvals had been lifted, but that no additional Reich, Land, or Reichsbahn projects would be recognized for RfAA basic subsidies; BAK, R2/18607, Niederschrift. Besprechung in der Hauptstelle [RfAA] mit den Sacharbeitern der LAA über Fragen der wertschaffenden Arbeitslosenfürsorge am 24. u. 25. Juli 1934; BAK, R2/18606, president RfAA to RFM, May 10, 1934, recapitulating the May

7 meeting; president RfAA to LAA presidents, June 20, 1934; RAM to RFM, May 19, 1934; RAM to president RfAA, June 29, 1934, Schnellbrief; NSDAP, Deputy Führer (signed Martin Bormann) to state secretary Reinhardt [RFM], May 22, 1934, Private! Personal!

41. Exceptions were made, and the RM 3 rate remained in force for the Göring Plan in Berlin, and was later extended to Hamburg, Cologne, Munich, Leipzig, Essen, Dresden, and Breslau. See BAK, R2/18606, president RfAA to RAM (with copy to RFM) June 7, 1934; RAM to president RfAA, June 11, 1934; RFM to RAM, June 15, 1934.

42. BAK, R2/18607, Niederschrift. Besprechung in der Hauptstelle [RfAA] mit den Sacharbeitern der LAA über Fragen der wertschaffenden Arbeitslosenfürsorge am 24. u. 25. Juli 1934.

43. BAK, R2/18607, president RfAA to LAA presidents, Dec. 8, 1934; president RfAA to RFM, Dec. 12, 1934; StADü, IV/1859, Auszug aus der Niederschrift über die Besprechung mit den Landräten und Oberbürgermeistern in Gegenwart der Polizeipräsidenten vom 19. Nov. 1934; BAK, R2/18607, Regierungspräsident [Düsseldorf] to RAM, Dec. 3, 1934, concerning financing of public work creation measures in the western border areas; BAK, R2/18607, Vermerk über das Ergebnis der Besprechung, "Restfinanzierung der öffentlichen Notstandsarbeiten" (undated, probably Jan. 10, 1935); RAM to president RfAA, Feb. 14, 1935; president RfAA to RAM, Feb. 22, 1935; RFM to RAM, March 11, 1935; R2/18608, president RfAA to president LAA Rheinland, April 26, 1935.

44. Copies of Frick's decree can be found in StAN, LRA Schwabach 1984, 4282, and StAD, 609/28, Reich and Prussian Interior minister to Land governments, April 11, 1935, "Ausgaben der Gemeinden u. Gemeindeverbände für Zwecke der Arbeitsbeschaffung," marked "not for release to the press." For reference to Syrup's order to discontinue approval of new applications for RfAA basic subsidy, see StAN, LRA Schwabach 1984, 4282, president LAA Bayern to AA directors, May 3, 1935.

45. StAN, LRA Schwabach 1984, 4282, president LAA Bayern to AA directors, May 3, 1935; GStAPK, 151/2369, Prussian finance ministry, Vermerk, Aug. 26, 1935; Reich and Prussian interior minister to Prussian finance minister, Nov. 12, 1935, enclosing copy of NSDAP, Reichsleitung, Stellvertreter des Führers (signed Hess), *Rundschreiben* 118/35, June 14, 1935, not for publication.

46. BAK, R2/18609, Reich and Prussian minister of labor, "Vermerk über das Ergebnis der Besprechung im Reichs- und Pr. Arbeitsministerium am 14 Februar 1936," Feb. 19, 1936; RFM memorandum, Jan. 20, 1936, signed by Regierungsrat Gase, "Aufzeichnung über die Gestaltung des Haushalts der Reichsanstalt für AV und AV"; president RfAA to RAM, Abt. IIc, Feb. 4, 1936, concerning "Gestaltung der wertschaffenden Arbeitslosenfürsorge f. das Haushaltsjahr 1936"; RFM, Vermerk, Feb. 24, 1936, indicating disagreement between the Reich interior ministry, the RfAA, and the Reich finance ministry as to the amount available for RfAA

emergency relief projects during fiscal year 1936; RFM memorandum of May 4, 1936, addressed to RFM, compilation of all sums provided by the Reich budget, the RfAA, the Reichsautobahnen-Gesellschaft, Öffa, and other financing institutions for the purpose of "work creation" during fiscal year 1936–37. Of a total of RM 1,431 million, RM 210 million, presumably from the RfAA budget, was earmarked for emergency relief projects. *Autobahnen* construction was to receive RM 500 million, Reich roads RM 180 million, and waterways RM 112 million. Housing and *Kleinsiedlung* (RM 182 million) and agricultural land improvement (RM 210 million) were the other recipients of major "work creation" investment. "Added to this are the funds for armaments," whose sum was not known to the writer of the memorandum.

47. BAK, R2/18609, RFM, Vermerk, March 4, 1936; Vermerk über die Sitzung des Preußischen Staatsministeriums vom 26. 2. 1936; Vermerk, March 16, 1936.

48. R. J. Overy, *The Nazi Economic Recovery, 1932–1938* (London: Macmillan, 1982), p. 44.

49. For summaries of the development of German price control policy, see Maxine Sweezy, *The Structure of the Nazi Economy* (Cambridge, Mass.: Harvard University Press, 1941), pp. 96–98; Nathan, *Nazi Economic System*, pp. 214–215; Lurie, *Private Investment*, pp. 49–53. See Arthur Schweitzer, "Die wirtschaftliche Wiederaufrüstung Deutschlands von 1934–1936," *Zeitschrift für die gesamte Staatswissenschaft* 114 (1958), p. 612, for the assertion that Goerdeler was appointed at Schacht's insistence. At the time of his appointment as price czar, Wagner served as Gauleiter of both Westfalen-Süd and Silesia.

50. Lurie, *Private Investment*, pp. 47–48, 149; Nathan, *Nazi Economic System*, pp. 26–27; Schweitzer, *Big Business*, pp. 302, 321, citing statements by Reich economics minister Kurt Schmitt and Reich Commissar for Price Supervision Karl Goerdeler. See also, HHStA, Abt. 485, 248, Reichskommissar f. Preisüberwachung, Rundschreiben no. 45, concerning "Preisüberwachung im Bauwesen," Jan. 19, 1935. Vertraulich! Sofort! Nicht für die Presse! The most comprehensive examination of Nazi policy on performance and wages is found in Tilla Siegel, *Leistung und Lohn in der nationalsozialistischen "Ordnung der Arbeit"* (Opladen: Westdeutscher Verlag, 1989).

51. Overy, *Nazi Economic Recovery*, p. 44.

52. Kroll, *Von der Weltwirtschaftskrise zur Staatskonjunktur*, p. 577.

53. Karl Mandelbaum, "An Experiment in Full Employment: Controls in the German Economy, 1933–1938," in Oxford University Institute of Statistics, *The Economics of Full Employment* (Oxford: Basil Blackwell, 1944), p. 192; Rüdiger Hachtmann, "Lebenshaltungskosten und Reallöhne während des 'Dritten Reiches'", *Vierteljahrschrift für Sozial- und Wirtschaftsgeschichte* 75 (1988), pp. 32–73, especially p. 70, Table 10, and *Industriearbeit*, pp. 158–159. Hachtmann's "corrected" net weekly real income figures (1932 = 100) indicate an increase to 101.5 in

1935, followed by a dip to 100.2 in 1936. According to the Reich Statistical Office, real income by the end of 1934 had made up for nearly half of the loss incurred during the economic crisis. See BAK, R43II/323, memoranda by Franz Willuhn, April 18, 1935, and June 20, 1936.

54. For an excellent summary of Hugenberg's views on agricultural policy, see BAK, Nachlaß Hugenberg 129, including "Die Rettung des Bauern," May 17, 1933, draft of an article for the *Berliner Börsenzeitung;* May 20, 1933, speech given at the opening of the Wanderausstellung der Deutschen Landwirts-Gesellschaft, Berlin; May 21, 1933, press release, "Gerechter Preis—ein Beitrag zur Arbeitsbeschaffung." Hugenberg claimed he sought not a real increase in prices, but only "the creation of just prices," equalization of agricultural prices with the general price level.

55. BAK, R43II/323, "Vermerk über den Stand der Preise in Deutschland," Nov. 19, 1934, prepared by Franz Willuhn. According to the Reich Statistical Office, the cost of living had risen by 5.7 percent between May 1933 and May 1936. Food prices were up by 8.5 percent, clothing prices up by 12.6 percent, and housing costs unchanged. Costs for heating and electricity had fallen by 0.2 percent. See BAK, R43II/323, memoranda by Franz Willuhn, April 18, 1935, and June 20, 1936. For other estimates of cost of living increases, see Hachtmann, "Lebenshaltungskosten und Reallöhne." These estimates diverge from official estimates, especially for years after 1935. Barkai, *Nazi Economics,* pp. 144–146, 153, claims a strong Nazi ideological commitment to the peasantry, rather than economic considerations, produced significant increases in agricultural prices 1933–1935.

56. Mandelbaum, "Experiment in Full Employment," pp. 191–192.

57. *Akten der Reichskanzlei,* pt. 1, vol. 2, p. 786, Schacht's remarks before the Generalrat der Wirtschaft, Sept. 20, 1933.

58. BAK, R2/18675, D.R.d.F. [RFM], Vermerk, July 11, 1933, describing a meeting held July 1 in the offices of Öffa. Representatives of Öffa, the RFM, RAM, and the Deutsche Bau- u. Bodenbank A.G. all agreed to the finance ministry's proposal, but it was not implemented.

59. BAP, 31.01, 10100, RWM to Reichsverband der Deutschen Ton- u. Ziegelindustrie e.V., etc., Jan. 29, 1934.

60. HHStA, Abt. 485, 246, Der Generalinspektor für das deutsche Straßenwesen to Direktion der Gesellschaft "Reichsautobahnen," June 5, 1934, with enclosure, Der Generalinspektor für das deutsche Straßenwesen to Reichsverband des Ingenieurbaues E.V., Fachgruppe Straßenbau, June 5, 1934.

61. HHStA, Abt. 485, 248, Reichskommissar für Preisüberwachung, Rundschreiben no. 45, concerning "Preisüberwachung im Bauwesen," Jan. 19, 1935. Vertraulich! Sofort! Nicht für die Presse!

62. Ibid.

63. Ibid.

64. For information on price development and its impact on the German hand-icrafts industries, see HHStA, Abt. 485, 250, pamphlet titled "Die Preisentwicklung des Handwerks im Jahr 1935, prepared by the Reichsstand des Deutschen Hand-werks, May 1936. Statistics presented in this pamphlet were drawn in part from the publication *Wirtschaft und Statistik.*

65. HHStA, Abt. 485, 250, RWM to RFM, April 1, 1936, responding to RFM letter of Dec. 13, 1935 (not found in file). Schacht cited the development of the price of brick on the Berlin market. For the period 1930–1932, the general price was RM 17 to 18 per 1,000, with lows sometimes reaching the RM 14 to 16 range. In the spring of 1933, the labor trustees intervened with a new wage and price schedule that raised wages by 8 to 10 percent and boosted the price of brick to RM 22 per 1,000. The price of brick three years later, RM 23 to 24 on a virtually sold-out Berlin market, indicated to Schacht that the brick industry was not making "exceptional profits" from the construction boom.

3. National Socialist Work Creation from Theory to Practice

1. Henry Ashby Turner, Jr., *Big Business and the Rise of Hitler* (New York, Oxford: Oxford University Press, 1985), p. 71.

2. Ibid.

3. Harold James, *The German Slump* (Oxford: Clarendon Press, 1986), p. 347. For brief summaries of Hitler's economic ideas, see James, *German Slump*, pp. 345–353; Turner, *Big Business*, pp. 71–83.

4. Avraham Barkai, *Nazi Economics. Ideology, Theory, and Policy*, trans. Ruth Hadass-Vashitz (New Haven: Yale University Press, 1990), pp. ix, 18, 20, 226, 244.

5. BAK, R43II/308, Funk interview with *New York Times* correspondent Guido Enderis (Deutsches Nachrichtenburo, Berlin), April 14, 1939. Funk granted this interview in response to complaints from the United States concerning Germany's foreign trade policy.

6. James, *German Slump*, p. 347.

7. James, "Economic Reasons for the Collapse of the Weimar Republic," in *Weimar: Why Did German Democracy Fail?* ed. Ian Kershaw (New York: St. Martin's Press, 1990), p. 52; Turner, *Big Business*, p. 81.

8. Turner, *Big Business*, p. 62. Feder had described himself as "the ideologist of the movement" after Hitler made him responsible for the "preservation of the foundations of the [NSDAP] program" in Feb. 1926. See Albrecht Tyrell, "Gott-fried Feder and the NSDAP," in Peter D. Stachura, ed., *The Shaping of the Nazi State* (London: Croom Helm, 1978), p. 70. Feder was appointed state secretary in the Reich economics ministry on June 29, 1933, the same day Kurt Schmitt replaced

Alfred Hugenberg as Reich economics minister. His influence on policy proved to be inconsequential. He was placed on leave on Aug. 2, 1934, and was retired from the post on Nov. 16, 1934.

9. BAP, 25.01, Bd. 2/6788, Statistische Abteilung der Reichsbank, memorandum, "Zu Gottfried Feder: Das Radikalmittel," Nov. 11, 1930, with photocopy of Feder's "Das Radikalmittel," *Süddeutsche Monatshefte* (Feb. 1919), pp. 307–320. Feder advocated elimination of interest payments only on domestic debt. Germany would still have to meet its foreign obligations.

10. Ibid. Here and elsewhere, references to "the Reichsbank" refer to ideas and opinions expressed by the individual who prepared the memorandum cited.

11. BAP, 25.01, Bd. 2/6788, Statistische Abt. d. Reichsbank, memorandum (untitled), Feb. 27, 1932, report of Reichsbank employee who, on behalf of the statistical office, attended NSDAP Vortragsabend, Fachgruppe Bankwesen, Berlin, Feb. 26, 1932.

12. BAP, 25.01, Bd. 2/6788, Volkswirtschaftliche und Statistische Abt. d. Reichsbank, untitled memorandum dated Feb. 8, 1934, prepared by Director Dr. Müller at Schacht's request. Müller cited Feder's statements of Aug. and Oct. 1933, in which Feder spoke of a reduction of interest rates to a level at which the rate for "loan capital" would be lower than the rates for "production capital." This represents a notable shift from his earlier demands for the outright abolition of interest on loan capital. The memorandum quotes Feder's final remarks in a *Deutsche Welle* conversation with the social democrat Erik Nölting in Jan. 1931: "While today you laugh at our range of ideas, Herr Professor, the utopians (as you call them) of today are the realists of tomorrow. History will one day decide who was right in the end."

13. BAP, 25.01, Bd. 2/6788, Statistische Abt. d. Reichsbank, memorandum dated Nov. 15, 1930, "Die nationalsozialistischen Reichsanträge vom 15.–30. Oktober 1930." Turner, *Big Business*, p. 70, notes that even on the eve of Hitler's appointment to the chancellorship, "the statements of Nazi [Reichstag] deputies contributed little toward a clarification of the NSDAP's position."

14. BAP, 25.01, Bd. 2/6788, Statistische Abt. d. Reichsbank, memorandum dated Nov. 15, 1930, "Die nationalsozialistischen Reichsanträge vom 15.-30. Oktober 1930."

15. For recent references to the NSDAP's 1932 *Sofortprogramm* and *Aufbauprogramm*, see Barkai, *Nazi Economics*, pp. 40–48; Turner, *Big Business*, pp. 250, 288–289; James, *German Slump*, p. 350. As James notes, the Nazis may have valued reemployment not as an economic weapon but rather as a means to overcome class divisions and achieve political integration.

16. Tyrell, "Gottfried Feder and the NSDAP," pp. 74–76. Hitler had appointed Wagener head of the new economic policy department of the NSDAP's Reich command in Dec. 1930. For more on Wagener, see Henry A. Turner, Jr., ed.,

Hitler—Memoirs of a Confidant, trans. Ruth Hein (New Haven: Yale University Press, 1985).

17. For Strasser's organizational reforms, see Dietrich Orlow, *The History of the Nazi Party: 1919–1933* (Pittsburgh: University of Pittsburgh Press, 1969), pp. 256–276; Tyrell, "Gottfried Feder and the NSDAP," p. 76; Turner, *Big Business*, p. 285. Orlow (p. 264) notes that, until the Sept. 1932 reorganization, all of the Reich Economic Council's members were businessmen and corporation executives.

18. Tyrell, "Gottfried Feder and the NSDAP," pp. 76–77; Turner, *Big Business*, pp. 284–285; Martin Broszat, *The Hitler State: The Foundation and Development of the Internal Structure of the Third Reich* (New York: Longman, 1981), p. 52. The motives for Hitler's reorganization order of Sept. 22, 1932, are obscure. Broszat (p. 52) claimed that, whatever the motive, the order "subsequently had no particular significance."

19. Orlow, *History of the Nazi Party: 1919–1933*, p. 275.

20. HHStA, Abt. 483, 10924, NSDAP Reichsleitung, Reichsorganisationsleitung, Hauptabt. IV (Wirtschaft), Der Beauftragte f. das Wirtschaftsgebiete Mitte, Herbert v. Obwurzer, Dresden, to Dr. [Max] Ludewig, [NSDAP authorized agent (*Beauftragte*) for Germany's southwest economic region], Wiesbaden, Aug. 29, 1932.

21. Barkai, *Nazi Economics*, pp. 34, 45.

22. HHStA, Abt. 483/10924, NSDAP Reichsleitung, Der Reichsorganisationsleiter [signed Gregor Strasser], to Beauftragten der H. A. IV [Haupt-Abteilung IV (Wirtschaft)], to all Gau Wirtschafts-Referenten u. wirtschaftliche Fachberater, Oct. 10, 1932, Rundschreiben no. 4. Strasser appears to have been trying to use the period of confusion to assert his own authority over NSDAP economic policy.

23. HHStA, Abt.483/10924, NSDAP, Gau Baden, Hauptabteilung IV (Wirtschaft), Abteilung: Arbeitsbeschaffung, Karlsruhe, Sept. 15, 1932, Rundschreiben no. 2. Dienstausweisung f. die Fachberater f. Arbeitsbeschaffung.

24. Orlow, *History of the Nazi Party: 1919–1933*, pp. 290–291.

25. HHStA, Abt. 483/10924, NSDAP Reichsleitung, Kommission f. Wirtschaftsfragen. Unterkom. A: Wirtschaftspolitik. Der Geschäftsführer to Dr. Max Ludewig, Wiesbaden, Jan. 13, 1933, with two enclosures. The first of these was a copy of NSDAP Reichsleitung, Wirtschaftsberater des Führers Walther Funk, Rundschreiben, Jan. 12, 1933. The second enclosure was described as a copy of a "memorandum of the Führer of 15./20. 12. 1932," which formed the basis for Funk's Rundschreiben of Jan. 12, 1933. See Adolf Hitler, "Denkschrift über die inneren Gründe für die Verfügungen zur Herstellung einer erhöhten Schlagkraft der Bewegung," part 1, Dec. 15, 1932; part 2, Jan. 20, 1932. Hitler's memorandum is discussed, but not reproduced, in Orlow, *History of the Nazi Party: 1919–1933*, pp. 294–296.

26. Hitler, "Denkschrift," pt. 1.

27. Ibid.

28. Ibid., pt. 2.

29. StADü, Ebel 8, NSDAP Reichsleitung, III. Kommission f. Wirtschaftsfragen, Unterkommission B (signed Feder), Anordnung Nr. 1/33, Jan. 24, 1933, which describes Hitler's reorganization order of Dec. 15, 1932; NSDAP, Reichsleitung, Wirtschaftsberater des Führers Walther Funk, Rundschreiben, Jan. 12, 1933, listing the appointment of ten party members as "economic deputies of the NSDAP Reich executive" on the basis of Hitler's Dec. 15, 1932, reorganization order. The appointed economic deputies were Werner Daitz, Dr. Freiherr von Gregory, Wilhelm Keppler, Bernhard Köhler, Dr. Max Ludewig, Herbert von Obwurzer, Fritz Reinhardt, Dr. Theodor Adrian von Renteln, Walther Schuhmann, and Erich Winnacker. The former "Gau economic experts" (Gauwirtschafts-Referenten) were henceforth to be known as "Gau economic advisers" (Gauwirtschaftsberater). Orlow, *History of the Nazi Party: 1919–1933*, p. 295, indicates that Hitler dissolved both Main Department IV and the Reich Economic Council, "and merely retained Funk and Feder as his personal economic advisers." He makes no mention of the role of Funk and Feder in the new Third Commission for Economic Questions.

30. StADü, Ebel 8, NSDAP, Reichsleitung, Wirtschaftsberater des Führers Walther Funk, Rundschreiben, Jan. 12, 1933.

31. StADü, Ebel 8, NSDAP, Reichsleitung, III. Kommission f. Wirtschaftsfragen, Unterkommission B (signed Feder), Anordnung no.. 1/33, Jan. 24, 1933.

32. HHStA, Abt. 483, 10924, NSDAP Reichsleitung, Wirtschaftsberater des Führers Walther Funk to Wirtschaftsbeauftragten u. Gauwirtschaftsberater der NSDAP, Rundschreiben no. 2, Feb. 22, 1933.

33. Ibid.; Wirtshaftsberater des Führers Walther Funk, communication of Feb. 22, 1933, concerning opposition from Volksbund zum Schutz ersparten Vermögens, apparently sent to party Wirtschaftsbeauftragten and Gauwirtschaftsberater.

34. HHStA, Abt. 483, 10924, Funk's Rundschreiben no. 2, Feb. 22, 1933, quoting from unspecified Hitler speech (between Jan. 5 and Jan. 15, 1933) in Lippe during the Lippe-Detmold Landtag electoral campaign. Hitler campaigned heavily for Nazi party candidates in Lippe, with rewarding results. NSDAP candidates won 39.6 percent of the popular vote. See Max Domarus, ed., *Hitler Reden und Proklamationen, 1932–1945*, vol. 1, *Triumph, 1932–1938* (Neustadt a. d. Aisch: Verlagsdruckerei Schmidt, 1962), pp. 176–180. The passage quoted here is not found in the brief excerpts contained in Domarus's edition.

35. HHStA, Abt. 483, 10924, Funk's Rundschreiben no. 2, Feb. 22, 1933.

36. HHStA, Abt. 483, 10929, clipping from *Der Deutsche,* Dec. 12, 1933, "Ein Vortrag von Werner Daitz: Die Wirtschaftsprogrammatik der Nationalsozialismus." The press account does not cite Daitz's words directly. More extensive coverage of Daitz's remarks in the Dec. 4, 1933, issue of the *Völkischer Beobachter* makes no mention of the twenty-five-point program.

37. HHStA, Abt. 483, 10929, Dr. Fritz Nonnenbruch, "Rasse, Gesinnung, Führung in der Wirtschaft," clipping from *Völkischer Beobachter,* Jan. 30, 1934.

38. HHStA, Abt. 483, 10928, Dr. Fritz Nonnenbruch, "Das erste Ziel unserer Wirtschaftspolitik," clipping from *Frankfurter Volksblatt,* Feb. 17, 1935.

39. BAP, 25.01, vol. 2, no. 1863, "Nicht Kapitalismus, sondern Sozialismus," clipping from *Berliner Börsen Courier,* Oct. 27, 1933, speech to Reichsverband der Wirtschaftsleiter by Bernhard Köhler, Leiter der Wirtschaftspolitischen Kommission der NSDAP, on the theme of "Das Dritte Reich und der Kapitalismus." Associated with the Nazi movement since 1919, Köhler, an academically trained political economist specializing in the theory and propaganda of work creation, did not enter the NSDAP's inner circle of economic experts until 1930.

40. HHStA, Abt. 483, 10937, "Das Recht auf Arbeit als Wirtschaftsprinzip," clipping from *Völkischer Beobachter,* June 24, 1934.

41. HHStA, Abt. 483, 10937, "Arbeitsdenken besiegt Kapitaldenken," account from *Wirtschaftspolitischer Pressedienst* (WPD), Sept. 26, 1934, speech in Königsberg. As state secretary in the Reich economics ministry, Gottfried Feder was also proclaiming the "sovereignty of work over finance capital." See HHStA, Abt. 483, 10928, "Der Ausbau der deutschen Wirtschaft," clipping from *Berliner Morgenpost,* Aug. 20, 1933, account of Feder's speech in Danzig.

42. HHStA, Abt. 483, 10928, Fritz Nonnenbruch, "Die nationalsozialistische Wirtschaftspolitik," clipping from *Völkischer Beobachter,* Oct. 27, 1933.

43. Ibid.

44. Ian Kershaw has developed the general notion of a "Hitler myth" in *The "Hitler Myth": Image and Reality in the Third Reich* (Oxford: Clarendon Press, 1987), which originally appeared as *Der Hitler-Mythos: Volksmeinung und Propaganda im Dritten Reich* (Stuttgart: Deutsche Verlags-Anstalt, 1980).

45. BAK, R43II/536, "Besprechung mit Industriellen über Arbeitsbeschaffung," May 29, 1933; *Akten der Reichskanzlei,* pt. 1, vol. 1, pp. 506–527. For Hitler's opening remarks, see pp. 506–514.

46. BAK, R2/18677, RFM Vermerk on reallocation of Reinhardt program funds, Oct. 25, 1933; R2/18679, RFM Vermerk, Nov. 1933.

47. Rüdiger Hachtmann, *Industriearbeit im "Dritten Reich"* (Göttingen: Vandenhoeck & Ruprecht, 1989), pp. 283–284.

48. The sole reference to the absence of road construction in the original version of the Reinhardt program known to this author is found in Jürgen Stelzner, *Arbeitsbeschaffung und Wiederaufrüstung, 1933–1936* (Tübingen: Tübingen University dissertation, 1976), pp. 87, 241–242. He indicates (pp. 87, 238) that the Reich finance ministry felt that road construction already had received significant funding in the Papen and Gereke programs, and asserts that "construction of housing and roads did not in the least interest most of the industrialists." For an emphasis on the role of motorization and housing in Germany's economic recovery, see R. J. Overy, *The*

Nazi Economic Recovery, 1932–1938 (London: Macmillan, 1982), pp. 48–50; idem, "Cars, Roads and Economic Recovery in Germany, 1932–8," *Economic History Review*, 2nd ser., 28 (1975), pp. 466–483; idem, "Unemployment in the Third Reich," *Business History* 29 (1987), pp. 253–281; Charles S. Maier, *In Search of Stability: Explorations in Historical Political Economy* (New York: Cambridge University Press, 1987), pp. 97–99; G. F. R. Spencerley, "R. J. Overy and the Motorisierung: A Comment," *Economic History Review* 32 (1979), pp. 100–106; Overy's response, "The German Motorisierung and Rearmament: A Reply," *Economic History Review* 32 (1979), pp. 107–113; Timothy W. Mason, private correspondence with author, May 10, 1988. In *War and Economy in the Third Reich* (Oxford: Clarendon Press, 1994), Overy has somewhat softened his earlier emphasis on motorization as the key to Germany's economic recovery.

49. N-WHStA, Reg. Aachen 16849, Leopold Peill to Reg. Präsident Eggert Reeder, Oct. 24, 1933.

50. N-WHStA, Reg. Aachen 16857, president RfAA to LAA presidents, April 21, 1933, enclosing the results of a meeting of top RfAA officials: Referentenbesprechung über Arbeitsbeschaffung am 24. März 1933, Berlin, March 31, 1933, with report on "Jahresplan 1933. Ergebnisse"; president LAA Rheinland to AA directors, May 11, 1933, "Arbeitsbeschaffung, Jahresplan 1933." Political considerations—the desire to disperse throughout the countryside potentially dangerous left-leaning masses of the urban unemployed—may have played a role in defining the strategy for 1933.

51. Barkai's contention in *Nazi Economics* that Nazi agricultural policy and resettlement policy was driven primarily by ideological considerations is not well supported by the evidence. Land improvement and resettlement was viewed prior to Hitler's assumption of power as the only practical method of dealing with massive unemployment. RM 200 million of the original RM 500 million Gereke program was earmarked for *Bodenkulturarbeiten* and other projects connected with agricultural improvements. Because of onerous financing terms, there was "relatively little demand" from local authorities for these funds during the spring of 1933. See N-WHStA, Reg. Aachen 16857, president RfAA to LAA presidents and Bezirkscommissioners for FAD, March 4, 1933 (Beilage zum Reichs-Arbeitsmarkt-Anzeiger no. 5, March 8, 1933); president RfAA and Reich Commissioner for the FAD to LAA presidents, April 27, 1933.

52. For details on the unfolding of work creation programs under Hitler, see Dan P. Silverman, "National Socialist Economics: *The Wirtschaftswunder* Reconsidered," in Barry Eichengreen and T. J. Hatton, eds., *Interwar Unemployment in International Perspective* (Dordrecht: Kluwer Academic Publishers, 1988), pp. 185–220.

53. BAK, R43II/536, letters of RAM to state secretary in Reich Chancellery, April 22, 1933, "Vorschlage des Reichsarbeitsministers zur Arbeitsbeschaffung," and April 27, 1933, concerning "Arbeitsbeschaffung." The April 27 document

appears in *Akten der Reichskanzlei*, pt. 1, vol. 1, pp. 400–415. In contrast to Reinhardt, a trusted Nazi Old Fighter, Seldte joined the NSDAP on April 26, 1933.

54. BAK, R43II/536, RAM to state secretary in Reich Chancellery, April 27, 1933, "Arbeitsbeschaffung"; *Akten der Reichskanzlei*, pt. 1, vol. 1, pp. 400–415. For an analysis of Germany's housing shortage and attempts to relieve it, see Dan P. Silverman, "A Pledge Unredeemed: The Housing Crisis in Weimar Germany," *Central European History* 3 (1970), pp.112–139.

55. For Hitler's meeting with industrialists, see *Akten der Reichskanzlei*, pt. 1, vol. 1, pp. 506–527, "Besprechung mit führenden Industriellen, 29. Mai 1933." Bavaria's representative to the Reich government and the Reichsrat reported work creation proposals from both the RFM (RM 675 million) and the RAM (RM 1 billion to 1.5 billion) on May 26 and 29, 1933. He had heard (May 29) that an agreement had been reached between the RFM and the RAM, under which "in the main, the Reinhardt program [RFM] shall be pursued." See BHStA, MA 106743, Bayerische stellv. Bevollmächtigte zum Reichsrat, Ministerialdirektor Dr. [Paul] Hammer, to [Bavarian] Minister-president, May 26, 1933, with enclosure, "Entwurf eines Gesetzes zur Verminderung der Arbeitslosigkeit vom —— Mai 1933"; Hammer to Bavarian minister-president Ludwig Siebert, May 29, 1933. For similar reports from Württemberg's representative in Berlin, see HStAS, E130b, Bü 3221, Württembergische Bevollmächtigte zum Reichsrat, Ministerialdirektor Dr. [Rudolf] Widmann, to Württ. economics ministry, May 12, 1933, with enclosure, "Anmeldungen zum Arbeitsbeschaffungsprogramm in der [RAM] Sitzung am 9. Mai 1933"; Württ. Gesandtschaft, Berlin, to Württ. economics ministry, May 23, 1933.

56. BAK, R2/18675, "Anmeldung zum Arbeitsbeschaffungsprogramm in der Sitzung am 9. Mai 1933," prepared by RAM; RAM to state secretary in the Reich chancellery, May 11, 1933, with enclosure, "Vermerk über das Ergebnis in der Besprechung im Reichsarbeitsministerium am 9. Mai," signed by RAM Ministerialrat Dr. Werner Stephan.

57. BAK, R2/18675, RFM, "Vermerk" signed by Ministerialrat Stephan Poerschke, May 10, 1933. Reinhardt participated in this meeting. The RFM may have taken its cue from Reichsbank president Hjalmar Schacht, who feared credit requirements would overwhelm the Reichsbank's capacity. See BHStA, MA 106743, Bayerische stellv. Bevollmächtigte zum Reichsrat, Ministerialdirektor Hammer, to [Bavarian] minister-president Ludwig Siebert, May 29, 1933.

58. BAK, R43II/536, RWM (signed Hugenberg) to state secretary in the Reich Chancellery (Lammers), May 11, 1933, "Denkschrift über die Finanzierung der Arbeitsbeschaffung"; BAK, R43II/536, state secretary in the Reich Chancellery to RAM, etc., June 3, 1933, with enclosure: "Vermerk über die Chefsbesprechung am 31. Mai 1933 . . . über Arbeitsbeschaffung"; *Akten der Reichskanzlei*, pt. 1, vol. 1, p. 533.

59. The cabinet approved the first "Reinhardt program" in a "Chefsbesprechung

über Arbeitsbeschaffung," May 31, 1933. See *Akten der Reichskanzlei*, pt. 1, vol. 1, pp. 530–534.

60. See BAK, R43II/536, R2/18675, RWM to all Reich ministers and state secretary in Reich chancellery (Lammers), June 28, 1933, Schnellbrief, "Arbeitsbeschaffungsmaßnahmen auf Grund des Gesetzes zur Verminderung der Arbeitslosigkeit vom 1. Juni 1933." Hugenberg's absence is noteworthy. When he sought to have himself added to the committee as a voting member, he was firmly rebuffed by Krosigk and Schacht. See BAK, R43II/536, RWM to RFM (copy to state secretary in Reich chancellery Lammers), June 21, 1933, "Durchführungsbestimmungen zum Gesetz zur Verminderung der Arbeitslosigkeit"; Lammers to RFM, June 26, 1933, supporting Hugenberg's request; RFM to Lammers, June 30 and July 6, 1933; *Akten der Reichskanzlei*, pt. 1, vol. 1, p. 533.

61. For the amounts requested and the June 27, 1933, allocation schedule, see BAK, R43II/536, RAM to Reich chancellor (copies to RFM, Reichsbank president), June 8, 1933, pp. 254–255; "Vorschläge des Herrn Reichsverkehrsministers," p. 294; "Vorschlage des Herrn Reichsministers für Ernährung u. Landwirtschaft," p. 294; RFM to all Reich ministers and state secretary in Reich chancellery, Schnellbrief, June 28, 1933, p. 291.

62. "Verordnung zur Durchführung der Arbeitsbeschaffungsmaßnahmen auf Grund des Gesetzes zur Verminderung der Arbeitslosigkeit vom 28. Juni 1933, RGBl, 1933, vol. 1, p. 425; N-WHStA, Reg. Aachen 16848, Reich food and agriculture minister to governments of Länder, etc., July 24, 1933, concerning "Meliorationskredite." Although Hugenberg's departure from the cabinet is generally attributed to Hitler's annoyance at an inflammatory speech on colonial policy that Hugenberg delivered at the World Economic Conference in London, his obstructionist position on work creation must have been an equally important factor in his removal.

63. HStAS, E130b, Bü3321, pp. 455, 460, Württ. Gesandschaft, Berlin, to Württ. economics ministry, Stuttgart, May 23, 1933; Vertretung Württ. beim Reich to Württ. economics ministry, June 19, 1933. Owing to the condition of Germany's capital markets and the diminishing tax base, funding for "luxury roads," so-called *nur-Autostraßen*, had been expressly prohibited under the Gereke *Sofortprogramm*.

64. Todt cited the ending of the rails versus roads conflict as one of the virtues of the *Reichsautobahnen* program. See BHStA, MWi 8682, clipping from *Münchner Neuste Nachrichten*, Aug. 4, 1933, "Großzugige Straßenbau-Politik."

65. See Chapter 7 for funding of road construction.

66. This housing program resulted not from any thorough analysis of the requirements of either the housing or labor markets, but rather as a response to a tax-reduction proposal submitted to the Reich Chancellery by Reich finance minister Krosigk only five days earlier. For details see Dan P. Silverman, "National Socialist

Economics: The *Wirtschaftswunder* Reconsidered," in Eichengreen and Hatton, eds., *Interwar Unemployment*, pp. 195–196.

67. HHStA, Abt. 483, 10928, Fritz Nonnenbruch, "Die Führung der Wirtschaft durch den Staat," clipping from *Völkischer Beobachter*, March 7, 1935. Schleicher's policy, in the form of Günther Gereke's *Sofortprogramm*, was in fact continued and completed by the Hitler government. The significance of Nonnenbruch's failure to mention Franz von Papen's economic policies can be only a matter of speculation.

4. Work Creation in Action

1. GStAPK, 90/1079, *Nationalsozialistische Aufbauarbeit in Ostpreußen: Ein Arbeitsbericht. Auf Grund amtlicher Quellen herausgegeben im Auftrage des Ober-präsidiums Königsberg Pr.* (Königsberg Pr.: Sturm-Verlag G.m.b.H., 1934), pp. 17–18; BAK, R43II/534, Aug. 16, 1933 telegram, Oberpräsident Ostpreußen to Reich chancellor; StAD, 102/1687, clipping from *Mitteilungen des deutschen Städtetages*, Nov. 20, 1933, no. 11, p. 516, "Kommunale Sozialpolitik," with subtitle, "Arbeitsbeschaffung." Koch also notified Prussian minister-president Hermann Göring that "within a month we have succeeded in creating work for all of the unemployed in the province of East Prussia. In the city of Königsberg alone more than 30,000 willing-to-work men and women have been provided work." See GStAPK, 90/1079, Deutsche Reichspost, telegram, Oberpräsident [East Prussia] to Ministerpräsident Göring, Aug. 15, 1933. As a result of the success of his work creation measures, Koch "was considered by Hitler as a model Gauleiter and Oberpräsident." See Peter Hüttenberger, *Die Gauleiter: Studie zum Wandel des Macht-gefüges in der NSDAP*, Schriftenreihe der Vierteljahrshefte für Zeitgeschichte, 19 (Stuttgart: Deutsche Verlags-Anstalt, 1969), p. 108.

2. *Nationalsozialistische Aufbauarbeit in Ostpreußen*, p. 17. The claim of single-minded Nazi leadership was pure fiction. See Hüttenberger, *Die Gauleiter*, p. 108, and GStAPK, 90/1079, Dr. E. Brandes, Preußischer Staatsrat, Zaupern-Insterburg [East Prussia] to minister for agriculture and forests, Darré, Sept. 26, 1933. Stimmungsbericht, for Koch's bitter conflicts with Richard-Walter Darré (who was both Reich and Prussian agriculture minister and leader of the Reich Food Estate—Reichsnährstand), and the SA. The latter conflict involved "preventive arrests" and prompted Brandes to report that "the economic recovery of the province suffers under this discord."

3. StAD, 102/1687, *Mitteilungen des deutschen Städetages*, Nov. 20, 1933, p. 516, "Kommunale Sozialpolitik." The private sector received no public subsidies for these new jobs. During 1933, Königsberg's unemployed virtually disappeared over-night, and soon began to reappear. End-of-month statistics for 1933: Jan., 32,315; June, 24,536; July, 21,464; Aug., 1,076; Sept., 1,089; Oct. 3,630; Nov., 6,654; Dec.,

13,525. In 1934, the number of unemployed in Königsberg never fell below 3,115 (September).

4. Ibid.; *Nationalsozialistische Aufbauarbeit in Ostpreußen*, p. 18. The wage set by the Trustee was RM 0.36 per hour for single unskilled workers, and RM 0.40 per hour for married unskilled laborers. *Autobahnen* construction workers in Bavaria who complained that "Hitler should work for 50 Pfennige per hour!" were in fact well paid compared with these East Prussian laborers. See BHStA, MA106767, AA Rosenheim, Situationsbericht for July 31, 1934, prepared Aug. 8, 1934.

5. *Nationalsozialistische Aufbauarbeit in Ostpreußen*, pp. 18, 28–29.

6. StAD, 102/1687, *Mitteilungen des deutschen Städetages*, Nov. 20, 1933, "Kommunale Sozialpolitik."

7. See, for example, N-WHStA, Reg. Aachen, 16899, Vorsitzende des Kreisausschußes [Landrat Classen] to president RfAA, Feb. 16, 1934; AA Aachen to Reg. Pres. Aachen, Feb. 17, 1934; Vorsitzende des Landkreis Aachen, Kreiswohlfahrtsamt [Landrat Classen] to Reg. Präs., monthly reports Dec. 9, 1933, April 9 and July 10, 1934. It was reported that the *Landhilfe*, which recruited single young men and women up to age 21, was taking in entire families of agricultural laborers in East Prussia. How, or whether, East Prussian authorities obtained an exception for this procedure was not indicated. See StAD 102/1687, *Mitteilungen des deutschen Städetages*, Nov. 20, 1933, "Kommunale Sozialpolitik." For regulations governing the placement of youths in the *Landhilfe*, see N-WHStA, Reg. Aachen 16858, president RfAA to LAA and AA, March 3, 1933; AA Erkelenz 3, p. 29, Preßedienst der LAA Rheinland, March 22, 1933, "Die Landhilfe für bäuerliche Betriebe."

8. GStAPK, 90/1079, Oberpräsident of Province Ostpreußen to Reich chancellor—Reichskommissar für das Land Preußen, Jan. 24, 1933, "Notstandsmaßnahmen für die Provinz Ostpreußen," an eleven-page report with three appendices.

9. GStAPK, 90/1079, and BAP 39.05, 127, Prussian minister-president to Reich interior minister, Feb. 16, 1933 (signed v. Papen as Reich commissioner for Prussia; Hitler appointed Hermann Göring Prussian minister-president on April 10, 1933); Reich interior minister (signed Pfundter) to state secretary in the Reich chancellery, etc., Feb. 18, 1933, Schnellbrief inviting Reich and Prussian officials to Feb. 24 "provisional deliberation" on the East Prussian situation; memorandum, "Ergebnis der kommissarischen Beratung vom 24. Februar 1933 über die Notlage Ostpreußens"; Reich interior minister (signed Pfundter) to Reich Commissar for Prussia, Feb. 25, 1933, Schnellbrief, containing (on reverse of letter) proposal for a press release. See also BAP 39.05, 127, Prussian finance minister v. Popitz to Prussian minister president (K.d.I.), Feb. 6, 1933.

10. GStAPK, 90/1079, Prussian minister for agriculture, domains, and forests to Reich commissioner for Prussia (Prussian minister-president), March 3, 1933; GStAPK, 90/1079, RFM to Reich minister for food and agriculture, March 4,

1933; Reich minister for food and agriculture to Reich interior minister, March 11, 1933; RAM to Reich interior minister, April 19, 1933.

11. GStAPK, 90/1079, press clipping from Wolf's Telegraphisches Büro, Berlin, July 5, 1933, "Großzügige Aktion zur Rettung Ostpreußens"; RFM to Reichswehr minister, Aug. 19, 1933; RFM to president of Landesfinanzamt in Königsberg, Aug. 19, 1933.

12. *Akten der Reichskanzlei*, pt. 1, vol. 1, pp. 618–624, Chefsbesprechung vom 5. Juli 1933. Present, among others, were Hitler, Frick, Krosigk, Blomberg, Funk, and Koch.

13. BAP, 39.03, 225, Vermerk, July 26, 1933, signed by Dr. Zschucke, RfAA, concerning arrangements for East Prussian work creation program.

14. Ibid.

15. BAP, 39.03, 225, "Verteilung der für Flußregulierung vorgesehen 100 millionen RM," RFM decree of June 28, 1933; Reich minister for food and agriculture (signed Darré) to governments of Länder, July 24, 1933, explaining change in definition of *"Flußregulierung;* Niederschrift über die Besprechung vom 29. Juli 1933 betreffend Beteiligung der Provinz Ostpreußen an dem Arbeitsbeschaffungsprogramm (Reinhardt-Programm)"; president RfAA to president LAA Ostpreußen, Aug. 3, 1933, concerning Reinhardt program, "Sondermitteln für Ostpreußen."

16. GStAPK, 90/1079, Oberpräsident of Province East Prussia (signed Gauleiter Erich Koch) to minister-president (Göring), Sept. 3, 1934, with enclosure, *Nationalsozialistische Aufbauarbeit in Ostpreußen.*

17. *Nationalsozialistische Aufbauarbeit in Ostpreußen*, pp. 10–14. See also Dr. Hans Bernhard v. Grünberg, "Die Hauptgrundsätze des Ostpreußenplanes," in *Das nationalsozialistische Ostpreußen* (Königsberg: Ostdeutsche Verlagsanstalt u. Druckerei Gebr. Kaspereit, 1934), pp. 7–42.

18. GStAPK, 151/2369, "Ostpreußenprogramm: Denkschrift zu den Beschlüßen des Ostpreußenausschußes in der Sitzung vom 27. Oktober 1936," submitted by the Oberpräsident of the province East Prussia. Confidential, (no date; probably late 1936 or early 1937). Sixteen-page memorandum with five appendices.

19. BAP, 39.03, "Niederschrift über die am 8. 8. 33 vorm 10 Uhr abgehaltene Besprechung mit den Präsidenten der LAA über die Unterbringung von Arbeitslosen," chaired by Syrup, remarks by East Prussian LAA president Gassner; BAP, 39.03, 233, memorandum on East Prussian Landdienst, Oct. 12, 1933, signed by Regierungsrat Gisevius.

20. Information on East Prussian *Kameradschaftslagern* is found in BAP, 39.03, 225, "Niederschrift über die am 8. 8. 33 vorm 10 Uhr abgehaltene Besprechung mit den Präsidenten der LAA über die Unterbringung von Arbeitslosen"; BAP, 39.03, 220, two unsigned, undated memoranda on "Die zukünftige Entwicklung der Notstandsarbeiten."

21. BAP, 39.03, 220, memoranda on "Die zukünftige Entwicklung der Notstandsarbeiten."

22. BAP, 39.03, 225, "Niederschrift über die am 8. 8. 33 vorm 10 Uhr abgehaltene Besprechung mit den Präsidenten der LAA über die Unterbringung von Arbeitslosen"; BAP, 39.03, 220, memoranda on "Die zukünftige Entwicklung der Notstandsarbeiten"; RfAA Vermerk, March 5, 1934, describing March 3 meeting of Syrup, Oberregierungsrat v. Hertzberg, and Count Büdingen of the Verein "Arbeitsdank."

23. BHStA, MWi 3135, Staatsministerium des Innern to the Regierungen, Kammern des Innern, and to the Kommandatur of Dachau concentration camp, Nov. 22, 1934.

24. BAP, 39.03, 220, memorandum, "Die zukünftige Entwicklung der Notstandsarbeiten"; N-WHStA, Reg. Aachen 16849, Oberpräsident Rheinprovinz to Reg. Präs. in Aachen, Koblenz, Köln, Düsseldorf, Trier, July 25, 1933, with Aktenvermerk dated Aug. 2 on reverse; HHStA, Abt. 483/10929, press clipping from *Völkischer Beobachter,* Aug. 19, 1933, "Das neue Wachstum in der Wirtschaft."

25. For Düsseldorf-Mettmann unemployment statistics, see monthly reports in N-WHStA, Reg. Aachen, 16876; Oberpräsident Rheinprovinz to Vorsitzenden des Kreisausschußes in Düren, Sept. 28, 1933, with copy of unidentified press notice, "Starker Rückgang der Arbeitslosigkeit im Kreise Düsseldorf-Mettmann." Of all Landkreise in the Rhineland, Düsseldorf-Mettmann ranked highest in the number of unemployed. It lay adjacent to the city of Düsseldorf and was later consolidated with the Stadtkreis.

26. N-WHStA, Reg. Aachen, 16899 and StAD, 102/1687, Oberpräsident Rheinprovinz to Reg. Präs. Rheinprovinz, Sept. 4, 1933, with five appendices, each describing an aspect of the "Tapolski Plan."

27. Ibid.

28. Ibid.

29. N-WHStA, Reg. Aachen 16899, president RfAA to LAA presidents, Aug. 19, 1933, containing reference to RFM Aug. 7 letter to Prussian interior ministry.

30. N-WHStA, Reg. Aachen 16899, Oberpräsident Rheinprovinz to Reg. Präs., Oct. 11, 1933, citing reports received from president LAA Rheinland. The Oberpräsident asked that district welfare authorities bring their subsidies in line with those paid under the Reich Landhilfe program.

31. N-WHStA, Reg. Aachen 16899, Landrat Landkreis Aachen to Industrieverband in Stolberg, Oct. 17, 1933; Landrat Monschau to Oberpräsident in Koblenz, Sept. 30, 1933. See also, among many others, Vorsitzende Kreisausschuß Geilenkirchen-Heinsberg to Oberpräsident Rheinprovinz, Sept. 28, 1933; Reg. Präs. Aachen to Oberpräsident Rheinprovinz, Oct. 19, 1933; Vorsitzende Kreisausschuß Düren to Oberpräsident Rheinprovinz, Sept. 20 and 30, 1933.

32. BAK, R2/18676, RAM to RFM, July 28, 1933, "Arbeitsbeschaffung in Ber-

lin"; R2/18679, Oberpräsident of province Brandenburg and of Berlin to Staatssekretär Reinhardt, RFM, Oct. 10, 1933.

33. For the development of the Göring Plan, see BAK, R2/18606, Prussian minister for economics and labor to Staatskommissar der Hauptstadt Berlin et al., May 11, 1934, "Berliner Plan zur Bekämpfung der Arbeitslosigkeit" (Göring Plan); R2/18606, Prussian Regierungsrat [Hans Bernd] Gisevius to Ministerialrat Raps (RFM), April 24, 1934; Prussian minister-president Göring to RAM (copy to RFM), May 4, 1934. The May 15, 1934, meeting that approved the plan is detailed in R2/18606, RFM, Vermerk, May 17, 1934. For the final plan, see BAK, R2/18606, and StAN, LRA Rothenburg 1975, Fach 645, 9^I, pamphlet, published by the RfAA, "Beschäftigung von Notstandsarbeitern aus Groß-Berlin bei auswärtigen Maßnahmen: Göring-Plan." The East German historian Lotte Zumpe has attributed the plan to Staatskommissar der Reichshauptstadt Dr. Julius Lippert; Göring's name simply lent it the weight needed to see it through. See Lotte Zumpe, "Die Entwicklung der Arbeitslosigkeit in Berlin 1932 bis 1935 und die Maßnahmen zu ihrer Verringerung (Vom 'Papen-Plan' bis zum 'Göring-Plan'), *Jahrbuch für Wirtschaftsgeschichte*, Sonderband, *Zur Wirtschafts- und Sozialgeschichte Berlins vom 17. Jahrhundert bis zur Gegenwart* (Berlin: Akademie-Verlag, 1986), p. 193.

34. BAK, R2/1806, memorandum dated July 20, 1934, prepared by Prussian Regierungsrat Gisevius for July 23 meeting to discuss implementation of the Göring Plan; BAK, R2/18607, account of "Besprechung in der Hauptstelle [of RfAA] mit der Sacharbeitern der Landesarbeitsämter über Fragen der wertschaffenden Arbeitslosenfürsorge am 24. und 25. Juli 1934." Number of Berlin unemployed reporting to employment offices (end of month): *1933:* Jan.: 654,878; March: 627,043; June: 601,511; Sept.: 531,116; Dec.: 582,562. *1934:* Jan.: 504,430; March: 424,511; June: 356,995; Sept.: 279,427; Dec.: 277,267. *1935:* Jan.: 303,146; March: 262,167; June: 218,210; Sept.: 197,123; Dec.: 244,558. The lows for 1936 (126,232) and 1937 (73,994) were reached in Sept.

35. BAP, 33.09, 221, AA Torgau to president LAA Mitteldeutschland, Nov. 19, 1934. BAP 39.03, 238 contains numerous applications for RfAA loans for airport projects that would employ Berliners.

36. BAK, R2/18607, Oberpräsident of Provinz Brandenburg and Grenzmark Posen-Westpreußen to Prussian interior minister, Sept. 27, 1934.

37. GStAPK, 90/1718, Oberbürgermeister Berlin to Ministerialrat Gramsch, Preußische Staatsministerium, Sept. 7, 1934, containing enclosure, a copy of the minutes of a Sept. 3 meeting concerning the "inclusion of Reichsautobahnen projects in the Göring-Plan." The minutes are identified as follows: Berlin, Sept. 4, 1934, "Vermittlung von Berliner Arbeitslosen zur Reichsautobahn. Ergebnis der Besprechung am 3. 9. 1934."

38. GStAPK, 90/1718, "Vermittlung von Berliner Arbeitslosen zur Reichsautobahn: Ergebnis der Besprechung am 3. 9. 1934." The terms negotiated between

Berlin authorities and inspector general Todt are also found in HHStA, Abt. 485/ 259, Reichsbahnen Direktion to all oberste Bauleitungen [district headquarters, oberste Bauleitung für den Bau der Kraftfahrbahn, OBK] Oct. 8, 1934, with enclosure, "Richtlinien für den Einsatz Berliner Arbeitsloser." These guidelines explicitly stated that "the employment of Berlin unemployed on the Reichsautobahnen takes place within the framework of the Berlin battle for work, known as the Göring-Plan."

39. GStAPK, 90/1718, "Vermittlung von Berliner Arbeitslosen zur Reichsautobahn: Ergebnis der Besprechung am 3. 9. 1934"; HHStA, Abt. 485/259, OBK Frankfurt/M to Reichsautobahnen Direktion Berlin, Oct. 17, 1934 (draft).

40. In one case, married Berliners employed on the Bremen-Hamburg stretch walked off the job when their employer sought to reduce payments for family support. Of the workers, 32 were arrested, and 107 were dismissed and sent home to Berlin, where welfare authorities promptly suspended their support payments. The DAF asked Göring to intervene and lay down guidelines for decent conditions for the workers and their dependents in Berlin, "so as not to allow the measures bearing your name to appear antisocial." See GStAPK, 90/1718, Deutsche Arbeitsfront, Reichsbetriebsgemeinschaft Bau, to Prussian minister-president Göring, Oct. 19, 1934, with enclosure, "Bericht über Vorkommnisse beim Bau der Reichsautobahnstraße Bremen-Hamburg."

41. Todt cited the example of one contractor on the Berlin-Eberswalde stretch who had to dismiss 100 of 300 laborers drawn from the greater Berlin area. See HHStA, Abt. 485/262, Reichsautobahnen Direktion Berlin to all OBK, June 1, 1934; Abt. 485/259, General inspector for German roads to president RfAA, Oct. 24, 1934 (copy); president RfAA to LAA presidents, Nov. 28, 1934 (copy), recapping Todt's complaints and asking LAA to comply with the general-inspector's requests; Reichsautobahnen Direktion Berlin to all OBK, Jan. 29, 1935, outlining the agreement between Todt and the RfAA. Attempts to place jobless men from other large cities in *Autobahnen* construction produced similar complaints. In June and July 1934, Bavarian *Autobahnen* construction firms refused to take laborers from Munich after their "unfavorable experience" with them. One AA director recommended that the political police be assigned to oversee the workers. See BHStA, MA/ 106765, Situationsberichte of AA Trauenstein, June 11, 1934; AA Holzkirchen/ Oberbayern, June 10, 1934; AA München, June 30, 1934; AA Rosenheim, July 1, 1934.

42. BAK, R2/18606, president RfAA to RFM, June 4, 1935. If Syrup's figures are correct, then very little of the decline in the number of Berlin unemployed (n. 34) can be attributed to the Göring Plan.

43. HHStA, Abt. 485/259, Reichsautobahnen Direktion Berlin to all OBK, letters of Aug. 16 and Sept. 16, 1935.

44. See numerous documents in HStAS, E130b, Bü 3221, Bü 3222.

45. StAN, LRA Schwabach 1984, No. 4282, Bavarian minister-president (signed Siebert) to all Reg. Präs., July 3, 1933, announcing his intention to launch a "comprehensive" Bavarian work creation program for fall and winter; BHStA, MA 106743, state finance ministry to state ministries, Aug. 25, 1933. After studying law, Siebert entered the Bavarian civil service and later served as mayor of Lindau. After the Nazi takeover, he was appointed provisional Bavarian finance minister in March 1933. The following month, he was named Bavarian minister-president and finance minister. In 1936, he was also entrusted with the duties of Bavarian economics minister. Although NSDAP records indicated he entered the party in 1931, Siebert claimed he joined "officially" in 1930, and had campaigned for a Reichstag seat in 1926 as an NSDAP candidate at the request of the Lindau Nazi organization. See BHStA, MA 107593, Siebert to Reich and Prussian minister of interior, c/o State Secretary Pfundter, Oct. 14, 1936.

46. The Bavarian Handwerkskammertag held on Sept. 14 agreed that all member organizations would contribute to a RM 200,000 loan repayable with 4½ percent interest to enable the state to carry out its work creation program. Local chambers lacking liquid funds were to borrow their share of the contribution. See BHStA, MWi 3132, Bavarian state economics ministry, division for commerce, industry and trade to state finance ministry, Sept. 21, 1933; Nuremberg chamber of industry and commerce to Bavarian state economics ministry, division for commerce, industry, and trade, Sept. 14, 1933; Handwerkskammer of upper Bavaria to state economics ministry, Sept. 20, 1933.

47. BHStA, MWi 3132, Ministerialsitzung vom 19. Sept. 1933; MA 106743, clipping from *Gesetz- und Verordnungs- Blatt für den Freistaat Bayern*, Sept. 30, 1933, containing "Gesetz zur Bekämpfung der Arbeitslosigkeit in Bayern vom 22. September 1933," and "Verordnung zur Sicherstellung ausreichender Arbeitskräfte für die Landwirtschaft (Erweiterte Landhilfe in Bayern) vom 29. September 1933."

48. BHStA, MWi 3132, Ministerialsitzung vom 19. Sept. 1933; Ministerialsitzung vom 14. Nov. 1933; MA 106743, clipping from *Gesetz- und Verordnungs- Blatt für den Freistaat Bayern*, "VO zur Sicherstellung ausreichender Arbeitskräfte für die Landwirtschaft (Erweitete Landhilfe in Bayern) vom 29. September 1933"; for Landhilfe statistics, MA 106743, Landesarbeitsamt Bayern, *Arbeit und Arbeitslosigkeit in Bayern im Jahre 1934* (LAA Bayern, Munich, 1934), pp. 58–60; StAN, Regierung von Oberfranken und Mittelfranken, Kammer des Innern, Abg. 1978 (hereafter Reg. O.u.M, KdI), no. 3440, [Bavarian] State economics ministry, department of agriculture, to Vorstände der Bezirksämter, May 18 and June 6, 1934.

49. BHStA, MWi 5955, Vormerkung über eine Besprechung bei Herrn Ministerpräsidenten Siebert über die Denkschrift des Bayerischen Industriellen-Verbandes, "Durch Starkung. . .," dated Sept. 7, 1933; Aufzeichnung über die Bespre-

chung über Industreifragen am Freitag, den 29. 9. 33, im Staatsministerium für Wirtschaft, Abt. f. Handel, Industrie und Gewerbe; MWi 3132, Ministerialsitzung vom 14. Nov. 1933.

50. BHStA, MWi 5955, "Ergebnis der von der Landesgruppe Bayern des Reichsstandes der Deutschen Industrie veranlassten Rundfrage bei den bayerischen Industreiunternehmungen betreffend Arbeitsbesschaffung," Aug. 1933. Of the 1,590 industrial firms employing 226,392 persons responding, 995 firms employing 125,014 persons indicated they could not take on any additional workers over the winter of 1933–34. Another 456 firms employing 85,670 indicated willingness to take on 12,000 under "appropriate conditions."

51. BHStA, MWi 5955, Aufzeichnung über die Besprechung über Industreifragen am Freitag, den 29. 9. 33, im Staatsministerium für Wirtschaft, Abt. f. Handel, Industrie und Gewerbe.

52. BHStA, MWi 5955, "Verordnung über Kredithilfe zur Arbeitsbeschaffung in industriellen und gewerblichen Betrieben," Nov. 15, 1933; MWi 3132, Ministerialsitzung vom 14. Nov. 1933. The Reichsbank, apparently fearing many similar demands, stipulated that news of its agreement to rediscount the bills be withheld from the public.

53. BHStA, MWi 5955, press clipping, *Bayr. Staatszeitung,* Feb. 13, 1934, "Staatliche Kredithilfe für Industrie und Gewerbe"; Bayerischer Industriellen-Verband EV, "Die Staatliche Kredithilfe in Bayern," Aug. 31, 1934. The Bavarian state government had limited its guarantee to only 50 percent of the total credits approved.

54. BHStA, MWi 5955, Seyboth [Bavarian ambassador in Berlin] to Bavarian state economics ministry, department for trade, industry, and commerce, Feb. 6, 1933, reporting that further pursuit of the matter in Berlin was "entirely hopeless." See also Bavarian deputy plenipotentiary to the Reichsrat, Ministerialdirektor Dr. Paul Hammer, to Herr Blum [Ministerialdirektor, Bavarian state finance ministry], Jan. 10, 1934; Bavarian state finance ministry [Siebert] to Bavarian state economics ministry, department for trade, industry, and commerce, Jan. 16, 1933.

55. Personal rivalries and alleged incompetence among Siebert's colleagues in the Bavarian state and party hierarchy may have contributed to the difficulties encountered by Siebert's plan. Hans Dauser, the head of the Bavarian state economics ministry labor and social welfare department, was charged with incompetence (he was not a professional civil servant and had no prior experience in matters dealing with labor and welfare) and treason to the ideals of the Nazi movement by permitting former members of the Social Democratic Party and the Volkspartei to continue working in his department. Siebert supported Dauser's opponents but was rebuked by Reich Statthalter in Bavaria, General Franz Xavier Ritter von Epp. See BHStA, MA 107593. Siebert was no match for Dauser, an SS regimental leader *(Standartenführer)* who held party membership number 10,158. See BAK, Personalabteilung

des Reichsführers-SS, *Dienstaltersliste der Schutzstaffel der N.S.D.A.P.*, Stand vom 1. Juli 1935 (München, Buchdruckerei Birkner). The author was denied permission to examine a seemingly relevant file on Bavarian economics minister Hermann Esser, BHStA, MA 107585, on the grounds that it is "a personnel file, and has nothing to do with economics."

56. BHStA, MWi 5955, Bavarian deputy plenipotentiary to the Reichsrat, Ministerialdirektor Dr. Paul Hammer, to Herr Blum [Ministerialdirektor, Bavarian finance ministry], Jan. 10, 1934 (excerpt); BHStA, 3132, Bavarian state minister for economics (signed Hermann Esser) to Bavarian minister-president Ludwig Siebert, Oct. 19, 1933.

57. Karl Mandelbaum, "An Experiment in Full Employment: Controls in the German Economy, 1933–1938," in Oxford University Institute of Statistics, *The Economics of Full Employment* (Oxford: Basil Blackwell, 1944), pp. 183, 201. For the development of Germany's international trade statistics, see Réne Erbe, *Die nationalsozialistische Wirtschaftspolitik im Lichte der modernen Theorie* (Zurich: Polygraphischer Verlag, 1958), p. 82; Maxine Y. Sweezy, *The Structure of the Nazi Economy* (Cambridge, Mass.: Harvard University Press, 1941), pp. 122–123.

58. Since 1945, analysts have differed on the impact that devaluation might have had on Germany's trade problems. See Erbe, *nationalsozialistische Wirtschaftspolitik*, pp. 188–189; Mandelbaum, "Experiment in Full Employment," p. 201.

59. Heinrich Steubel, "Die Finanzierung der Aufrüstung im Dritten Reich," *Europa-Archiv* 6 (1951), p. 4136.

60. See numerous documents in BAK, R28/57, R28/58, R28/59; James, *German Slump*, pp. 403–405; Arthur Schweitzer, *Big Business in the Third Reich* (Bloomington: Indiana University Press, 1964), pp. 307–308. In Oct. 1933, the Conversion Office for German Foreign Debt (Konversionskasse für deutsche Auslandsschulden) stipulated that Germany's foreign creditors were to receive no more than 50 percent of their funds due in cash, and the remainder in scrip. Schweitzer and other commentators have referred to the scrip system as a policy of depreciating the assets of foreign creditors. Germany had instituted the *Zusatzausfuhrverfahren* at the turn of the year 1932–33.

61. BAK, R28/60, Reichsbank-Direktorium to all Reichsbank branch offices, etc., April 21, 1934, signed by Schacht and Dreyse; BAK, R28/62, RWM (signed Schmitt) to highest Reich officials (obersten Reichsbehörden), etc., June 7, 1934. Also found in HHStA, Abt. 485, 246. Philipp Kessler, chairman of the board of a utilities corporation and "Führer der deutschen Wirtschaft" from March to July 1934, also urged industrial leaders to promote exports, "even if that meant a sacrifice from them." See BAK, R43/II/323, Bl. 46, Willuhn memorandum of May 2, 1934.

62. BAK, R28/65, Nr. 70, Reichsstelle für Devisenbewirtschaftung an alle Überwachungsstellen [signed Wohlthat], March 14, 1935; BAK, R28/66, and HStAS, E130b, Bü3044, "Bestimmungen des Reichswirtschaftsministers über die Förde-

rung zusatzlicher Ausfuhr," [June] 1935. Streng Vertraulich!; HStAS, E130b, Bü3044, RWM to foreign office and governments of *Länder,* July 9, 1935, with enclosure marked "Confidential," "Erläuterung zum Gesetz über Erhebung von Umlagen in der gewerblichen Wirtschaft von 28. Juni 1935" (RGBl, 1935, vol. 1, p. 812). Wohlthat headed both the Reich Office for Allocation of Foreign Exchange (Reichsstelle für Devisenbewirtshaftung) and the department for foreign exchange allocation in the Reich economics ministry. For details on Schacht's appointment of Wohlthat to these positions, see Willi Boelcke, *Die deutsche Wirtschaft, 1930–1935: Interna des Reichswirtschaftsministeriums* (Düsseldorf: Droste Verlag, 1983), p. 88.

63. See, for example, BAK, R43/323, p. 113, "Vermerk betreffend Stand der wirtschaftspolitischen Beziehungen Deutschlands im Jahre 1934," Jan. 13, 1935, memorandum written by Franz Willuhn, an economics expert in the Reich chancellery, stating that "Germany does not want to be and will not become autarkic or self-sufficient, because it [Germany] wants a share of all of the fruits produced by this earth, with which our country is not provided or not sufficiently provided, and because the reduction of imports also results in a reduction of exports." Dr. Carl Lüer, provisional president of the Frankfurt am Main–Hanau chamber of industry and commerce, and a member of the Nazi party, explained that "a service in return for its equivalent" *(Leistung gegen Gegenleistung)* is the goal of national socialist autarky policy. See HHStA, Abt. 483, 10925, clipping from *Frankfurter Volksblatt,* April 24, 1933, "Die Neugesaltung der Wirtschaft," account of meeting of National Sozialistische Arbeitsgemeinschaft für berufsständliche Wirtschaftsgestaltung, Gau Hessen-Nassau-Süd. Gauleiter Jacob Sprenger (Hesse-Nassau) warned that boosting exports would take precedence over "piling up profits." See HHStA, Abt. 483, 10925, clipping from *Frankfurter Volksblatt,* March 24, 1935, "Arbeitstagung der Kreiswirtschaftsberater," account of a meeting held in Frankfurt am Main.

64. BAK, R28/59, Reichsbank-Direktorium to all Reichsbank branch offices, etc., March 16, 1934; BAK, R23/63, Aussprach des Herrn Reichsbankpräsidenten Dr. Schacht auf der Betriebsversammlung der Beamten, Angestellten u. Arbeiter der Reichsbank am 19. Oktober 1934 in Berlin; C. W. Guillebaud, *The Economic Recovery of Germany From 1933 to the Incorporation of Austria in March 1938* (London: Macmillan, 1939), p. 67; Dieter Petzina, *Autarkiepolitik im Dritten Reich: Die nationalsozialistische Vierjahrplan,* Schriftenreihe der Vierteljahrshefte für Zeitgeschichte, no. 16 (Stuttgart: Deutsche Verlags-Anstalt, 1968), pp. 15–16.

65. Documents relating to trade agreements with the South African government, for example, are found in BAK, R28/64, R28/65, and R28/67. Items covered included animal products, grain, fruit, chromium ore, manganese ore, scrap metal, asbestos, and industrial diamonds.

66. See, for example, N-WHStA, BR1015/80-II, Der Regierungspräsident, Düsseldorf, to RAM, July 3, 1934; BHStA, MA106712, Bezirksamt Münchberg to

Geheime Staatspolizei, Staatspolizeistelle München, April 30, 1937, contained as a supplement to "Monatsbericht des Regierungspräsidenten von Oberfranken u. Mittelfranken für April 1937."

67. BAP, 25.01, Bd. 2, 6579, "Rohstofflage und Beschäftigung nach den Berichten der Treuhänder der Arbeit. Erlaüterung der anliegenden Tabellen. I. Die Bedrohung der Beschäftigungslage durch Schließung von Betrieben mangels Rohstoffe," prepared Sept. 6, 1935, in the Reichsbank. Between Oct. 1, 1934, and July 31, 1935, a total of 2,272 plants, employing 115,952 workers, fully or partially closed down under AOG section twenty provisions. Only 218 of those plant closings, and 7,702 of the worker layoffs, were attributable to raw material shortages. Small plants, and larger plants that did not expect to lay off more than 50 employees or 10 percent of their workforce, were not required under the AOG (RGBl, 1934, vol. 1, p. 45) to give labor trustees prior notice of plant closings and layoffs.

68. BAK, R2/18626, president RfAA to RAM, Abt. IVa, Sept. 27, 1934, concerning carrying out of *Notstandsarbeiten* in the winter of 1934–35; president RfAA to LAA and AA, Runderlaß concerning carrying out of *Notstandsarbeiten* in winter 1934–35, Oct. 8, 1934; RAM, "Vermerk über das Ergebnis der Besprechung im RAM am 8. Oktober d.Js.," Oct. 9, 1934, sent to RWM; [RFM], "Aufzeichnung für die Chefsbesprechung über Fragen der Arbeitsbeschaffung am 6. 11. 34," Nov. 1934; president RfAA to LAA presidents, Nov. 24, 1934, guidelines concerning the promotion of private firms; N-WHStA, Reg. Aachen, 16852, president LAA Rheinland to Regierungspräsident in Aachen, Feb. 18, 1935, containing "Richtlinien zur Förderung von Privatunternehmungen aus Mitteln der RfAA (wertschaffende Arbeitslosenhilfe)."

69. For additional information on Keppler, see Hans Kehrl, *Krisenmanager im Dritten Reich* (Düsseldorf: Droste Verlag, 1973), pp. 60–62; R. J. Overy, *Goering: The "Iron Man"* (London: Routledge & Kegan Paul, 1984), pp. 37, 41–42. Keppler had gained prominence as Hitler's special representative for economic questions. At the end of Oct. 1934, Hitler gave him responsibility for developing domestic substitutes for foreign raw materials. Keppler clashed with both Krosigk and Schacht over the issue of enhanced development of iron ore resources, development of synthetic materials and fuels, and autarkist policy in general. The fact that it was never clear whether Keppler's office was a state agency, a party agency, or something else, was viewed by Keppler and his top aide, Hans Kehrl, as an advantage, "for the certain lack of clarity permitted us a broad interpretation of our authority." With Hitler's appointment of Göring to head a new Raw Materials Office in April 1936, Keppler's influence was eclipsed.

70. For this jurisdictional aspect of the import-substitution subsidy program, see BAK, R2/18626, RAM to Stellvertreter des Führers der NSDAP, etc., Oct. 23, 1934, Schnellbrief, concerning promotion of domestic production.

71. BAK, R2/18626, "Niederschrift über die zweite Sitzung des Auschußes vom

18. Januar 1935"; D.R.d.F [RFM] to president RfAA, Vermerk, and draft of letter concerning "Förderung von Privatunternehmungen, Nutzbarmachung einheimischer Gebrinden," March 23, 1935.

72. BAK, R2/18627, "Niederschrift über die vierte Sitzung des Ausschußes vom 14. Mai 1935." The following account is taken from documents in this file as well as R2/18626, president RfAA to Geheimen Regierungsrat Dr. [Stephan] Poerschke, RFM, May 6, 1935, Schnellbrief, with appendices. See Anlage 9, Arbeitsamt Hamburg, Landesarbeitsamt Nordmark, Förderung von Privatunternehmungen. Antrgagsteller: Michelmotor G. m. b. H., Hamburg.

73. It is possible that the government was trying to force Michel-Motor, which lacked the resources to produce the engines, to sell or license its patent to Deutsche Werft, which did have the facilities required for the production of the engines. In the awarding of military contracts in 1934 and 1935, the services consistently favored larger firms that could reliably meet short delivery deadlines.

74. BAK, R2/18677, Dr. Feder, state secretary in the RWM, to state secretary in the RFM, F. Reinhardt, Aug. 22, 1933; D.R.d.F. [RFM, signed Reinhardt] to state secretary in the RWM, Dr. Feder, Sept. 9, 1933 [draft]; R2/18678, D.R.d.F [RFM] to RWM, Oct. 24, 1933 [draft], approving a grant of RM 800,000 out of Reinhardt program funds; RWM to Oberpräsident of Rheinprovinz [Prussia], Oct. 26, 1933. Reinhardt's response was "to be written in the form of a private letter," indicating that this arrangement might be considered as a favor from one good friend and Nazi to another, rather than as a pure business transaction.

75. BAK, R2/18628, president RfAA to RAM, Section IIc, Sept. 4, 1935, concerning support of private firms, here: extension of the range of persons to be supported; Reichskriegsminister u. Oberbefehlshaber der Wehrmacht to RFM and the Beauftragter d. Führers f. Wirtschaftsfragen W. Keppler, Sept. 27, 1935; D.R.d.F [RFM] Vermerk (signed Gase), Oct. 21, 1935; BAK, R2/18629, president RfAA to RAM, Nov. 25, 1935, concerning promotion of private firms. The RfAA estimated that, up to the end of December 1935, it would spend about RM 350,000 on work that was technically ineligible for support. A total of 77 projects costing the RfAA over RM 3 million had been approved by the committee. The projects currently employed 1,500 workers, but were expected to place about 7,000 workers in permanent employment.

76. BAK, R2/18628, Reichskriegsminister u. Oberbefehlshaber der Wehrmacht to RFM and the Beauftragter des Führers f. Wirtschaftsfragen W. Keppler, Sept. 27, 1935.

77. BAK, R2/18628, D.R.d.F. [Reich finance ministry], Vermerk (signed Gase), Oct. 21, 1935; BAK, R2/18629, RAM to Beauftragten des Führers u. Reichskanzlers f. Wirtschaftsfragen [Keppler], etc., Dec. 14, 1935, "Vermerk über das Ergebnis der Besprechung im Reichs und Pr. Arbeitsministerium vom 12 Dezember 1935

über die Förderung von Privatunternehmungen"; Der Beauftragte des Führers u. Reichskanzlers f. Wirtschaftsfragen W. Keppler to RFM, Dec. 18, 1935.

78. BAK, R2/18629, RAM to RWM, RFM, etc., Jan. 6, 1936; D.R.d.F [RFM] to Beauftragter des Führers u. Reichskanzlers f. Wirtschaftsfragen [Keppler], Jan. 28, 1936 [draft]; RFM (signed Gase), Vermerk, Feb. 22, 1936.

79. BAK, R2/18630, "Niederschrift über die 11. Sitzung des Ausschußes am 12. März 1936"; president RfAA to LAA and AA, June 9, 1936, concerning Förderung von Privatunternehmungen zur Erschließung von deutschen Rohstoffen; "Richtlinien über die Gewahrung von Reichsmitteln an Privatunternehmungen," June 1, 1936, issued by Keppler's office; D.R.d.F. [RFM], Vermerk, concerning granting of Reich funds to private firms, June 10, 1936.

80. BAK, R28/55, RFM to all Reichsbank offices, etc., Feb. 8, 1933, concerning "Bevorzugung deutscher Arbeit u. deutscher Erzeugniße."

81. N-WHStA, Reg. Aachen, 16857, Der Regierungspräsident. Bezirkswohnungskommissar to Landräte des Bezirks, etc., March 11, 1933. Economic relations with the Netherlands were a matter of particular concern to Hitler's government from the beginning. Germany depended heavily on fats imported from Holland, and also imported significant quantities of wood, eggs, cheese, and milk from its neighbor. Hitler had to renegotiate an expiring trade agreement with Holland shortly after his appointment to the chancellorship. Many workers crossed the German-Dutch border in both directions to get to their jobs, and the two governments negotiated a six-month agreement covering the situation in Sept. 1935, renewed after new negotiations in March 1936. See BAK, R43II/1481, Bd. 2, Sitzung des Wirtschaftspolitischen Ausschuß der Reichsregierung, Feb. 1 and 2, 1933; N-WHStA, Reg. Aachen, 16848, RAM to foreign office, etc., April 3, 1936, concerning German-Netherlands agreement on the utilization of labor.

82. BHStA, MA106773, Reich minister for food and agriculture to Reich defense minister, etc., July 17, 1933.

83. Petzina, *Autarkiepolitik im Dritten Reich*, p. 24. If Petzina is correct, then Schacht apparently did not always have his way.

5. Race Policy, Agricultural Policy, and Work Creation

1. StAW, LRA Marktheidenfeld, Nr. 4171, "Denkschrift zur Besserung und Hebung der wirtschaftlichen und kulturellen Verhältnisse in Rhön und Spessart. Dr. Hellmuth-Plan," Nov. 15, 1933, signed by Hasslinger. Dr. Otto Hellmuth, a dentist by profession (he married another dentist, Erna Maria Stamm, in June 1936) and a Nazi "old fighter," had been a Nazi party member since 1925 (membership number 22,815) and Gauleiter of the Bavarian district of Unterfranken (Mainfranken) since 1927. After Hitler's assumption of the Reich chancellorship, he was

named Regierungspräsident of Unterfranken and Aschaffenburg. Headquarters for both his political and governmental activities was the city of Würzburg. At war's end, Hellmuth was brought before a military tribunal at Dachau, where he was charged with and convicted of responsibility for the shooting of Allied airmen forced to make an emergency landing in Sept. 1944. His sentence of death by hanging was commuted to life imprisonment. In Landsberg prison he served as prison dentist. In 1951 his sentence was reduced to twenty years, and in 1955 Hellmuth was released from prison. He settled in Reutlingen, and in preference to twenty-one other candidates, was licensed to practice dentistry once again. In April 1968 Hellmuth died at age 72. See Dieter W. Rockenmaier, *Das Dritte Reich und Würzburg: Versuch einer Bestandsaufnahme* (Würzburg: Mainpresse Richter Druck & Verlags-GmbH, 1983), pp. 237–240. In Rockenmaier's opinion (p. 237), "Hellmuth certainly was not one of the 'wild' and inhuman Gauleiters like Julius Streicher in Nürnberg and Fritz Sauckel in Thüringia; Albert Speer counted him as one of the 'rational' among the Nazi leaders." He was careful to add the observation that "such judgements are nevertheless relative."

2. BDC, minister-president Marschler to Oberste Parteigericht der N.S.D.A.P, II. Kammer, Sept. 16, 1934.

3. Robert L. Koehl, *RKFDV: German Resettlement and Population Policy, 1939–1945* (Cambridge, Mass.: Harvard University Press, 1957), provides an account of the development of wartime resettlement policy in areas added to the Reich after 1938. There is no major work on internal settlement policy within Germany between 1933 and 1938.

4. For Bavarian programs and plans for road construction and land improvement in Rhön and Spessart, see BHStA, MWi 5934, 5935; Joachim S. Hohmann, *Landvolk unterm Hakenkreuz: Agrar- und Rassenpolitik in der Rhön*, 2 vols. (Frankfurt am Main: Peter Lang, 1992), provides plentiful evidence that Bavarian authorities had tried to address the Rhön's problems prior to the Nazi era.

5. StAW, LRA Marktheidenfeld, 4171, Wirtschaftsberater der Gauleitung, "Denkschrift . . . Dr. Hellmuth–Plan," Nov. 15, 1933 (signed Hasslinger).

6. Ibid.

7. StAW, LRA Mellrichstadt, 1371, press clipping from the National Socialist newspaper *Mainfrankische Zeitung* (Würzburg), Nov. 8, 1937; article from the *Volkischer Beobachter,* Dec. 31, 1934, "Der Aufbau von Rhön und Spessart," conversation with Gauleiter Dr. Hellmuth and his Gau economic adviser Hasslinger. The statements are attributed to Hellmuth and Hasslinger, although the article quotes none of the interview directly.

8. StAW, LRA Marktheidenfeld, 4171, Hasslinger, "Denkschrift . . . Dr. Hellmuth–Plan."

9. Prior to the Nazi takeover of Bavaria, the budget committee of the Bavarian Landtag approved a Bavarian Volkspartei petition for the voluntary resettlement of

excess population in Spessart. See BHStA, MWi 5935, Bayerischer Landtag, I. Tagung 1932–33, Jan. 24, 1933, Beilage 232, Antrag Dr. Stang, Kurz.

10. StAW, LRA Mellrichstadt, 1371, article from *Würzburger General-Anzeiger,* Oct. 12, 1934, "Rhon und Spessart im Aufbau," quotation from Hasslinger's contribution to collection published on occasion of Rhön-Spessart-Ausstellung in Berlin; article from *Volkischer Beobachter,* Dec. 31, 1934, "Der Aufbau von Rhön und Spessart. Unterredung mit Gauleiter Dr. Hellmuth und seinem Gauwirtschaftsberater Hasslinger."

11. BHStA, MWi 5935, Kurt Hasslinger, Gauwirtschaftsberater der NSDAP, Gau Mainfranken, *4 Jahre Dr. Hellmuth–Plan* (Würzburg, undated, probably Oct. 1937), p. 6.

12. Hohmann, *Landvolk unterm Hakenkreuz,* pt. 1, pp. 160–191, discusses many of these studies.

13. See invitations for two tours in BAK, R2/18606; BAP, 39.03, 130.

14. The exhibition, planning for which began on Feb. 27, 1934, in the rooms of the Staatsarchiv Würzburg, opened in Berlin and ran through Sept.–Oct. 1934. See StAW, LRA Marktheidenfeld, 4171, circular from Kreisleiter, "Lieber Volksgenosse!" Jan. 5, 1934; BAP, 39.03, 129, "Rhön und Spessart," 36-page pamphlet distributed at the Berlin exhibition in the Europahaus, prepared by the Rhön-Spessart Werbestelle, Würzburg.

15. BAP, 39.03, 130, "Bericht über die Besichtigung des Notstandsgebietes der Rhön in der Zeit vom 24. bis 26. Juli 1934," signed by Regierungsrat Dr. Kruschke, RfAA Hauptstelle; BHStA, MA106772, Reich food and agriculture minister to Prussian minister-president, etc. [including Hellmuth], Aug. 24, 1934.

16. Hohmann, *Landvolk unterm Hakenkreuz,* repeatedly stresses the argument that Hellmuth's plan coincided precisely with Darré's "blood and soil" ideology and "Nazi" race, agricultural, and settlement policy. He then makes the unwarranted assumption that Darré and the rest of the Nazi hierarchy supported Hellmuth's program. This assumption leads Hohmann to believe that opposition to Hellmuth's program came not from Hellmuth's Nazi colleagues (with the exception of Thuringian minister-president Wilhelm Marschler), but only from the Rhöners themselves, incited by their Roman Catholic bishops and priests. Hohmann has failed to grasp the intensity of opposition to Hellmuth's plan from Reich and NSDAP officials in Berlin.

17. In recent works, some German historians have characterized Hitler as a "weak dictator." A thoughtful and sensitive summary of such arguments and counterarguments can be found in Ian Kershaw, *The Nazi Dictatorship* (London: Edward Arnold, 1985). A similar question arises at the level of the Gauleiters. The fate of the Hellmuth plan not only helps to illuminate the role of the Gauleiters in the Nazi system but also by implication illustrates some of the factors that may have limited Hitler's exercise of power in certain matters of domestic policy. For an overview of

the functions and authority of various Gauleiters, see Peter Hüttenberger, *Die Gauleiter: Studie zum Wandel des Machtgefüges in der NSDAP*, Schriftenreihe der Vierteljahrshefte für Zeitgeschichte, 19 (Stuttgart: Deutsche Verlags-Anstalt, 1969).

18. BAP, 39.03, 129, Reich food and agriculture minister to Gauleiter Dr. Hellmuth, Feb. 20, 1934, requesting cost estimate; Reich ministry for food and agriculture, April 4, 1934, "Vermerk über die Besprechung vom 28. März 1934, betreffend die Kultivierung der Rhön," statement by Dr. Bardow (RfAA) reiterating Syrup's statement at the Feb. 19 meeting; StAW, LRA Mellrichstadt, 1366, Der Generalinspektor für das deutsche Straßenwesen (signed Dr. Todt) to Bayerische Staatsministerium des Innern, Feb. 19, 1934

19. BAP, 39.03, 129, "Voranschlag für den Dr. Hellmuth–Plan zur Verbesserung der wirtschaftlichen Verhältnisse in Rhön und Spessart, Abschnitt Rhön," prepared by Kreisbauernschaft Würzburg, March 5, 1934; Der Gauwirtschaftsberater [Hasslinger], memorandum concerning "Rhön u. Spessart-Aufbau. hier, Rhönplan."

20. BAP, 39.03, 129, Reich ministry for food and agriculture, April 4, 1934, "Vermerk über die Besprechung vom 28. März 1934, betreffend die Kultivierung der Rhön; "Arbeitsplan für den Dr.–Hellmuth Plan: Abschnitt I Rhön," dated March 18, 1934

21. BAP, 39.03, 129, Reich ministry for food, "Vermerk über die Besprechung vom 10. April 1934 betreffend die Kultivierung der Rhön mit Vertretern der Preußischen Landesregierung," undated, unsigned.

22. StAW, LRA Mellrichstadt, 1366, Deutscher Arbeitsdienst, Arbeitsgau 28 (Franken), Würzburg, "Niederschrift über die Besprechung bezüglich Beteilung des Arbeitsdienstes an der Durchführung des Dr. Hellmuth–Planes (Rhön-Ausbau-Plan)," im Hause der Arbeitsgauleitung 28 (Würzburg), May 16, 1934. In his 1937 progress report, Hasslinger confirmed that "in order to avoid any setbacks, this plan, whose objective was in reality the restoration of the entire Gau, was at first limited to the Rhön." See BHStA, MWi 5935, Hasslinger, *4 Jahre Hellmuth-Plan*, p. 5.

23. BHStA, MA 106772, Reich minister for food and agriculture to Prussian minister-president, etc. (including Hellmuth), Aug. 24, 1934. Hellmuth had the Würzburg office responsible for the clearing of fields draw up a land-improvement plan for a group of ten Rhön towns; 9,343 hectares with 5,453 landowners were affected. The necessary implementing ordinance was not issued by the Bavarian state ministry until March 9, 1936. The "miniplan" was part of a slightly larger plan to bring 12,000 hectares of Rhön wasteland under cultivation. See BHStA, MWi 5935, Hasslinger, *4 Jahre Hellmuth–Plan*.

24. BHStA, MA 106772, Reichskommissar für das Siedlungswesen (signed by deputy commissar J. Wilhelm Ludovici) to Bayerische Staatsministerium, Aug. 24, 1934.

25. The following account is based on BAP, 31.01, 10106, RWM (Schmitt) to

RAM (Seldte), Jan. 18 and 25, 1934; Deutsche Arbeitsfront, Heimstättenamt (signed Ludovici) to Ministerialrat Ronde, RWM, Feb. 20, 1934, claiming that Deputy Führer Rudolf Hess had issued the order establishing the Heimstättenamt; RWM, "Vermerk für den Herrn Minister," prepared by Regierungsrat Holtz, March 2, 1934; Reich chancellor (signed Adolf Hitler) to RWM, etc., March 29, 1934, announcing appointment of Feder as Reich commissar for settlement affairs; BAP, 25.01, vol. 2, 6788, Kundgebung des Reichssiedlungskommissars. Vortrag von Herrn Staatssekretär Gottfried Feder, dated May 30, 1934. For an excellent discussion of Robert Ley's attempts to enlarge the empire of his Deutsche Arbeitsfront by taking over all responsibility for "homesteads and settlement," see Ronald Smelser, *Robert Ley: Hitler's Labor Front Leader* (Oxford: Berg, 1988), pp. 199–201. Some documents relating to the jurisdictional conflict over settlement policy and to Feder's appointment as commissioner, can be found in *Akten der Reichskanzlei*, pt. 1, vol. 2, pp. 1225–1227.

26. Claiming "far-reaching full powers" in settlement policy, Schacht decreed on July 5, 1934, that all large settlement projects required prior authorization from his Reich economics ministry. See N-WHStA, Reg. Aachen, 16851, RWM to governments of Länder, housing and settlement departments, July 6, 1934; RWM and Prussian minister for economics and labor to [Prussian] Oberpräsidenten, July 19, 1934, with enclosure, to be published in local newspapers, Entwurf der Presseveröffentlichung, explaining the RWM's July 5 decree on nonagricultural settlements and housing. Hitler's decree of Dec. 12, 1934, removed jurisdiction over housing and settlements from the RWM and placed it back in the RAM, from which it had been transferred after Hitler's appointment to the chancellorship.

27. "The modern big city is the death of the nation," proclaimed Feder. He planned to create new cities and rural towns as part of a new social organization that would replace decadent cities. See BAP, 25.01, vol. 2, 6788, Kundgebung des Reichssiedlungskommissars. Vortrag von Herrn Staatssekretär Gottfried Feder, dated May 30, 1934.

28. BAK, R2/18607, Reich and Prussian minister for food and agriculture to Reich interior minister, RFM, the Reichsforstamt, and the Prussian Landforstamt, Feb. 21, 1935, with enclosure, "Aufzeichnung von der Besprechung . . . am 12. Februar 1935 über Maßnahmen zur Hebung der gewerblichen Wirtschaft in der Rhön (Hellmuth Plan)." Also found in BHStA, MA 106772.

29. BAK, R2/18607, Reich and Prussian minister for food and agriculture to Reich interior minister, etc., Feb. 21, 1935, "Aufzeichnung von der Besprechung . . . am 12. Februar 1935 über Maßnahmen zur Verbesserung der Verkehrseinrichtungen."

30. Hellmuth's afforestation proposals for the Rhön were modest compared with schemes suggested for other regions of Germany. In July 1933, the Reich Federation of German Woodland Owners Associations proposed a massive afforestation project

covering up to two-and-a-half million hectares of wasteland. The five-to-ten-year project envisioned the afforestation of about 400,000 hectares per year, employing around 200,000 workers for a portion of each year. See BAP, 39.03, 233, Reichsverband Deutscher Waldbesitzerverbände, July 20, 1933, "Denkschrift betr. Aufstellung eines nationalen Aufforstungs-planes zur Ergänzung des Gesetzes zur Verminderung der Arbeitslosigkeit," copy to RAM, July 20, 1933.

31. Ibid., "Aufzeichnung von der Besprechung . . . über Massnahmen zur Verbesserung der Verkehrseinrichtungen," Feb. 12, 1935.

32. BHStA, MWi 5935, Reich and Prussian minister for food and agriculture to Bavarian state economics ministry, department of agriculture, Nov. 6, 1935; Bavarian minister-president to all state ministries, Nov. 28, 1935.

33. StAW, LRA Marktheidenfeld, Nr. 4171, Hasslinger, "Denkschrift . . . Dr. Hellmuth–Plan," Nov. 15, 1933; Bezirksamt Marktheidenfeld to Regierung von Unterfranken und Aschaffenburg, Kammer des Innern, Jan. 16, 1934, reporting on a Jan. 10 meeting held at Marktheidenfeld concerning the implementation of the Hellmuth Plan; StAW, LRA Mellrichstadt, 1366, Der Generalinspektor für das deutsche Straßenwesen (signed Dr. Todt) to Bayerische Staatsministerium des Innern, Feb. 19, 1934 (copy); BAP, 39.03, 129, [Herbert] Backe, state secretary in Reich food ministry, to state secretary Reinhardt, etc., Feb. 14, 1934.

34. BAK, R2/18607, Reich minister for food and agriculture to RWM, etc., Nov. 27, 1934, concerning "Maßnahmen für die Wirtschaft in der Rhön"; BAK, R2/ 18607, BAP, 39.03, 130, and BHStA, MA106772, RFM, "Niederschrift über die Besprechung im Reichsministerium für Ernährung und Landwirtschaft am 6. Dezember 1934, betreffend Maßnahmen für die Hebung der Wirtschaft in der Rhön," Dec. 8, 1934; BHStA, MA106772, Reich minister for food and agriculture to RWM, etc., Dec. 13, 1934, containing Darré's account of the Dec. 6, meeting; BAK, R2/18607, RFM, Vermerk (undated; written on reverse of Reich ministry for food and agriculture's invitation to Dec. 6, 1934 meeting), RFM account of the meeting, also found in BHStA, MA 106772; BAP, 39.03, 130, Vermerk, betr. Hellmuth plan (Rhön u. Spessart), Dec. 6, 1934, signed by Bardow, who represented the RfAA at the meeting. See also BHStA, MWi 5935 and MA 106772, Vertretung Bayerns in Berlin to [Bavarian] state economics ministry, department of agriculture, Dec. 6, 1933, for another eyewitness account of the Dec. 6 meeting.

35. In connection with the March 29, 1935, "Law on regulation of land requirements of the state," responsibility for "Landesplanung" was assigned to the Reichsstelle für Raumordnung, a new agency established under a Reich chancellor decree of June 26, 1935. Reich minister without portfolio Hanns Kerrl headed the new office. Hellmuth's plan, insofar as it related to land use and settlement, now had to contend with yet another layer of bureaucracy. See RGBl, 1935, vol. 1, p. 468, *Gesetz über die Regelung des Landbedarfs der öffentliche Hand vom 29. 3. 35.* For Hitler's

June 26, 1935, decree creating the Reichsstelle für Raumordnung, see RGBl, 1935, vol. 1, p. 793.

36. BAP, 39.03,129, Reich food ministry, Vermerk über die Besprechung vom 10. April 1934 betreffend die Kultivierung der Rhön mit den Vertretern der Preußischen Landesregierung, undated, unsigned; Reich food ministry, "Vermerk über die Besprechung vom 12.4.1934 betreffend die Kultivierung der Rhön mit den Vertretern der Bayerischen Landesregierung," undated, unsigned. The official cited here is Ministerialrat Blum, Bavarian finance ministry.

37. BAK, R2/1807, and BAP, 39.03, 130, RFM, "Niederschrift über die Besprechung im Reichsministerium für Ernährung und Landwirtschaft am 6. Dezember 1934, betreffend Maßnahmen für die Hebung der Wirtschaft in der Rhön," Dec. 8, 1934; BAP, 39.03, 129, Thuringian economics ministry to Reich minister for food and agriculture, Feb. 22, 1934. National Socialists had played a direct role in Thuringia's government since Wilhelm Frick's appointment as Thuringian interior minister after the NSDAP won 11.3 percent of the vote in the state parliamentary elections of Dec. 8, 1929. In 1932, Gauleiter Fritz Sauckel was named Thuringian minister-president and interior minister. Sauckel gave up his post as minister-president when Hitler appointed him Reich Governor in Thuringia in 1933. His successor as minister-president was NSDAP comrade Wilhelm Marschler.

38. BAP, 39.03, 129, Thuringian economics ministry (signed Marschler), "Denkschrift über die thüringische Rhön. Stellungnahme zur Denkschrift des Wirtschaftsberaters der Gauleitung zu Würzburg . . . vom 15. November 1933," March 19, 1934.

39. BAP, 39.03, 129, Reich minister for food and agriculture to Thuringian economics ministry, April 25, 1934.

40. BAP, 39.03, 129, Reich food and agriculture ministry, "Vermerk über die Besprechung vom 11. 5. 1934, betreffend die Kultivierung der Rhön, mit den Vertretern der Thüringischen Landesregierung."

41. Ibid.

42. Ibid.

43. BDC, Hellmuth file, NSDAP, Gauleitung Unterfranken, the Gauleiter [Hellmuth], to Reichsleitung of NSDAP, c/o Reichsleiter Pg. Grimm, July 29, 1934.

44. BDC, Hellmuth file, Thuringian minister-president to Reich minister for people's enlightenment and propaganda Dr. Goebbels, July 17, 1934.

45. BDC, Hellmuth file, minister president Marschler to Oberste Parteigericht der N.S.D.A.P, II. Kammer, Sept. 16, 1934. Marschler cited documents and statements from Reich officials, including Reich food and agriculture minister Darré's Aug. 24, 1934, letter to the Prussian minister president and Hellmuth (cited earlier), as evidence that Reich officials, too, believed the Hellmuth plan was "fantasy."

46. BDC, State Secretary and head of the Reich chancellery (Lammers) to Reich

Governor Sauckel, Sept. 30, 1934; NSDAP, Gauleitung Thüringen, the Gauleiter (signed by Sauckel's adjutant) to Oberste Parteigericht, c/o Reichsleiter Grimm, Oct. 15, 1934. Hellmuth claimed that Hitler had commissioned him to prepare a memorandum on the Rhön and Spessart, so that implementation of plans for economic revival could begin immediately. See BHStA, MWi 5935, press clipping from the *Fränkische Zeitung,* March 22, 1934, "Rhön und Spessart: Neue Aufbaupläne," press conference remarks attributed to Hellmuth.

47. StAW, LRA Mellrichstadt 1371, article from *Meininger Kreisanzeiger,* Oct. 13, 1936. Although not directly attributed to Marschler, such remarks in the Nazi-controlled press can be taken as a reflection of Marschler's views.

48. BAP, 39.03, 130, president LAA Mitteldeutschland to president RfAA, Jan. 11, 1936; [Thuringian economics ministry], "Rhönplan," Dec. 10, 1935; Reich and Prussian ministry for food and agriculture to Thuringian economics minister, Feb. 25, 1936; Generalinspektor for German roads to Thuringian economics ministry, May 16, 1936.

49. Hohmann, *Landvolk unterm Hakenkreuz,* pt. 1, pp. 7–14, 23, 33–36.

50. BAK, R2/18607, Reich and Prussian minister for food and and agriculture to Reich interior minister, etc., Feb. 21, 1935, with enclosure, "Aufzeichnung von der Besprechung . . . am 13. Februar 1935 über Maßnahmen zur Umgestaltung der land- und forstwirtschaftliche Verhältnisse in der Rhön (Hellmuth–Plan)." The "Aufzeichnung" is also found in BAP, 39.03, 130.

51. StAW, LRA Mellrichstadt, 1371, Landwirtschaftsstelle Bad Neustadt a. Saale (im Auftrage und mit Genehmigung des Kreisleiters, Kreisleitung der NSDAP Neustadt a. S./Mellrichstadt), Rundschreiben an die Bürgermeister des Kreises Neustadt-Mellrichstadt!, Nov. 22, 1938, concerning "Durchführung des Hellmuth-Planes."

52. BAP, 39.03, 129, president RfAA to president LAA Bayern, concerning Kultivierung der Rhön, May 17, 1934, with enclosure, Deutsche Reichspost, Telegram: Gauleiter Hellmuth to President Syrup, Reichsanstalt, May 14, 1934.

53. StAW, LRA Mellrichstadt 1367, Bezirksamt Mellrichstadt, memorandum of May 3, 1935; Kulturbauamt Schweinfurt to Bezirksamt Neustadt a.d. Saale, May 24, 1935; Regierung Unterfranken und Aschaffenburg to [Bavarian] state economics ministry, department of agriculture (signed by Hellmuth), June 22, 1935. The latter two reports were based on figures supplied by Hasslinger. The immediate work creation value of this RM 708,000 project was modest. At the beginning of Oct. 1935, 150 persons were employed on *Rhönstraße* construction. The Kulturbauamt Schweinfurth asked for 250, and predicted that with an average workforce of 200, the road would be completed during the fall of 1937. See StAW, LRA Mellrichstadt 1367, Kulturbauamt Schweinfurth to AA Schweinfurth, Oct. 2, 1935.

54. StAW, LRA Mellrichstadt 1367, NSDAP Kreisleitung Mellrichstadt,

Maßnahme des Rhön-Aufbau-Planes (Dr. Hellmuth Plan). Hochrhön-Straße, May 7, 1934, material in support of application for RfAA basic subsidy. Not until March 1937 did the Reich and the Bavarian state governments agree on a formula for sharing the costs of subsidizing the plan. The Reich government assumed responsibility for 45 percent of the subsidy costs, the Bavarian state government 25 percent, the Regierung Unterfranken 20 percent, and local residents 10 percent. See StAW, LRA Mellrichstadt 1371, Niederschrift über die am 18. März 1937 vorm. 11½ Uhr in Wirtschaftsministerium [Munich] staatgefundene Besprechung, concerning Wirtschaftliche Hebung der Rhön; Bavarian state economics ministry to Reich and Prussian minister for food and agriculture (signed by minister-president Siebert), Jan. 25, 1938, a 14-page progress report on the "Wirtschaftliche Hebung der Rhön."

55. BHStA, MWi 5935 [Staatsministerium f. Wirtschaft], Vormerkung, Nov. 25, 1937, concerning economic situation of Mellrichstadt.

56. What follows is based on numerous documents in BHStA, MWi 5935, including a sixteen-page pamphlet authored in Dec. 1936 by Diplom.-Volkswirt Kurt Hasslinger, Gauwirtschaftsberater der NSDAP, Gau Mainfranken, "Die Förderung des Rhön-Aufbaues (Dr. Hellmuth–Plan) durch die Industrieverlagerung der Siemens-Schuckert-Werke."

57. BHStA, MWi 5935 "Denkschrift der Stadt und Bezirks Mellrichstadt vom 31. Dezember 1936," prepared by the mayor and Bezirksoberamtsmann, sent to Gauleiter and Regierungspräsident of Mainfranken, Dr. Hellmuth, Dec. 31, 1936.

58. StAW, LRA Mellrichstadt, 1371, Oberamtsmann Unger (Bezirksamt Mellrichstadt) to Dr. Gerhard Ritter, Amt für Deutsche Roh- und Werkstoffe, Berlin, Dec. 23, 1936.

59. BHStA, MWi 5935 [Bavarian economics ministry], Vormerkung concerning economic opening up of the Rhön, Dec. 23, 1936, indicating that Mellrichstadt officials believed they had an agreement with Siemens-Schuckert to locate in Mellrichstadt; StAW, LRA Mellrichstadt, 1371, numerous documents, including Oberamtsmann Unger (Bezirksamt Mellrichstadt) to Herr [Konrad] Bildstein, Landesplannungsgemeinschaft Bayern, Zweigstelle Würzburg, Jan. 30, 1937, indicating that, "recently, it is said that the planned [Siemens-Schuckert] factory will be built in Bad Neustadt rather than in Mellrichstadt"; Unger to Dr. Gerhard Ritter, Amt für Deutsche Roh- und Werkstoffe, Berlin, Dec. 23, 1936; Unger to Justizrat Wagner, IG Farben, Ludwigshafen/Rhein, Dec. 11, 1936; Koehn to Major a. D. Nebel, Telefunken-Gesellschaft für drahtlose Telegraphie m. b. H, Berlin, Dec. 15, 1936; Koehn to Unger, Dec. 17, 1936.

60. BHStA, MWI 5935, Denkschrift der Stadt und Bezirks Mellrichstadt vom 31. Dezember 1936.

61. BHStA, MWi 5935 [Bavarian economics ministry], Vormerkung, concerning

economic opening up of the Rhön, Dec. 23, 1936; [Bavarian economics ministry], department for trade, industry, and commerce to president LAA Bayern, March 1, 1937.

62. StAW, LRA Mellrichstadt, 1371, Kreisleiter, Bad Neustadt a/Salle, Gedanken zur Denkschrift der Stadt und des Bezirks Mellrichstadt vom 31. Dez. 1936, dated Jan. 30, 1937, sent to Oberamtsmann Unger, Mellrichstadt, on Feb. 2, 1937.

63. BHStA, MWi5935, Hasslinger pamphlet "Die Förderung des Rhön-Aufbaues (Dr. Hellmuth–Plan) durch die Industrieverlagerung der Siemens-Schuckert-Werke," Dec. 1936.

64. Ibid.

65. Ibid.

66. BHStA, MWi 5935, Auszug aus dem Monatsbericht des Regierungspräsidenten von Unterfranken u. Aschaffenburg [Hellmuth] vom 8. 1. 37, Nr. 12; [Bavarian economics ministry], Vormerkung, concerning economic opening up of the Rhön, Dec. 23, 1936.

67. BHStA, MA 106712, Bavarian economics ministry, department for trade, industry, and commerce, to RWM, April 17, 1937.

68. BHStA, MWi 5935, clipping from *Völkische Beobachter,* Dec. 16, 1938, "Die Vierjahresplansiedlung in Bad Neustadt."

69. BAP, 39.03, 130, typewritten copy of Hellmuth announcement appearing in *Deutsche Siedlung,* no. 30, April 27, 1938, Berichte und Bemerkungen.

70. StAW, LRA Mellrichstadt 1371, [Bavarian] Staatsministerium f. Wirtschaft to Reich minister for food and agriculture, Jan. 25, 1938 (signed Siebert).

71. Ibid. Werner Willikens, state secretary in the Reich food and agriculture ministry, drew different conclusions from the facts presented by Siebert. He advised Siebert to select only a few areas for settlement after completion of land improvements, and to reserve the rest for common cow pastures. See StAW, LRA Mellrichstadt 1371, Reich and Prussian minister for food and agriculture to [Bavarian] state economics ministry, May 2, 1938, concerning economic revival of the Rhön.

72. BHStA, MWi5935, Konrad Bildstein, "Der Hellmuth–Plan," pp. 48–51; Wilhelm Hüttlinger, "Die Schutzwaldanlagen des Dr. Hellmuth–Plans," p. 87; Fritz Scherer, "Der Einsatz des Reichsarbeitsdienstes in Mainfranken," p. 67; Hugo Maurer, "Neuordnung der Basalt-Industrie in der Rhön," 97, all in *Raumforschung und Raumordnung,* Monatsschrift der Reichsarbeitsgemeinschaft für Raumforschung, 2. Jahrgang, part 2 (Feb. 1938), published in Heidelberg.

73. BHStA, MWi5935, Dr. Gieselher Wirsing, editor-in-chief, *Münchner Neuste Nachrichten,* to [Bavarian] minister-president, Dec. 22, 1938, including special edition of *Münchner Neuste Nachrichten,* Dec. 18, 1934, "Der Großangriff auf der Rhön. Zwischenbilanz des Dr.–Hellmuth–Planes," by Dr. Wolfgang Höpker. Given the opposition to the plan and the delays in implementing it, some of these claimed achievements are more impressive than one might have expected.

74. StAW, LRA Mellrichstadt, 1371, Niederschrift über die Rhönberatung am 2. Mai 1939 beim Flurbereinigungsamt in Würzburg; Niederschrift über die Rhönberatung am 3. Mai 1939 in Dr. Hellmuth–Lager-Fladungen.

75. StAW, NSDAP Gau Mainfranken, Nr. 9, report of Gau economic adviser, Wirtschaftsbericht no. 6, Nov. 23, 1939.

76. BHStA, MWi 5935 [Bavarian state economics ministry], Vormerkung, May 9, 1938, concerning Truppenübungsplatz in der Rhön; StAW, LRA Mellrichstadt 1371, Stellv. Gen. Kdo. des XIII. A.K., Nuremberg, to Bavarian state economics ministry, Nov. 3, 1939, concerning Wirtschaftl. Hebung d. Rhön; hier, Freimachung von Arbeitsdienstlagern; Bavarian state economics ministry, department of agriculture, to Stellv. Gen. Kdo. des XIII. A.K., Nuremberg, Nov. 21, 1939, concerning economic revival of the Rhön.

77. Hohmann, *Landvolk unterm Hakenkreuz*, p. 181. Wildflecken was converted into an American military base after the Second World War. Hohmann, a native of the Rhön, argues that military bases brought no benefits to the Rhön either during the Nazi period or after the war. He emphasizes the destructive impact of the bases on the Rhön's social fabric.

78. StAW, LRA Mellrichstadt 1371, [Bavarian] state ministry for economics, department of agriculture, to Reich minister for food and agriculture, May 7, 1941, enclosing a letter from the Reichstreuhänder der Arbeit für das Wirtschaftsgebiet Bayern, Aug. 16, 1940.

79. StAW, NSDAP Gau Mainfranken, Nr. 9, 1. Bericht über Sonderfragen für das Gaugebiet u. einzelne Bezirke, 15. 9. 1939. Marktheidenfeld and Mellrichstadt attracted the attention of firms considering relocation.

80. StAW, LRA Marktheidenfeld, 4171, Landesplannungsgemeinschaft Bayern, Bericht über die Gründungsversammlung, Aug. 18, 1936, in the Deutsche Museum, Munich. The words quoted are those of the report writer who provided an account of Epp's remarks.

81. StAN, LRA Hilpolstein, 1971, 46^I, Deutscher Gemeindetag, Der Geschäftsführer (signed Jesserich) to the cities, etc., July 24, 1933.

82. BAP, 39.03, 229, RFM to president RfAA, Dec. 2, 1933.

83. BHStA, MWi 5935, Dr. Gieselher Wirsing, editor-in-chief, *Münchner Neuste Nachrichten,* to [Bavarian] minister-president, Dec. 22, 1938, including special edition of *Münchner Neuste Nachrichten,* Dec. 18, 1934, "Der Großangriff auf der Rhön. Zwischenbilanz des Dr.–Hellmuth-Planes," by Dr. Wolfgang Höpker; [Bavarian minister-president] to Dr. Gieselher Wirsing, editor-in-chief of *Münchner Neuste Nachrichten,* Dec. 29, 1938. Personal; BHStA, MA106772, Dr. Gieselher Wirsing, editor-in-chief, *Münchner Neuste Nachrichten,* to [Bavarian] minister-president, Dec. 30, 1938.

84. BAK, R43/II/537, Dec. 6, 1933, "Chefsbesprechung im Reichsarbeitsministerium," on the subject of combatting unemployment during 1934. Also found in

Akten der Reichskanzlei, pt. 1, vol. 2, p. 1001. Present were the ministers for labor, finance, and transportation, and representatives from the ministries for economics, food and agriculture, and labor. Wilhelm Keppler represented Hitler.

6. Local and Regional Efforts in the "Battle for Work"

1. The pre-Hitler Gereke *Sofortprogramm* of January 1933 encountered strong resistance from regional and local authorities who considered its terms too onerous and its benefits too meager. Württemberg's economics minister Dr. Reinhold Maier (Deutsche Demokratische Partei) referred to the program as a "swindle." See HStAS, E130b, Bü3221, p. 417, Auszug aus der Niederschrift über die Sitzung des Staatsministeriums vom 7. Februar 1933.

2. There are few accounts of local efforts in the battle for jobs, 1933–1936. Among contemporary works are two studies prepared for the VI. Internationalen Gemeindekongress in Berlin, June 1936, by Stuttgart's Nazi mayor Dr. Karl Strölin: *Die Bekämpfung der Arbeitslosigkeit durch den Gemeinden* (Berlin, Munich, 1936), and *Der Kampf gegen die Arbeitslosigkeit in der Stadt Stuttgart* (Stuttgart: Stuttgarter Buchdruckerei-Gesellschaft, 1936). Recent works include two by Birgit Wulff, "The Third Reich and the Unemployed: National Socialist Work Creation Schemes in Hamburg 1933–4," in Richard J. Evans and Dick Geary, eds., *The German Unemployed* (New York: St. Martin's Press, 1987), pp. 281–302, and *Arbeitslosigkeit und Arbeitsbeschaffungsmaßnahmen in Hamburg, 1933–1939: Eine Untersuchung zur nationalsozialistischen Wirtschafts- und Sozialpolitik* (Frankfurt/M: Peter Lang, 1987); Dieter Pfliegensdörfer, *Vom Handelszentrum zur Rüstungsschmiede: Wirtschaft, Staat und Arbeiterklasse in Bremen 1929 bis 1945* (Bremen: Universität Bremen, 1986). The cases of Hamburg and Bremen cannot be considered "typical," since both cities depended heavily upon international trade, which remained artificially depressed under autarkic Nazi economic policy.

3. N-WHStA, Reg. Aachen, 16852, Reichsnährstand, Landesbauernschaft Rheinland, Verwaltungsamt Bonn, to Regierungspräsident in Aachen, July 10, 1935, concerning construction of a water supply system in Kreis Monschau; StAD, 500/433, press clipping from *Mitteilungen des deutschen Städtetages*, April 8, 1933, "Lohnanteil und wirtschaftliche Bedeutung von Notstandsarbeiten."

4. N-WStAM, Oberpräsidium 5711, Regierungspräsident in Münster (signed Dr. Pünder) to Prussian minister for economics and labor, Feb. 12, 1933.

5. RGBl, 1933, vol. 1, p. 647, Gemeindeumschuldungsgesetz vom 21. 9. 1933.

6. According to Reich chancellery Ministerialrat Franz Willuhn, German cities rescheduled RM 3.2 billion in short-term obligations during the period 1933–1936. Prussian municipalities and municipal organizations, which rescheduled two-thirds of their short-term obligations, accounted for 80 percent of the total, and saved interest payments of between 40 and 50 million Reich marks. See BAK, R43II/323,

Vermerk über die Umschuldung der Gemeinden, Dec. 12, 1936. Statistics used by the Association of German Municipal Governments (Deutsche Gemeindetag) indicated that German municipal governments reduced spending on debt service by RM 584 million between 1931 and 1934. But the decline had begun in 1932, suggesting that the 1933 debt restructuring scheme was not the only factor involved. See StADü, Ebel 96, Niederschrift über die Sitzung der Arbeitsgemeinschaft der Kämmerer der rheinischen Städtkreise im Stadtverordneten-Sitzungssaal des Rathauses zu Trier, Oct. 12, 1935, point two: report on the meeting of the Deutsche Gemeindetag finance committee in Munich.

7. BAK, R2/18701, RFM memorandum, "Die Arbeitsbeschaffungsmaßnahmen der Reichsregierung 1932 bis 1935," [April] 1937.

8. Wulff, *Arbeitslosigkeit in Hamburg*, p. 163; StAD, 500/432, clipping from *Mitteilungen des deutschen Städtetages*, June 15, 1934, "Arbeitsbeschaffung und Wohlfahrtshaushalt," by lord mayor Sperling, Quedlinburg. The cost-benefit ratio (work creation spending/savings on welfare payments) was generally favorable to municipalities, but "the yield deteriorates if the state welfare subsidy declines along with the number of welfare-unemployed reinstated in employment." See 500/433, clipping from *Mitteilungen des deutschen Städetages*, April 8, 1933, "Lohnanteil und wirtschaftliche Bedeutung von Notstandsarbeiten," by Stadtbaurat Dr. Trauer, Breslau. One 1936 estimate indicated that German cities spent an average of RM 600 a year on welfare support for an unemployed person. Employing such persons on work creation projects cost the cities between RM 3,500 and 6,000 per head per year for wages and material, depending on the type of work. See HStAS, E130b, Bü3212, "Die Bekämpfung der Arbeitslosigkeit durch die Lokalverwaltungen," speech by mayor Strölin before the VI. International Congress of Cities, Berlin, June 9, 1936.

9. On July 15, 1933, enrollment in the Reich Landhilfe stood at 144,981, of whom about one-quarter were female. In August 1933, the Reich finance minister imposed a restriction of 200,000 on the number of Landhelpers. In May, 1934, RfAA president Syrup indicated that the limit on Landhelpers had been reduced to 160,000. See StAD, 500/445, and StAN, LRA Hilpolstein, 46^{II}, president RfAA to LAA presidents, Aug. 3, 1933; StAD, 500/445, clipping from *Mitteilungen des deutschen Städetages*, no. 16, Aug. 22, 1934, p. 499. RfAA president Syrup insisted that "reporting for the Landhilfe is voluntary. The unemployed person can refuse a Landhelper position without giving any reason." See N-WHStA, Reg. Aachen 16858, president RfAA to LAA and AA, March 3, 1933, circular letter explaining Landhilfe regulations.

10. StAD, 500/434, flyer, "Jüngere Siedler Gesucht!"; AA Duisburg to Fürsorgeamt, attention Herr Nienhoff, July 20, 1933, concerning Siedlungsanwärter f. Ostpreußen.

11. StAD, 500/434, Oberpräsident East Prussia to head AA Duisburg, Oct. 24,

1

1933, concerning Landdienst; provisional head Duisburg AA to Oberpräsident East Prussia, Nov. 13, 1933, concerning Landdienst; Oberpräsident East Prussia to Magistrat der Stadt Dusbirg (sic), welfare office Duisburg, Dec. 12, 1933, concerning clothing for Landdienst. East Prussia also sent home 1,400 FAD volunteers who did not wish to remain in East Prussia after the expiration of their service commitment in April 1934. See StAD, 500/445, Duisburg Wohlfahrtsamt (signed Birkenbuel) to Kreisstelle, April 4, 1934.

12. StAD, 500/445, Oberpräsident Rheinprovinz to Landräte and mayors of district, July 21, 1934, concerning placement of youths and assignment to agriculture; Duisburg [Wohlfahrtsamt] (signed Birkenbuel) to mayor, Aug 10, 1934.

13. See Chapter 4 for a discussion of East Prussia's successful Landhilfe program.

14. N-WHStA, Reg. Aachen, 16899, mayor Aachen to Regierungspräsident, April 10, 1934, monthly report.

15. BHStA, MWi 3132, Ministerialsitzung vom 19. September 1933; Ministerialsitzung vom 14. November 1933; MA 106743, clipping from Gesetz- und Verordnungs- Blatt für den Freistaat Bayern, "VO zur Sicherstellung ausreichender Arbeitskräfte für die Landwirtschaft (Erweiterte Landhilfe in Bayern) vom 29. September 1933"; for Landhilfe statistics, MA 106743, Landesarbeitsamt Bayern, Arbeit und Arbeitslosigkeit in Bayern im Jahre 1934 (LAA Bayern, Munich, 1934), pp. 58–60; StAN, Regierung von Oberfranken und Mittelfranken, Kammer des Innern, Abg. 1978, Nr. 3440, [Bavarian] State economics ministry, department of agriculture, to Vorstände der Bezirksämter, May 18 and June 6, 1934.

16. StAS, HA-09/107, Stuttgart. Niederschrift der Wohlfahrtsabt. des Gemeinderats vom 13. November 1933, Nichtöffentlich. Nr. 11., Einrichtung der "Stuttgarter Landhilfe" and Wohlfahrtsamt Stuttgart to Gemeinderat, Nov. 7, 1933; Niederschrift . . . vom 4. Dezember 1933, Nr. 41, Wohlfahrtsamt Stuttgart to gemeinderätliche Wohlfahrtsabteilung, Nov. 30, 1933; Niederschrift . . . vom 16. April 1934, Nr. 34, Wohlfahrtsamt Stuttgart to gemeinderätliche Wohlfahrtsabteilung, April 12, 1934; Bürgermeisteramt 1933–1945, Nr. 119, Die Stadt Stuttgart im Jahre 1934, p. 86; Verwaltungsbericht der Stadt Stuttgart für 1934, p. 41; Strölin, Der Kampf gegen die Arbeitslosigkeit in der Stadt Stuttgart, p. 57.

17. See Chapter 7 for details of efforts by cities to place their unemployed on Autobahnen construction sites.

18. StadtAN, C25/I, F Reg., 665, president RfAA, Anerkennung no. 809, recognizing electrification of Augsburg-Nuremberg and Munich-Dachau lines as eligible for basic subsidy; Stadtrat Nürnberg to RAM, Sept. 6, 1933; Vormerkung, account of Sept. 22, 1933, meeting in Nuremberg between city officials and Reichsbahn officials; Stadtrat Nürnberg to Geschäftsstelle des Bayerischen Gemeindetages, Munich, Nov. 8, 1933.

19. BHStA, MA 106957, Bayer. Staatsministerium f. Wirtschaft, Abteilung f. Handel, Industrie u. Gewerbe to Hauptverwaltung der Deutschen Reichsbahn-

Gesellschaft, July 22, 1935; Bayer. Staatsministerium der Finanzen (signed Siebert) to Staatsministerium f. Wirtschaft, Abt. f. Handel, Industrie u. Gewerbe, July 31, 1935.

20. StAS, HA-09, 107, Stuttgart. Niederschrift der Wohlfahrtsabt. des Gemeinderats vom 18. Februar 1935, Nr. 27; Niederschrift . . . vom 17. Dezember 1934, Nr. 265; Bü Amt 121, Verwaltungsbericht der Stadt Stuttgart für 1935, p. 33; Bü Amt 119, Bü Amt Stuttgart, Arbeitsbeschaffungsamt, Tatigkeitsbericht auf 31. Dezember 1934 (dated Jan. 12, 1935); Karl Strölin, "10 Jahre nationalsozialistische Stadtverwaltung," final draft dated Feb. 19, 1943.

21. StadtAN, C25/I, F Reg., 689, Stadtrat Lindau (Bodensee) to Stadtrat-Bezirksfürsorgeverband Nürnberg, Feb. 20, 1934; Niederschrift über eine Besprechung, March 12, 1934; Entwurf einer Vereinbarung, undated; Stadtrat Lindau to Stadtrat Nürnberg, April 13, 1934; Städt. Wohlfahrtsamt Nürnberg to Stadtrat Lindau, April 28, 1934; Stadtrat Lindau to Stadtrat Nürnberg, June 16, 1934; Städt. Wohlfahrtsamt Nürnberg to Städt. Wohlfahrts- und Jugendamt, Abt. Arbeitsfürsorge, München, June 25, 1934; Städt. Wohlfahrtsamt Nürnberg to Stadtrat Lindau, July 14, 1934. Dornier stipulated that the Nuremberg welfare office would have to verify the "national trustworthiness" of any trainees provided for aircraft production. This seems to be a case of rearmament disguised as "work creation," thus making Nuremberg's successful defense of its intransigent attitude all the more difficult to explain.

22. Heidrun Homburg, "From Unemployment Insurance to Compulsory Labour: The Transformation of the Benefit System in Germany 1927–1933," in Richard J. Evans and Dick Geary, eds., *The German Unemployed* (New York: St. Martin's Press, 1987), p. 85.

23. Ibid., p. 93–97. For welfare work in Duisburg, for example, see StAD, 500/455, Duisburg-Hamborn Wohlfahrtsamt, Arbeitsfürsorge, memoranda of Jan. 11 and July 31, 1934. Duisburg *Fürsorgearbeiter* worked 32 to 48 hours per week, depending on marital status and number of children, and earned either 61 or 70 Pfennige per hour, depending on the type of work involved. Outdoor construction and maintenance work paid less than office work, for which Nazi "old fighters" were given preference. *Pflichtarbeiter* worked two days a week for a total of six hours, for which they received locally available welfare benefits, plus a weekly bonus of perhaps 40 or 80 Pfennige. Some also received an additional 40 Pfennige for lunch, and a monthly certificate worth RM 25 to cover basic necessities.

24. StAD, 500/432, Duisburg-Hamborn, Arbeitsfürsorge, Feb. 11, 1933, response to questionnaire from Deutscher Verein für öffentliche und privat Fürsorge, Frankfurt/M, Jan. 20, 1933.

25. Homburg, "From Unemployment Insurance to Compulsory Labour," p. 100.

26. StAD, 500/452, Auszug aus der Niederschrift über die Versammlung der Kreisstellenleiter [of welfare office] am 24. Oktober 1935, section 8: Einweisung

von Juden in Pflichtarbeit. In 1936, it was still possible to win some small conces-sions for Jews. Duisburg's welfare office granted the city rabbinate's request to excuse Jewish compulsory laborers from work for a week during the "Jewish Easter celebration" (Passover). See StAD, 500/452, Rabbinat der jüdischen Gemeinde zu Duisburg to städtische Fürsorgeamt Duisburg, March 12, 1936, with response noted at bottom and on reverse, March 14 and 16.

27. Duisburg officials rejected requests from a local SA unit and a local unit of the League of German Girls for the assignment of compulsory laborers to build and repair housing for the units. See StAD, 500/452, Sturm 29/43 and NSDAP Standort 43, Duisburg-Hamborn, to Oberbürgermeister Duisburg-Hamborn, June 21 and 28, 1934; Wohlfahrtsamt Duisburg-Hamborn to SA der NSDAP, Standort 43, Hamborn, Aug. 31, 1934; Bund der deutscher Mädel, Jungmädel-Ring I/236 to Stadtverwaltung Duisburg-Hamborn, Oct. 29, 1934, with response of Oct. 3, 1934. Duisburg officials cited the Reich interior minister's decree of May 22, 1934, which prohibited local governments from supporting agencies of the NSDAP, SA, and SS in any manner.

28. StAD, 500/432, Arbeitsfürsorge Duisburg-Hamborn, Feb. 11, 1933, response to questionnaire , "Frage-Schema für eine gutachtliche Äusserung," circulated Jan. 20, 1933, by the Deutscher Verein für öffentliche und privat Fürsorge, Frank-furt/M.

29. StAD, 500/452, Pflichtarbeiter der Baustelle Wedau-Regattabahn, Bauburo Kalkweg, to Wohlfahrtsdezernenten Duisburg-Hamborn, July 9, 1930, and to Stadtverordnetenkollegium, Aug. 1, 1930; Duisburg-Hamborn Fürsorgeamt to Pfli-chtarbeiter der Baustelle Wedau-Regattabahn, Aug. 16, 1930; Duisburg-Hamborn Fürsorgeamt, Nov. 24, 1931 memorandum on meeting held Nov. 23 dealing with Pflichtarbeiter petitions; "Fort mit Strafarbeit," flyer distributed by Die zentrale Kampfleitung der Pflicht- und Wohlfahrtsarbeiter, undated (probably May–June 1932). For other references to passive resistance, evasion, low productivity, and strikes by compulsory workers, see the following in Evans and Geary, eds., *The German Unemployed:* Evans, "Introduction: The Experience of Unemployment in the Weimar Republic," p. 15; Homburg, "From Unemployment Insurance to Com-pulsory Labour," p. 98; Harvey, "Youth Unemployment and the State: Public Pol-icies towards Unemployed Youth in Hamburg during the World Economic Crisis," pp. 155–157.

30. Wulff, *Arbeitslosigkeit in Hamburg,* pp. 109, 361, 365; StadtAN, C25/I, F Reg., 694, Städt. Wohlfahrtsamt Nürnberg, memorandum, "Die Arbeitslosenfürsorge in deutschen Städte," June 1, 1935, table taken from *Statistisches Jahrbuch Deutscher Gemeinden,* 1935, p. 149. Of twenty-four cities listed, twelve registered fewer than 10 percent of their welfare unemployed as compulsory laborers, five registered between 10 and 20 percent, three between 20 and 30 percent, two between 30 and 40 percent, one between 40 and 50 percent, and one over fifty percent.

31. After compulsory labor was introduced in Stuttgart, hundreds of welfare recipients, apparently having found work, left the welfare rolls. See StAS, Bü Amt 145, "Vier Jahre nationalsozialistische Gemeindearbeit in Stuttgart," Strolin's speech to assembled townspeople in the Liederhalle, April 9, 1937.

32. For volunteers for compulsory labor, see StAD, 500/432, Duisburg-Hamborn, Arbeitsfürsorge, Feb. 11, 1933, response to questionnaire from Deutscher Verein für öffentliche und privat Fürsorge, Frankfurt/M, Jan. 20, 1933. As Reich criteria for classifying recognized WE tightened, the number of such persons reported in official statistics undoubtedly diminished. Realistic percentages of WE engaged in compulsory labor should be calculated from the total number of WE, both "recognized" and nonrecognized.

33. StadtAN, C25/I, F Reg., 694, Städt. Wohlfahrtsamt Nürnberg, memorandum, "Die Arbeitslosenfürsorge in deutschen Städte," June 1, 1935, table taken from *Statistisches Jahrbuch Deutscher Gemeinden*, 1935, p. 149; *Statistische Beilage zum Reichsarbeitsblatt*, 1934, Nr. 7, p. 12, Table XV, p. 15, Table XXIV; StAD, 500/432, table, "Im Arbeitsdienst und in der produktiven Arbeitslösenfürsorge beschäftigte Personen seit Anfang 1933," taken from *Das nationalsozialistische Rathaus*, no. 1, Oct. 1, 1935, p. 16.

34. Elizabeth Harvey has argued that workers' opposition to local compulsory labor schemes forced Hamburg's municipal welfare authorities to consider the voluntary labor service as an "alternative model for occupying the unemployed" by the autumn of 1932. See Harvey, "Youth Unemployment and the State," in Evans and Geary, *The German Unemployed*, p. 157.

35. StAS, HA-09,107, Wohlfahrtsamt Stuttgart to Gemeinderätliche Wohlfahrtsabteilung, Nov. 9, 1933, concerning Stuttgarter Haushilfe, contained in Stuttgart, Niederschrift der Wohlfahrtsabt. des Gemeinderats vom 13. November 1933. Nichtöffentlich, Nr. 12. Einrichtung der "Stuttgarter Haushilfe"; Wohlfahrtsamt Stuttgart to Gemeinderätliche Wohlfahrtsabt., Nov. 13, 1933, in Niederschrift . . ., vom 4. Dezember 1933, Nr. 40; Bü Amt, 119, Bü Amt Stuttgart, Arbeitsbeschaffungsamt, Tätigkeitsbericht auf 31. Dezember 1934 (dated Jan. 12, 1935), Section 13: Stuttgarter Haushilfe. For the decline in unemployment in "household service," see Bü Amt 1933–1945, 121, *Die Stadt Stuttgart im Jahre 1935*, p. 69, "Verteilung der Arbeitslosen auf die einzelnen Berufsgruppen."

36. StAD, 102/1687, memorandum, "Städtische Arbeitsbeschaffungsstelle," undated, prepared at the request of the mayor dated April 6, 1934, for inclusion in the *Verwaltungsbericht* for 1933.

37. For the creation and activity of the Duisburg Arbeitsbeschaffungs- G.m.b.H., see voluminous documentation in StAD, 102/1687.

38. HHStA, Abt. 483, 10951, clipping from *Frankfurter Zeitung*, Jan. 12, 1934, "Rhein-Main-Gau im Werden. Möglichkeiten regionaler Zusammenarbeit."

39. Ibid.; HHStA, Abt. 483, 10951, clipping from *Frankfurter Zeitung*, May 5,

1934, "Wie das Rhein-Main-Gebiet entstand. Die wichtigsten Etappen aus der Arbeit des Reichsstatthalters"; clipping from *Rhein-Mainische Wirtschafts-Zeitung* (official organ of the Rhine-Main chamber of industry and commerce, the Rhine-Main region export office, and the economic chamber of Hesse, edited by Carl Lüer), May 5, 1936, "Drei Jahre nationalsozialistischer Wirtschaftsführung im Rhein-Main Gebiet."

40. HHStA, Abt. 483, 10951, clipping from *Frankfurter Volksblatt*, June 22, 1937, "Der rhein-mainische Wirtschaftsraum in seiner Aufbauarbeit," remarks by Prof. Dr. Carl Lüer to June 21 meeting of Wirtschaftskammer Hessen.

41. HHStA, Abt. 483, 10925, *Fränkische Tageszeitung* (Beilage), n.d., probably September 1937, article by Gau economic advisor Karl Eckardt, "Wirtschafts-Aufbau in Hessen-Nassau"; 10951, typewritten statistical summary for Land Hessen, "Rednerinformation," dated March 28, 1938; HHStA, Abt. 483, 10951, *Rhein-Mainische Wirtschafts-Zeitung*, May 5, 1936, issue titled "Drei Jahre nationalsozialistischer Wirtschaftsführung im Rhein-Main-Gebiet." Since the boundaries of Land Hesse and the Gau Hesse-Nassau did not exactly coincide, statistics compiled from the two sources are not completely identical.

42. HHStA, Abt. 483, 10951, *Rhein-Mainische Wirtschafts-Zeitung*, May 5, 1936, section titled "Die Entwicklung des Bergbaues und der Hochofenindustrie an Lahn, Dill und in Oberhessen seit 1933"; *Frankfurter Volksblatt* (F. V.), Jan. 18, 1935, "186 v.H. Belegschaftsvermehrung. Der Eisensteinbergbau an Lahn, Dill und in Oberhessen." The figure of 186 percent refers to the increase in employment from the end of 1932 to the end of 1934.

43. HHStA, Abt. 483, 10951, clipping from *Frankfurter Volksblatt*, June 22, 1937, "Der rhein-mainische Wirtschaftsraum in seiner Aufbauarbeit."

44. N-WHStA, Reg. Aachen, 16851, mayor of Aachen to Regierungspräsident, Nov. 5, 1934, concerning "Elektro-Angriff 1934–35."

45. StAD, 102/1687, D.O.B. [Duisburg Oberbürgermeister] to Niederrheinische Industrie- und Handelskammer Duisburg-Wesel, in Duisburg-Ruhrort, Dec. 15, 1933, response to chamber's request for information on Duisburg's municipal work creation effort; questionnaire of Reichsverband der Elektrizitätsversorgung, "Erhebung über Arbeiten, die zur Durchführung eines großzügigen Arbeitsbeschaffungsprogramm auf dem Gebiet der Elektrizitätsversorgung . . . auszuführen wären," included in Reichsverband circular of Feb. 3, 1934; response of Gas- Wasser- und Elektrizitätswerke der Stadt Duisburg (G.W.E.-Werke), Feb. 27, 1934; G.W.E.-Werke Duisburg to Stadtamt 11, A St., March 14, 1934, with copy of completed questionnaire.

46. StAD, 102/1687, Treuhänder der Arbeit Westfalen, "Richtlinien für die Arbeitsbeschaffungsfront," Jan. 1934.

47. Ibid.

48. For Schwabach's committee for the relief of unemployment, established on

the initiative of NSDAP Kreisleiter Engelhardt, see StAN, LRA Schwabach 1984, 4282, Arbeitsausschuß zur Behebung der Arbeitslosigkeit im Stadt und Bezirk Schwabach, to 1. Bürgermeister in Schwabach, Roth, Spalt, Wendelstein, Abenberg, Aug. 15, 1933. For the Lippe's Fighting Organization Against Unemployment, see N-WStAD, L76Gr.E, 1a, letter on Arbeitsamt Detmold letterhead, signed I.A. des Staatsminister, to Staatsminister [Hans-Joachim] Riecke, Detmold-Regierung, Aug. 3, 1933, copies apparently sent to all public officials in Lippe; communication on Arbeitsamt Detmold letterhead, signed by Gaukommissar of NSDAP, Aug. 24, 1933, apparently sent to all Nazi party offices in the district. Local Nazi leaders were asked to set up "fighting organizations against unemployment." In cities, membership was to include one employer, one laborer, one handicraftsman, one female, and one industrialist. In small towns, the organization was to consist of one farm owner, one agricultural laborer, one handicraftsman, and one female.

49. N-WStAD, L76, Gr.E, 1a, AA Detmold to president LAA Westfalen, Oct. 3, Nov. 2, Dec. 2, 1933, with labor market reports for Sept., Oct., and Nov. 1933. The November report indicated "great activity" by the AA in the matter of finding jobs for unemployed SA personnel; 47 members of national military organizations were placed in "stable positions."

50. BHStA, MA 106743, president RfAA to LAA presidents, Aug. 19, 1933; Runderlaß of Prussian interior minister to Regierungspräsidenten, Sept. 1, 1933; RAM to Länder governments, May 19, 1934; StAD, 102/1687, Regierungspräsident [Regierungsbezirk Düsseldorf], Niederschrift über die Besprechung mit den Landräten und Oberbürgermeistern vom 23 .11. 1933, section 4, Arbeitsbeschaffung.

51. BAP, 39.03, 233, NSDAP Kreisleitung Kirchheimbolanden/Pfalz to RfAA, Oct. 20, 1933; president RfAA to NSDAP Kreisleitung Kirchheimbolanden, Oct. 31, 1933 (draft).

52. BAP, 31.01, 17948, Bd. 11, president RfAA to RAM, Abt. IV, im Hause, Oct. 20, 1932; Mittelstands-Vereinigung Duisburg-Nord E. V. to RWM Hugenburg, Feb. 22, 1933; clipping from *Rheinisch-Westf. Ztg.*, April 30, 1933.

53. N-WStAM, Oberpräsidium 6834, NSDAP Gauleitung Westfalen-Süd to Oberpräsident Provinz Westfalen, Sept. 7, 1933, with enclosure, Stadtverwaltung Dortmund to NSDAP Gauleiter, Westfalen-Süd (signed Malzbender, Oberbürgermeister), undated copy; handwritten memorandum, D. O. P. [the Oberpräsident], (signed Lüninck), Sept. 13, 1933.

54. BAP, 31.01, 17948, Bd. 11, RWM (Schmitt) to Bavarian interior minister, Adolf Wagner, April 23, 1934; Stellungnahme of Dr. Vögler, presented to RAM; Der Sonderbeauftragte des Reichswirtschaftsministers Dr. R. Scheer-Hennings to RWM Dr. Kurt Schmitt, July 22, 1933, with enclosure, "Kurzbericht über die bisher geführten Verhandlungen zwecks Wiederinbetriebnahme der Hütte Ruhrort-Meiderich," reports of discussions of July 13 and 17, 1933; "Besprechung am 23.

August 1933 bei Herrn Gauleiter Terboven," concerning Hütte Ruhrort-Meiderich, dated Aug. 24, 1933, signed by Vögler.

55. StAN, LRA Uffenheim 1971, 448, [Bavarian] Staatsministerium f. Wirtschaft, Abt. f. Handel, Industrie u. Gewerbe to the Regierungen, K.d.I, March 28, 1934, enclosing copy of RWM circular of March 1, 1934, "Kauf am Ort- Propaganda"; idem., June 7, 1934, enclosing copy of letter of RWM to Reichsstand des deutschen Handwerks, April 27, 1934.

56. N-WHStA, Reg. Aachen, 16849, Landestelle Rheinland des Reichsminister- iums f. Volksaufklärung u. Propaganda to Regierungspräsident, Aachen, Sept. 5, 1933, containing copy of form sent to Grevesmühlen employers by the Landrat and NSDAP Kreisleiter, Aug. 2, 1933; D.R.P. [Regierungspräsident Aachen], Vermerk, Sept. 27, 1933; StAN, LRA Hilpoltstein, 46^{II}, Bezirksamt Hilpoltstein to communal authorities, Aug. 30, 1933, concerning the battle against unemployment; N- WHStA, Reg. Aachen, 16899, Landrat [Classen] of Landkreis Aachen to Indus- treiverband, Stolberg, Oct. 17, 1933. Despite Classen's earlier offer of a RM 30 premium for each new worker hired, Stolberg's thirty-five firms, employing 7,830 workers, had agreed to hire only 69 of the district's unemployed. If local businesses failed to "voluntarily" hire new workers, Classen threatened to levy compulsory special taxes on local businesses to finance public employment projects. He warned that public officials would not be able to resist the public demand for action, if the local press publicized the situation.

57. The mayor of Duisburg admitted that many accusations against workers, either employed or unemployed, resulted from long-standing personal feuds. See StAD, 102/1687, memorandum of Oberbürgermeister als Ortspolizeibehörde to Stadtamt 11, Oct. 20, 1933, concerning *Schwarzarbeit*.

58. BHStA, MWi 3135, Staatsministerium des Innern to the Regierungen, Kam- mern des Innern, and to the Kommandatur of Dachau concentration camp, Nov. 22, 1934. Sending "work-shy" welfare recipients to Dachau was a relatively costly solution to local welfare problems. The welfare authority had to pay the concentra- tion camp command a fee of RM 1.20 per day for each inmate, payable in advance each month. Either purging work-shy persons from the welfare rolls or enlisting them in local compulsory labor provided a less costly solution.

59. BHStA, Statthalter 472, Bavarian state economics ministry (signed Esser) to RWM, Aug. 7, 1934. Esser's involvement with the Nazi movement dated from 1921, when he served as an editor on the *Völkischer Beobachter*. Prior to his service as Bavarian economics minister (March 1, 1934, to March 23, 1935), he headed the newly created Bavarian Staatskanzlei established with Bavaria's Nazi cabinet of April 12, 1933.

60. This argument is fully developed in Wulff, *Arbeitslosigkeit in Hamburg*.

61. StAD, Niederrheinische Industrie- und Handelskammer Duisburg-Wesel zu Duisburg-Ruhrort, "Kurzer Bericht über die Tätigkeit der Niederrheinischen

Industrie- und Handelskammer Duisburg-Wesel im Jahre 1933," pp. 4–7; "Die Tätigkeit . . . im Jahre 1934," pp. 8, 12; "Die Tätigkeit . . . im Jahre 1935," p. 9. Wulff, *Arbeitslosigkeit in Hamburg,* indicates that Hamburg received little assistance from Reich programs and policies that were either irrelevant or damaging to the city's interests.

62. The use of Reinhardt program funds to construct a school on the Bavarian-Czechoslovakian border was one of the measures "which on the grounds of border policy serve special requirements in the general national interest." See BHStA, MWi 3132, RAM to Bavarian state ministry for education and religion, Jan. 6, 1934.

63. N-WHStA, Reg. Aachen 16852, Regierungspräsident Köln (signed Diels) to Generalinspektor für das deutsche Straßenwesen, Nov. 29, 1934. The removal of army garrisons at Cologne, Bonn, and Bensberg cost this district an estimated RM 30 million annually in lost revenues. *Autobahnen* construction was delayed in the district, and Cologne's brown coal industry was forced to make a significant capital contribution to the construction of a hydrogenation plant in Mitteldeutschland, but was prohibited on national security grounds from building such a plant locally.

64. N-WHStA, Reg. Aachen 16852, Clemens Bruckner, Syndikus der Industrie-u. Handelskammer für den Regierungsbezirk, to Regierungspräsident, May 9, 1934, enclosing Vertraulicher Bericht über die Tagung des Gauwirtschaftsrats der NSDAP Gau Köln-Aachen, May 7, 1934.

65. StADü, Ebel 96, Niederschrift über die Vorstandssitzung der Provinzialdienststelle Rheinland u. Hohenzollern des Deutschen Gemeindetages, June 27, 1935.

66. BHStA, MWi 8682, Vertretung Bayerns beim Reich to [Bavarian] Staatsministerium f. Wirtschaft, Abt. f. Handel, Industrie u. Gewerbe, Sept. 7, 1933; Bayer. Staatsmin. f. Wirtschaft, Abt. f. Handel, Industrie u. Gewerbe to Vertretung Bayerns beim Reich, Oct. 20, 1933; Vertretung Bayerns beim Reich to Staatsmin. f. Wirtschaft, Abt. f. Handel, Industrie u. Gewerbe, Nov. 2 and 17, 1933; Vormerkung zur Aufzeichnung über die Besichtigungsreise in die Rheinpfalz vom 29. XI.-2.XII. 1933.

67. N-WHStA, Reg. Aachen, 16852, Regierungspräsident in Köln to Generalinspektor für das deutsche Straßenwesen, Nov. 29, 1934.

68. N-WHStA, Reg. Aachen, 16849, Regierungspräsident Aachen [Eggert Reeder] to RWM, Sept. 20, 1933, concerning Wurm-Ruhr-Abkommen; RWM to Rheinisch-Westfälische Kohlensyndikat, Oct. 10, 1933; Regierungspräsident Aachen to Prussian interior minister, Nov. 3, 1933; Regirungspräsident Aachen to Dr. Fritz Thyssen, Prussian Staatsrat, Nov. 4, 1933. It is not clear that Aachen coal interests were sacrificed by this agreement. During the depression, Aachen's major coal producer had cut prices drastically and increased Aachen's output from 5.5 million to 7.5 million tons between 1928 and 1932. Thus, "while the Ruhr's pro-

duction was a mere 68 percent of 1913 levels, Aachen's was 231 percent." See John Gillingham, *Industry and Politics in the Third Reich: Ruhr Coal, Hitler and Europe* (New York: Columbia University Press, 1985), pp. 35–36.

69. N-WHStA, Reg. Aachen, 16849, Regierungspräsident Aachen to Prussian interior minister, Nov. 3, 1933, concerning work creation in Landkreis Aachen.

70. N-WHStA, Reg. Aachen, 16850, Treuhänder der Arbeit f. das Wirtshchaftsgebiet Rheinland to Regirungspräsident Aachen, Nov. 23, 1933; N-WHStA, Reg. Aachen, 13885, Clemens Bruckner, Syndikus der Industrie- und Handelskammer f. den Regierungsbezirk Aachen to Regierungspräsident Aachen, May 9, 1934, enclosing report of meeting, Vertraulicher Bericht über die Tagung des Gauwirtschaftsrats der NSDAP Gau Köln-Aachen, May 7, 1934.

71. Kelter's remarks in StAD, 100A/1/22, Niederschrift über die nichtöffentliche Sitzung der vorläufigen Gemeinderäte am 16. Juni 1934. For statistics on the number of welfare-supported persons in Duisburg, see StAD, 500/209, numerous statistical tables, especially, "Bericht über die öffentliche Wohlfahrtspflege der Stadt Duisburg," June 8, 1935, signed Birkenbuel.

72. StAD, 500/209, "Bericht über die öffentliche Wohlfahrtspflege." From 132.6 per 1,000 receiving cash support on Jan. 31, 1933, the ratio declined to 76.5 per 1,000 by April 1, 1935. Corresponding ratios for Duisburg's closest "competitor," Dortmund, were 131.1 per 1,000 and 62.5 per 1,000. Düsseldorf's welfare office provided cash assistance to only 50.3 per 1,000 on April 1, 1935.

73. StAD, C/159, Städtischen Statischschen Amt, "Statistischer Vierteljahresbericht der Stadt Duisburg-Hamborn," 1932–1935, showing that employment of males accounted for the entire increase in total employment, while female employment declined during the period; StAD, 100/A/1/23, Anlage zur Niederschrift über die erste Sitzung der Ratsherrn am 2. Oktober 1934, Kelter's speech; Niederschrift über die nicht öffentliche Sitzung der Ratsherrn der Stadt Duisburg-Hamborn am 30. März 1935, item no. 51, Haushaltssatzung für das Rechnungsjahr 1935.

74. StAD, 609/28, Die Beteilung der Stadt Duisburg an den Maßnahmen zur Bekämpfung der Arbeitslosigkeit in der Zeit vom 1. 4. 1933 bis 30. 3. 1935 bezw. bis 31. 3. 1936," report signed by city councillor Holke, Dec. 1, 1935.

75. StADü, IV/12519, Deutscher Gemeindetag to Düsseldorf mayor, Nov. 6, 1936, asking for information on the contribution of cities to the battle for jobs since 1933; Düsseldorf response, consisting of an undated five-page chart depicting size and cost of work creation projects, 1933 through 1935. As Düsseldorf's commitment to these projects increased, Reich support decreased. The city's entire 1933 work creation program, totaling 13,800 man-days of work, was carried out as Reich-supported emergency relief work *(Notstandsarbeiten)*. In 1935, only 800 of 30,950 man-days were carried out as emergency relief projects.

76. Strölin, *Der Kampf gegen die Arbeitslosigkeit in der Stadt Stuttgart*, p. 57.

7. Road Building

1. For the importance of "motorization" in Germany's economic recovery, see the works of R. J. Overy, especially "Cars, Roads, and Economic Recovery in Germany, 1932–8," *Economic History Review* 28 (1975), pp. 466–483.

2. The following summary of Todt's plan is drawn from BAK, R65I/1a, "Straßenbau und Straßenverwaltung," 49-page memorandum, signed by Fritz Todt, Munich, Dec. 1932.

3. The plan adopted by the Hitler government in 1933 called for an *Autobahnen* network of 6,900 kilometers. By mid-Dec. 1938, 3,000 kilometers had been constructed and opened for traffic. The incorporation of Austria and Czechoslovakia into the Reich in 1938 considerably increased the planned network to between 12,000 and 15,000 kilometers. See various materials in BHStA, MA 106949.

4. Ibid., p. 40. Todt soon found that he was mistaken on this point. See later discussion.

5. HStAS, E130b, Bü3321, pp. 455, 460, Württembergische Gesandschaft, Berlin, to Württemberg economics ministry, Stuttgart, May 23, 1933, and Vertretung Württemberg beim Reich to Württemberg economics ministry, June 19, 1933.

6. N-WHStA, Reg. Aachen, 16857, Reichsausschuß der Kraftverkehr, Berlin, to Länderregierungen, Feb. 11, 1933.

7. *Akten der Reichskanzlei*, pt. 1, vol. 1, pp. 331–332, 463–464.

8. Ibid., pp. 543–544.

9. GStAPK, 90/1718, Reich transportation minister to state secretary in the Reich chancellery, June 2, 1933, with enclosure of draft law on creation of an Unternehmens "Reichsautobahnen"; Reich transportation minister to state secretary in Reich chancellery, June 7, 1933, with enclosure, "Begründung" for draft law; Reich transportation minister to state secretary in Reich chancellery, June 21, 1933, enclosing Section 11 revised according to Hitler's request; Prussian economics and labor minister to Reich transportation minister, June 12, 1933; Prussian Staatsministerium, Vermerk, betr. Entwurf eines Gesetzes über die Errichtung eines Unternehmen "Reichsautobahnen," June 22, 1933; *Akten der Reichskanzlei*, pt. 1, vol. 1, pp. 552, 560–561.

10. The decision to establish the RAB and create the position of general inspector of German roads was taken in the Reich cabinet meeting of June 23, 1933. For an account of the cabinet's discussion, see *Akten der Reichskanzlei*, pt. 1, vol. 1, pp. 584–585. For the law promulgated by the government, see RGBl, 1933, vol. 2, pp. 509–510, Gesetz über die Errichtung eines Unternehmens "Reichsautobahnen" vom 27. Juni 1933. The concentration of authority in Todt's hands produced

some undesired consequences. Believing that responsibility for maintenance of *Landstraßen* and *Kreisstraßen* would soon be taken over by either Todt or some other agency, state and local authorities discontinued expenditures on normal maintenance work. Todt ordered all road maintenance authorities to spend at least as much in 1934 as they had spent during 1933. See Generalinspektor to all Länder and Prussian provinces, July 3, 1934, Rundschreiben no. 106, concerning work on Kreis and Land roads.

11. BAK, R2/18677, Prussian interior minister to RAM, July 13, 1933. For the June 28 regulations, see RGBl, 1933, vol. 1, p. 425.

12. For Krosigk's rejection of funding requests for roads considered strategically important by Reich defense minister General Werner von Blomberg, see BAK, R2/18676, Reich food and agriculture minister to RFM, July 13, 1933; R2/18677, Prussian interior minister to RAM, July 13, 1933; Reich defense minister to RAM, July 29, 1933; RAM to RFM, *Schnellbrief,* Aug. 5, 1933; Reich transportation minister to RFM, Aug. 24, 1933; RFM to Reich transportation minister (copies to Reich defense minister, RAM, General Inspector for German Roads), Aug. 30, 1933 (draft).

13. BAK, R2/18677, D.R.d.F. [RFM] to Reich transportation minister [with copies to Reich ministers for defense and labor, and the general inspector for German roads], Aug. 30, 1933. These agricultural roads were considered an aspect of land improvement projects and thus eligible for support from the Reinhardt program. For additional details, see StAN, LRA Hilpoltstein, 46^{II}, [Bavarian] economics ministry, department of agriculture, to the departments of the interior of the [Bavarian] Regierungen, Nov. 22, 1933.

14. Todt's idea of a "winter program" was neither new nor "Nazi." The Reich transportation minister had asked state and local officials to continue road construction work and work in the stone quarries in Dec. 1932. See StAN, LRA Hilpolstein 1971, 46^I, Reich transportation minister to Bavarian interior ministry, etc., Dec. 19, 1932.

15. Ibid.; BAP, 39.03, 228, RfAA, Vermerk, Sept. 16, 1933 (signed Zschucke), account of Sept. 15 meeting; Öffa to president RfAA, Sept. 18, 1933, with enclosed memorandum, "Verwendung der Reserven," account of Sept. 15 meeting; BAP, 39.03, 229, RfAA, Vermerk, Sept. 22, 1933, account of Sept. 20 Sonderbesprechung on financing of *Autobahnen,* held in the offices of Öffa; Generalinspektor für das Deutsche Straßenwesen, Rundschreiben, Sept. 29, 1933, "Winterarbeiten im Straßenbau 1933 aus Kraftfahrzeugsteuermittel"; Generalinspektor, Rundschreiben, Sept. 30, 1933, "Winterarbeiten im Straßenbau 1933 aus Öffa-Mitteln"; president RfAA to presidents of LAA, Oct. 10, 1933. The reference to the financing of *"Autobahnen"* in the RfAA Vermerk of Sept. 22 was in error; the funds were to be employed in the construction or reconstruction of state and provincial roads, not for *Autobahnen* construction.

16. BAP, 39.03, 241, Generalinspektor to RfAA, Dec. 2, 1933, with memorandum, "Stand der Straßenbauarbeiten am 1. Dezember 1933 im allgemeinen Straßenbau"; BAP, 39.03, 229, RFM to president RfAA, Oct. 25, 1933, with enclosure concerning financing of work creation measures under the Reinhardt program, which lists RM 55 million for "Straßenbauvorhaben"; president RfAA to presidents of LAA, Dec. 6, 1933, with Todt's indication that a total of RM 55 million was available for road construction under the Reinhardt program (also found in N-WStAM, Oberpräsidium, 5717); BAK, R2/18677, RFM, Vermerk, Oct. 25, 1933, in which "Straßenbau" sums of RM 25, 40, and 45 million are listed and crossed out before the final sum of RM 55 million is registered; BAK, R2/18685, Dr. K. Wilhelmi [Öffa] to *Ministerialrat* Dr. Panzeram, Rechnungshof des Deutschen Reiches, Aug. 28, 1934, with enclosure, "Übersicht über die in den 3 Arbeitsbeschaffungsprogrammen von der Öffa zu finanzierenden Kredite," indicating that RM 58.6 million had been earmarked for "Straßenbauten" under the Reinhardt program. Jürgen Stelzner, *Arbeitsbeschaffung und Wiederafrüstung 1933–1936* (Tübingen: Tübingen University dissertation, 1976), pp. 87, 242, indicates that the RFM approved RM 106 million for road construction early in Nov. 1933. RM 41 million was to come from increased automobile tax revenues, and RM 65 million from Reinhardt program funds earmarked for *Tiefbau* (earthmoving projects).

17. BAP, 39.03, 229, RfAA, Vermerk, Sept. 22, 1933, account of Sept. 20 special discussion on financing of Autobahnen, held in the offices of Öffa.

18. See, for example, N-WStAM, Oberpräsidium, 5716, Öffa to Oberpräsident Provinz Westfalen, Nov. 7, 1933; D.O.P. [Der Oberpräsidium] to Öffa, Dec. 1, 1933, concerning Reinhardt-Programm, Winterarbeiten im Straßenbau 1933; D.O.P to Regierungspräsidenten der Provinz [Westfalen], Dec. 1, 1933.

19. In the Prussian Rhine province, only 20 percent of the stone industry's labor force was employed at the end of Sept. 1933. See N-WHStA, Reg. Aachen 16849, Oberpräsident Rheinprovinz to Regierungspräsidenten, Aug. 3, 1933; N-WHStA, Reg. Aachen 16849, Oberpräsident Rheinprovinz to Regierungspräsidenten, Aug. 3, 1933; BAP, 39.03, 131, Generalinspektor to RAM, Oct. 24, 1933, where Todt indicated a sum of RM 80 million was available for winter work; HHStA, Abt. 485, No. 824, Generalinspektor to Gesellschaft "Reichsautobahnen" Direktion, Berlin, Dec. 8, 1933; BAP, 39.03, 139, Bezirksleitung der Deutschen Arbeitsfront, Bezirk Hessen und Hessen-Nassau, to Zentralburo der Deutschen Arbeitsfront, June 6, 1934; N-WHStA, Reg. Aachen, 16851, Verband Westdeutscher Hartsteinwerke E.V. Bonn, to Regierungspräsident zu Aachen, July 3, 1934, with enclosure, "Entschließung," dated July 3, 1934.

20. See N-WStAM, Oberpräsidium, 5717, Generalinspektor to [no addressee named; general letter to all concerned agencies], with enclosed Rundschreiben, Nov. 2, 1933.

21. *Akten der Reichskanzlei,* pt. 1, vol. 2, pp. 1120–1121, Chefsbesprechung vom 9. Februar 1934.

22. Ibid; BAK, R2/18682, D.R.d.F. [RFM], Vermerk, March 29, 1934, account of March 29 meeting, attended by Reinhardt, Todt, Director Willy Hof of the RAB, Director Homberger of the Reichsbank, representatives of the RFM, and a representative of the Reich accounting office (Rechnungshof), in which Todt gave this version of the Feb. 9 meeting; *Akten der Reichskanzlei,* pt. 1, vol. 1, p. 1121n3, Todt letter to Lammers, Feb. 23, 1934.

23. BAK, R2/18682, D.R.d.F. [RFM], Vermerk, March 29, 1934, account of March 29 meeting; D.R.d.F. [RFM] to Gesellschaft "Reichsautobahnen," March 29, 1934 (draft).

24. StADü, IV/1859, Generalinspektor to Wegunterhaltungspflichtigen Länder und Provinzen, Aug. 11, 1934, *Runderlaß* no. 123.

25. Ibid.

26. GStAPK 90/1718, Reichsautobahnen, Drucksache Nr. 4, 18.9.1933, zur 2. Sitzung des Verwaltungsrats der Reichsautobahnen am 19. September 1933, "Voranschlag der Gesellschaft "Reichsautobahnen" für das Geschäftsjahr 1933," and "Erläuterung"; *Akten der Reichskanzlei,* pt. 1, vol. 2, pp. 740–743, "Vermerk des Ministerialrats Willuhn über eine Besprechung zur Finanzierung der Reichsautobahnen und des sonstigen Straßenbaus am 18. September 1933"; GStAPK 90/1718, Reichsautobahnen. Niederschrift über die 2. Sitzung des Verwaltungsrats der Gesellschaft "Reichsautobahnen" in Berlin am 19. September 1933; BAP 39.03, 132, RfAA, Vermerk, concerning Reichsautobahnen, by Dr. Bardow, March 6, 1934.

27. *Akten der Reichskanzlei,* pt. 1, vol. 2, pp. 741–742; GStAPK 90/1718, Reichsautobahnen. Niederschrift über die 2. Sitzung des Verwaltungsrats . . . am 19. September 1933, Todt's account of Sept. 18 meeting of officials with Hitler.

28. *Akten der Reichskanzlei,* pt. 2, vol. 2, p. 742.

29. *Akten der Reichskanzlei,* pt. 1, vol. 2, p. 743n10, which cites Dorpmüller's report to the third meeting of the "Reichsautobahnen" corporation administrative council, Nov. 27, 1933.

30. BAP, 39.03, 131, Generalinspektor to RfAA, Oct. 4, 1933, addressed to Dr.-Ing. Bardow, confirming telephone conversations of Sept. 30 and Oct. 2, in which the RfAA agreed to provide basic subsidies for *Autobahnen* construction.

31. N-WStAM, Oberprasidium, 5716, Öffa to Oberpräsident Provinz Westfalen, Feb. 14 and 21, 1934; D.O.P. [Der Oberpräsident, Provinz Westfalen] to Öffa, Feb. 26, 1934.

32. BAP 39.03, 132, RfAA, Vermerk, concerning Reichsautobahnen, by Dr. Bardow, March 6, 1934.

33. BAP 39.03, 132, RfAA, Vermerk, concerning Reichsautobahnen, Dr. Bardow, April 25, 1934.

34. In his autobiography, *My First Seventy-six Years*, trans. Diana Pyke (London: Allan Wingate, 1955), p. 304, Schacht claims he approved a credit of RM 600 million for *Autobahnen* construction. These funds were to be repaid to the Reichsbank out of the Reich budget in future years.

35. *Akten der Reichskanzlei*, pt. 1, vol. 2, p. 741. A substantial portion of funds earmarked for the *Autobahnen* between 1934 and 1941 went to debt service rather than construction. Michael Wolffsohn, "Arbeitsbeschaffung und Rüstung im nationalsozialistischen Deutschland: 1933," *Militärgeschichtliche Mitteilungen* 19 (1977), p. 16, seems to be in error when he says that "it is little noted that construction of the Autobahnen was financed mainly not from money from the purely state work creation programs, but out of the funds of the Reichsbahn's work creation programs. The Reichsbahn was the sole member of the Reichsautobahn enterprise."

36. Karl Lärmer, *Autobahnbau in Deutschland 1933 bis 1945—Zu den Hintergründen* (Berlin: Akademie-Verlag, 1975), p. 31.

37. Richard J. Overy, *War and Economy in the Third Reich* (Oxford: Clarendon Press, 1994), p. 60.

38. Estimate of the Reichsausschuß der Kraftverkehr. See N-WHStA, Reg. Aachen 16857, Reichsausschuß der Kraftverkehr, Berlin, to Länderregierungen, Feb. 11, 1933.

39. See, for example, BAK, R2/18686, Generalinspektor to RFM, Dec. 1, 1933, concerning "road construction in the interest of border defense," in which Todt admitted the project in question could not be justified on the basis of economic value alone. The RFM authorized Öffa to issue a RM 250,000 loan for reconstruction of a stretch of road between Reetz and Kallies. See D.R.d.F. [RFM] to Öffa, Feb. 12, 1934. For the military road requirements in East Prussia, see *Akten der Reichskanzlei*, pt. 1, vol. 2, pp. 1120–1121, Chefsbesprechung vom 9. Februar 1934.

40. BAK, R65III/1, Generalinspektor to Prussian minister-president [Göring], the Reichsstatthalter, Nov. 30, 1933.

41. BHStA, MWi 8682, numerous documents from the period Sept.–Dec. 1933, including communications between the Bavarian state chancellery and the Bavarian economics ministry, and between the Vertretung Bayerns beim Reich and the Bavarian economics ministry; BAP 39.03, 131, president LAA Rheinland to president RfAA, Dec. 1, 1933; Generalinspektor to president RfAA, Dec. 21, 1933.

42. Overy, *War and Economy*, p. 81.

43. BHStA, MWi 6966, Reichsverband der Automobilindustrie e.V. to Reich chancellor, etc., Aug. 16, 1932, seven-page proposal for a work creation program based on the revival of the motor vehicle industry.

44. Ibid.

45. BHStA, MWi 6966, Stadtrat der Landeshauptstadt München to Bayerische Staatsministerium des Äußern, für Wirtschaft und Arbeit, Oct. 1, 1932.

46. GStAPK 90/1718, "Gezuvor," Gesellschaft zur Vorbereitung der Reichsautobahnen e.V., Berlin, *Jahresbericht 1933.* The name change and adoption of the Führer principle took place at the August 17, 1933 meting.

47. GStAPK 90/1718, Gesellschaft "Reichsautobahnen," *Geschäftsbericht der Gesellschaft "Reichsautobahnen,* 1933 (Berlin: 1934).

48. GStAPK 90/1718, Verwaltungsrat der Gesellschaft "Reichsautobahnen," Geschäftsordnung des Verwaltungsrats der Gesellschaft "Reichsautobahnen," first meeting of administrative council, Aug. 25, 1933.

49. HHStA, Abt. 485, Findbuch, introductory material on the history and organization of the Gesellschaft "Reichsautobahnen" and the Frankfurt/Main district headquarters.

50. Ibid.

51. BHStA, MA106949, invitations for opening ceremonies.

52. BHStA, Reichsstatthalter 553, Generalinspektor to Reichsstatthalter General Ritter von Epp, Munich, Oct. 13, 1933, with enclosure, "Bericht der Generalinspektor . . . an d. Herrn Reichsstatthalter," Oct. 13, 1933.

53. *Akten der Reichskanzlei,* pt. 1, vol. 1, pp. 676–678.

54. HHStA, Abt. 485, 247, Der Generalinspektor f. das deutsche Straßenwesen, "Richtlinien für die Vergebung beim Bau der Reichsautobahnen," Feb. 22, 1934.

55. Ibid.; Reichsautobahnen Direktion to all OBK, July 1, 1935.

56. HHStA, Abt. 485, 248, Reichsautobahnen Direktion to all OBK, Dec. 6, 1934.

57. *Akten der Reichskanzlei,* pt. 1, vol. 1, pp. 676–678; HHStA, Abt. 485, 246, Deutsche Reichsbahn-Gesellschaft, Reichsbahndirektion Frankfurt/M, to die Ämter und Direktionsbüro, Aug. 1, 1933, with enclosures: Reich cabinet guidelines of July 14, 1933, and RWM [Schmitt], Runderlaß of July 19, 1933, explanation of guidelines. Schmitt pointed out that about RM 20 billion in foreign capital still helped keep the German economy afloat. Furthermore, because a "not insubstantial amount" of German capital was invested abroad, Schmitt wished to avoid retaliatory measures.

58. HHStA, Abt. 485, 246, Reich interior minister (signed Frick) to Obersten Reichsbehörden, etc., Jan. 17, 1934.

59. HHStA, 246, NSDAP, Gauleitung Hessen-Nassau-Süd, Der Gaufachbearbeiter f. Wirtschaftstechnik u. Arbeitsbeschaffung, to Oberste Bauleitung der Kraftfahrbahn (FfM-Heidelberg), Reichsbahndirektion Frankfurt/M, March 6, 1934.

60. StAD 500/209, Duisburg, Wohlfahrtsamt, "Die öffentliche Wohlfahrtspflege der Stadt Duisburg seit 1933," in Bericht über die öffentliche Wohlfahrtspflege der Stadt Duisburg, June 8, 1935. Comparable rates for other industrial centers in the region were Dortmund, 131.1; Essen, 115.8; Düsseldorf, 113.2; Frankfurt/M, 104.1; Cologne, 103.7.

61. StAD, 609/48, numerous documents, including Reichsautobahnen Oberste

Bauleitung Essen to Oberbürgermeister Duisburg-Hamborn, June 28, 1934, and Aug. 2, 1934, and an undated memorandum describing the July 4, 1934, meeting, signed by Duisburg Stadtrat Holke.

62. BAP 39.03, 131, president LAA Hessen to president RfAA, Nov. 28, 1933, and April 3, 1934. The employment of these nonsupported persons violated regulations on work creation projects, which required that 80 percent of those employed on projects subsidized by RfAA funds had to be supported unemployed. By the end of Feb. 1934, according to the Hessen LAA president, all of the nonsupported *Autobahnen* laborers on this particular stretch had been placed in regular jobs and replaced by supported unemployed.

63. HHStA, Abt. 485, 246, Oberbürgermeister Heidelberg to Direktion der Reichsautobahn, Frankfurt/M, Sept. 12, 1934; Abt. 485, 259, Oberbürgermeister Heidelberg to Generalinspektor Todt and Gesellschaft "Reichsautobahnen," Oct. 29, 1934; OBK internal memorandum of Nov. 3, 1934, directed to "Herrn Dezernent K 11 ergebenst." The mayor pointed out that he was under pressure from the NSDAP Kreisleitung and the DAF to place Heidelberg unemployed on *Autobahnen* construction sites.

64. BAP, 39.03, 131, and HHStA, Abt. 485, 824, RAM to Generalinspektor, Jan. 24, 1934; BAP 39.03, 131, Generalinspektor to RAM, April 9, 1934, in reference to Seldte's Jan. 24 letter; HHStA, Abt. 485, 824, Generalinspektor to Gesellschaft "Reichsautobahnen" Direktion, Jan. 30, 1934; Reichsautobahn Direktion, Berlin, to Oberste Bauleitungen für den Bau der Kraftfahrbahnen in Altona, etc., Feb. 5, 1934.

65. In 1935, for example, the *Autobahnen* district construction office (OBK) at Frankfurt/M was drawing workers supplied by five different AA, in Frankfurt, Mannheim, Karlsruhe, Heidelberg, and Kaiserslautern.

66. BAP 39.03, 132, Generalinspektor to president RfAA, July 14, 1934; Generalinspektor to Oberregierungsrat Dr. Bardow, RfAA, July 23, 1934, enclosing Todt's compromise version of the "Sozialpolitische Bedingungen für die Vergebung und Leistungen bei der Reichsautobahnen."

67. HHStA, Abt. 485, 259, Reichsautobahnen, Oberste Bauleitung Nürnberg, to Direktion der Reichsautobahnen, Berlin, July 10, 1935.

68. HHStA, Abt. 485, 262, Generalinspektor to Gesellschaft "Reichsautobahnen" Direktion, March 2, 1936, citing directive issued by president of RfAA, Nov. 26, 1935. An exception to the rule was the agreement to employ one hundred Saarlanders on *Autobahnen* construction in Nov. 1934, a patent attempt to influence the outcome of the Saar plebiscite scheduled for Jan. 1935. Although they were given exceptionally favorable terms of employment, most of them quit their jobs on the second day of work. They had been misled into thinking they would be placed in high-paying, relatively comfortable factory work rather than in low-paid, strenuous outdoor labor in inclement weather. See HHStA, Abt. 485, 259, Reichsauto-

bahnen Direktion Berlin to OBK Frankfurt/M, Nov. 10, 1934; Treuhänder der Arbeit für das Wirtschaftsgebiete Bayern, Der Beauftragte für die Rheinpfalz, Neustadt a.d. Haardt, to Reichsautobahn, OBK Frankfurt/M, Nov. 15, 1934; Reichsautobahnen, Kraftfahrbahn-Bauabteilung beim Straßen- und Flußbauamt Kaiserslautern, to OBK, Frankfurt/M, Jan. 5, 1935.

69. StAS, HA-09, Nr. 8, Beilage zur Niederschrift des Gemeinderates vom 11. Januar 1935, mayor Strölin informs municipal council of subsidization of Stuttgart-Ulm and Stuttgart-Heilbronn Reichsautobahnen stretches, Nov. 21, 1933–Aug. 10, 1934; Stuttgart. Niederschrift des Gemeinderates vom 11. Januar 1935. Nichtöffentlich., Nr. 34, Stuttgart's contribution to Reichsautobahnen stretches Stuttgart-Ulm and Stuttgart-Heilbronn; HA-09, Nr. 10, Stuttgart. Niederschrift der Hauptabteilung des Gemeinderates vom 10. April 1934, Nr. 218, Reichsautobahn Stuttgart-Heilbronn; Niederschrift . . . 4. Sept. 1934, Nr. 377; Niederschrift . . . 16. Oct. 1934, Nr. 421; Bü Amt, 119, *Verwaltungsbericht der Stadt Stuttgart für 1934*, p. 42; Bürgermeisteramt Stuttgart, Arbeitsbeschaffungsamt, Tätigkeitsbericht auf 31. Dezember 1934 (dated Dec. 1, 1935). It is not clear that Stuttgart received all of the workplaces that the city paid for. On the Stuttgart-Ulm stretch, where the 30 percent quota should have guaranteed 626 jobs, only about 220 Stuttgarters were employed.

70. StadtAN, C25/I, F Reg., 686, Stadtrat Nürnberg to president LAA Bayern, Sept. 13, 1934; president LAA Bayern to Oberste Bauleitung Nürnberg der Reichsautobahnen and AA Nürnberg, Oct. 3, 1934.

71. StadtAN, C25/I, F Reg., 686, Städt. Wohlfahrtsamt Nürnberg, Vormerkung für das Reichsautobahnen, 2. Bericht, Oct. 4, 1934.

72. StAD, 500/432, Duisburg, Oct. 31, 1936, memorandum prepared by Stadtrat Birkenbuel, "Ergebnis der Besprechung am 30. October beim Landesarbeitsamt in Köln." Birkenholz ultimately agreed with the director of the Duisburg AA that it was "totally out of the question" that 2,300 *Autobahnen* workers would be dismissed on Nov. 15, 1936. Layoffs would have to be spread out, a hundred or so at a time. When told of prevailing wage rates in regions where Duisburg workers might be reassigned, Duisburg city councillor Birkenbuel told Birkenholz that "we could not expect our Duisburg workers to work in other areas for such a low hourly wage."

73. Lärmer, *Autobahnbau*, pp. 58–59, 86–87.

74. HHStA, Abt. 485, 246, Reichsautobahnen Direktion, Berlin, to OBK Altona, Essen, Frankfurt/M, Köln, Königsberg (Pr), München, und Stettin, Nov. 29, 1933. On the reverse of this document, a notation by the OBK Frankfurt-Heidelberg-Mannheim, dated Dec. 6, 1933, indicates that excavation work in that district was being done "only by manual labor."

75. HHStA, Abt. 485, 250, Generalinspektor to Gesellschaft "Reichsautobahnen" Direktion, Berlin, July 6, 1936; BHStA, MWi 8682, *Geschäftsbericht des Unter-*

nehmens "Reichsautobahnen" über das 5. Geschäftsjahr 1937 (Berlin, 1938), pp. 3, 34, 42.

76. HHStA, Abt. 485, 259, Generalinspektor to das Zentralamt der Deutschen Arbeitsfront, Aug. 2, 1934.

77. Tilla Siegel, *Leistung und Lohn in der nationalsozialistischen "Ordnung der Arbeit"* Schriften des Zentralinstituts für Sozialwissenschaftliche Forschung der Freien Universität Berlin, vol. 57 (Opladen: Westdeutscher Verlag, 1989), pp. 39–40, 55, 57.

78. Lärmer, *Autobahnbau*, p. 60.

79. Rüdiger Hachtmann, "Lebenshaltungskosten und Reallöhne während des 'Dritten Reiches,' " *Vierteljahrschrift für Sozial- und Wirtschaftsgeschichte* 75 (1988), p. 46.

80. BHStA, MA106949, [Bavarian] Ministerialrat Sommer to [Bavarian] minister-president, June 7, 1934. The "free market" wage paid to Munich laborers on Bavarian *Autobahnen* construction sites was 45–50 Pf. per hour, or RM 3.60 to 4.00 per eight-hour day. One AA reported road-construction workers shouting, "Hitler should work for 50 Pf. an hour!" See BHStA, MA 106765, AA Rosenheim, Situationsbericht July 31, 1934.

81. HHStA, Abt. 485, 262, Reichsautobahnen Direktion Berlin to all OBK, Aug. 9, 1934, asking for reports showing the impact of "special regulations" of wages made by TdA up to that date; OBK Frankfurt/M, report compiled Aug. 13, 1934, "Nachweisung über Tarif- und Streckenlöhne der Unternehmerarbeiter bei der OBK Frankfurt (M)." Individual firms paid different wage rates, apparently reflecting their varying cost structures and/or the amount bid for the contract.

82. HHStA, Abt. 485, 265, Frankfurt/M, Der Stellvertreter des Treuhänders der Arbeit, "Aktennotiz!" dated Aug. 5, 1936, concerning Tarifordnung für den Bau der Reichsautobahnen, Strecke Frankfurt/Main-Limburg-Köln; Hachtmann, "Lebenshaltungskosten und Reallöhne," p. 46.

83. HHStA, Abt. 485, 246, RAM [signed by Dr. Mansfeld] to all TdA, and to Reich ministers for finance, economics, and transportation, March 16, 1934.

84. HHStA, Abt. 485, 246, RAM to all TdA, Nov. 5, 1934.

85. HHStA, Abt. 485, 246, Grün u. Billfinger A.G., Bauunternehmung, Mannheim, to OBK, Reichsbahndirektion Frankfurt/M, Nov. 14, 1933, enclosing copy of report sent directly to Todt concerning the labor force at Frankfurt-Niederrad work site. One of the officials who examined this report underlined the "Tiefbauarbeiter" entry.

86. Lärmer, *Autobahnbau*, pp. 60, 69. See pp. 60–70 for working and living conditions. Despite Lärmer's annoying references to the evils of "fascist monopoly capital," his assessment of social conditions for the *Autobahnen* workers is fundamentally accurate.

87. BAP 39.03, 132, president LAA Hessen to president RfAA, May 24, 1934.

88. BHStA, MA106765, AA Traunstein, Situationsbericht, July 11, 1934.

89. HHStA, Abt. 485, 259, Generalinspektor to das Zentralamt der Deutschen Arbeitsfront, Aug. 2, 1934.

90. HHStA, Abt. 485, 259, Generalinspektor to president LAA Berlin, Aug. 29, 1935, based on report from RAB headquarters. It is not clear whether the workers themselves set the fire.

91. BHStA, Reichsstatthalter 553.

92. Calculated from monthly statistics from annual *Geschäftsberichte* of Gesellschaft "Reichsautobahnen," covering the period Dec. 1933 through Dec. 1938.

8. The "Voluntary" Labor Service under National Socialism

1. Hitler speeches of Feb. 1 and May 1, 1933, in Max Domarus, ed., *Hitler: Reden und Proklamationen 1932–1945*, vol. 1, *Triumph, 1932–1938* (Neustadt a.d. Aisch: Verlagsdruckerei Schmidt, 1962), p. 193, 262.

2. RGBl, 1935, vol. 1, p. 769, RAD-Gesetz of June 26, 1935.

3. For earlier works on the German labor service, see Henning Köhler, *Arbeitsdienst in Deutschland: Pläne und Verwirklichungs-formen bis zur Einführung der Arbeitsdienstpflicht im Jahre 1935* (Berlin: Duncker & Humblot, 1967); Wolfgang Benz, "Vom freiwilligen Arbeitsdienst zur Arbeitsdienstpflicht," *Vierteljahreshefte für Zeitgeschichte* 16 (1968), pp. 317–346.

4. Whether Roosevelt modeled his CCC plan after the German system remains unclear. Garraty recently emphasized the similarities between the CCC and the German FAD, without arguing for any direct influence of the German program on New Deal policies. See John A. Garraty, *The Great Depression* (Garden City, N. Y.: Doubleday Anchor Books, 1987), pp. 189–190. Despite similarities with the German Labor Service, "Roosevelt always warmly denied that it [the FAD] had ever influenced his thinking on the CCC." See John A. Salmond, *The Civilian Conservation Corps, 1933–1942: A New Deal Case Study* (Durham: Duke University Press, 1967), p. 5. Roosevelt had good reason to deny any connection between the German FAD and his own CCC. William Green, president of the American Federation of Labor, complained that the CCC bill originally presented to Congress "smacks, as I see it, of fascism, of Hitlerism, of a form of sovietism." For the text of the original bill and hearing testimony, see *Unemployment Relief: Joint Hearings Before the Committee on Education and Labor, United States Senate, and the Committee on Labor, House of Representatives, 73rd Congress, First Session, on S. 598, March 23 and 24* (Washington: Government Printing Office, 1933).

5. For the administrative history of the FAD, see BHStA, MA106753, Staatsministerium f. Wirtschaft, Abt. f. Arbeit u. Fürsorge, to [Bavarian] minister-president, Feb. 14, 1934, with memorandum, "Denkschrift über die Verhältnisse im

Arbeitsdienst," prepared at the request of minister-president Ludwig Siebert; Köhler, *Arbeitsdienst,* pp. 90–91, 94.

6. Benz, "Vom freiwilligen Arbeitsdienst zur Arbeitsdienstpflicht," pp. 330–331. Sponsorship of FAD organizations varied regionally within Germany. Statistics for Dec. 1932 indicate the following distribution of FAD projects and enlistees in the Rhineland: public corporations (including municipal and district governments) 60 percent of projects, 45 percent of enlistees; church and welfare organizations, 18 percent and 25 percent respectively; youth and sports organizations, 10 percent and 13 percent; land settlement and allotment societies, 3 percent and 2 percent; military associations such as the Stahlhelm, 1 percent and 5 percent; various other associations, 8 percent and 10 percent. In Bavaria (including the Palatinate), the percentage of recruits provided by various types of sponsors for 816 FAD projects in Dec. 1932 was as follows: municipal and district governments, 38 percent; sports organizations, 24 percent; Catholic organizations (including the Deutsche Jugendkraft), 14 percent; the Volksbund, 6 percent; evangelical organizations, 3 percent; the Stahlhelm, 2 percent; various other providers of enlistees, 14 percent. See N-WHStA, Kalkum branch, AA Erkelenz, 3, Pressedienst des LAA Rheinland, Feb. 7, 1933, "Der rheinische Arbeitsdienst im Monat Januar 1933"; press clipping from *Kölnischer Volkszeitung,* Dec. 13, 1932, "Der freiwillige Arbeitsdienst in Bayern."

7. Hierl complained about the popular perception that only laggards and "workshy" elements served (involuntarily) in the FAD. The FAD, he argued, was an honorable service *(Ehrendienst).* See StAN, LRA Hilpolstein, 1971, 46[I]; Regierung Oberfranken/Mittelfranken, 3440, Reichsleitung des Arbeitsdienstes (signed Hierl) to interior ministries of Länder, Oct. 23, 1933.

8. For an analysis of the nazification of the RfAA, see Silverman, "Nazification of the German Bureaucracy Reconsidered: A Case Study," *Journal of Modern History* 60 (1988), pp. 496–539.

9. Benz, "Vom freiwilligen Arbeitsdienst zur Arbeitsdienstpflicht," pp. 332–333; BAK, R43I/1459, and *Akten der Reichskanzlei,* pt. 1, vol. 1, p. 32, Ministerbesprechung vom 2. Februar 1933; HStAS, E130b, Bü 3243, RAM to Reichsrat, Feb. 4, 1933; Württ. economics ministry to Staatsministerium, Feb. 7, 1933; Staatsministerium to Staatspräsident, Feb. 8, 1933; Württ. Gesandschaft to Württ. Staatsministerium, Feb. 16, 1933.

10. Köhler, *Arbeitsdienst,* pp. 88, 123; N-WStAM, clipping from *Vossische Zeitung,* Jan. 10, 1933, "Der Sinn der Arbeitsdienstes," account of Reich labor minister Syrup's speech before the Westfälisch-Lippischen Wirtschaftsbund, Bielefeld, Jan. 9, 1933; N-WHStA, Kalkum branch, AA Erkelenz, 3, clipping from *Kölnische Zeitung,* Jan. 17, 1933, "Syrup zum Arbeitsdienst."

11. Köhler, *Arbeitsdienst,* p. 252, noted that, given its earlier significant activity in the FAD, the Stahlhelm had a far stronger claim to FAD leadership than did Hierl.

12. *Akten der Reichskanzlei*, pt. 1, vol.1, p. 140; R2/4538, "Diktat von Oberst a.D. Hierl über Einführung und Organization des staatlichen Arbeitsdienstes," March 1, 1933; Köhler, *Arbeitsdienst*, p. 253.

13. HStAS, E130b, Bü3248, Reichsleitung des Arbeitsdienstes (signed Hierl) to Reich minister for food and agriculture, May 30, 1933.

14. N-WStAM, Oberpräsidium 6710, Reichskommissar d. Arbeitsdienst to Oberpräsident Provinz Westfalen, April 11, 1933, invitation to conference on FAD; D.k.O.P [Der kommissarische Oberpräsident], April 18, 1933, Niederschrift über die Besprechung am Samstag, den 15. 4. 1933 über Freiwilligen Arbeitsdienst; N-WStAD, L80 ID, XIX, 1, Nr. 1, Bd. II, Memorandum to Dr. jur. Spelge, 1. Oberregierungsrat, April 19, 1933, describing the April 15 discussion with Mahnken; BHStA, MA106753, Der Gesandte [to Ausgleichstelle der Länder, Berlin] to [Bavarian] Staatsministerium f. Wirtschaft, Abt. f. Handel, Industrie und Gewerbe, June 23, 1933.

15. RGBl, 1932, vol. 1, p. 352, Verordnung über den freiwilligen Arbeitsdienst, July 16, 1932; Köhler, *Arbeitsdienst*, pp. 115, 121; Willi Hemmer, *Die "unsichtbaren" Arbeitslosen: Statistische Methoden—Soziale Tatsachen* (Zeulenroda: Bernhard Sporn, 1935), p. 189; HstAS, E130b, Bü3248, Reichsrat, Jan. 21, 1933, Antrag Anhalts betreffend Bereitstellung von Mitteln für den freiwilligen Arbeitsdienst und dessen weiteren Ausbau; BHStA, MWi 3135, Bayer. Staatsmin. f. Wirtschaft, Abt. II to Abt. I, March 2, 1933.

16. BAP 39.03, 224, AD Reichsleitung (signed by Hierl) to Reich minister for food and agriculture, May 30, 1933, and undated document, "Forderung der Reichsleitung des Arbeitsdienstes an einem Vierjahresplan für Landeskulturarbeiten"; *Akten der Reichskanzlei*, pt. 1, vol. 1, p. 288, Chefsbesprechung vom 4. April 1933; BAK, R2/4538, RFM to RAM, June 26, 1933 (draft), describing Hitler's position during a June 16 meeting of high government officials; R2/4539, state secretary for labor service (Hierl) to RAM Seldte, Feb. 16, 1934, budget request for 1934; *Akten der Reichskanzlei*, pt. 1, vol. 1, p. 559n7; R2/4539, RFM, Vermerk (signed Poerschke), May 12, 1934, describing May 8 meeting with Hierl in RFM. Benz, "Vom freiwilligen Arbeitsdienst zur Arbeitsdienstpflicht," pp. 336–337, blames Seldte's behind-the-scene intervention for much of the delay in the preparation of an FAD budget.

17. BAK, R2/4538, RFM, Vermerk of Aug. 28 and 31, and Sept. 18, 1933, describing meetings of Aug. 28 and Sept. 15 and 16; RAM (signed Seldte) to State secretary in the Reich chancellery (Lammers) and concerned ministers, Nov. 17, 1933; *Akten der Reichskanzlei*, pt. 1, vol. 2, p. 933n5 for Seldte to Reich Chancellery, Oct. 19, 1933.

18. BAK, R2/4538, Reich defense minister (signed Blomberg) to RFM, Sept. 20, 1933; Reich interior minister to RAM, Nov. 27, 1933, in response to Seldte's Nov. 17 letter to the Reich chancellery raising the possibility of creating a special

Reich commissioner for the FAD; Benz, "Vom freiwilligen Arbeitsdienst zur Arbeitsdienstpflicht," pp. 338–339. Any decision concerning the FAD, particularly the introduction of compulsory labor service, potentially affected the recruiting base of the armed forces. According to Köhler, *Arbeitsdienst*, p. 251, the SA, functioning as "auxiliary police" to secure the Nazi revolution, had little interest in the FAD after Hitler's appointment to the chancellorship.

19. BHStA, MA106753, Reich interior minister (signed Frick) to highest Reich authorities, etc., July 26, 1934.

20. BAK, R2/4539, State secretary for labor service [Hierl-RAM] to Reich minister Seldte, Feb. 16, 1934, concerning 1934 budget; RFM to state secretary for labor service, Feb. 24, 1934 (draft); RFM, Vermerk (signed Poerschke), May 12, 1934, describing meeting between Hierl and two other FAD officials with Krosigk, state secretary Fritz Reinhardt (RFM), and Ministerialrat Stephan Poerschke (RFM).

21. BAP 39.03, 220, president LAA Rhineland to president RfAA, Jan. 17 and April 26, 1934; AA Essen to LAA Rhineland, Jan. 4, 1934; chairman of Kreisausschuß of Landkreis Düsseldorf-Mettmann to mayors of Kreis (signed Tapolski, Landrat), April 10, 1934; BAK, R2/4539, state secretary for FAD, RAM [Hierl] to Mein Führer!, May 2, 1934; State secretary in Reich chancellery [Lammers] to RFM, May 28, 1934; RFM to RAM, June 6, 1934 (draft); state secretary for FAD, RAM, to RFM, June 7, 1934; RFM to state secretary for FAD, July 7, 1934 (draft); RFM to state secretary in Reich chancellery, July 9, 1934 (draft); RFM to Rechnungshof des Deutschen Reiches, July 2, 1935, indicating that the 1934 FAD budget had been set at RM 195 million in Dec. 1934.

22. Köhler, *Arbeitsdienst*, pp. 261–262.

23. Benz, "Vom freiwilligen Arbeitsdienst zur Arbeitsdienstpflicht," pp. 333–334; GStAPK, 84a/354, Die Reichsleitung des Arbeitsdienstes (signed Hierl) to Reichskanzlei, etc., Nov. 25, 1933.

24. BHStA, MA106753, [Bavarian] Staatsministerium f. Wirtschaft, Abt. f. Arbeit u. Fürsorge, to minister-president, Feb. 14, 1934, with copy of "Denkschrift über die Verhältnisse im Arbeitsdienst"; Reichskommissar f. den Arbeitsdienst (signed Hierl) to Bezirksführer and Bezirkskommissäre f. den Arbeitsdienst, April 8, 1933; N-WHStA, Kalkum branch, AA Erkelenz 1, II, Der Bezirkskommissar f. den Arbeitsdienst im Bezirk des LAA Rheinland to Vorsitzenden der AA im Bereich LAA Rheinland, April 12, 1933; Konstantin Hierl, *Ausgewählte Schriften und Reden* (Munich: F. Eher, 1941), vol. 2, p. 109, Aug. 1, 1933, interview with the *Hamburger Fremdenblatt*, response to a June 13 committee report of the Geneva disarmament conference. The German foreign office expressed concern about "the foreign policy perspective on the buildup of the German labor service." See *Akten der Reichskanzlei*, pt. 1, vol. 1, pp. 554–559, Auswärtige Amt to RAM, June 10, 1933.

25. Köhler, *Arbeitsdienst*, p. 253. In the "open" camp system, FAD enlistees lived

at home with their families and commuted each day to a nearby work site. In the "closed" camp system, labor service volunteers were billeted in barracks near a work site. In Dec. 1932, the Rheinland LAA president had already decided to fund only "closed" camps, and the LAA in Westphalia had begun to close down projects being carried out under the "open" system. See N-WHStA, Kalkum branch, AA Erkelenz, 1, I, Der Bezirkskommissar f. den FAD im Bezirk des LAA Rheinland to Vorsitzenden der AA im Bereich des LAA Rheinland, Dec. 3, 1932; N-WStAD, L80Id, XIX 1, Nr. 1, Bd. II, Der Stadtrat Lage, Abt. V, to Lippische Landesregierung, Abt. II, Jan. 4, 1933; StAN, LRA Eichstätt 1981, 3163, Bezirksleitung des Arbeitsdienstes f. den Bezirk Bayern West, Anlage to letter of June 6, 1933.

26. N-WHStA, Kalkum branch, AA Erkelenz 1, II, Bezirksleitung f. den Arbeitsdienstbezirk Rheinland, "Verfugung: Weiterer Aufbau des Arbeitsdienstes," July 25, 1933, summarizing July 21, 1933, Erlaß no. D394/33 of Reichskommissar f. den FAD (Hierl); BHStA, Statthalter 496, Reichsarbeitsdienst, Bezirksleitung Bayern-Ost, Der Bezirksführer, July 28, 1933, "Auszug aus dem Erlaß des Reichskommissars f. den FAD, Nr. D394/33 von 21. 7. 33;" MA106753, [Bavarian] Staatsministerium f. Wirtschaft, Abt. f. Arbeit u. Fürsorge to minister-president, Feb. 14, 1934, with Beilage: "Denkschrift über die Verhältnisse im Arbeitsdienst," which contains a section on the administrative history of the AD; StAN, LRA Hilpoltstein, 1971, 46^I, Bezirksleitung des Arbeitsdienstes f. den Bezirk Bayern-West, Betreff: Amtsbereich (apparently circular letter), July 20 and 29, 1933.

27. Der Beauftragte f. den Arbeitsdienst der NSDAP (signed Hierl) to the Führer, Sept. 12, 1933, copies of which are found in BHStA, MA106753, Hierl to [Bavarian] state minister without portfolio and head of the state chancellery Hermann Esser, and HStAS, E130b, Bü32348, Hierl to Württemberg minister-president Mergenthaler, both dated Sept. 12, 1933.

28. Hierl ordered district leaders to limit barracks cost to RM 35,000 because "the AD already suffers from rumors spread by its opponents that it presses for such a great expenditure on lodging, that it is much more practical for sponsors to have projects carried out as emergency relief works." See BAP 39.03, 228, AD Reichsleitung (signed by Hierl) to AD Bezirksleitungen, Aug. 11, 1933. In Lippe, new FAD barracks generally cost RM 80,000, far more than the amount allowed by financing institutions. The FAD Reichsleitung eventually made available plans for less expensive portable barracks. See N-WStAD, L80ID, Gr. XVII, 2, Nr. 11, Anl. 22, Landrat Kreis Lemgo to Lippische Landesregierung, Abt. I, June 15, 1934. At the end of Oct. 1933, increasing costs of labor and material forced financing institutions to raise the spending limit on FAD barracks construction to RM 50,000. See BAP 39.03, 226, Deutsche Rentenbank-Kreditanstalt to Dr. Zschucke, RfAA, Oct. 30, 1933, with enclosure, "Richtlinien für die Gewährung von Darlehen für Meliorationen—bei denen einen völlig oder teilweise Mitfinanzierung der Kosten für die Unterkünfte des Arbeitsdienstes kommt in Frage."

29. Bavarian Regierungsbaurat Salisko charged the FAD leadership with being

more interested in constructing barracks than in finding work for the men to be housed in them. See BHStA, MA106753, [Bavarian] Staatsmin. f. Wirtschaft, Abt. f. Arbeit u. Fürsorge, to Ministerpräsident, Feb. 14, 1934, with enclosure, "Denkschrift über die Verhältnisse im Arbeitsdienst," which reproduces report, Regierungsbaurat Salisko im Staatsmin. d. Innern to Ministerialrat Ziegler, Staatsmin. f. Wirtschaft, Abt. f. Arbeit u. Fürsorge, Jan. 9, 1934, the "Salisko Report." For Hierl's offer to pay rent on barracks not yet completed, see StAN, LRA Scheinfeld, 271, Bayerischer Gemeindetag im Deutschen Gemeindetag to all member communities with population over 2,000, Jan. 5, 1934, enclosing copy of Dec. 15 AD Reichsleitung order [signed Hierl].

30. BHStA, MA106753, Lagebericht (Halbmonatsbericht) des Regierungs-Präsident von Schwaben und Neuburg, Augsburg, Nov. 21, 1933, report of Stadtrat Lindau, indicating that an FAD barracks, "constructed at great cost," may have to be torn down owing to insufficient work to occupy a standard FAD unit of 216 men; BHStA, MA106753 and StAN, LRA Scheinfeld/271 Deutscher Arbeitsdienst, Arbeitsgau 28-Franken (signed Arbeitsgauführer Fritz Schinnerer) to [Bavarian] minister-president, June 18, 1934, enclosing June 14 Standortsrundschreiben no. 27, which reproduces May 24 Rundschreiben of Deutsche Gemeindetag, Landesdienststellen Bayern. Schinnerer claimed that the Deutsche Gemeindetag's information was incorrect.

31. Hierl to Führer, Sept. 12, 1933, cited n27.

32. N-WHStA, Reg. Aachen 16858, president LAA Rheinland to AA presidents, May 17, 1933; president LAA Rheinland to Oberpräsident Rheinland, etc., May 23, 1933, urging greater usage of emergency relief projects; Reg. Aachen 16848, Oberpräsident Rheinprovinz to Reg. Präsident in Aachen, Oct. 9, 1933; StAN, LRA Scheinfeld 271, Bayerischer Gemeindetag im Deutschen Gemeindetag to all Mitgliedsgemeinden over 2,000 population, etc., Jan. 5, 1934; HHStA, Abt. 485/824, Arbeitsgau 22 Hessen-Nord, Kassel, to Oberpräsident der Provinz Hessen-Nassau, etc., Jan. 22, 1934. Vigorous complaints from community administrators forced Hierl to modify this demand.

33. BAK, R2/4522, AD Reichsleitung to RAM (copy to State secretary Fritz Reinhardt, RFM, Dec. 18, 1933).

34. BAP 33.09, 221, president RfAA to RAM and RFM, Nov. 20, 1934; RfAA Vermerk, Nov. 29, 1934, concerning "Lagerverlegung des AD zwecks Freimachung der Umgegend von Städten für Notstandsarbeiten (verheiratete Erwerbslose)"; [RfAA] president Dr. Syrup to state secretary Hierl, Jan. 8, 1935; RfAA Vermerk, Jan. 15, 1935, signed Bardow; RfAA, continuation of Vermerk of Jan. 15, 1935; Reich and Prussian ministry for food and agriculture, "Niederschrift über die Besprechung . . . vom 14. 1. 1935 über den Einsatz des Reichsarbeitsdienstes und von Notstandsarbeiten bei Wasserwirtshafts- und Landeskultur- Maßnahmen," Jan. 19, 1935.

35. BAP, 31.05, 41, AD Reichsleitung (signed by Tholens) to RFM, with copy

to Reich Commissioner for Work Creation, asking for his support, June 10, 1933; BHStA, Statthalter 496, "Regelung des Arbeitseinsatzes des Arbeitsdienst" [signed Hierl], June 27, 1934, distributed as Anlage to *Verordnungsblatt* 64, no. 469, July 4, 1934. Other copies of this regulation are found in BAP 39.03, 220, and HHStA, Abt. 485, Nr.247, Arbeitsgauleitung 25, Hessen-Süd, Wiesbaden, to Oberste Bauleitung der Reichsautobahnen, Frankfurt/Main, Dec. 3, 1934, enclosing a copy of Hierl's regulation at the request of the OBK. It is not clear that top Reich officials accepted Hierl's definition of the FAD's sphere of activity, and he apparently issued the regulations without consulting some of them, including the Reich finance minister. See BAP 39.03, 221, RfAA Vermerk, July 16, 1934.

36. HHStA, Abt. 485/824, Generalinspektor f. das deutsche Straßenwesen to Reichsleitung d. Arbeitsdienstes, Jan. 24, 1934; Todt to Gesellschaft Reichsautobahnen, Berlin, Jan. 24, 1934.

37. See, for example, HHStA, Abt. 485/824, for the response of Neubauamt Darmstadt, which rejected the employment of FAD units on five possible projects in Jan. and Feb. 1934.

38. HHStA, Abt. 485/824, Reichsautobahnen Direktion, Berlin, to Reichskommissar f. den FAD, Reichsleitung, Sept. 10, 1934; HHStA, Abt. 485/824, Reichsautobahnen Direktion, Berlin, to all OBK, Dec. 22, 1934, enclosing copy of agreement concluded with Hierl, "Grundsätze f. den Einsatz des Arbeitsdienstes bei der Reichsautobahnen," Dec. 22, 1934. It had to be demonstrated that the cost of using FAD units would be 50 percent below the cost of employing private contractors. Work requiring the use of heavy equipment was to be performed only by expert private contractors, and any exemption from this regulation required Todt's approval. See HHStA, Abt. 485/824 and 825.

39. HHStA, Abt. 485/246, Reichsautobahnen, Vorstand des Kraftfahrbahn-Neubauamtes Frankfurt/Main, to OBK Frankfurt/Main, Nov. 4, 1933, enclosing a copy of "Sondervorschrift über den Bedarf an Arbeitskräften f. die Autobahn," undated, apparently issued by Reich authorities during the autumn of 1933.

40. HHStA, Abt. 485/248, Der Generalinspektor f. das deutsche Straßenwesen to Gesellschaft "Reichsautobahnen" Direktion, Sept. 27, 1934, enclosing copy of "Sozialpolitische Bedingungen f. die Leistungen bei der Reichsautobahnen"; president RfAA to LAA presidents, Nov. 1, 1934, enclosing copy of "final version" of Generalinspektor's "Sozialpolitische Bedingungen."

41. Hemmer, *Die "unsichtbaren" Arbeitslosen*, pp. 43, 55–56; Dan P. Silverman, "National Socialist Economics: The *Wirtschaftswunder* Reconsidered," in Barry Eichengreen and T. J. Hatton, eds., *Interwar Unemployment in International Perspective* (Dordrecht: Kluwer Academic Publishers, 1988), p. 208 ff. Beginning Sept. 30, 1934, *Autobahnen* and canal construction workers were no longer counted either as emergency relief workers or as "looking for work." They were considered as having a "normal" contract relationship between private employers and their employees, and were no longer counted as "substitute" *(zusätzliche)* employed. See

Karl Lärmer, *Autobahnbau in Deutschland 1933 bis 1945—Zu den Hintergründen* (Berlin: Akademie-Verlag, 1975), p. 54.

42. For examples of labor problems on *Autobahnen* construction sites, see GStAPK, 90/1718, Deutsche Arbeitsfront, Reichsbetriebsgemeinschaft Bau, to Prussian minister-president Hermann Göring, Oct. 19, 1934, with enclosure, "Bericht über Vorkommnisse beim Bau der Reichsautobahnstraße Bremen-Hamburg"; HHStA, Abt. 485/259, General inspector for German roads [Fritz Todt] to president RfAA, Oct. 24, 1934 (copy). For the Dec. 1934 arrangement between Todt and Syrup, see HHStA, Abt. 485/247, 248, president RfAA to LAA presidents, Dec. 3, 1934 and April 17, 1935.

43. Köhler, *Arbeitsdienst*, pp. 261–262.

44. BHStA, MA106753, [Bavarian] Staatsmin. f. Wirtschaft, Abt. f. Arbeit u. Fürsorge, to minister-president, Feb. 14, 1934, with Nov. 25, 1933, memorandum prepared at minister-president's request, "Denkschrift über die Verhältnisse im Arbeitsdienst." On one Bavarian drainage project that was begun as an FAD project and completed as an emergency relief project using emergency relief workers, the cost per hectare drained by the FAD was 130 percent higher than for those drained by emergency relief workers. See StAN, LRA Rothenburg 1975, Fach 645, Nr. 9^{I}, Bericht über die Prüfung der Verwendung von Darlehen zu Arbeitsbeschaffungsmaßnahmen . . . im Bereich der Bezirksämter Weissenburg, Rothenburg, u. Ansbach (copy, excerpt), undated, probably Sept. or Oct. 1935.

45. BHStA, MA106753, Reichsleitung des Arbeitsdienstes to all Land governments, Oct. 10, 1933; HStAS, E130b, Bü 3248, Badischer Finanz- u. Wirtschaftsminister to Reichsleitung des Arbeitsdienstes (and copy to Württembergische Staatsministerium), Nov. 16, 1933; Württ. economics ministry to interior ministry, Dec. 30, 1933.

46. Benz, "Vom freiwilligen Arbeitsdienst zur Arbeitsdienstpflicht," p. 339.

47. BHStA, MA106753, Staatsmin. f. Wirtschaft, Abt. f. Arbeit u. Fürsorge, to minister-president, Feb. 14, 1934, with two enclosures: "Denkschrift über die Verhältnisse im Arbeitsdienst," and Regierungsbaurat Salisko im Staatsministerium des Innern to Ministerialrat Ziegler, Staatsministerium f. Wirtschaft, Abt. f. Arbeit u. Fürsorge, Jan. 9, 1934 ("Salisko report"). Among those lodging complaints about the FAD with minister-president Siebert was Siebert's son, the mayor of Lindau. For a damaging report on the FAD from Saxony's labor and welfare ministry, supported by several Nazi Gauleiters and Prussian Oberpräsidenten, see Benz, "Vom freiwilligen Arbeitsdienst zur Arbeitsdienstpflicht," p. 339.

48. HHStA, Abt. 483/2713, Reichsleitung des Arbeitsdienstes [signed Hierl] to Bezirksleitungen des Arbeitsdienstes, May 13, 1933; Reichsleitung des Arbeitsdienstes [signed Hierl] to Prussian minister for agriculture, May 31, 1933, in which Hierl asked the Prussian agriculture ministry for the loan of ten Regierungsbauräte for one year.

49. Zahnow became active in the FAD during the autumn of 1931, and joined

the NSDAP in July 1932. After the Nazi takeover, he was furloughed from state service, became a full-time FAD official, and by Oct. 1935 held the position of Oberstarbeitsführer and Leiter der Abteilung Plannung for Arbeitsgau XXV (Hessen-Süd). See HHStA, Abt. 483/2713, Lebenslauf prepared by Zahnow. Zahnow's writings, including several versions of his proposal for a Generalstab der Arbeit, are collected in HHStA, Abt. 483/2723.

50. HHStA, Abt. 483/2723, p. 214, "Entwicklung des Arbeitsdienstes: Plannung"; Zahnow to Dr. Hellmuth Stellrecht, Aug. 28, 1942. In part because Hierl had appointed and supported Tholens, Zahnow never considered Hierl as a suitable head of his proposed Generalstab der Arbeit. In 1941, his choice to head a Generalstab was either Reich marshal Hermann Göring, who had directed Hitler's 1936 Four Year Plan, or Fritz Todt, general inspector of German roads who now headed the Ministry for arms and munitions as well as the Organization Todt, which controlled the construction sector of Germany's economy.

51. HHStA, Abt. 483/2723, Feder to Zahnow, July 8, 1940, in response to Zahnow to Feder, June 24, 1940, enclosing copy of "Generalstab der Arbeit." Zahnow sought Feder's advice on whether to pressure the government for action by having his proposal published in the press.

52. BHStA, MA106753, Staatskanzlei memorandum dated Jan. 17, 1935, placed before minister-president with accompanying memorandum, "Denkschrift über die Entwicklung im D.A.D." [signed Jos. Schmidt]. What follows immediately is taken from Schmidt's memorandum

53. Ibid. According to Schmidt, Stellrecht considered Hierl "incompetent and morally and spiritually inferior." Lancelle allegedly characterized Hierl as a "Polish Jew," and Dr. Will Decker, Lancelle's superior and head of the FAD's Führer schools, as a "swine." To avoid the appearance of smearing Hitler, Schmidt concluded that the Führer was unaware of the FAD's disastrous condition.

54. Hierl was certainly stretching the truth when he described recently solicited ratings of FAD performance by Nazi Gauleiters and by a number of government officials as "mostly very good, many were enthusiastic." He was either lying or deluding himself when he asserted that "through nothing other than our performance, we have won for ourselves a place in the sun." See Hierl, *Schriften u. Reden*, vol. 2, p. 165, remarks to Gauarbeitsführer and FAD department heads, May 3–4, 1934.

55. Benz, "Vom Arbeitsdienst zur Arbeitsdienstpflicht," p. 341.

56. BHStA, MA106753, Deutscher Arbeitsdienst, Arbeitsgau 28 (Franken), Der Arbeitsgauführer [signed Schinnerer], to minister-president Siebert, July 28, 1934, enclosing invitation to a celebration honoring his forty-five FAD units; Hierl's order in StAW, LRA Mellrichstadt 1371, Der Arbeitsgauführer [signed Schinnerer], N.S. Arbeitsdienst, Arbeitsgau 28 (Franken), Standortrundschreiben no. 33, Jan. 10, 1935. On the basis of this order, Schinnerer moved four FAD units.

57. HStAS, E130b, Bü3248, Stuttgart, May 1, 1934, Vierteljahresbericht vom 1.

Januar 1934–31. März 1934 über den Deutschen Arbeitsdienst im Gau 26 Württemberg, sent by Gauarbeitsführer Alfred Müller to Württ. Staatsministerium, May 9, 1934; BHStA, MA106765, AA Würzburg, Situationsbericht, May 31, 1934, describing an FAD advertising campaign in Arbeitsgau 28; BHStA, MA106765, AA Nuremberg, Situationsbericht for June 30, 1934, for a more successful advertising campaign in Nuremberg.

58. BAK, R2/4522, Reichskommissar f. den freiw. Arbeitsdienst, Reichsleitung [signed Seldte], to Arbeitsgauleitungen, etc., March 28, 1934; D.R.d.F. [RFM, signed Gase], memorandum, April 1934; D.R.d.F. to RAM [draft], May 7, 1934, concerning agricultural laborers in the FAD.

59. StAD, 500/445, Staatssekretär f. den Arbeitsdienst [signed Hierl] to RAM (copy), April 23, 1934. Hierl also suggested that farmers could help reverse the "flight from the land" by providing better accommodations for agricultural labor. See Hierl, *Schriften u. Reden*, vol. 2, pp. 166–167.

60. StAD, 500/445, Hierl to RAM, April 23, 1934; Hierl, *Schriften u. Reden*, vol. 2, p. 166, Hierl's remarks to May 3–4, 1934, meeting of thirty Gauarbeitsführer and the FAD Reichsleitung department heads. For the legal basis of the workplace exchange regulations, see the Aug. 10, 1934, "Verordnung über die Verteilung von Arbeitskräften," RGBl, 1934, vol. 1, p. 786. The RfAA issued implementing regulations in the Aug. 28, 1934, "Anordnung über die Verteilung von Arbeitskräften," *Deutscher Reichs- und Preussischer Staatsanzeiger*, 1934, no. 202. RfAA president Syrup gave Hierl no credit for originating these labor market initiatives. See Friedrich Syrup, *Hundert Jahre Staatliche Sozialpolitik, 1839–1939*, ed. Otto Neuloh (Stuttgart: Verlag W. Kohlhammer, 1957), pp. 419–420; Syrup, *Der Arbeitseinsatz und die Arbeitslosenhilfe in Deutschland* (Berlin: Otto Elsner Verlagsgesellschaft, 1936), pp. 105–108. The impact of these measures was muted by business opposition to workplace exchange, and the government's reluctance to block labor migration to urban centers. See Chapter 9.

61. Hierl, *Schriften u. Reden*, vol. 2, pp. 203–204, speech to meeting of Deutsche Arbeitsfront, Leipzig, March 28, 1935, shortly after the introduction of compulsory military service on March 16.

62. HStAS, E130b, Bü3248, Reich interior minister [signed Frick] to Länderregierungen, July 3, 1933; RAM to Regierungen der Länder, Oct. 13, 1933, enclosing Hierl's Aug. 3, 1933, directive, "an die Bezirksleitungen f. den Arbeitsdienst"; Reich minister for public enlightenment and propaganda to Länderregierungen, March 24, 1934.

63. BAK, R2/4533, RFM [Schacht], to Reich and Prussian interior minister and all other ministers, March 28, 1935, Schnellbrief, following March 26 discussion of draft Reichsarbeitsdienstgesetz; RAM to Reich and Prussian interior minister, March 28, 1935, Confidential!, Schnellbrief. See also Köhler, *Arbeitsdienst*, p. 261, and Benz, "Vom freiwilligen Arbeitsdienst zur Arbeitsdienstpflicht," p. 344.

64. BAK, R2/4533, Reich and Prussian interior minister to State secretary and

head of the Reich chancellery, May 13, 1935; BAK, R43I, Sitzung des Reichsministeriums, June 26, 1935, for minutes of the cabinet meeting; RAD-Gesetz of June 26, 1935, RGBl, 1935, vol. 1, p. 769; Hierl, *Schriften u. Reden*, vol. 2, pp. 208–209. The law provided for at least six months of mandatory labor service for both men and women, to be performed at some point between age 19 and 25. Compulsory service for young women was included "in order to underline for foreign consumption the nonmilitary character of the labor service." Implementation of this provision, however, would be delayed "for a few years" because of the lack of funding and a proper organizational structure for young women in the AD.

65. Benz, "Vom freiwilligen Arbeitsdienst zur Arbeitsdienstpflicht," p. 341.

66. Hierl, *Schriften u. Reden*, vol. 2, p. 211, speech at NSDAP Gautag at Hanover, June 30, 1935.

9. From Creating Jobs to Allocating Labor

1. Frieda Wunderlich, *Farm Labor in Germany, 1810–1945* (Princeton: Princeton University Press, 1961), p. 292. To bolster her position, Wunderlich noted that the term "labor market" was dropped in favor of the "allocation of labor," indicating the role that the state intended to play in directing manpower.

2. RGBl, 1934, vol. 1, p. 381.

3. R. J. Overy, *War and Economy in the Third Reich* (Oxford: Clarendon Press, 1994), pp. 45–50.

4. In pursuing this course, Germany's National Socialist government mirrored labor market policy in fascist Italy. See Gianni Toniolo and Francesco Piva, "Unemployment in the 1930s: The Case of Italy," in Barry Eichengreen and T. J. Hatton, ed., *Interwar Unemployment in International Perspective* (Dordrecht: Kluwer Academic Publishers, 1988), pp. 221–245.

5. Andreas Kranig, *Lockung und Zwang: Zur Arbeitsverfassung im Dritten Reich* (Stuttgart: Deutsche Verlags-Anstalt, 1983), p. 150.

6. Wunderlich, *Farm Labor*, p. 303.

7. Tim Mason has argued that Nazi attempts to remove women from regular employment were distinct from the campaign to increase marriage and child-bearing rates. "Despite the claims made about its impact upon the labour market, the marriage loan program," wrote Mason, "was primarily an instrument of family policy." See Tim Mason, "Women in Germany, 1925–1940: Family, Welfare and Work," in Tim Mason, *Nazism, Fascism and the Working Class*, ed. Jane Caplan (Cambridge: Cambridge University Press, 1995), p. 162.

8. BAP, 39.05, 41, RAM to all Reich ministers, June 13, 1933, concerning Frauenarbeit und Doppelverdienertum.

9. For a discussion of German antifeminism as a response to the "emancipation" of German women during the 1920s, see Mason, "Women in Germany," in Mason,

Nazism, Fascism and the Working Class, pp. 151–156. Jill Stephenson, *Women in Nazi Society* (London: Croom Helm, 1975), pp. 80–85, discusses the "growing campaign from the autumn of 1930 to replace women who had jobs by unemployed men."

10. BAP, 39.05, 41, RAM to all Reich ministers, June 13, 1933, concerning Frauenarbeit und Doppelverdienertum.

11. Dörte Winkler, *Frauenarbeit im "Dritten Reich"* (Hamburg: Hoffmann and Campe Verlag, 1977), pp. 43–44, 48, 53.

12. For the biological, hereditary, and racial examination of marriage loan applicants, see, for example, StAS, Bü117, Städt. Gesundheitsamt Stuttgart, Verwaltungsbericht für das städt. Gesundheitsamt für 1933.

13. Stephenson, *Women in Nazi Society,* p. 87. The loans were paid in the form of certificates redeemable in shops selling furniture and household goods. The Reich finance ministry estimated that each marriage loan created one new job in these industries. See StadtA Nürnberg, C25I/F Reg, 659, clipping from "N. Z." [*Nürnberger Zeitung*], Nov. 21, 1933. Because another job was "created" for an unemployed male head of household by the departing female worker, the RFM considered that the 60,000 marriage loans granted during August, September, and October 1933 had "relieved" the labor market by 120,000.

14. As noted by Andreas Kranig, *Lockung und Zwang,* pp. 60–61, by financing marriage loans with a new tax, the Reich government merely transferred purchasing power from single wage earners to married couples. Mason, "Women in Germany," in Mason, *Nazism, Fascism and the Working Class,* p. 163, indicates that the tax on the unmarried was "soon dropped on account of the resentment which it caused among working spinsters," who were unable to find partners as a result of the slaughter of young men in the Great War.

15. StAD, 102/1687, "Kommunal Sozialpolitik," clipping from *Mitteilungen des deutschen Städetages,* Nov. 20, 1933. Among the firms making such grants of RM 300 to 600 were several cigarette factories, chemical firms, and the Continental Gummi Werke. Stephenson, *Women in Nazi Germany,* pp. 87–88, cites the Reemtsma cigarette company, which offered a "substantial cash payment" to every female employee who participated in the Reich marriage loan plan.

16. BAK, R43/II/537, RFM, March 20, 1934, "Entwurf eines Gesetz zür Änderung des Gesetzes über Förderung der Eheschließungen," the justification clauses *(Begründung)* of which *(Akten der Reichskanzlei,* pt. 1, vol. 2, pp. 1187–1188) includes statistics on marriage loans made between Aug. 1933 and Feb. 1934; Stelzner, *Arbeitsbeschaffung und Wiederaufrüstung, 1933–1936* (Bamberg: Schadel & Wehle, 1976), pp. 101–102; Syrup, *Der Arbeitseinsatz und die Arbeitslosenhilfe in Deutschland* (Berlin: Otto Elsner Verlagsgesellschaft, 1936), pp. 124–127; Willi Hemmer, *Die "Unsichtbaren" Arbeitslosen: Statistische Methoden—Soziale Tatsachen* (Zeulenroda, Germany: Bernhard Sporn, 1935), pp. 86–87.

17. Mason, "Women in Germany," in Mason, *Nazism, Fascism and the Working Class,* p. 161.

18. StadtA Nürnberg, C25I/F Reg, 659, clipping from "N. Z." [*Nürnberger Zeitung*], Nov. 21, 1933; clipping from *Nürnberger Zeitung,* Feb. 28, 1934. In 1933, recorded marriages rose by 121,780 over 1932, and in 1934 the number of marriages rose by another 101,592. A large portion of this increase in marriages must have resulted from the improvement in economic conditions. During the last few months of 1933, more than half of all marriages were supported by marriage loans. During the following years, this fraction fell to 30 percent (1934), 24 percent (1935), and 28 percent (1936). For Britain and Belgium, see Mark Thomas, "Labor Market Structure and the Nature of Unemployment in Interwar Britain," and Martine Goossens, Stefaan Peeters, Guido Pepermans, "Interwar Unemployment in Belgium," in Barry Eichengreen and T. J. Hatton, eds., *Interwar Unemployment in International Perspective* (Dordrecht: Kluwer Academic Publishers, 1988), pp. 97–148, 289–324.

19. Overy, *War and Economy,* p. 49.

20. StAD, 500/432, Pressedienst des LAA Rheinland, "Der Kampf gegen die Arbeitslosigkeit im Rheinland," Sept. 19, 1933. The textile industry was singled out for particular attention.

21. StAD, 102/1687, "Kommunal Sozialpolitik," clipping from *Mitteilungen des deutschen Städtetages,* Nov. 20, 1933.

22. StAD, Duisburg-Hamborn, Personalamt 2, memorandum of Oct. 20, 1933. The *Gesetz zur Änderung von Vorschriften auf dem Gebiete des allgemeinen Beamten-, des Besoldungs- und des Versorgungsrechts vom 30. Juni 1933,* RGBl, 1933, vol. 1, p. 435, made it easier to dismiss and replace female civil servants, and males were given preference in new hiring. It is not clear that any of the women dismissed from Duisburg's municipal administration held civil service status.

23. StAD, 500/434, Arbeitshilfswerk der NSDAP und der NSBO, Duisburg, to Herrn Beigeordneten Pg. Birkenbuel [welfare office], Duisburg, Aug. 19, 1933; StAS, Bü, 117, Bericht über die öffentliche Sitzung des Gemeinderats um 27. März 1934, "Bericht über den Stand des Kampfes gegen die Arbeitslosigkeit," reported by Bürgermeister Dr. Sigloch.

24. Overy, *War and Economy,* p. 50.

25. BAK, R43II/529c, RFM to Reichskanzlei, Sept. 29, 1937, including draft for a third amendment to the marriage loan law; state secretary and head of the Reich chancellery to RFM, Oct. 16, 1937, indicating that no Reich minister had objected to the RFM's proposal.

26. For a discussion of the issue of multi-income families, see Mason, *Sozialpolitik im Dritten Reich,* pp. 134–135 (English ed., pp. 117–118). There was no general agreement on a definition of "double earning."

27. BAK, R28/57, circular from Reichsbank-Direktorium (signed by Schacht

and Dreyse), Sept. 4, 1933, "Doppelverdiener." Believing this was a matter for the appropriate Reich (not Nazi party) authorities, the Reichsbank directorate ordered its branch banks not to comply with such requests from local party officials.

28. BAK, R43II/537, RWM and RAM to state secretary in the Reich Chancellery, Oct. 26, 1933, "Das Doppelverdienertum und seine Regelung."

29. Ibid.

30. BAK, R28/58, RAM (signed Seldte) to Reichsbank-Direktorium, Dec. 4, 1933, enclosing copy of joint memorandum from RAM and RWM to highest Reich authorities, Nov. 20, 1933, "Doppelverdiener." The memorandum is reproduced in Syrup, *Der Arbeitseinsatz*, pp. 118–123.

31. Ibid.

32. Ibid.; BAP, 25.01, 6578, vol. 2, Volkswirtschaftliche und Statistische Abteilung der Reichsbank, memorandum on "Bestimmungen betreffend Doppelverdiener und Schwarzarbeiter," June 29, 1935.

33. *Akten der Reichskanzlei*, pt. 1, vol. 1, Chefsbesprechung im Reichsarbeitsministerium, Dec. 6, 1933, pp. 1001–1005. Original in BAK, R43II/537.

34. Overy, *War and Economy*, p. 64. For regional unemployment in 1933 and 1934, see Appendix, Tables 12 and 13.

35. Syrup, *Der Arbeitseinsatz*, p. 92.

36. While Overy, *War and Economy*, p. 43, and Mason, *Sozialpolitik*, p. 132 (English ed., p. 115), have emphasized the dramatic decline in unemployment among those under 25, Fritz Petrick has argued that official unemployment statistics overestimate the decline in youth unemployment by about 500,000 between June 1933 and Oct. 1935. The alleged discrepancy arises because official statistics did not count as "unemployed" members of the Labor Service, the Landhilfe, the Hitler Youth Landdienst, those serving their *Landjahr* in Prussia, and females serving their year as domestic household help. See Fritz Petrick, "Eine Untersuchung zur Beseitigung der Arbeitslosigkeit unter der deutschen Jugend in den Jahren von 1933 bis 1935," *Jahrbuch für Wirtschaftsgeschichte* (1967), pp. 289–290, 299.

37. Syrup, *Arbeitseinsatz*, pp. 90–91.

38. N-WHStA, Reg. Aachen 16857, president RfAA to LAA presidents, April 21, 1933, enclosing the results of a meeting of top RfAA officials: Berlin, March 31, 1933, "Referentenbesprechung über Arbeitsbeschaffung am 24. März 1933; Jahresplan 1933. Ergebnisse."

39. Syrup, *Arbeitseinsatz*, p. 92. Eight of Germany's largest cities still held a total of about one million unemployed in Jan. 1934, more than a half-million in Berlin alone.

40. Syrup, *Arbeitseinsatz*, pp. 92, 100–102. Industries declared off-limits for the employment of "agricultural" labor were mining, iron and steel, construction and related industries, the brick industry, and construction and maintenance for railways, tramways, and the Reich postal service. For the Gesetz zur Regelung des Arbeit-

seinsatzes, see RGBl 1933, vol. 1, p. 381. For RfAA orders barring immigration of workers into Berlin, Hamburg, and Bremen, and orders prohibiting agricultural laborers from accepting employment in mining, metallurgy, construction, masonry, and railway construction, see Friedrich Syrup, *Gesetz zur Regelung des Arbeitsein-satzes und die dazu ergangenen Anordnungen* (Berlin: Otto Elsner Verlagsgesellschaft, 1934).

41. Syrup, *Arbeitseinsatz*, p. 93; Wunderlich, *Farm Labor*, pp. 294–295.

42. Mason, *Sozialpolitik*, p. 137n34 (English ed., p. 120), regarded the ban on labor migration as "an effective remedial measure, especially in Berlin, where there were 650,000 unemployed in January 1933." Syrup, *Arbeitseinsatz*, p. 93, credited work creation, rather than the migration block, for the decline in Berlin's unemployment level. But without the block, he argued, as emergency relief projects and regular jobs put Berliners back to work, more unemployed workers would have streamed into the city and pushed the unemployment figure back up to its original level.

43. Syrup, *Arbeitseinsatz*, pp. 93–94. The strategy worked so well that it was possible to lift the ban on movement into the Saarland in the spring of 1936.

44. Syrup, *Arbeitseinsatz*, p. 94. Mason, *Sozialpolitik*, p. 137n34 (English ed., p. 120).

45. For the legal basis of the workplace exchange regulations, see the Aug. 10, 1934, "Verordnung über die Verteilung von Arbeitskräften," RGBl, 1934, vol. 1, p. 786. The RfAA issued implementing regulations in the Aug. 28, 1934, "Anord-nung über die Verteilung von Arbeitskräften," *Deutscher Reichs- und Preußischer Staatsanzeiger*, 1934, no. 202.

46. Syrup, *Arbeitseinsatz*, p. 106.

47. Mason, *Sozialpolitik*, pp. 133–134 (English ed., pp. 116–117); N-WStAM, AA Iserlohn 6, president LAA Westfalen, Nov. 6, 1934, Bericht über die Arbeitslage in den einzelnen Berufsgruppen für die Zeit vom 1. bis 31. Oktober 1934; BHStA, MA106767, AA Marktredwitz, Situationsbericht for Aug. 31, 1934, prepared Sept. 11, 1934; AA Schweinfurt, Situationsbericht for Dec. 31, 1934, prepared Jan. 12, 1935; AA Coburg, Situationsbericht for Jan. 1, 1935, prepared Jan. 10, 1935; AA Kaiserslautern, Situationsbericht for Jan. 1, 1935, prepared Jan. 11, 1935. The AA reported that the DAF was including evidence of AA attempts to enforce the job exchange directive in a collection of material to be used against the RfAA in some unspecified proceeding.

48. Syrup, *Arbeitseinsatz*, p. 108. Wunderlich, *Farm Labor*, p. 296, concluded that the unpopular order of Aug. 28, 1934, was not rigidly enforced, because "it resulted in the release of only 130,000 workers from October 1934 to October 1935." Mason, *Sozialpolitik*, p. 134 (English ed., p. 117), notes that many "voluntary" exchanges, usually under pressure from Nazi party organizations, had taken place prior to the promulgation of the Aug. 28, 1934, Directive on Manpower Distribution.

49. Syrup, *Arbeitseinsatz,* p. 108. The impact of the workplace exchange program on official labor market statistics cannot be established with any degree of certainty. It cannot be assumed that all of the older newly hired replacements had previously been counted as "unemployed," nor can it be ascertained how many of the displaced younger workers found alternative regular employment, joined the Land Helpers or Labor Service, or ended up on the unemployment rolls.

50. N-WStAM, AA Iserlohn 6, president LAA Westfalen, Nov. 6, 1934, Bericht über die Arbeitslage in den einzelnen Berufsgruppen für die Zeit vom 1. bis 31. Oktober 1934. The LAA reported over 15,000 young male and female workers in the district as suitable for job exchange, but lack of alternative placement opportunities was slowing down the exchange process.

51. N-WHStA, Reg. Aachen 16851, Oberpräsident der Rheinprovinz to Regierungspräsidenten, concerning placement of youthful manpower and the utilization of labor in agriculture, July 21, 1934.

52. BAK, R28/62, Reichsbank-Direktorium to Reichsbank branch offices, etc., Sept. 22, 1934; BAK, R43II/537, Mecklenburg-Strelitzsches Staatsministerium, Abteilung für Arbeitsbeschaffung, to Reich Chancellery, Aug. 11, 1933. The date of this commentary indicates that the practice of workplace exchange antedated the Aug. 10, 1934 decree.

53. Mason, *Sozialpolitik,* pp. 135–136 (English ed., pp.118–119) notes the success of these special initiatives for hiring Nazi veterans for new jobs and as replacements for "Marxists" holding existing jobs.

54. BHStA, MA106765, AA Nürnberg, Situationsbericht, May 31 and June 30, 1934; MA106767, AA Ingolstadt, Situationsbericht, July 31, 1934; AA Würzburg, Situationsbericht prepared Aug. 7, 1934, indicating that Old Fighters unsuited for their work were being laid off; AA Kaiserslautern, Situationsbericht, July 31, 1934, indicating that employers were not supporting AA attempts to find jobs for Nazi Old Fighters.

55. Gesetz zur Einführung eines Arbeitsbuches vom 26. 2. 1935, RGBl 1935, vol. 1, p. 311; Wunderlich, *Farm Labor,* pp. 306–307; Syrup, *Arbeitseinsatz,* pp. 117–118; idem, *Hundert Jahre Staatliche Sozialpolitik, 1839–1939,* Otto Neuloh, ed. (Stuttgart: Verlag W. Kohlhammer, 1957), pp. 436–441.

56. Syrup, *Arbeitseinsatz,* p. 117; Rüdiger Hachtmann, *Industriearbeit im "Dritten Reich": Untersuchungen zu den Lohn- und Arbeitsbedingungen in Deutschland, 1933–1945* (Göttingen: Vandenhoeck & Ruprecht, 1989), p. 43.

57. Kranig, *Locking und Zwang,* p. 66.

58. See Hachtmann, *Industriearbeit,* pp. 43–44, for a summary of labor market restrictions issued in conjunction with the implementation of the Four Year Plan during Nov./Dec. 1936 and Feb. 1937.

59. Syrup's statements cited in Hachtmann, *Industriearbeit,* p. 44.

60. Overy, *War and Economy,* p. 50; Hachtmann, *Industriearbeit,* pp. 44–45.

61. Hachtmann, *Industriearbeit,* p. 45.

62. Ibid., pp. 45–46.

63. Ibid., pp. 46–47.

64. Dieter Petzina, *Autarkiepolitik im Dritten Reich: Der nationalsozialistische Vierjahrplan,* Schriftenreihe der Vierteljahrsheft für Zeitgeschichte, no. 16 (Stuttgart: Deutsche Verlags-Anstalt, 1968), pp. 158, 160.

10. The Nazi Economic Achievement

1. Tim Mason, *Sozialpolitik im Dritten Reich* (Opladen: Westdeutscher Verlag, 1977), pp. 126–127, 134, 138–139. English edition: *Social Policy in the Third Reich: The Working Class and the "National Community,"* trans. John Broadwin; ed. Jane Caplan (Providence: Berg, 1993), pp. 111, 117, 120–121.

2. For Syrup's memorandum, see BAK, R41/5, president RfAA to RAM, Sept. 30, 1933, with enclosed memorandum, "Zur Entlastung des Arbeitsmarktes im Winter 1933/34." Seldte's memorandum can be found in several locations, including BAK, R43^{II}/ 534, 537; BHStA, MA106743; HHStA, Abt. 485, 824, RAM to obersten Reichsbehorden, etc., Nov. 15, 1933, with enclosed report, "Der Stand der deutschen Arbeitsschlacht," dated end of Oct. 1933. The HHStA copy is used here.

3. Ibid., p. 2. Seldte noted the unevenness in the labor market improvement based on gender, occupation, and region.

4. Ibid., pp. 3–4, 10–12. Seldte recognized (p. 11) that programs coincided and overlapped. He thus made no estimate of the total number of unemployed given jobs as of Sept. 30, 1933, under the Papen, Schleicher, and Reinhardt work creation programs, supplemented by RfAA support funds.

5. BAK, R2/18701, RAM to RFM, Dec. 5, 1934, with enclosed memorandum on work creation programs.

6. Seldte, "Der Stand der deutschen Arbeitsschlacht," dated end of Oct. 1933, p. 13.

7. *Akten der Reichskanzlei,* pt. 1, vol. 2, p. 1003, Chefsbesprechung im Reichsarbeitsministerium, 6. Dezember 1933. Original in BAK, R43II/537. Also found in R2/ 18679, as "Niederschrift über die Chefsbesprechung im Reichsarbeitsministerium am 6. Dezember 1933 zur Frage der Bekämpfung der Arbeitslosigkeit im Jahre 1934, Vertraulich!" Reich labor minister Seldte, Reich finance minister Krosigk, and Reich transportation minister Eltz-Rübenach shared Feder's priorities for 1934.

8. See, for example, BHStA, MWi 5637, Synopsis der Berichtes der Reichs-Kredit-Gesellschaft über Deutschlands wirtschaftliche Lage 1933/34, n.d., by Dr. Max Roosen and Werner Kertscher. The original 83-page report, "Deutschlands wirtschaftliche Lage an der Jahreswende 1933/34," Jan. 2, 1934, can be found in BAK, R43^{II}/309; BAK, R43^{II}/323, Franz Willuhn, Vermerk, "Wirtschaftstätigkeit

in Deutschland im Jahre 1933," Jan. 23, 1934. Willuhn was an economic analyst in the Reich chancellery.

9. BAK, R43^{II}/308, Wolff's Telegraphisches Büro account of Schmitt's July 13, 1933 speech to "an invited circle of leading personalities from the economy"; Wolff's Telegraphisches Büro, account of Schmitt's comments to domestic and foreign correspondents, dated Dec. 11, 1933. Schmitt had replaced Hugenberg as RWM on June 30, 1933.

10. BAK, R43^{II}/308, Deutsches Nachrichtenbüro, June 10, 1934, account of "Rede des Staatssekretärs Fritz Reinhardt auf der Tagung der Kommission für Wirtschaftspolitik der NSDAP."

11. Ibid.

12. Ibid.

13. BAK, R2/18606, president RfAA to state secretary Reinhardt, RFM, June 6, 1934, information provided to assist Reinhardt's preparation for the "upcoming conference of Gau economic advisors" to be held in Munich on June 10, 1934.

14. BAP 25.01, vol. 2, 6579, "Deutschlands wirtschaftliche und finanzielle Lage," Dec. 2, 1935. An attached note describes this as a draft for a speech or article by General Oshima, military attaché at the Japanese embassy in Berlin. It came to the Reichsbank from the Reich chancellery by way of Ministerialdirektor Wohltat (RWM).

15. BAP 25.01, 6578, vol. 2, Dr. Franz Döring, Reichsbank director, "Die wirtschaftliche und finanzielle Lage Deutschlands," final version of July 22, 1935.

16. Ibid.

17. Ibid.

18. BAK, R43^{II}/309a, Oswald Lehnich, "Nationalsozialistische Arbeitsbeschaffungspolitik," June 8, 1935, speech in Königsberg.

19. H. W. Richardson, *Economic Recovery in Britain, 1932–9* (London: Weidenfeld & Nicolson, 1967), p. 221.

20. W. R. Garside, *British Unemployment 1919–1939: A Study in Public Policy* (Cambridge: Cambridge University Press, 1990), p. 347; Roger Middleton, *Towards the Managed Economy: Keynes, the Treasury, and the Fiscal Policy Debate of the 1930s* (London: Methuen, 1985), pp. 139–140. Richardson, *Economic Recovery in Britain, 1932–9*, pp. 315–316, contended that British "fiscal policy was actively destabilizing both at the lower turning point [August-September 1932] and in 1936–7." On the other hand, S. N. Broadberry, *The British Economy Between the Wars: A Macroeconomic Survey* (Oxford: Basil Blackwell, 1986), p. 152, has argued that British fiscal policy "was probably broadly neutral through the 1930s, neither strongly stabilizing nor strongly destabilizing."

21. Richardson, *Economic Recovery in Britain, 1932–9*, pp. 219–220.

22. Ibid., pp. 27–29; G. D. N. Worswick, "The Sources of Recovery in the UK

in the 1930s," *National Institute Economic Review* 110 (Nov. 1984), pp. 87–88. In 1985, Barry Eichengreen and Jeffrey Sachs demonstrated a positive correlation between devaluation and economic revival for a number of countries in the 1930s. See Barry Eichengreen and Jeffrey Sachs, "Exchange Rates and Economic Recovery in the 1930s," *Journal of Economic History* 45 (1985), pp. 925–946. Eichengreen has continued his study of the gold standard and its impact on economic performance, culminating in his book *Golden Fetters: The Gold Standard and the Great Depression, 1919–1939* (New York: Oxford University Press, 1992).

23. G. D. N. Worswick, "Sources of Recovery," p. 91. Broadberry, *British Economy Between the Wars*, p. 129, estimates that the 13 percent depreciation of sterling during the year 1931–32 produced a gain of 3 percent to the GNP. Michael Kitson and Solomos Solomou, *Protectionism and Economic Revival: The British Interwar Economy* (Cambridge: Cambridge University Press, 1990), pp. 66, 89–90, calculate average tariff rates for manufactures under the Import Duties Act at over 14 percent in the period 1932–1937.

24. Worswick, "Sources of Recovery," p. 90.

25. Ibid., pp. 90–91. Kitson and Solomou, *Protectionism and Economic Revival*, pp. 90–91, point out that building society deposits grew faster during the 1920s than in the 1930s because of an increase in the proportion of savings going to the societies and to a peak in repayments of mortgages. They conclude that "the availability of funds in the 1930s was mainly due to the favorable conditions of the 1920s, not the monetary shift of 1932."

26. Worswick, "Sources of Recovery," pp. 91–93; N. H. Dimsdale, "Employment and Real Wages in the Interwar Period," *National Institute Economic Review* 110 (Nov. 1984), p. 95; Kitson and Solomou, *Protectionism and Economic Revival*, pp. 95–99. Kitson and Solomou have concluded that "it is not possible to distinguish a long-term relationship between real wages and economic growth."

27. Worswick, "Sources of Recovery," p. 93; Kitson and Solomou, *Protectionism and Economic Revival*, p. 99.

28. Garside, *British Unemployment, 1919–1939*, p. 314. Susan Howson, "Slump and Unemployment," in Roderick Floud and Donald McCloskey, eds., *The Economic History of Britain Since 1700*, vol. 2, *1860 to the 1970s* (Cambridge: Cambridge University Press, 1981), p. 280, argued that carrying out public works programs on the scale originally planned would have had little additional impact on the labor market.

29. Middleton, *Towards the Managed Economy*, p. 179. S. Glynn and P. G. Howells, "Unemployment in the 1930s: The 'Keynesian Solution' Reconsidered," *Australian Economic History Review* 20 (1980), p. 42; Mark Thomas, "The macroeconomics of the inter-war years," in Roderick Floud and Donald McCloskey, eds., *The Economic History of Britain Since 1700*, 2nd ed., vol. 2, *1860–1939* (Cambridge: Cambridge University Press, 1994), p. 350. Garside and Hatton have argued that

Keynesian pump-priming might have produced significant results. See W. R. Garside and T. J. Hatton, "Keynesian Policy and British Unemployment in the 1930s," *Economic History Review* 38 (1985), pp. 87–88.

30. Alan Booth, "The British reaction to the economic crisis," in W. R. Garside, ed., *Capitalism in Crisis: International Responses to the Great Depression* (London: Pinter Publishers, 1993), pp. 51–52.

31. Peter Fearon, "Hoover, Roosevelt and American economic policy during the 1930s," in W. R. Garside, ed., *Capitalism in Crisis*, p. 143.

32. John A. Garraty, *The Great Depression* (Garden City, N. Y.: Doubleday Anchor Books, 1987), pp. 187–188, 191–192, 199–200, 208.

33. Harold James, "Innovation and Conservatism in Economic Recovery: The Alleged 'Nazi Recovery' of the 1930s," in Thomas Childers and Jane Caplan, eds., *Reevaluating the Third Reich* (New York: Holmes & Meier, 1993), pp. 116–117. See also James's identically titled chapter in Garside, *Capitalism in Crisis*, p. 77; Silverman, "National Socialist Economics: The *Wirtschaftswunder* Reconsidered," in Barry Eichengreen and T. J. Hatton, eds., *Interwar Unemployment in International Perspective* (Dordrecht: Kluwer Academic Publishers, 1988) p. 188, estimated direct work creation expenditures at 2.5 percent of Germany's GNP for the three years 1933 through 1935.

34. Hellmut Wollmann, "Die Wohnungsbaupolitik des New Deal," in Heinrich August Winkler, ed., *Die große Krise in Amerika* (Göttingen: Vandenhoeck & Ruprecht, 1973), p. 166; Anthony J. Badger, *The New Deal: The Depression Years, 1933–1940* (New York: Farrar, Straus, & Giroux, 1989), pp. 240–241.

35. Michael M. Weinstein, "Some Macroeconomic Impacts of the National Industrial Recovery Act, 1933–1935," in Karl Brunner, ed., *The Great Depression Revisited* (The Hague: Martinus Nijhoff, 1981), pp. 274, 278–279. Weinstein acknowledges that the NIRA codes were not the only factor retarding recovery.

36. *Final Statistical Report of the Federal Emergency Relief Administration* (Washington, D. C.: Government Printing Office, 1942), pp. iii, 38 (calculated from Table 10), 49; Badger, *New Deal*, p. 191. The Federal Emergency Relief Act of 1933 authorized the use of federal funds for both direct relief and work relief. Of the $3,212,000,000 paid out between 1933 and the end of 1935, $1,230,000,000 (38 percent) represented work relief earnings, while $1,982,000,000 (62 percent) took the form of direct relief. But when Civil Works Administration (CWA) public works projects became available in Dec. 1933 and during the first three months of 1934, work relief earnings dropped to only 5 percent of FERA relief expenditures during those months.

37. Bonnie Fox Schwartz, *The Civil Works Administration, 1933–1934: The Business of Emergency Employment in the New Deal* (Princeton: Princeton University Press, 1984), p. 23.

38. Ibid., p. 38. Since the $400 million was shifted from the CWA appropriation,

no "new" money was being pumped into public works projects. Most of the funds were spent on projects that added value to the nation's stock of roads and public buildings.

39. Schwartz, *Civil Works Administration*, pp. 214–220; Badger, *New Deal*, pp. 199–200. German firms also complained of "unfair competition" from publicly funded operations.

40. Calculated from U. S. Department of Commerce, Bureau of the Census, *Historical Statistics of the United States, Colonial Times to 1970* (Washington, D.C.: Government Printing Office, 1975), pt. 1, p. 234, and Donald S. Howard, *The WPA and Federal Relief Policy* (New York: Russell Sage Foundation, 1943), p. 38.

41. Howard, *WPA and Federal Relief Policy*, pp. 129–130, 531. "WPA employment" as discussed here means employment on projects operated directly by the WPA, and does not include employment on projects of other federal agencies that were financed in part by WPA funds. Between Jan. 1936 and Jan. 1941, projects of other federal agencies employed an average of 512,000 relief workers, and the CCC and NYA assisted an average of 776,000 youths each month. Thus, an average of 3,348,000 persons worked each month on WPA, CCC, NYA, and other federal projects between 1936 and 1941. As a percentage of WPA expenditures, highways, roads, and streets led the way with 38.9 percent, followed by public buildings (10.2 percent) and recreational facilities (8.3 percent).

42. Badger, *New Deal*, pp. 211–212.

43. Peter Fearon, *War, Prosperity and Depression: The U.S. Economy 1917–45* (Lawrence, Kansas: University Press of Kansas, 1987), p. 250.

44. Gary D. Best, *Pride, Prejudice, and Politics: Roosevelt versus Recovery, 1933–1938* (New York: Praeger, 1991), pp. 17, 28, 63–64, 219, 222. Best's work is seriously flawed by a completely uncritical reading and acceptance of statements by businessmen and business organizations, bankers, and chambers of commerce who believed that their interests were threatened by Roosevelt's policies.

45. Michael A. Bernstein, *The Great Depression: Delayed Recovery and Economic Change in America, 1929–1939* (Cambridge: Cambridge University Press, 1987), pp. 28–31; idem, "Why the Great Depression Was Great: Toward a New Understanding of the Interwar Economic Crisis in the United States," in Steve Fraser and Gary Gerstle, ed., *The Rise and Fall of the New Deal Order, 1930–1989* (Princeton: Princeton University Press, 1989), pp. 32–54.

46. Ibid., pp. 197, 203.

47. David Abraham, *The Collapse of the Weimar Republic: Political Economy and Crisis* (Princeton: Princeton University Press, 1981). In the wake of a bitter controversy over Abraham's methodology and the substance of his argument, a second "corrected" edition appeared (New York: Holmes & Meier, 1987).

48. For Henry A. Turner, Jr., and Gerald D. Feldman, see *New York Times Book Review*, Sept. 13, 1987, pp. 60–61, letters to the editor, "Why Weimar Fell." For

Maier, see "The Vulnerabilities of Interwar Germany," *Journal of Modern History* 56 (1984), p. 93. Timothy W. Mason's review of Abraham's book appeared in the *American Historical Review* 87 (1982), pp. 1122–1123. Maier noted that some of the leading dynamic new industries were corporate subsidiaries of the basic iron and steel concerns, "with a tangle of interlocking interests and cross-cutting priorities." Mason's observation (p. 1123) that there were opposing factions within individual firms has been confirmed in the work of Peter Hayes on IG Farben. See Peter Hayes, *Industry and Ideology: IG Farben in the Nazi Era* (Cambridge: Cambridge University Press, 1987); idem, "Carl Bosch and Carl Krauch: Chemistry and the Political Economy of Germany 1925–1945," *Journal of Economic History* 47 (1987), pp. 353–363. In a review of the second edition, V. R. Berghahn, in *New York Times Book Review*, Aug. 2, 1987, pp. 12–13, found Abraham's structural analysis promising for future research.

49. Maier, "Vulnerabilities of Interwar Germany," p. 93.

50. James, "Innovation and Conservatism in Economic Recovery: The Alleged 'Nazi Recovery' of the 1930s," in Childers and Kaplan, *Reevaluating the Third Reich*, pp. 122, 123, 132; also in Garside, *Capitalism in Crisis*.

51. R. J. Overy, "Cars, Roads, and Economic Recovery in Germany, 1932–8," *Economic History Review* 28 (1975), pp. 466–483; idem, *War and Economy in the Third Reich* (Oxford: Clarendon Press, 1994), p. 12; Simon Reich, *The Fruits of Fascism: Postwar Prosperity in Historical Perspective* (Ithaca: Cornell University Press, 1990), pp. 107–130.

52. Reich, *Fruits of Fascism*, p. 111.

53. Overy, *War and Economy*, p. 79, table 2.6

54. Reich, *Fruits of Fascism*, p. 110.

55. Ibid., pp. 110–111.

56. Ibid. Daimler-Benz ultimately became a willing employer of slave labor and Jews, who were worked to exhaustion and then shipped to concentration camps. See Reich's summary of such charges and evidence, pp. 251–253. Turner has found no evidence that Daimler-Benz provided the Nazi movement any significant financial assistance during Hitler's struggle for the chancellorship. See Henry A. Turner, Jr., *German Big Business and the Rise of Hitler* (New York: Oxford University Press, 1985), pp. xx–xxi, 267.

57. Totals and percentages calculated from Overy, *War and Economy*, p. 75, table 2.5. Overy does not indicate the portion of "outside investment" provided directly by the Hitler government. That German commercial banks provided auto manufacturers with most of their outside funds seems unlikely in view of information on bank balance sheets cited by Samuel Lurie. Total business credits were lower at the end of both 1933 and 1935 than they had been at the end of 1932, and business credits as a portion of total commercial bank assets declined between December 1932 and December 1935. See Samuel Lurie, *Private Investment in a Controlled*

Economy: Germany, 1933–1939 (New York: Columbia University Press, 1947), p. 94, table 21. The government restricted the distribution of profits in an effort to promote the plowing back of profits. Daimler-Benz had less profit than Opel to reinvest, but this difference alone seems insufficient to explain the magnitude and portion of outside investment channeled to Daimler-Benz between 1933 and 1936, before rearmament dominated the economy.

58. James, "Innovation and Conservatism in Economic Recovery," in Childers and Kaplan, *Reevaluating the Third Reich*, p. 124; also in Garside, *Capitalism in Crisis*, p. 81; idem, *The German Slump* (Oxford: Clarendon Press, 1986), p. 378.

59. Peter Hayes, "Polycracy and Policy in the Third Reich: The Case of the Economy," in Childers and Caplan, *Reevaluating the Third Reich*, p. 192.

60. V. R. Berghahn, "Big Business in the Third Reich," *European History Quarterly* 21 (1991), p. 101, review of Hayes, *Industry and Ideology: IG Farben in the Nazi Era.*

61. Hayes, *Industry and Ideology:* p. xix.

62. Hayes, "Polycracy and Policy," in Childers and Caplan, *Reevaluating the Third Reich*, pp. 193, 198, 200, 205n18. In most instances, Hayes dates the implementation of Hitler's plan from 1933; here he suggests 1934 as the starting date. This is an important issue, since Germany's labor market improved significantly during 1933, even though Nazi work creation programs provided only very modest assistance until the end of 1933 and the spring of 1934.

63. Elizabeth Harvey, *Youth and the Welfare State in Weimar Germany* (Oxford: Clarendon Press, 1993), pp. 296–298.

64. Bernstein, *The Great Depression*, p. 205.

65. R. J. Overy, *The Nazi Economic Recovery, 1932–1938*, 2nd ed. (Cambridge: Cambridge University Press, 1996), pp. 34, 45.

66. R. J. Overy, "Transportation and Rearmament in the Third Reich," *Historical Journal* 16 (1973), p. 399; StAN, LRA Rothenburg 1975, Fach 645, Nr. 9^I, for statement of Todt's adviser on social policy, Dr. Carl Birkenholz; BHStA, MA 106947, "Rede des Herrn Reichsministers Rudolf Hess anlässlich des VII. internationalen Straßenkongress," undated [Munich, Sept. 3, 1934]; BHStA, MWi 6966, pamphlet, *Wille Wirkt Wunder.* Drei Reden zur Internationalen Automobil- und Motorrad- Ausstellung, Berlin, Hitler speech of Feb. 14, 1935.

67. R. J. Overy, "Unemployment in the Third Reich," *Business History* 29 (1987), p. 273. For other reports on employment trends in the construction sector, see BAK, R2/18701, Deutsche Bau- und Bodenbank AG, "Die Entwicklung der deutschen Bauwirtschaft und die Arbeitsbeschaffung im Jahre 1933," pp. 33–34; HStAS, E151dI, Bü 29, and E130b, Bü 3245, monthly labor market reports of LAA Südwestdeutschland.

68. Rüdiger Hachtmann, *Industriearbeit im "Dritten Reich"* (Göttingen: Vandenhoeck & Ruprecht, 1989), pp. 283–284. Experts in 1920 estimated that it would

take an annual net gain of 250,000 units to eliminate the shortage; by the end of 1938, RAM Seldte estimated the required net gain at 300,000 to 400,000 units annually. In 1938, Seldte admitted that the "Nazi revolution" had reduced the housing shortage by only 40,000 units since 1933. See Statistisches Reichsamt, *Wirtschaft und Statistik* (Berlin, 1928–1938); Franz Seldte, *Sozialpolitik im Dritten Reich* (Munich and Berlin: Beck Verlag, 1939), pp. 172–175; Dan P. Silverman, "A Pledge Unredeemed: The Housing Crisis in Weimar Germany," *Central European History* 3 (March 1970), pp. 119–120. Overy's housing construction statistics for 1928–1938 show an impressive increase in building activity after 1933. But his figures are misleading, for the number of dwellings constructed, both new and converted, exceeds the net gain (for which he provides no statistics) by 20,000 to 50,000 per year. Nor does Overy relate the annual net gains in housing to the housing needs of the German population. By this standard, the Nazi housing effort looks less impressive. See Overy, *War and Economy*, p. 63.

69. Overy, "Unemployment in the Third Reich," pp. 266–267; idem, *War and Economy*, p. 53.

70. Overy, *The Nazi Economic Recovery, 1932–1938*, 2nd ed., pp. 37–38, 48.

Sources

Unpublished Sources

Bayerisches Hauptstaatsarchiv (BHStA)
   MA 1957 (1933–1945) Staatskanzlei
   Mwi Staatsministerium für Wirtschaft und Verkehr
   Reichstatthalter Epp
Berlin Document Center (BDC)
   Personnel files of Gauleiter Otto Hellmuth
Bundesarchiv Koblenz (BAK)
   R 2 Reichsfinanzministerium (Reich Finance Ministry) (RFM)
   R 24 Statistisches Reichsamt (Reich Statistical Office)
   R 28 Dienststellen der Deutschen Reichsbank (German Reichsbank Branch
      Offices)
   R 41 Reichsarbeitsministerium (Reich Labor Ministry) (RAM)
   R 43II Reichskanzlei (Reich Chancellery)
   R 53 Stellvertreter des Reichskanzlers (Deputy Reich Chancellor)
   R 65I Generalinspektor für das deutsche Straßenwesen (General Inspector for
      German Roads)
   R 163 Reichsanstalt für Arbeitsvermittlung und Arbeitslosenversicherung
      (Reich Institution for Placement and Unemployment Insurance)
   NL Hugenberg
Bundesarchiv Potsdam (BAP)
   21.01 Reichsfinanzministerium (Reich Finance Ministry) (RFM)
   25.01 Deutsche Reichsbank (German Reichsbank)
   31.01 Reichswirtschaftsministerium (Reich Economics Ministry)(RWM)
   36.01 Reichsministerium für Ernährung und Landwirtschaft (Reich Ministry
      for Food and Agriculture)
   39.03 Reichsanstalt für Arbeitsvermittlung und Arbeitslosenversicherung
      (Reich Institution for Placement and Unemployment Insurance)

39.05 Reichskommissar für Arbeitsbeschaffung (Reich Commissioner for Work Creation)

Geheimes Staatsarchiv Preußischer Kulturbesitz (GStAPK), Berlin-Dahlem

Rep 87 Preußische Domänenakten; Reichsministerium für Ernährung und Landwirtschaft

Rep 90 Staatsministerium

Rep 151 Preußisches Finanzministerium

Hauptstaatsarchiv Stuttgart (HStAS)

E 130b Staatsministerium

E 130b, II. Teil

E 151d, I. Ministerium des Innern, Abt. IV. Kommunalangelegenheiten

Hessisches Hauptstaatsarchiv (HHStA), Wiesbaden

Abt. 411 Regierung Wiesbaden, Preußisches Landratsamt Limburg an der Lahn

Abt. 412 Regierung Wiesbaden, Presßisches Landratsamt des Oberlahnkreises in Weilburg

Abt. 483 NSDAP, Gauleitung Hessen-Nassau, Stabsamt

Abt. 485 Reichsautobahnen Oberste Bauleitung Frankfurt am Main

Nordrhein-Westfälisches Hauptstaatsarchiv (N-WHStA), Düsseldorf

Regierung Düsseldorf

212.06.2 Kommunalwesen

212.19.1 Handel und Gewerbe

215.16 Landratsamt Gummersbach (Oberberg. Kreis)

215.26.2 Kreisausschuß und Lanadratsamt Monschau

420.20 Rheinische Gemeindeverbände

Arbeitsamt Erkelenz

Arbeitsamt Moers

Arbeitsamt Eschweiler

Regierung Aachen

211.05 Handel und Gewerbe

Nordrhein-Westfälisches Staatsarchiv Detmold (N-WStAD)

Lippische Regierung

Bestand L 80 Ia Abt. des Innern

Bestand L 80 Id Mitwirkung der Abt. des Innern an Angelegenheiten andere Abteilungen

Bestand L 76 Reichsstatthalter für Lippe und Schaumberg-Lippe

Nordrhein-Westfälisches Staatsarchiv Münster (N-WStAM)

Oberpräsidium Provinz Westfalen

Arbeitsamt Bestwig

Arbeitsamt Dortmund

Arbeitsamt Gelsenkirchen

Arbeitsamt Iserlohn

Staatsarchiv Nürnberg (StAN)

Regierung von Oberfranken und Mittelfranken, Kammer des Innern, Abg.
1978

Bezirksamt Erlangen, Abg. 1978

NSDAP Gau Franken, Gauleitung

Landratsamt (LRA) Ansbach, Abg. 1961

LRA Dinkelsbühl, Abg. 1976

LRA Eichstätt, Abg. 1981

LRA Hilpoltstein, Abg. 1977

LRA Rothenburg o. T., Abg. 1975/76

LRA Scheinfeld, Abg. 1977

LRA Schwabach, Abg. 1984

LRA Uffenheim, Abg. 1956, 1971

LA Weißenburg, Abg. 1955

Staatsarchiv Würzburg (StAW)

NSDAP Gau Mainfranken, Hauptbestand. Beständegruppe III 8.0.1

LRA Alzenau

LRA Lohr

LRA Marktheidenfeld

LRA Mellrichstadt

LRA Obernburg, Generalakten, NS-Zeit

Stadtarchiv Duisburg (StAD)

Bestand 100A/1- Rats- und Ausschußprotokolle

Bestand 102

Bestand 500 Wohlfahrtsamt

Stadtarchiv Düsseldorf (StADü)

Bestand "Ebel." Quellen zur Geschichte des Nationalsozialismus im Raum
Düsseldorf. Akten des Stadtrates Horst Ebel

Ratsprotokolle

Stadtverwaltung (Tiefbauamt I)

Wohlfahrt

Stadtarchiv Nürnberg (StadtAN)

C25/I FReg., vol. 1 Akten des Städt. Wohlfahrtsamt

C25/I FReg., vol. 2 Fürsorgeregistratur

Rep. C29 Direktorium A (Oberbürgermeister Willi Liebel)

Stadtarchiv Stuttgart (StAS)

Bürgermeisteramt (Bü) Hauptaktei, 1933–1945

Hauptakatei, Gruppe O-9

Nachlaß [mayor Karl] Strölin

Printed Primary Sources

Achter Bericht der Reichsanstalt für Arbeitsvermittlung und Arbeitslosenversicherung für die Zeit 1. April 1935 bis zum 31 März 1936

Akten der Reichskanzlei: Die Regierung Hitler. Teil I: 1933/34. 2 vols. Edited by Karl-Heinz Minuth. Boppard am Rhein: Harald Boldt Verlag, 1983

Hitler: Reden und Proklamationen 1932–1945. Edited by Max Domarus. 2 vols. Neustadt a. d. Aisch: Verlagsdruckerei Schmidt, 1962

Reichsarbeitsblatt, 1933–1936

Reichsgesetzblatt, 1933–1938

Sechster Bericht der Reichsanstalt für Arbeitsvermittlung und Arbeitslosenversicherung für die Zeit 1. April 1933 bis zum 31 März 1934

Siebenter Bericht der Reichsanstalt für Arbeitsvermittlung und Arbeitslosenversicherung für die Zeit vom 1. April 1934 bis zum 31. März 1935

Statistische Beilage zum Reichsarbeitsblatt, 1928–1939

Statistisches Jahrbuch für das Deutsche Reich, 1933–1936

Wochenbericht des Instituts für Konjunkturforschung, 1933–1936

Index

ment Affairs, 103–104; on economic recovery, 221

Feldman, Gerald D., 8, 238

Fladungen, 109, 110, 115, 116

Ford motor company (Germany), 239, 240

Foreign exchange shortage, 87–89

Four Year Plan (1936), 10, 112, 114; impact on labor market, 216, 245

Frankenheim, 115

Frankfurt am Main, 132

Frick, Wilhelm, 40, 73; and FAD, 181, 197; 1935 decree on work creation expenditures, 224

Fulda, 98, 109

Funk, Walther, 49, 52, 53, 55, 56, 57, 58, 73

Fürsorgearbeit. See welfare work

Garraty, John A., 231–232

General Motors corporation, 239

Gereke, Günter, 2–3, 5, 32. *See also Sofortprogramm*

Gesellschaft zur Vorbereitung der Reichsautobahnen (GEZUVOR), 159

Gisevius, Friedrich, 75

Glynn, Sean, 230

Goebbels, Joseph, 107

Goerdeler, Karl, 41–42; on price controls, 45–46

Gold Discount Bank, 36

Göring, Hermann, 47, 69, 91, 152; assistance for East Prussia, 73, 75, 77, 81, 84, 119; seeks additional imports, 225

Göring Plan (Berlin), 69, 82–84, 87

Great Britain, 87, 205; economic recovery, 226–231; fiscal policy, 227, 229, 235; leaves gold standard, 228; monetary policy, 228; housing boom, 228; government role in recovery, 229; direct work creation, 229, 235; limited economic recovery, 229–231

Grevesmühlen, 139

Guillebaud, C. W., 11

Hachtmann, Rüdiger, 43, 170, 217

Hamburg, 141, 162, 164; compulsory labor, 129

Harvey, Elizabeth, 242

Hasslinger, Kurt, 97, 98, 99, 101, 102, 105, 106, 109, 110, 111, 112, 113

Hayes, Peter, 241, 242

Heidelberg: placement of unemployed on *Autobahnen* construction, 163–164

Heilbronn, 167

Heimstättenamt, 103–104, 118

Hellmuth, Otto, 69, 97, 98, 99, 100, 101, 102, 103, 105, 106, 107, 108, 109, 110, 111, 113, 116, 119

Hellmuth Plan, 69, 97–120; compulsory resettlement, 99, 102, 109, 114; racial policy, 99, 100, 108–109; industrial development, 111–114; results, 115–118; military development, 116

Hess, Rudolf, 104, 243

Hesse, 106, 132, 134

Hierl, Konstantin, 193; new image for FAD, 177–178; proposes Nazi labor service, 177; appointed RAM state secretary for FAD, 179; proposes four-year FAD program, 179; appointed Reich Commissioner for FAD, 181; submits action program to Hitler, 183–184; demands RfAA projects and funds, 185–186; claims sphere of activity for FAD, 186–187; creates FAD technical planning office, 192; on compulsory labor service, 196, 198

Hilpoltstein, 139

Hindenburg, Paul von, 52

Hitler, Adolf, 1, 2, 92, 93, 103, 104, 108, 114, 115, 117, 119, 120, 121, 139, 142, 144, 146, 154, 158, 168, 173, 177, 179, 189, 193, 200, 217; first cabinet, 6, 28; appointment as Reich chancellor, 7; on economic recovery, 8, 10; responsibility for economic recovery, 9, 10, 219, 245; ideas for economic recovery, 29, 48, 57, 62, 64, 88, 89; on balanced budget, 29; and Reichsbank, 32; rejects price controls, 42; on Nazi party organization, 52, 53, 54–56; bans NSDAP discussion of economic policy, 53; and myth, 61; May 1933 meeting with industrialists, 64; role in developing economic recovery program, 67; East Prussian assistance, 73, 74; on motorization, 147, 157; on road